NEGIMA!

21

Ken Akamatsu

TRANSLATED AND ADAPTED BY
Ikoi Hiroe

LETTERING AND RETOUCH BY
Steve Palmer

Negima! volume 21 is a work of fiction. Names, characters, places, and incidents are the products of the author's imagination or are used fictitiously. Any resemblance to actual events, locales, or persons, living or dead, is entirely coincidental.

A Del Rey Manga/Kodansha Trade Paperback Original

Published in the United States by Del Rey, an imprint of The Random House Publishing Group, a division of Random House, Inc., New York.

Publication rights arranged through Kodansha Ltd.

First published in Japan in 2008 by Kodansha Ltd., Tokyo

ISBN 978-0-345-50528-6

Printed in the United States of America

www.delreymanga.com

9 8 7 6 5 4 3 2 1

Translator/adapter—Ikoi Hiroe
Lettering and retouch—Steve Palmer

Honorifics Explained

Throughout the Del Rey Manga books, you will find Japanese honorifics left intact in the translations. For those not familiar with how the Japanese use honorifics and, more important, how they differ from American honorifics, we present this brief overview.

Politeness has always been a critical facet of Japanese culture. Ever since the feudal era, when Japan was a highly stratified society, use of honorifics—which can be defined as polite speech that indicates relationship or status—has played an essential role in the Japanese language. When addressing someone in Japanese, an honorific usually takes the form of a suffix attached to one's name (example: "Asuna-san"), is used as a title at the end of one's name, or appears in place of the name itself (example: "Negi-sensei," or simply "Sensei!").

Honorifics can be expressions of respect or endearment. In the context of manga and anime, honorifics give insight into the nature of the relationship between characters. Many English translations leave out these important honorifics and therefore distort the feel of the original Japanese. Because Japanese honorifics contain nuances that English honorifics lack, it is our policy at Del Rey not to translate them. Here, instead, is a guide to some of the honorifics you may encounter in Del Rey Manga.

-*san*: This is the most common honorific and is equivalent to Mr., Miss, Ms., or Mrs. It is the all-purpose honorific and can be used in any situation where politeness is required.

-*sama*: This is one level higher than "-san" and is used to confer great respect.

-*dono*: This comes from the word "tono," which means "lord." It is an even higher level than "-sama" and confers utmost respect.

-*kun*: This suffix is used at the end of boys' names to express familiarity or endearment. It is also sometimes used by men

among friends, or when addressing someone younger or of a lower station.

-chan: This is used to express endearment, mostly toward girls. It is also used for little boys, pets, and even among lovers. It gives a sense of childish cuteness.

Bōzu: This is an informal way to refer to a boy, similar to the English terms "kid" and "squirt."

Sempai/Senpai: This title suggests that the addressee is one's senior in a group or organization. It is most often used in a school setting, where underclassmen refer to their upperclassmen as "sempai." It can also be used in the workplace, such as when a newer employee addresses an employee who has seniority in the company.

Kohai: This is the opposite of "sempai" and is used toward underclassmen in school or newcomers in the workplace. It connotes that the addressee is of a lower station.

Sensei: Literally meaning "one who has come before," this title is used for teachers, doctors, or masters of any profession or art.

Anesan (or *nesan*): A generic term for a girl, usually older, that means sister.

Ojōsama: A way of referring to the daughter or sister of someone with high political or social status.

-[blank]: This is usually forgotten in these lists, but it is perhaps the most significant difference between Japanese and English. The lack of honorific means that the speaker has permission to address the person in a very intimate way. Usually, only family, spouses, or very close friends have this kind of permission. Known as *yobisute*, it can be gratifying when someone who has earned the intimacy starts to call one by one's name without an honorific. But when that intimacy hasn't been earned, it can be very insulting.

A Word from the Author

I'm pleased to present volume 21.

Negi and crew kick off their entry into the Magical World with a *major* incident. How will they find their way out of this mess? (^^;)

In these coming episodes, many mysteries surrounding Negi will be resolved, so stay sharp!

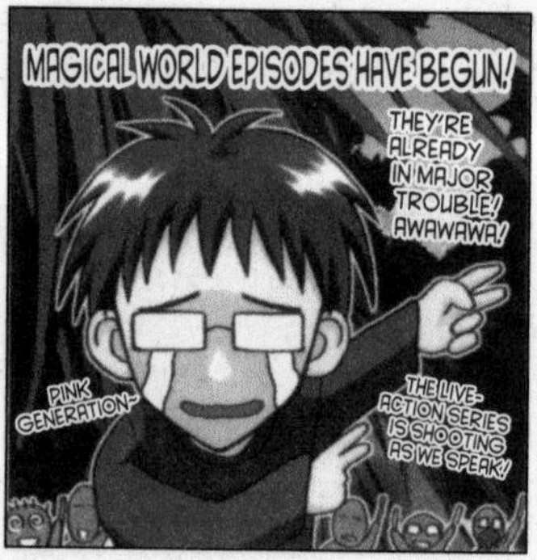
MAGICAL WORLD EPISODES HAVE BEGUN!
THEY'RE ALREADY IN MAJOR TROUBLE! AWAWAWA!
THE LIVE-ACTION SERIES IS SHOOTING AS WE SPEAK!
PINK GENERATION-

The shoots for the live-action drama version have been picking up steam! The drama series began in March of 2008! There will be cards available, similar to the manga series! I'm on fire!

Ken Akamatsu
www.ailove.net

21

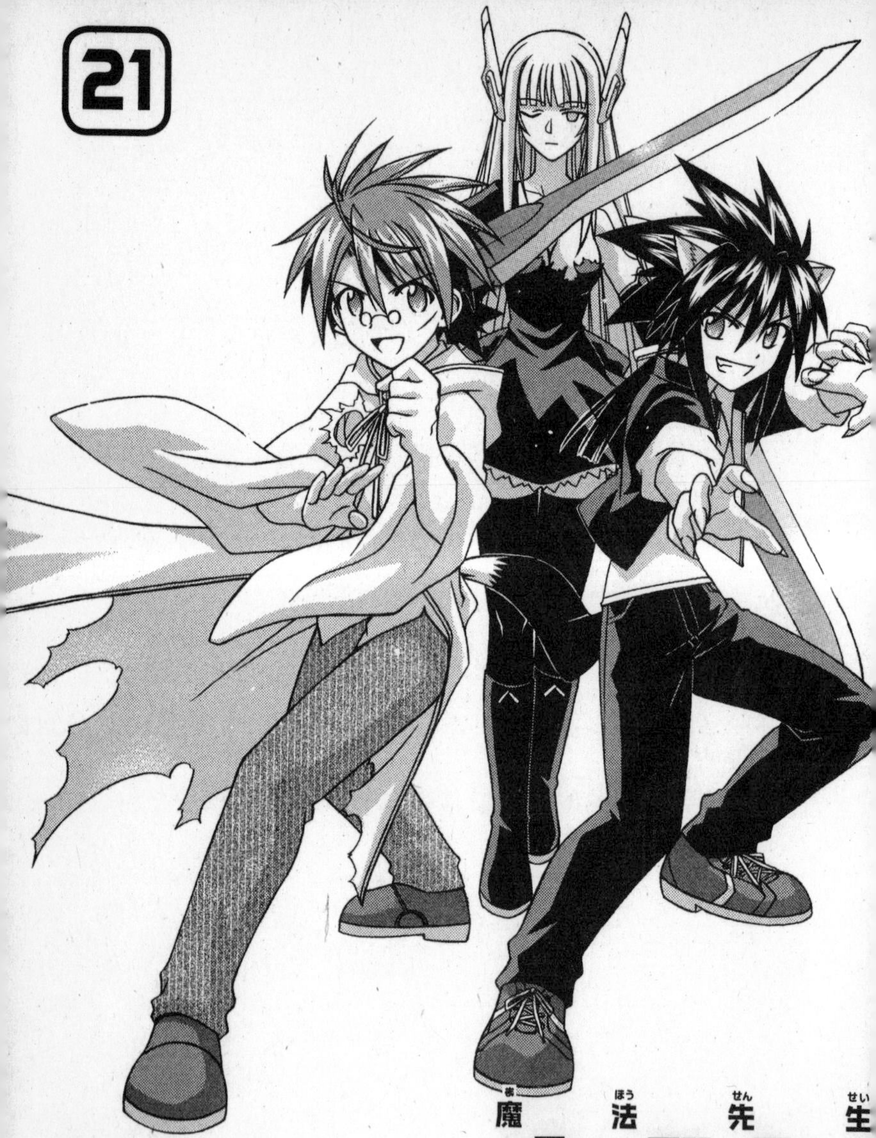

Ken Akamatsu

赤松 健

魔法先生ネギま!

MAGISTER NEGI MAGI

CONTENTS

87th Period – Fate Causes a Catastrophe........3

188th Period – Power Up, Negi Party!!........21

189th Period – Destruction! Negi Party!!........39

190th Period – Energy Recovered, 120% ♡........57

191st Period – Promise from the Past........75

192nd Period – Hero's Duty........91

193rd Period – Wanted!!........109

194th Period – Made in the Magical World........127

195th Period – 1,000,000 Dorakuma Repayment Plan........145

Fan Art Corner........164

Lexicon Negimarium........168

Class Roster........172

Cover Concept Sketches........174

Translation Notes........176

About the Creator........178

Preview of *Negima!* Volume 22........179

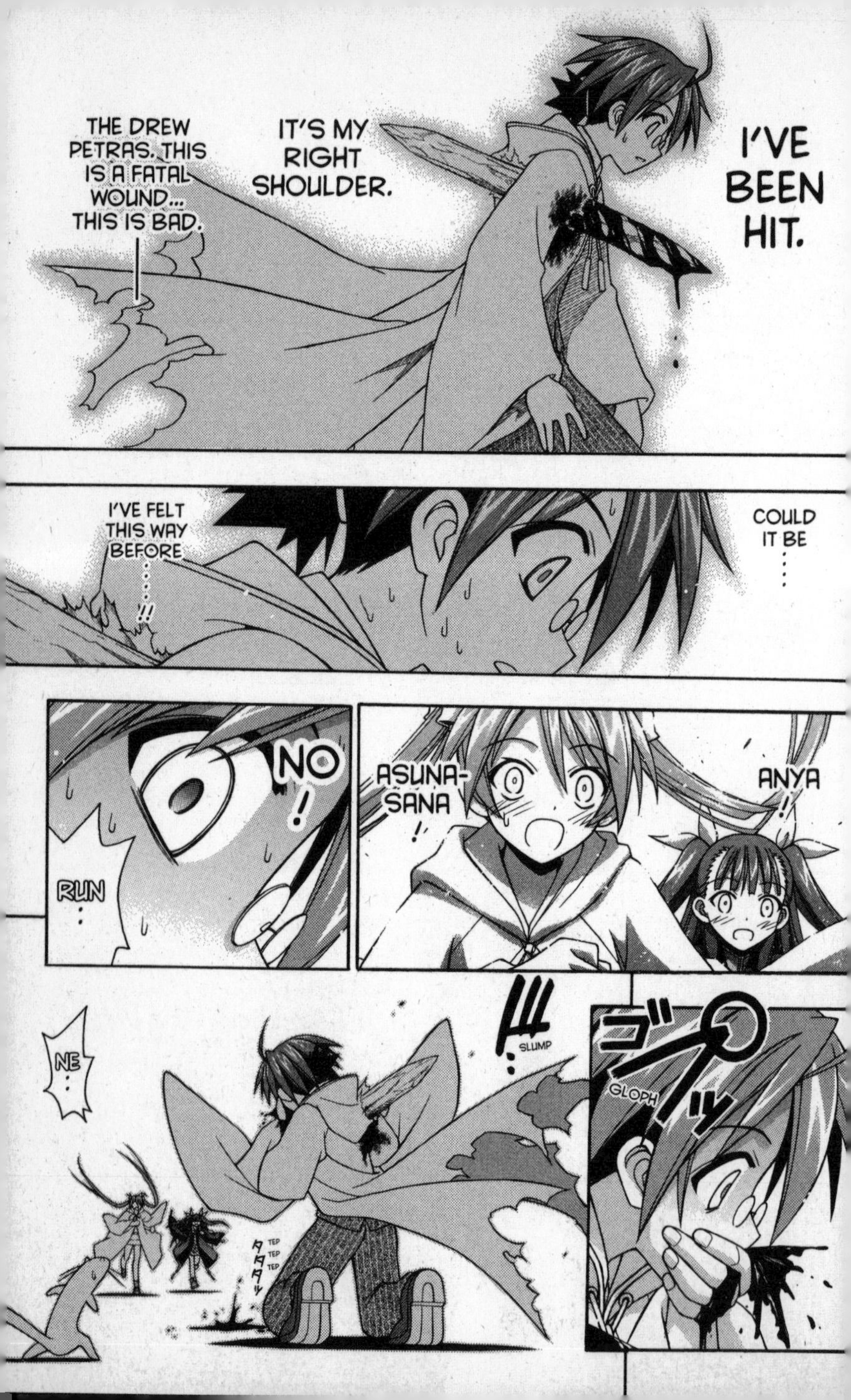
I'VE BEEN HIT.
IT'S MY RIGHT SHOULDER.
THE DREW PETRAS. THIS IS A FATAL WOUND... THIS IS BAD.
COULD IT BE....
I'VE FELT THIS WAY BEFORE......!!
ANYA!!
ASUNA-SANA!
NO!
RUN...
GLOPH
SLUMP
TEP TEP TEP
NE...

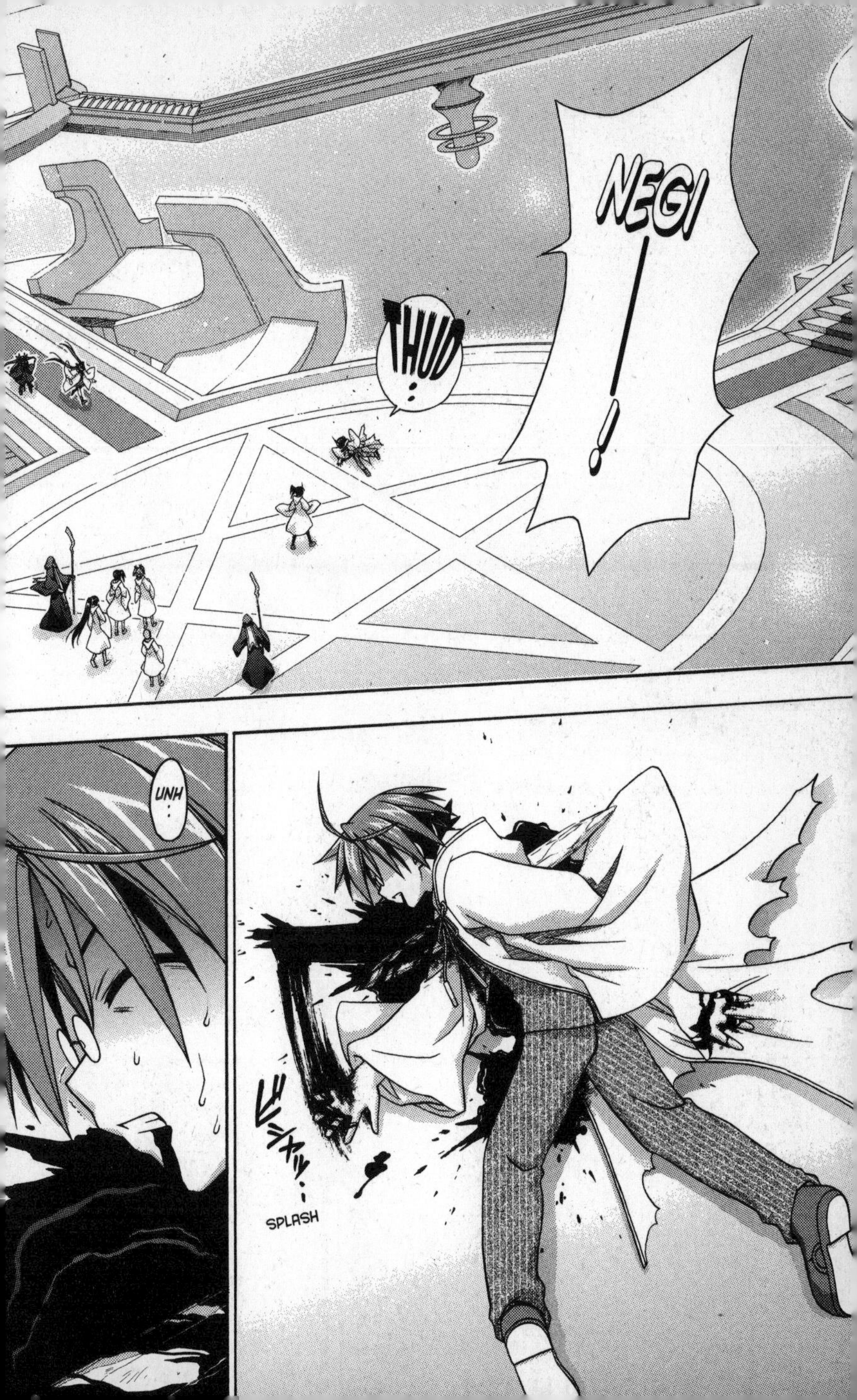
NEGI—!!
THUD...
ビシャッ...
SPLASH
UNH...

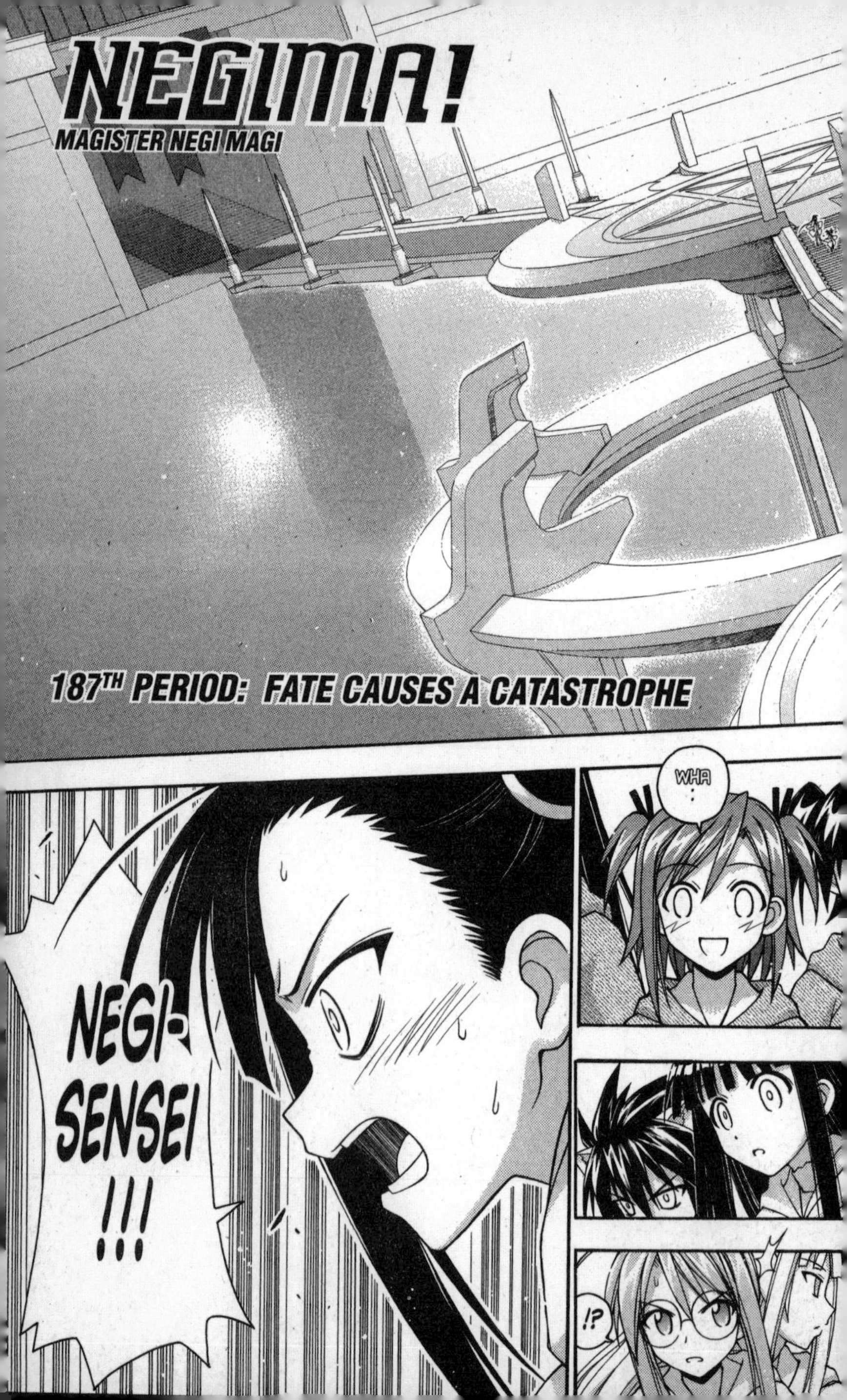
NEGIMA!
MAGISTER NEGI MAGI
187TH PERIOD: FATE CAUSES A CATASTROPHE
WHA :
!?
NEGI-SENSEI !!!

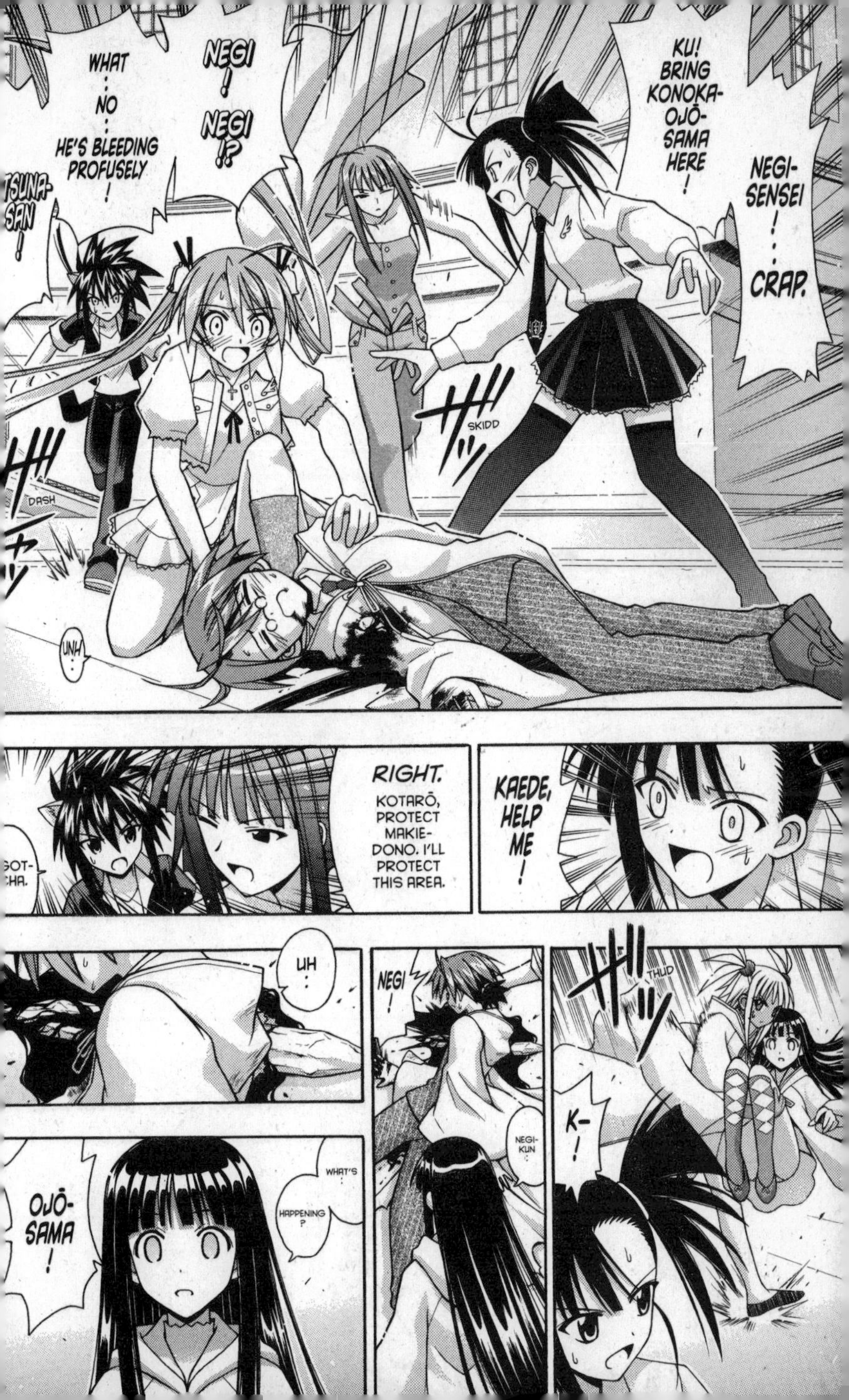

KU! BRING KONOKA-OJŌ-SAMA HERE!
NEGI-SENSEI! ... CRAP.
NEGI! NEGI!?
WHAT... NO... HE'S BLEEDING PROFUSELY!
TSUNA-SAN!
SKIDD
DASH
UNH...
KAEDE, HELP ME!
RIGHT.
KOTARŌ, PROTECT MAKIE-DONO. I'LL PROTECT THIS AREA.
GOT-CHA.
THUD
K-!
NEGI!
NEGI-KUN...
UH...
WHAT'S... HAPPENING?
OJŌ-SAMA!

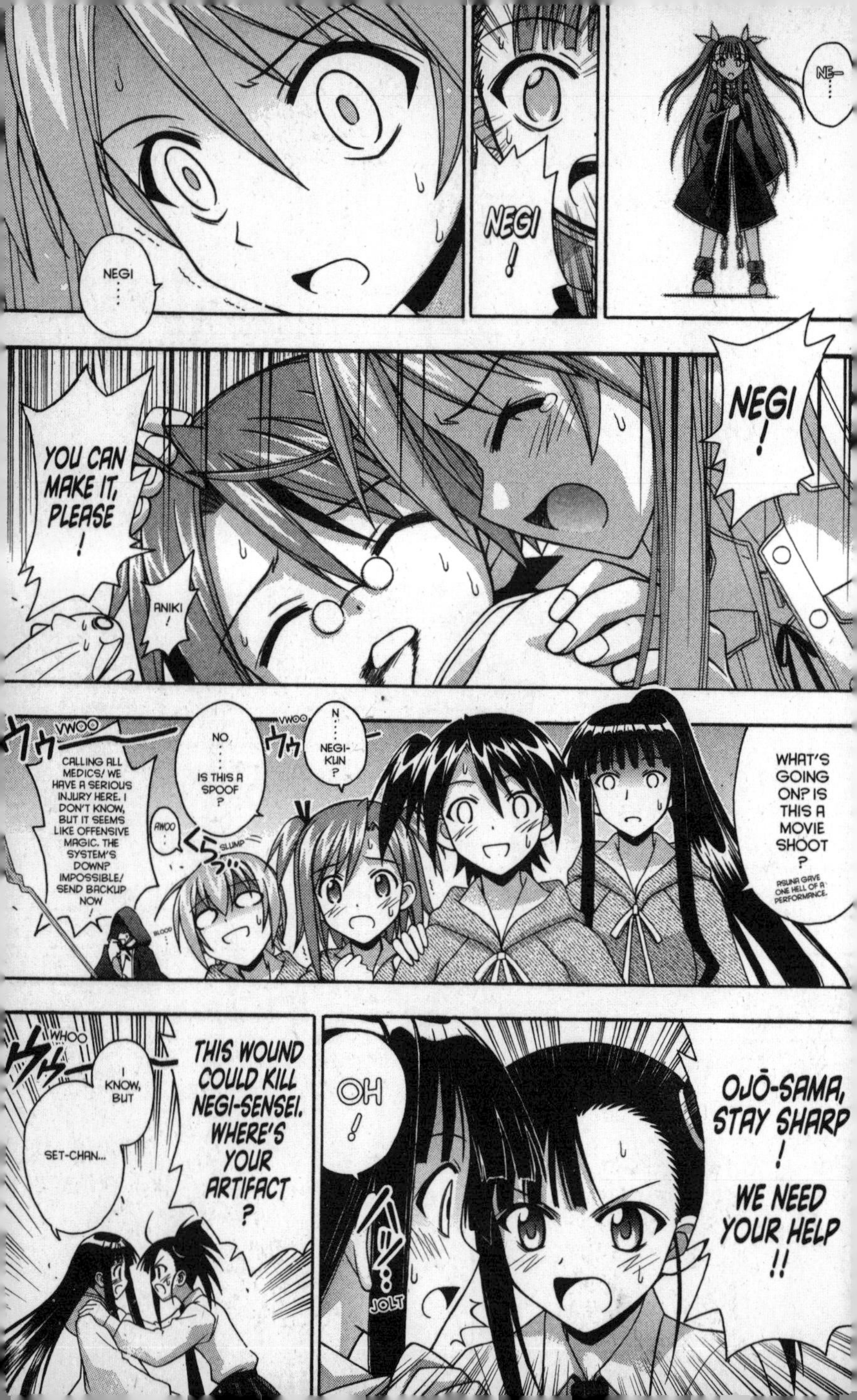
NE— ...
NEGI !
NEGI ...
NEGI !
YOU CAN MAKE IT, PLEASE !
ANIKI !
WHAT'S GOING ON? IS THIS A MOVIE SHOOT ?
ASUNA GAVE ONE HELL OF A PERFORMANCE.
N... NEGI-KUN ?
VWOO
NO ... IS THIS A SPOOF ?
AWOO ...
SLUMP
BLOOD ...
VWOO
CALLING ALL MEDICS! WE HAVE A SERIOUS INJURY HERE. I DON'T KNOW, BUT IT SEEMS LIKE OFFENSIVE MAGIC. THE SYSTEM'S DOWN? IMPOSSIBLE! SEND BACKUP NOW !
OJŌ-SAMA, STAY SHARP !
WE NEED YOUR HELP !!
OH !
JOLT
THIS WOUND COULD KILL NEGI-SENSEI. WHERE'S YOUR ARTIFACT ?
I KNOW, BUT
SET-CHAN...
WHOO

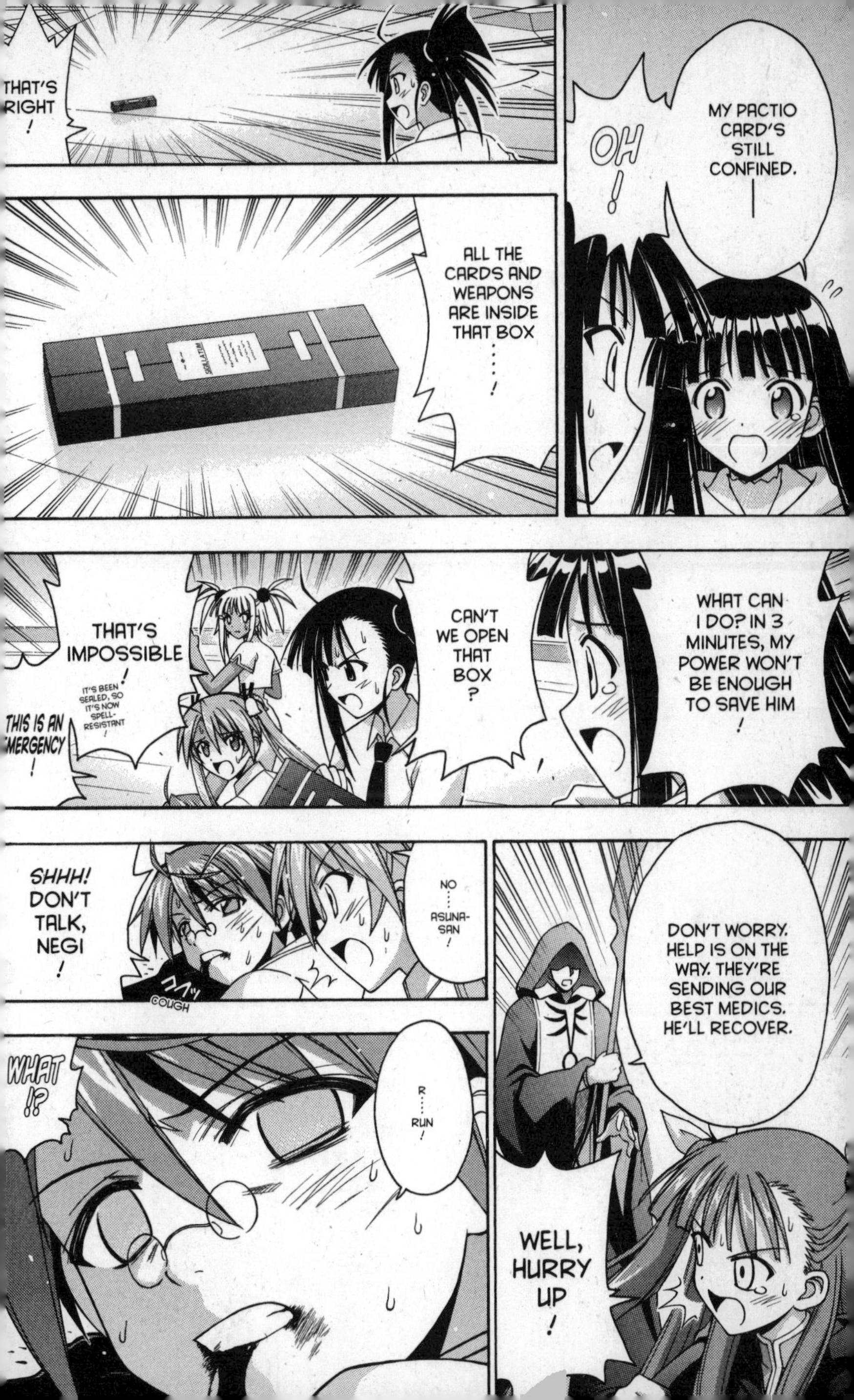
MY PACTIO CARD'S STILL CONFINED.
OH!
THAT'S RIGHT!
ALL THE CARDS AND WEAPONS ARE INSIDE THAT BOX.....!
WHAT CAN I DO? IN 3 MINUTES, MY POWER WON'T BE ENOUGH TO SAVE HIM!
CAN'T WE OPEN THAT BOX?
THAT'S IMPOSSIBLE!
IT'S BEEN SEALED, SO IT'S NOW SPELL-RESISTANT!
THIS IS AN EMERGENCY!
DON'T WORRY. HELP IS ON THE WAY. THEY'RE SENDING OUR BEST MEDICS. HE'LL RECOVER.
WELL, HURRY UP!
NO... ASUNA-SAN!
SHHH! DON'T TALK, NEGI!
COUGH
R... RUN!
WHAT!?

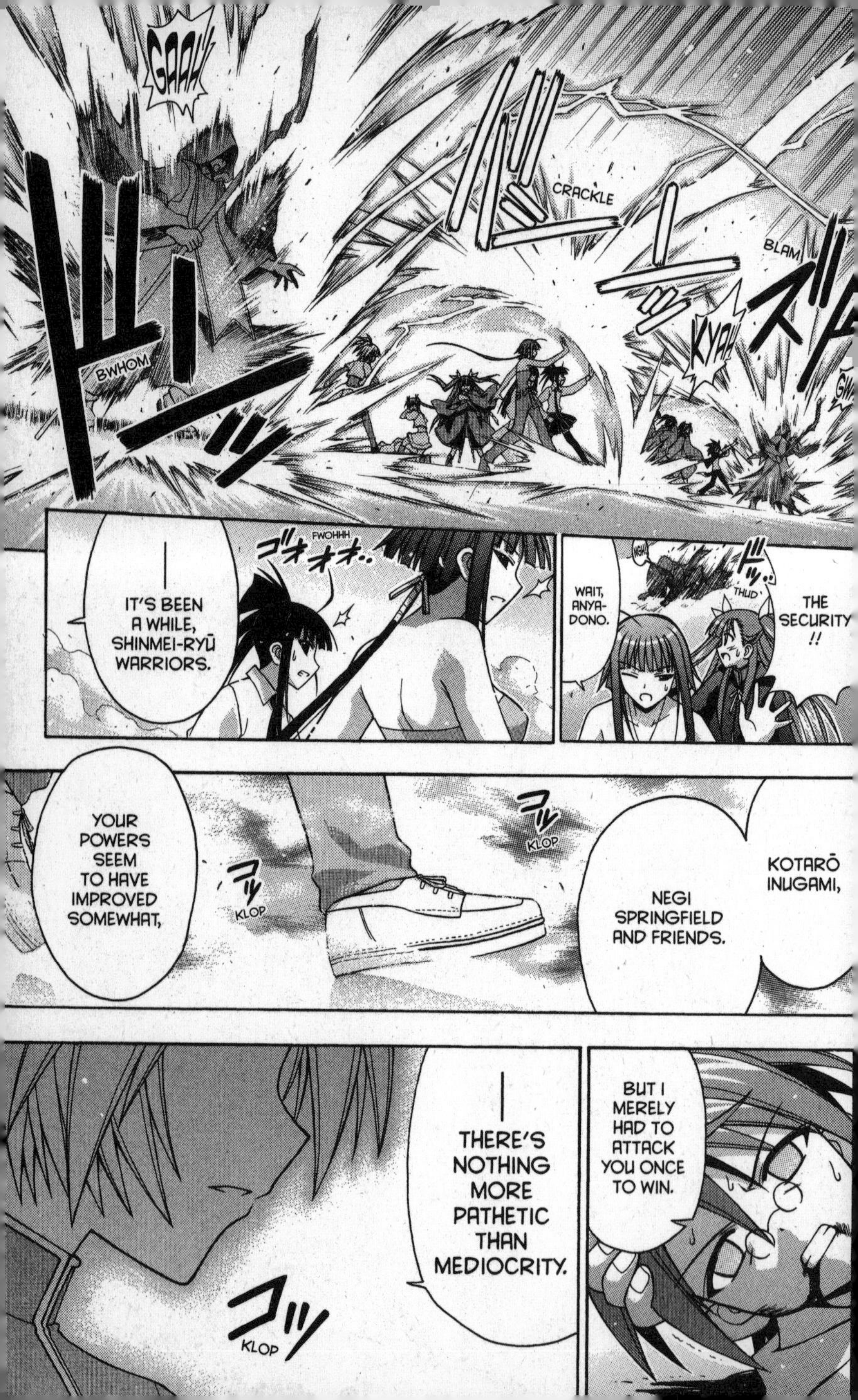
BLAM
KYAH
CRACKLE
GAAH
BWHOM
NGH!
THE SECURITY!!
THUD
WAIT, ANYA-DONO.
FWOHHH
IT'S BEEN A WHILE, SHINMEI-RYŪ WARRIORS.
KOTARŌ INUGAMI,
NEGI SPRINGFIELD AND FRIENDS.
KLOP
KLOP
YOUR POWERS SEEM TO HAVE IMPROVED SOMEWHAT,
BUT I MERELY HAD TO ATTACK YOU ONCE TO WIN.
THERE'S NOTHING MORE PATHETIC THAN MEDIOCRITY.
KLOP

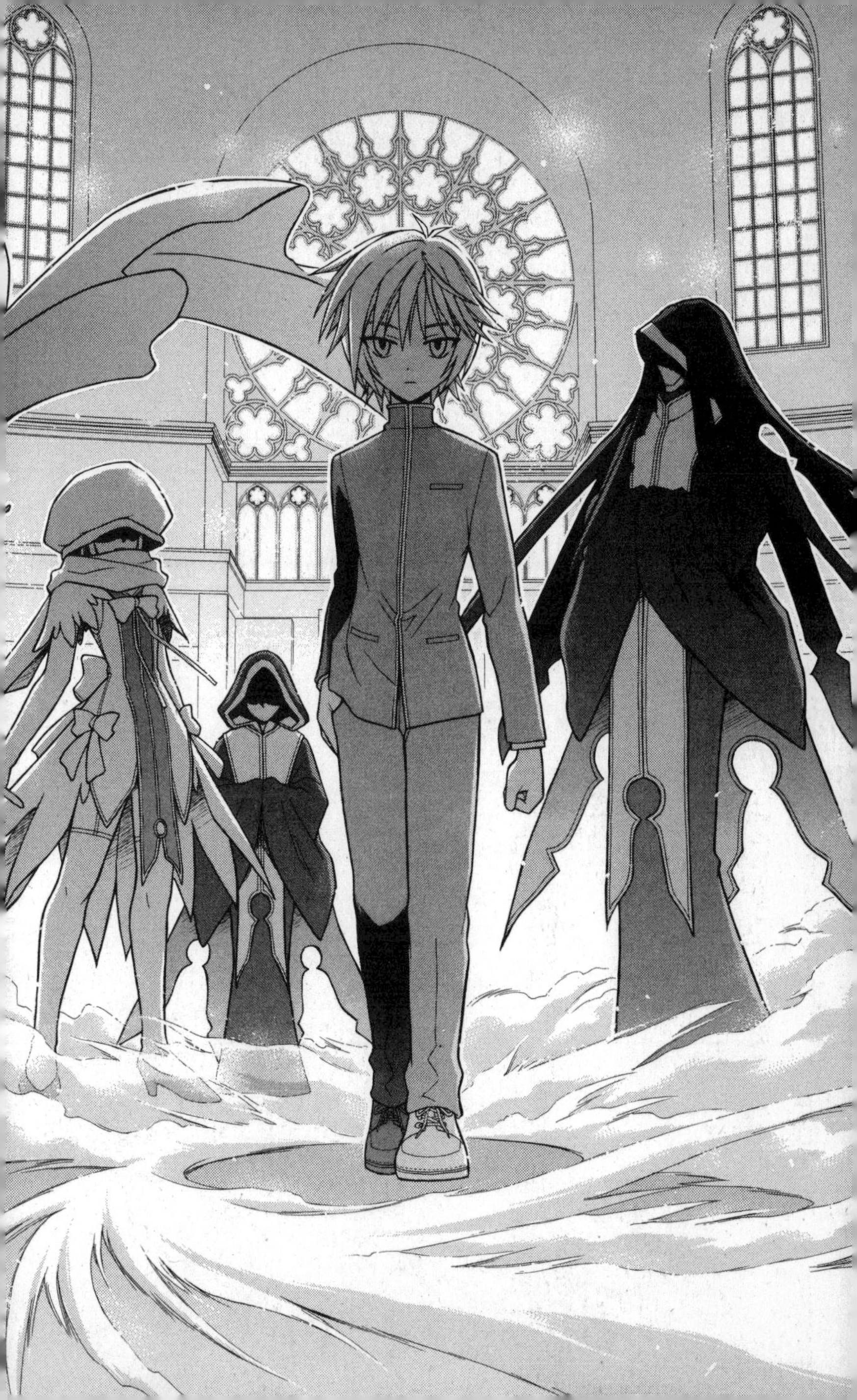

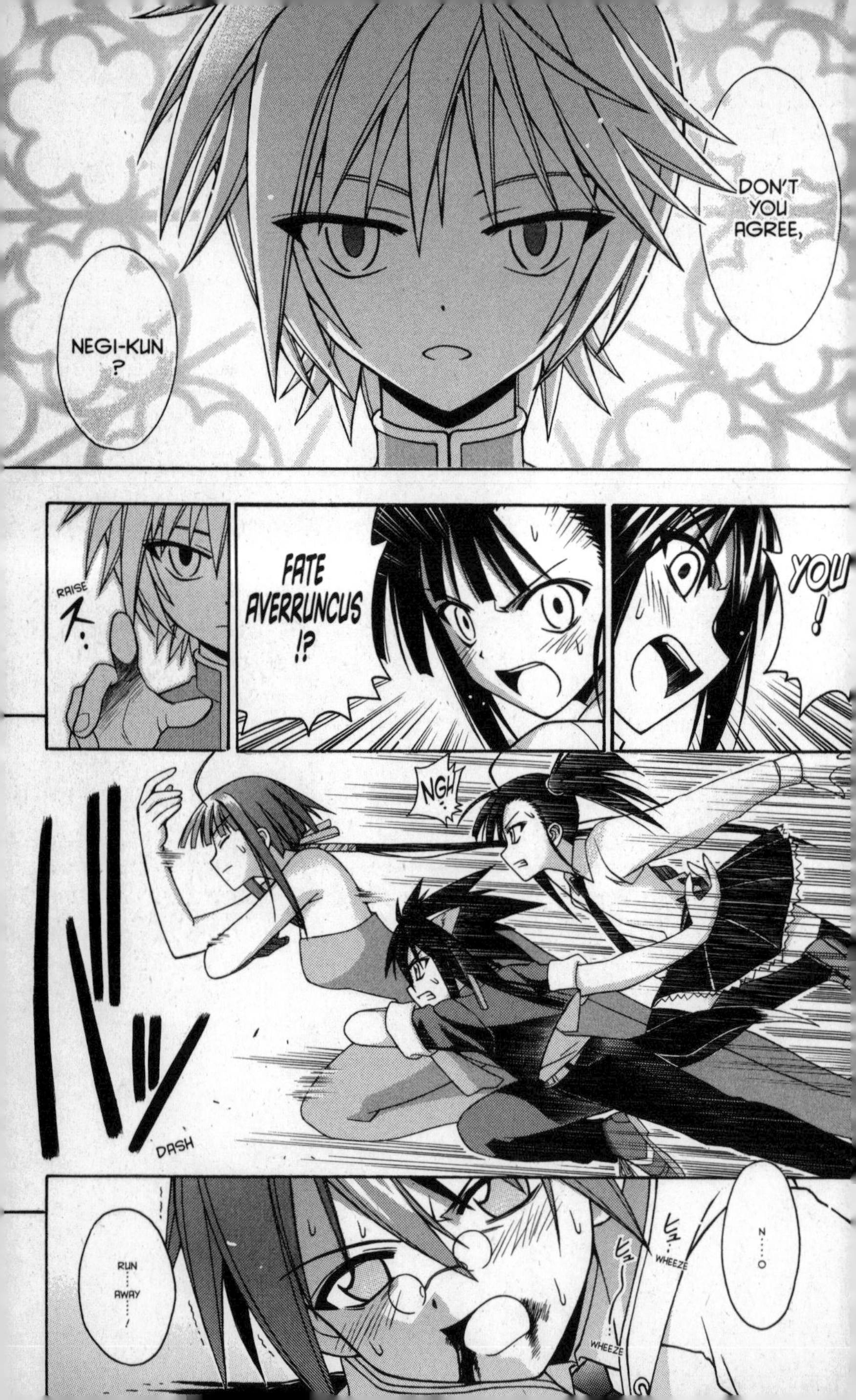
DON'T YOU AGREE,
NEGI-KUN ?
YOU !
FATE AVERRUNCUS !?
RAISE
NGH
DASH
N....O
WHEEZE
WHEEZE
RUN... AWAY...!

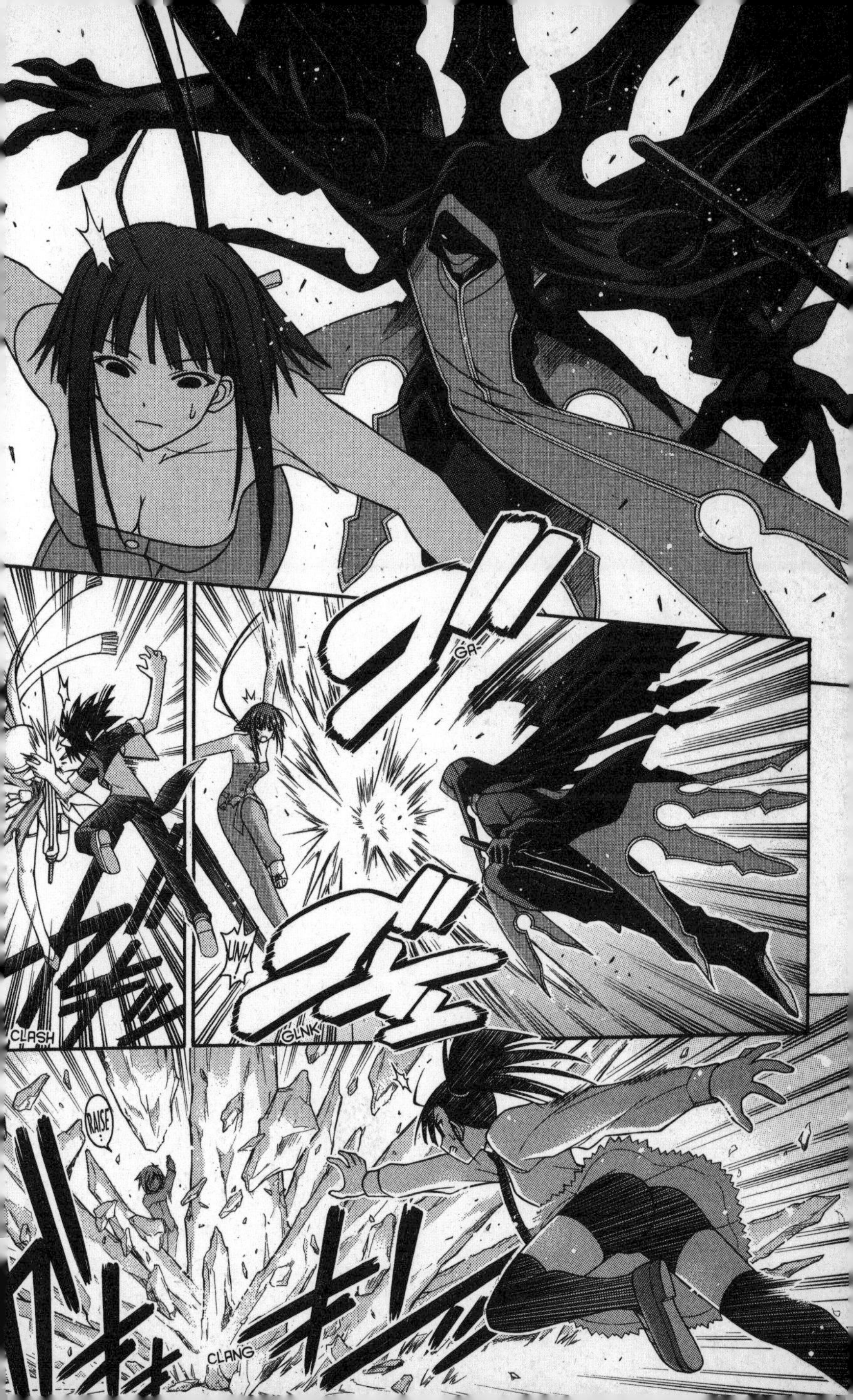
GA-
UNH!
GLNK
CLASH
RAISE
CLANG

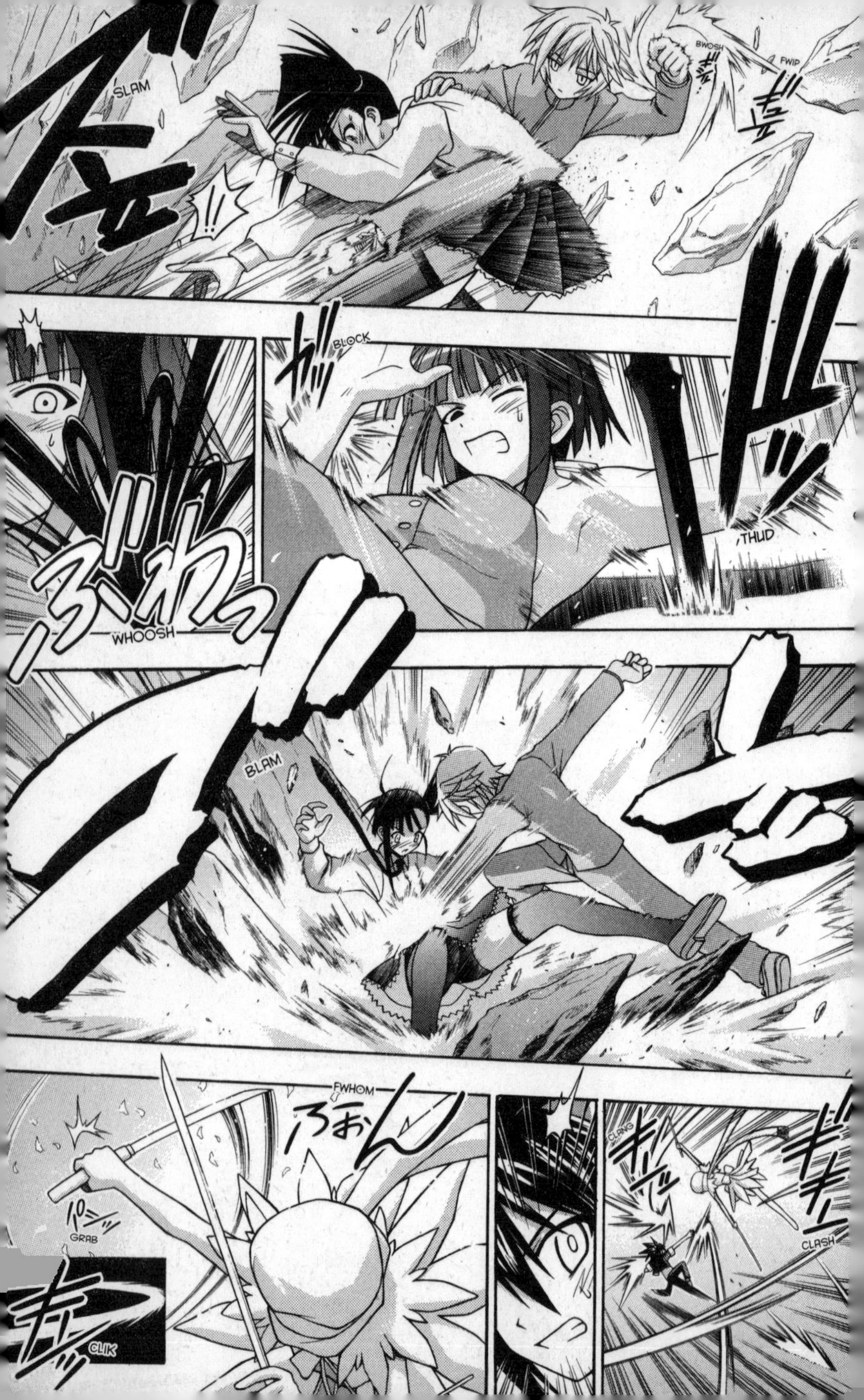
FWIP
BWOSH
SLAM
BLOCK
THUD
WHOOSH
BLAM
CLANG
CLASH
FWHOM
GRAB
CLIK

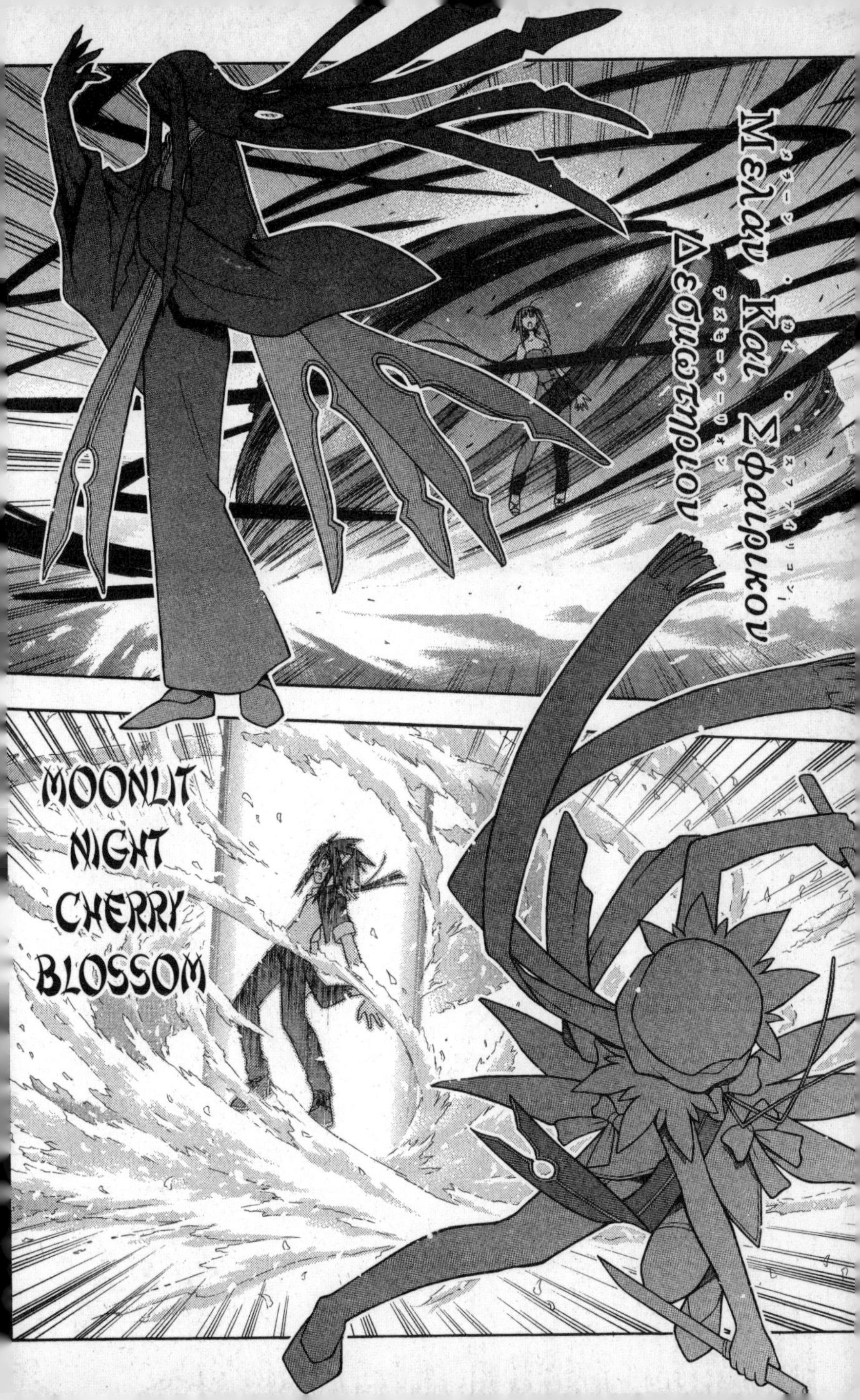
Μελαν · Και · Σφαιρικον Δεσμωτηριον
MOONLIT NIGHT CHERRY BLOSSOM

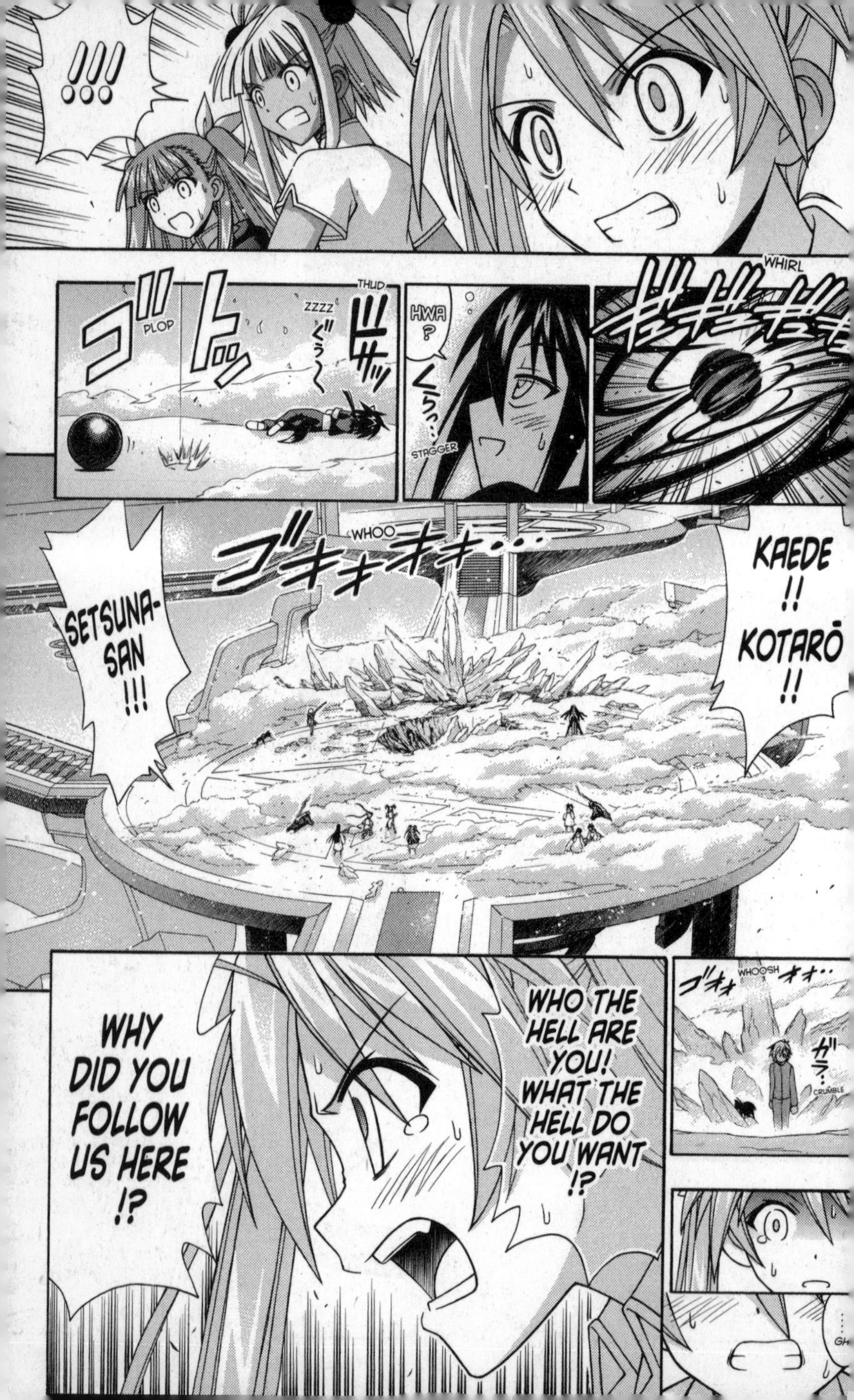
!!!!
WHIRL
HWA?
STAGGER
THUD
ZZZZ
PLOP
WHOO
KAEDE!! KOTARŌ!!
SETSUNA-SAN!!!
WHOOSH
CRUMBLE
...GH
WHO THE HELL ARE YOU! WHAT THE HELL DO YOU WANT!?
WHY DID YOU FOLLOW US HERE!?

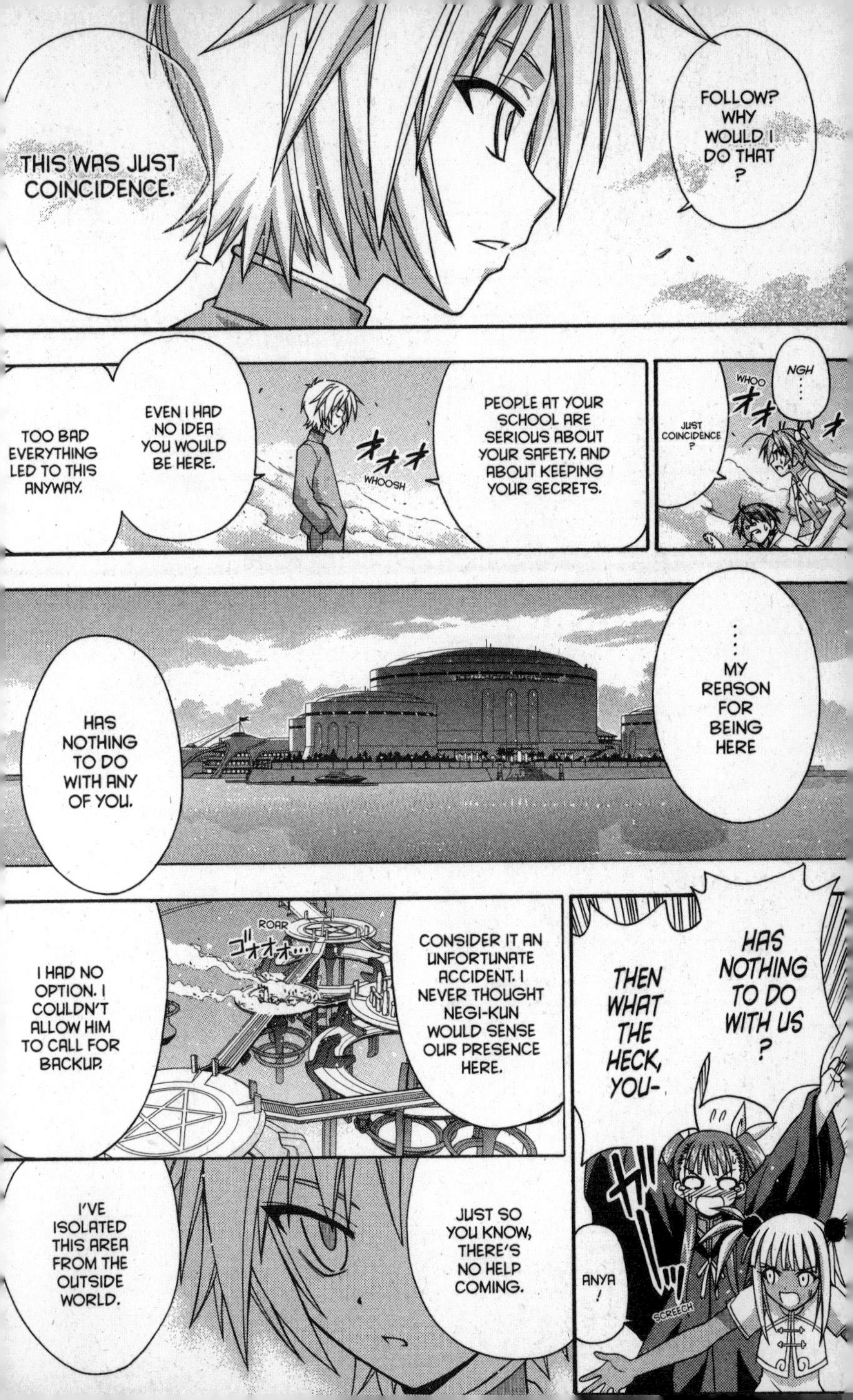
FOLLOW? WHY WOULD I DO THAT ?
THIS WAS JUST COINCIDENCE.
NGH .....
WHOO
JUST COINCIDENCE ?
PEOPLE AT YOUR SCHOOL ARE SERIOUS ABOUT YOUR SAFETY. AND ABOUT KEEPING YOUR SECRETS.
WHOOSH
EVEN I HAD NO IDEA YOU WOULD BE HERE.
TOO BAD EVERYTHING LED TO THIS ANYWAY.
..... MY REASON FOR BEING HERE
HAS NOTHING TO DO WITH ANY OF YOU.
HAS NOTHING TO DO WITH US ?
THEN WHAT THE HECK, YOU-
SCREECH
ANYA !
CONSIDER IT AN UNFORTUNATE ACCIDENT. I NEVER THOUGHT NEGI-KUN WOULD SENSE OUR PRESENCE HERE.
ROAR
I HAD NO OPTION. I COULDN'T ALLOW HIM TO CALL FOR BACKUP.
JUST SO YOU KNOW, THERE'S NO HELP COMING.
I'VE ISOLATED THIS AREA FROM THE OUTSIDE WORLD.

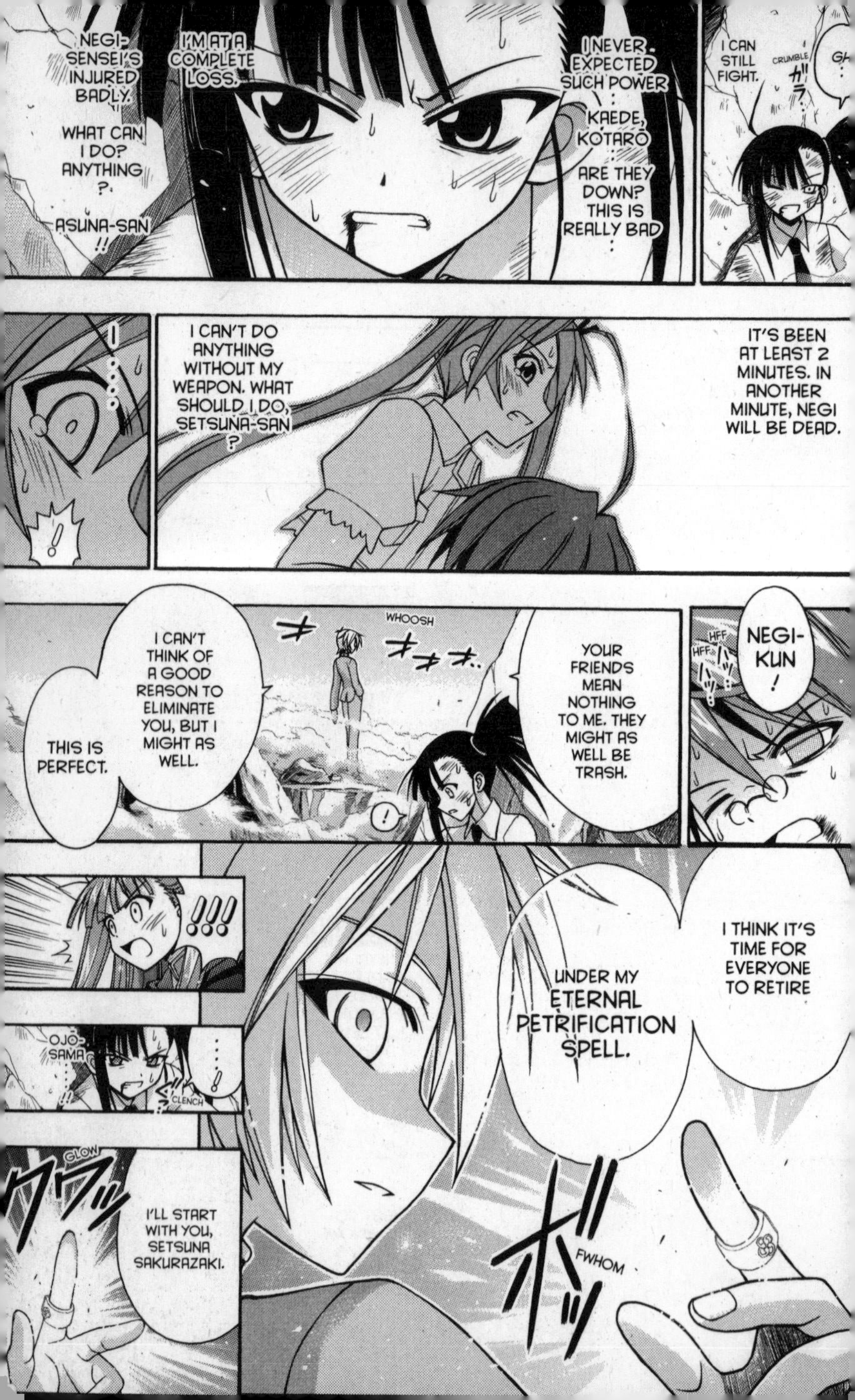
I CAN STILL FIGHT.
CRUMBLE
GH...
I NEVER EXPECTED SUCH POWER... KAEDE, KOTARO... ARE THEY DOWN? THIS IS REALLY BAD...
I'M AT A COMPLETE LOSS.
NEGI-SENSEI'S INJURED BADLY. WHAT CAN I DO? ANYTHING?.. ASUNA-SAN!!
IT'S BEEN AT LEAST 2 MINUTES. IN ANOTHER MINUTE, NEGI WILL BE DEAD.
I CAN'T DO ANYTHING WITHOUT MY WEAPON. WHAT SHOULD I DO, SETSUNA-SAN?
I....
!
HFF HFF
NEGI-KUN!
YOUR FRIENDS MEAN NOTHING TO ME. THEY MIGHT AS WELL BE TRASH.
WHOOSH
!
I CAN'T THINK OF A GOOD REASON TO ELIMINATE YOU, BUT I MIGHT AS WELL.
THIS IS PERFECT.
I THINK IT'S TIME FOR EVERYONE TO RETIRE
UNDER MY ETERNAL PETRIFICATION SPELL.
FWHOM
!!!
...!
OJO-SAMA...!!
CLENCH
I'LL START WITH YOU, SETSUNA SAKURAZAKI.
GLOW

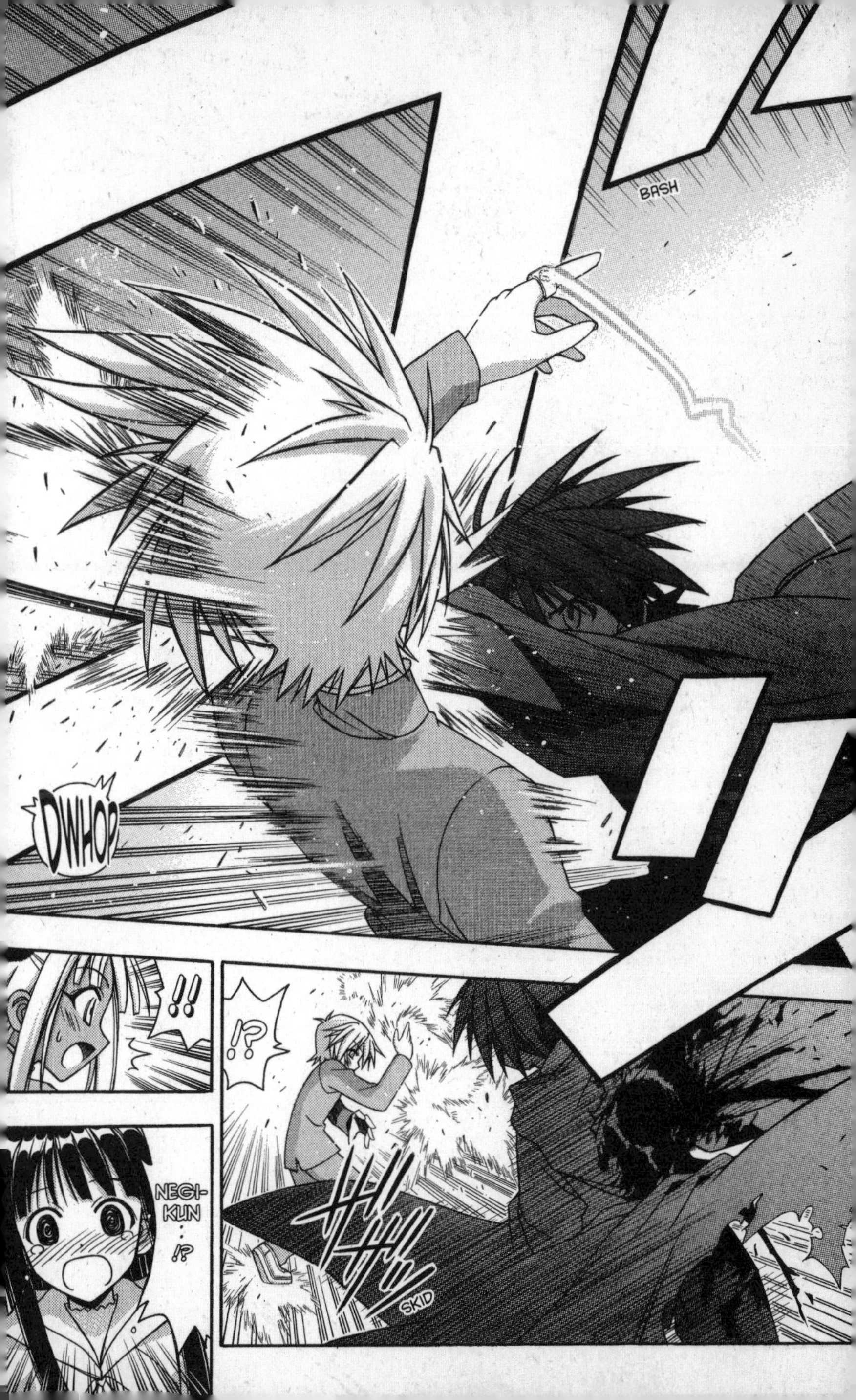
BASH
DWHOP
!?
SKID
!!
NEGI-KUN ...!?

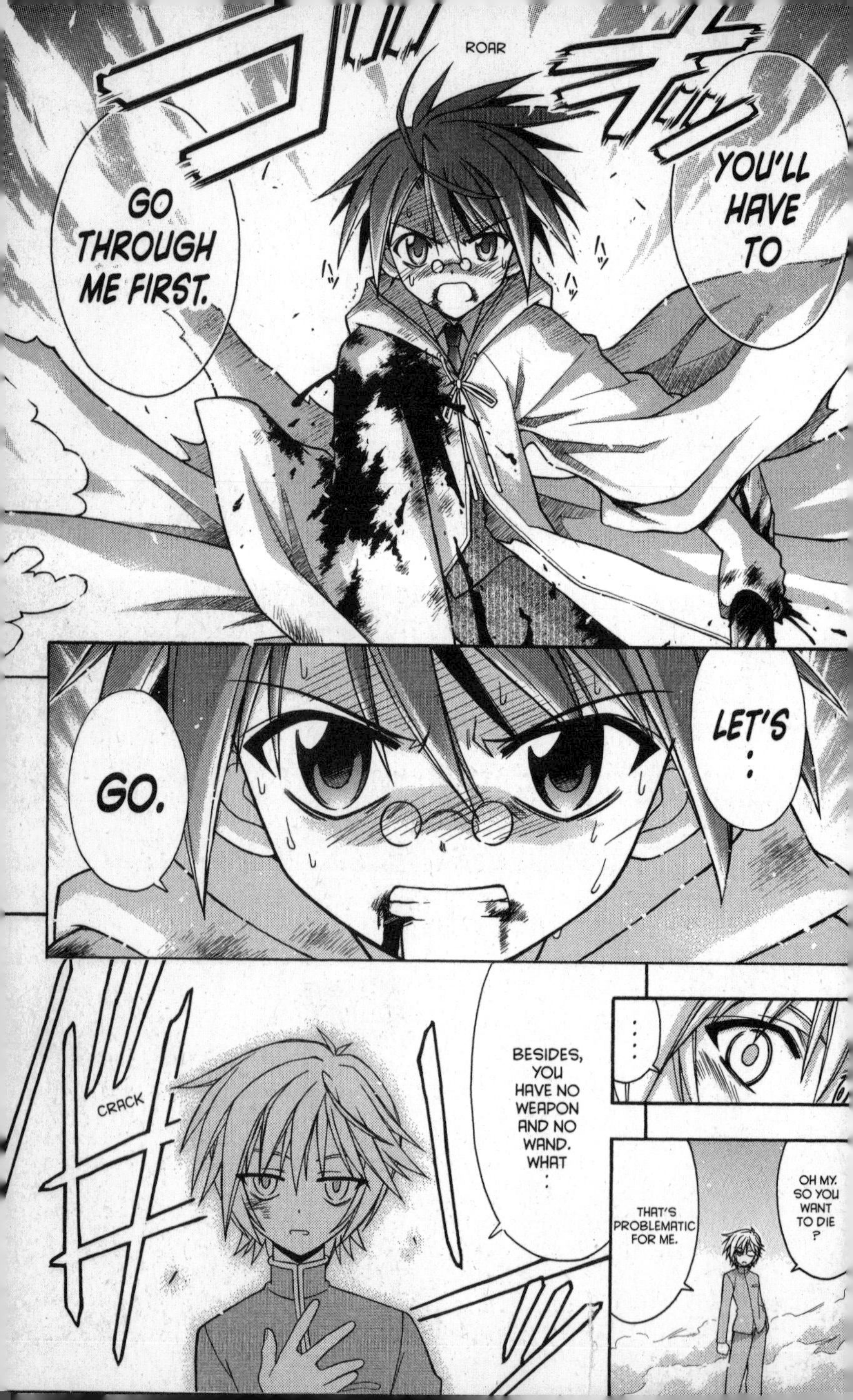
ROAR
YOU'LL HAVE TO
GO THROUGH ME FIRST.
LET'S...
GO.
....
OH MY. SO YOU WANT TO DIE?
THAT'S PROBLEMATIC FOR ME.
BESIDES, YOU HAVE NO WEAPON AND NO WAND. WHAT...
CRACK

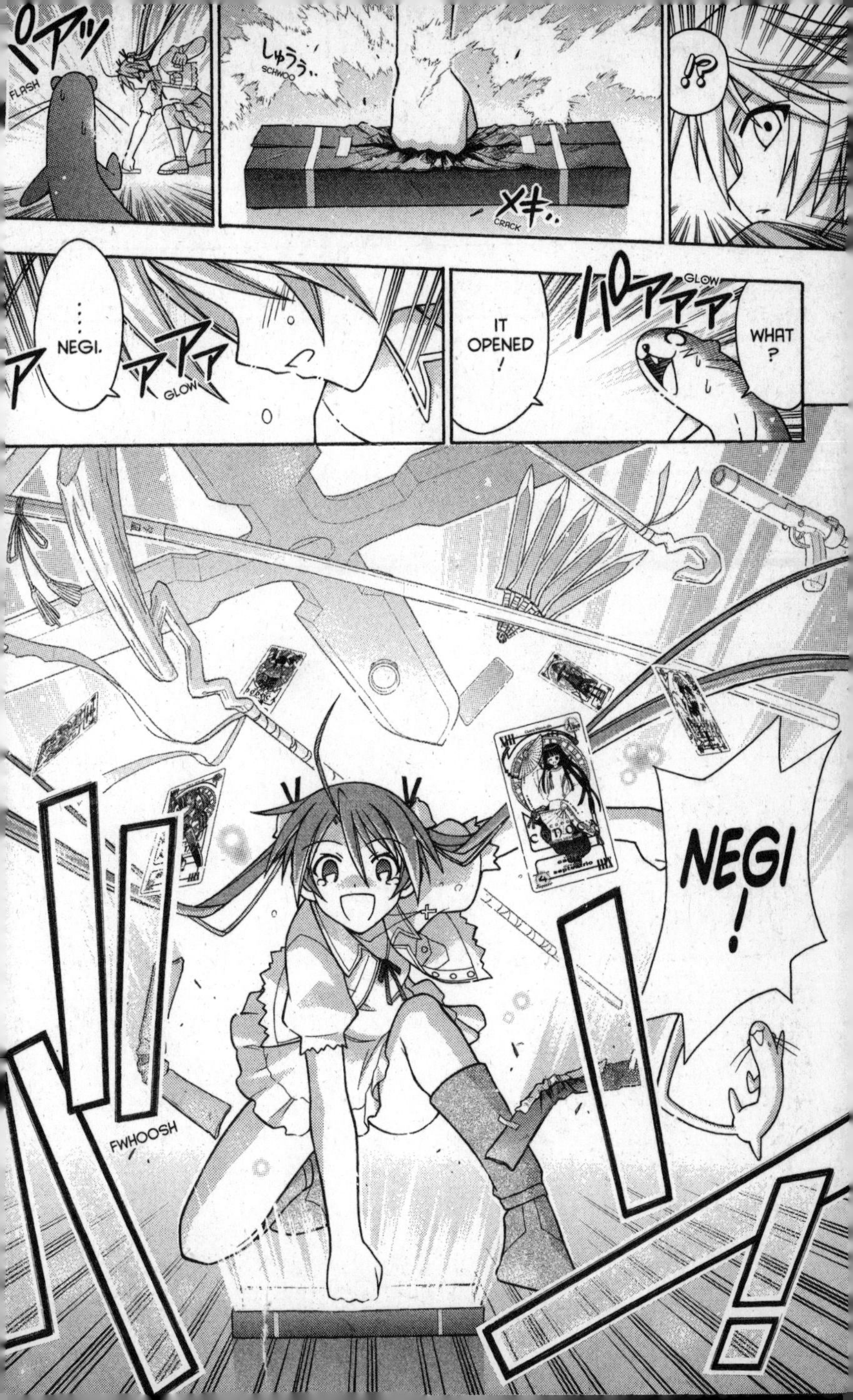

!?
しゅうう..
SCHWOO
メキ..
CRACK
パアッ
FLASH
WHAT?
パアアア
GLOW
IT OPENED!
...NEGI.
GLOW
NEGI!
FWHOOSH

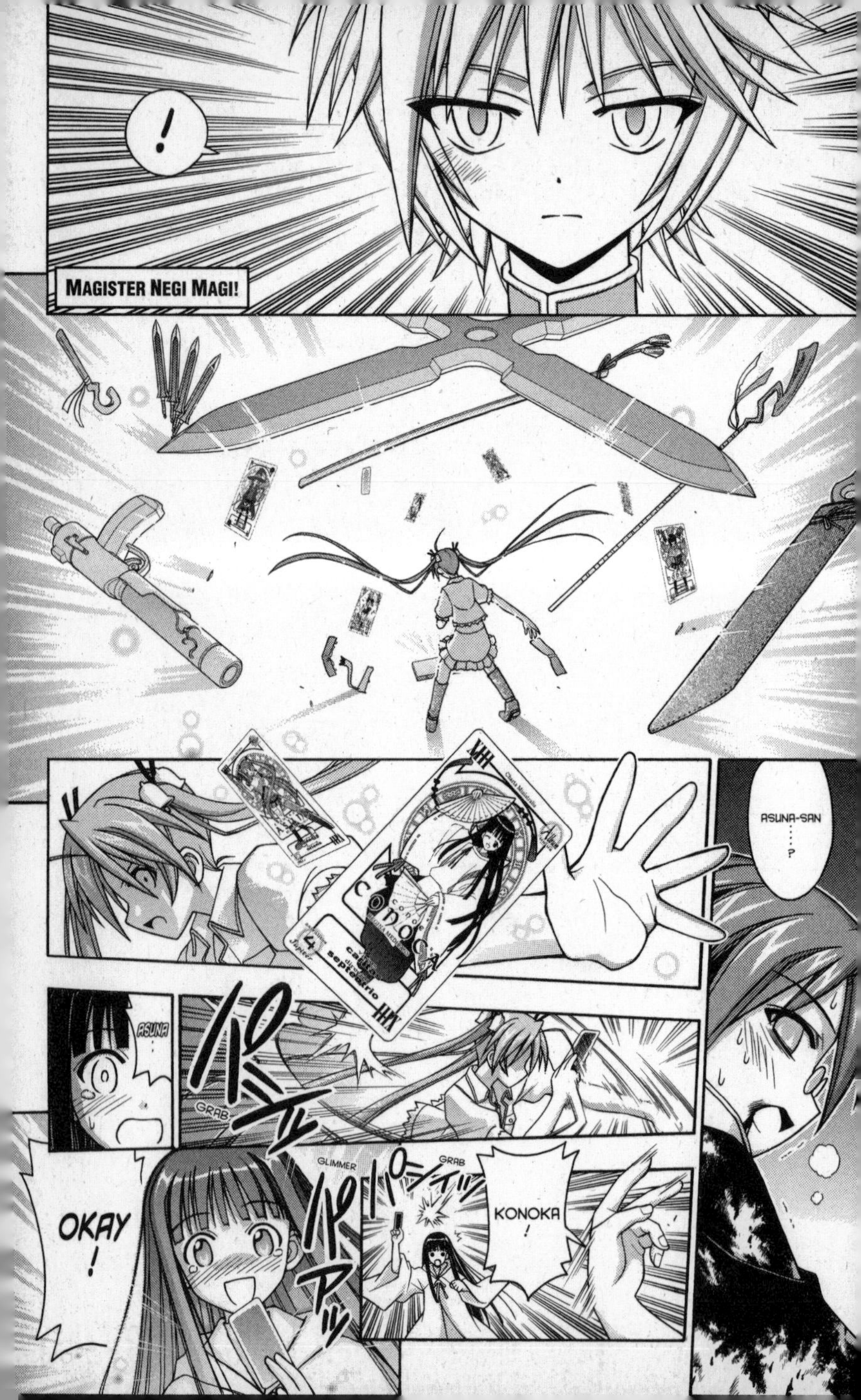
!
MAGISTER NEGI MAGI!
ASUNA-SAN....?
GRAB
ASUNA
GRAB
KONOKA!
GLIMMER
OKAY!

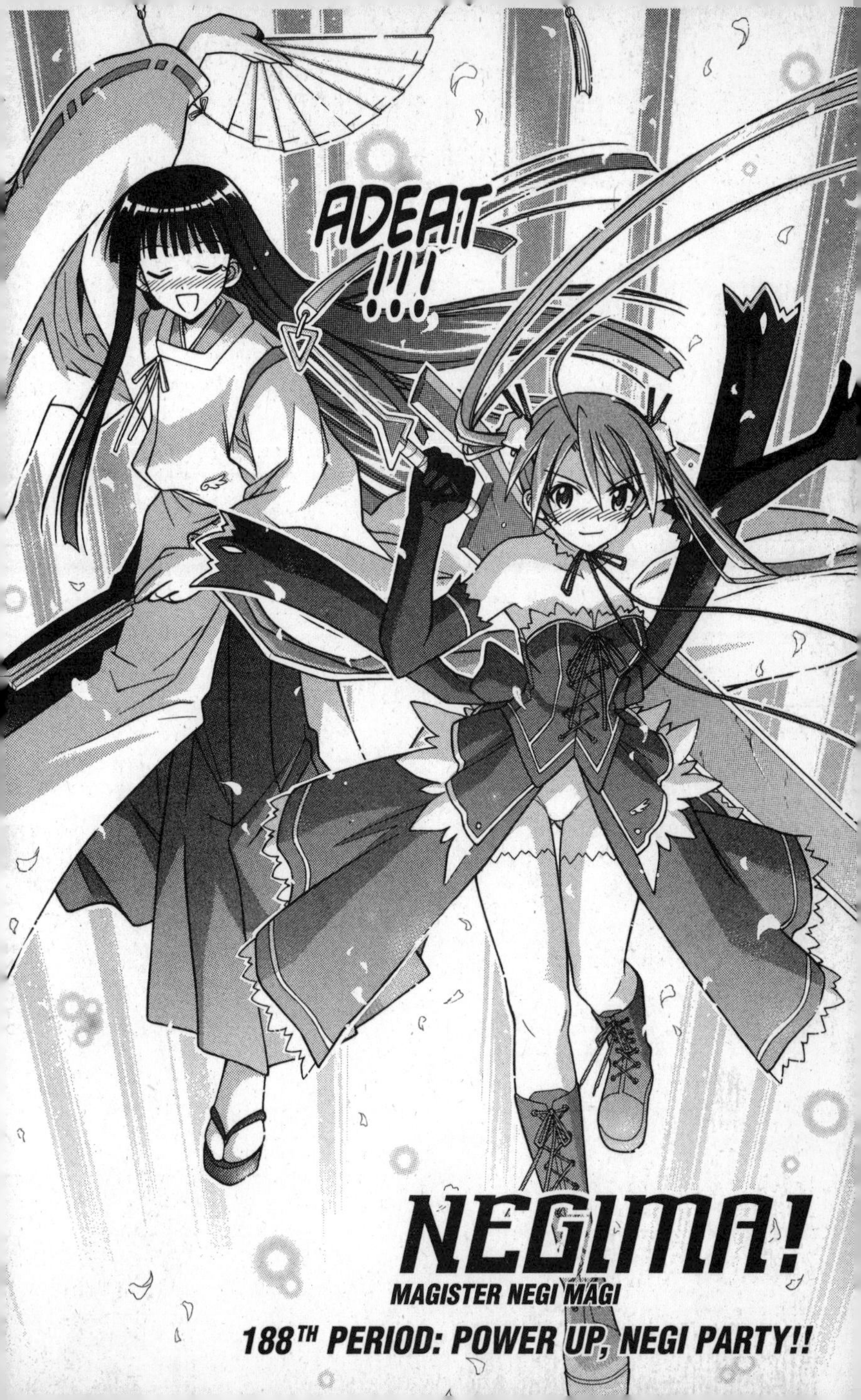
ADEAT!!!

NEGIMA!

MAGISTER NEGI MAGI

188TH PERIOD: POWER UP, NEGI PARTY!!

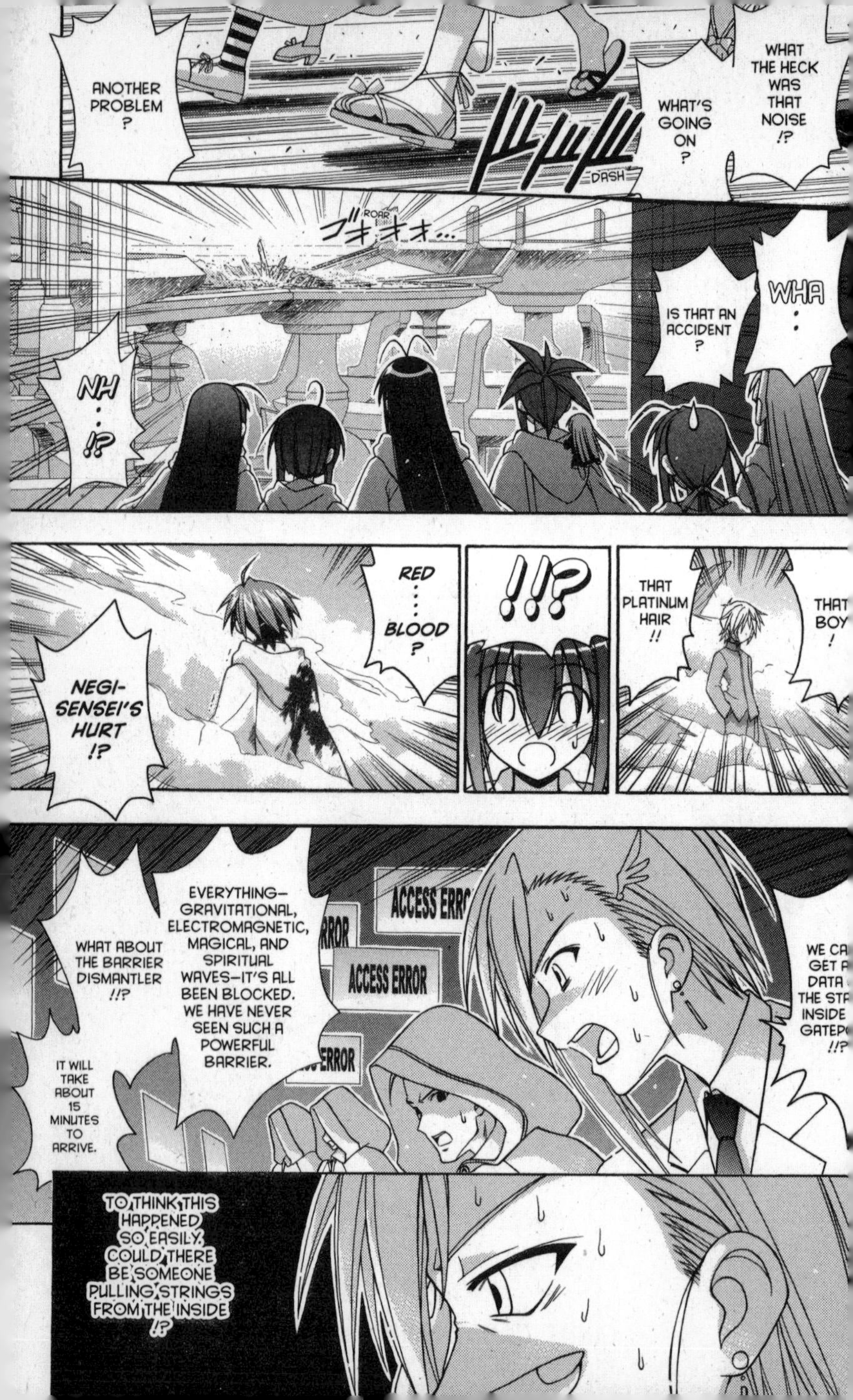
WHAT THE HECK WAS THAT NOISE !?
WHAT'S GOING ON ?
DASH
ANOTHER PROBLEM ?
WHA . .
IS THAT AN ACCIDENT ?
ROAR
NH . . !?
THAT BOY !
THAT PLATINUM HAIR !!
!!?
RED . . . . BLOOD ?
NEGI-SENSEI'S HURT !?
WE CA GET A DATA THE STA INSIDE GATEPO !!?
ACCESS ERRO
ACCESS ERROR
RROR
ERROR
EVERYTHING—GRAVITATIONAL, ELECTROMAGNETIC, MAGICAL, AND SPIRITUAL WAVES—IT'S ALL BEEN BLOCKED. WE HAVE NEVER SEEN SUCH A POWERFUL BARRIER.
WHAT ABOUT THE BARRIER DISMANTLER !!?
IT WILL TAKE ABOUT 15 MINUTES TO ARRIVE.
TO THINK THIS HAPPENED SO EASILY. COULD THERE BE SOMEONE PULLING STRINGS FROM THE INSIDE !?

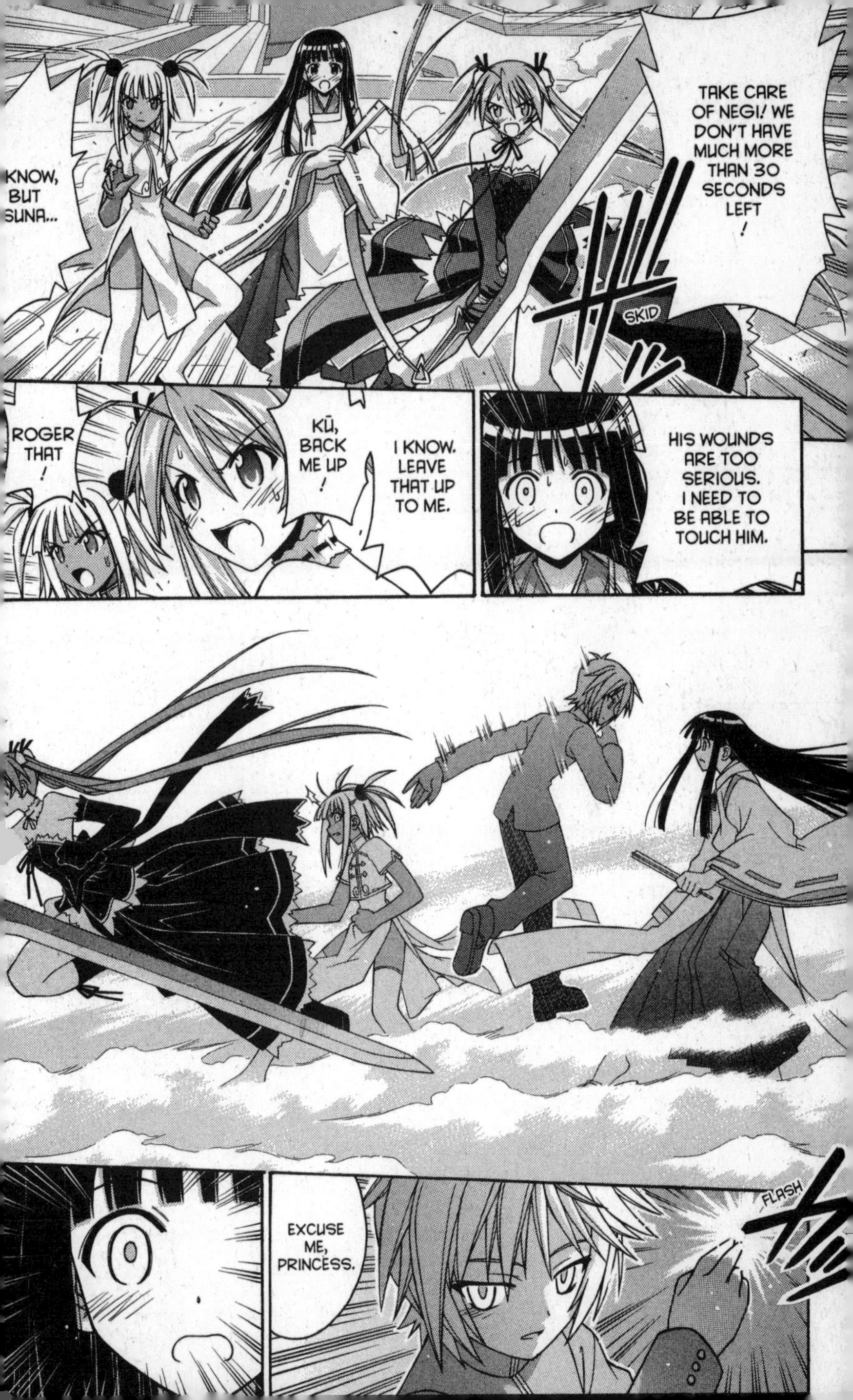
TAKE CARE OF NEGI! WE DON'T HAVE MUCH MORE THAN 30 SECONDS LEFT!
SKID
KNOW, BUT SUNA...
HIS WOUNDS ARE TOO SERIOUS. I NEED TO BE ABLE TO TOUCH HIM.
I KNOW. LEAVE THAT UP TO ME.
KŪ, BACK ME UP!
ROGER THAT!
FLASH
EXCUSE ME, PRINCESS.

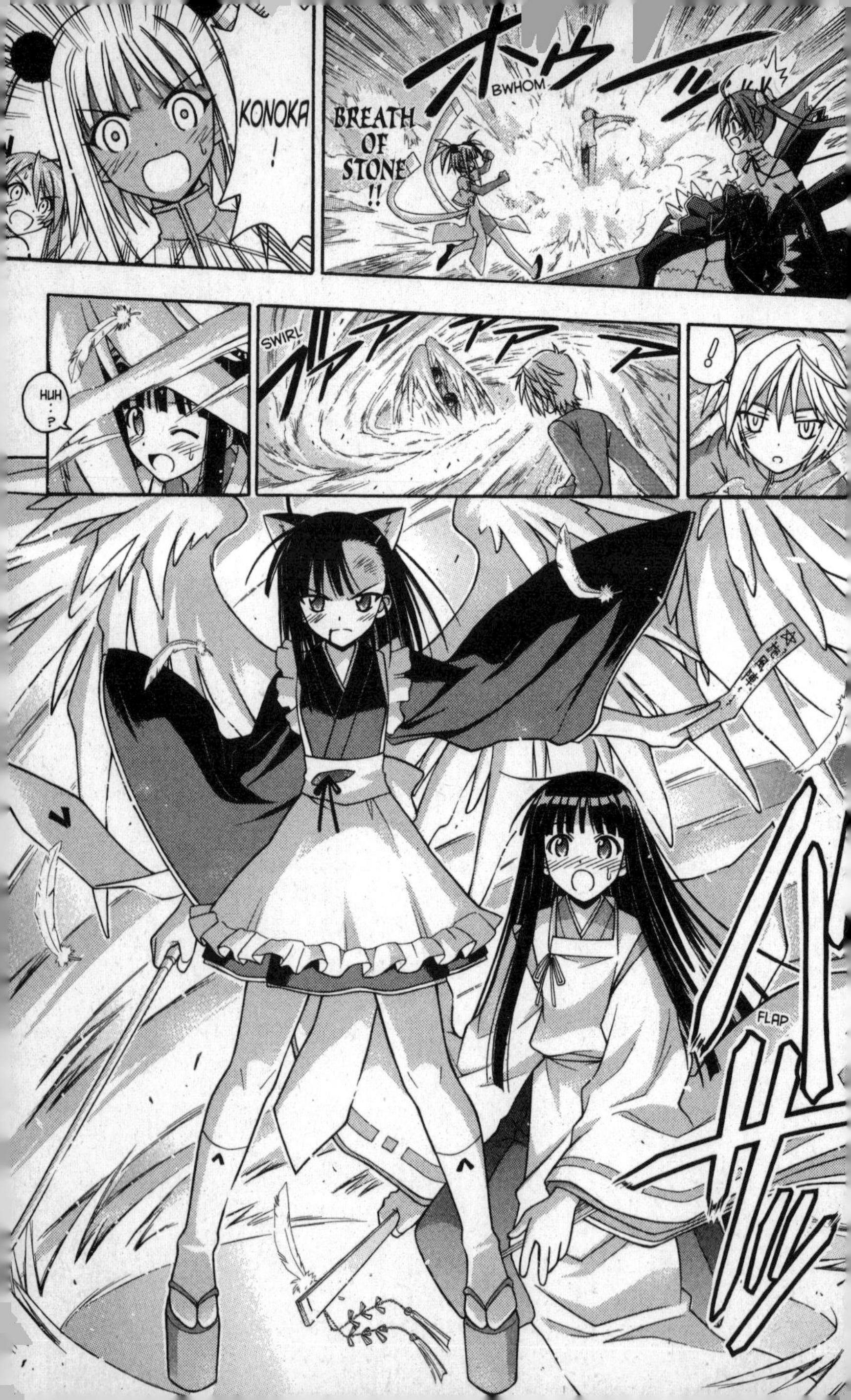
BWHOM
BREATH OF STONE!!
KONOKA!
!
SWIRL
HUH..?
FLAP

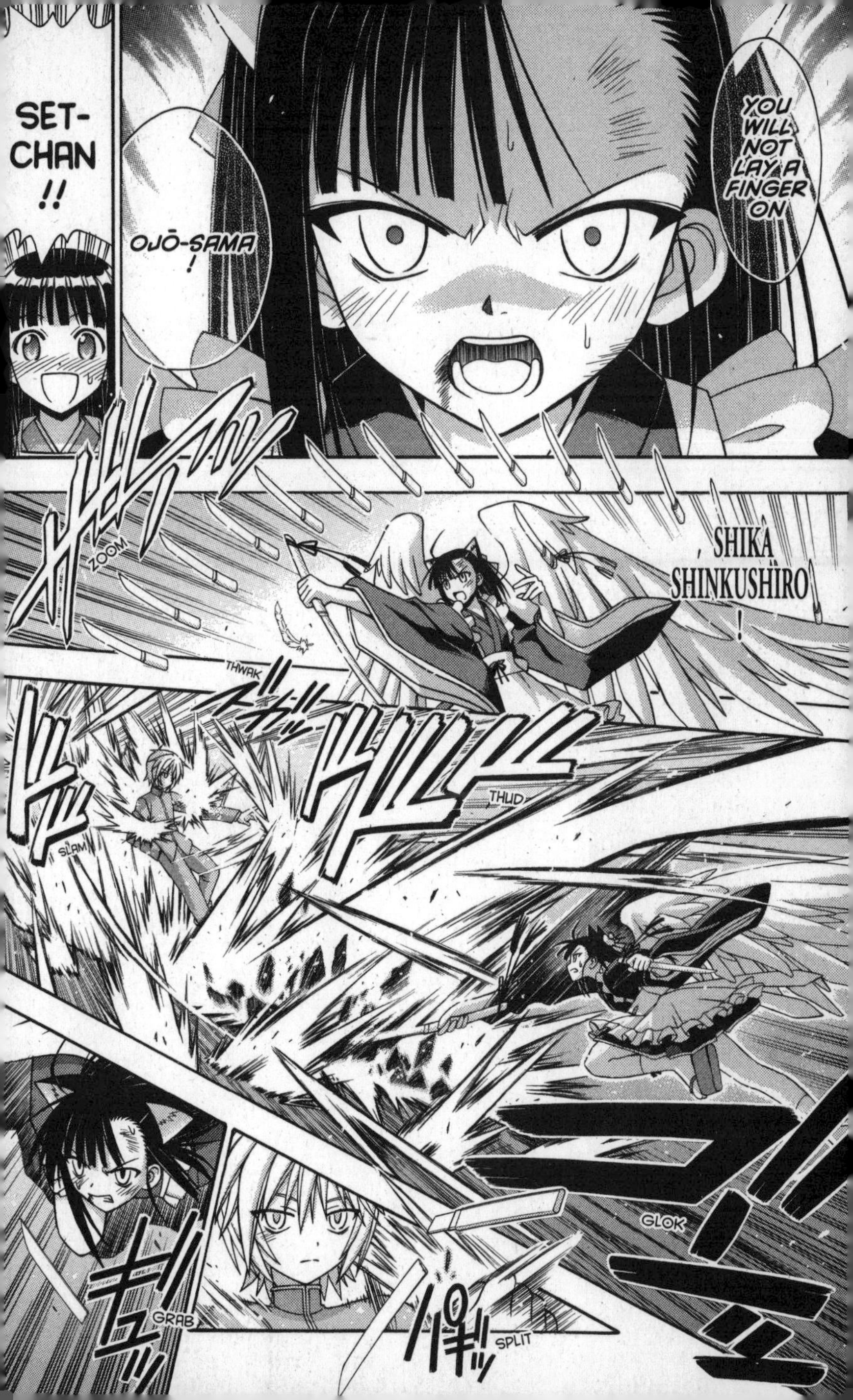

YOU WILL NOT LAY A FINGER ON
OJŌ-SAMA!
SET-CHAN!!
SHIKA SHINKUSHIRO!
ZOOM
THWAK
THUD
SLAM
GLOK
SPLIT
GRAB

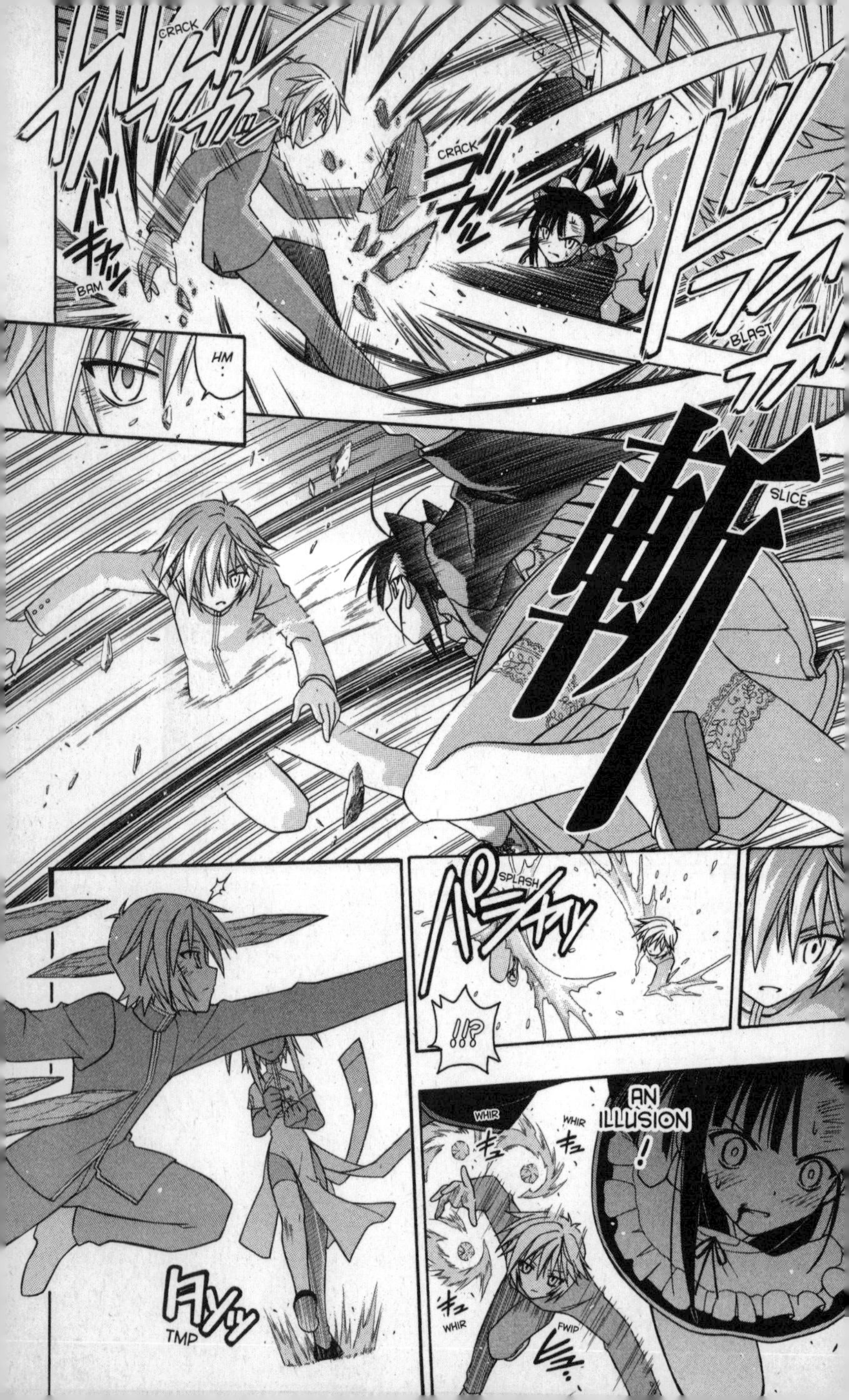
CRACK
CRACK
BAM
BLAST
HM
...
SLICE
SPLASH
!!?
TMP
AN ILLUSION!
WHIR
WHIR
WHIR
FWIP

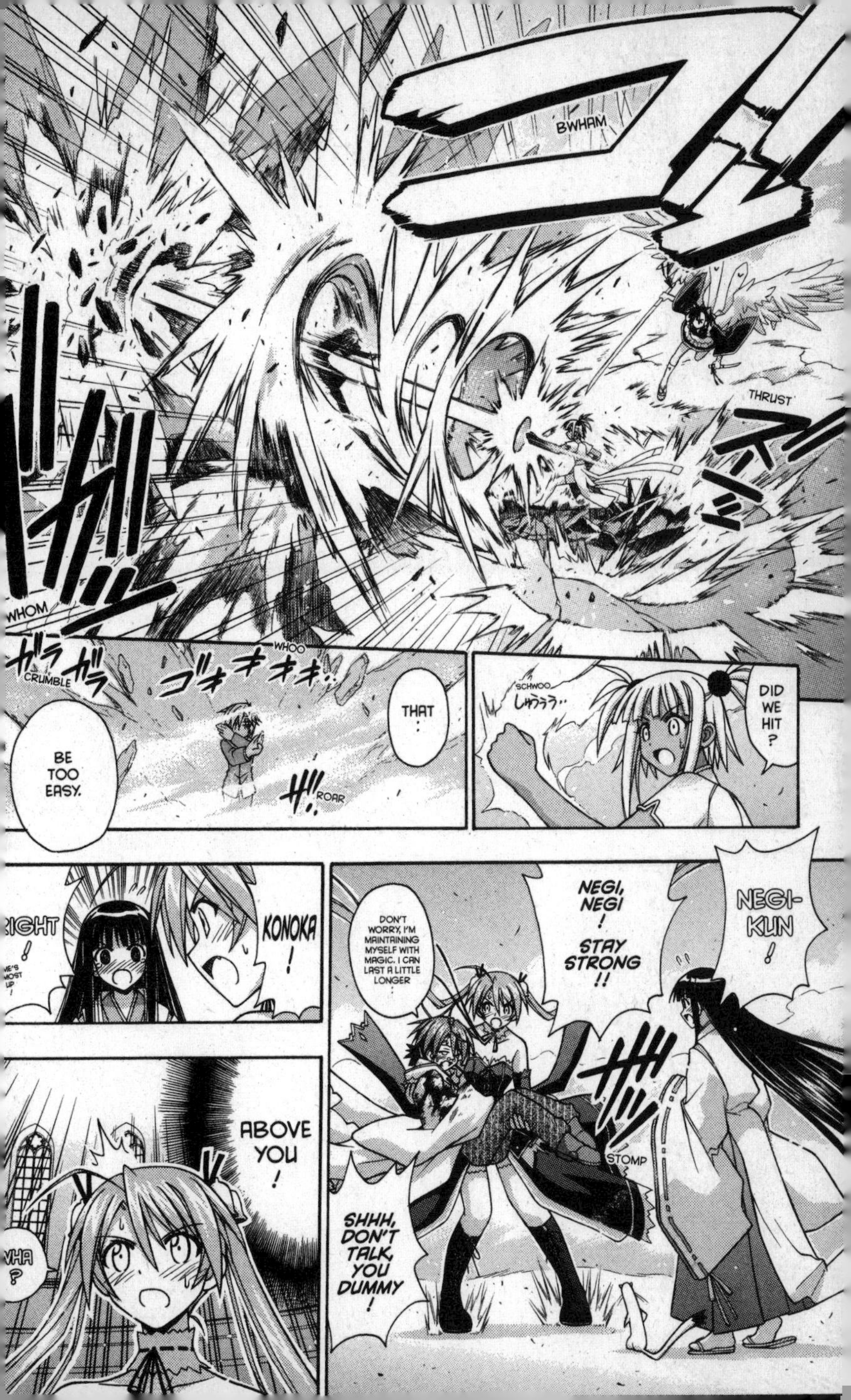
BWHAM
THRUST
WHOM
SCHWOO
DID WE HIT?
WHOO
CRUMBLE
THAT...
BE TOO EASY.
ROAR
NEGI-KUN!
NEGI, NEGI! STAY STRONG!!
DON'T WORRY, I'M MAINTAINING MYSELF WITH MAGIC. I CAN LAST A LITTLE LONGER...
STOMP
SHHH, DON'T TALK, YOU DUMMY!
KONOKA!
ABOVE YOU!
WHA?

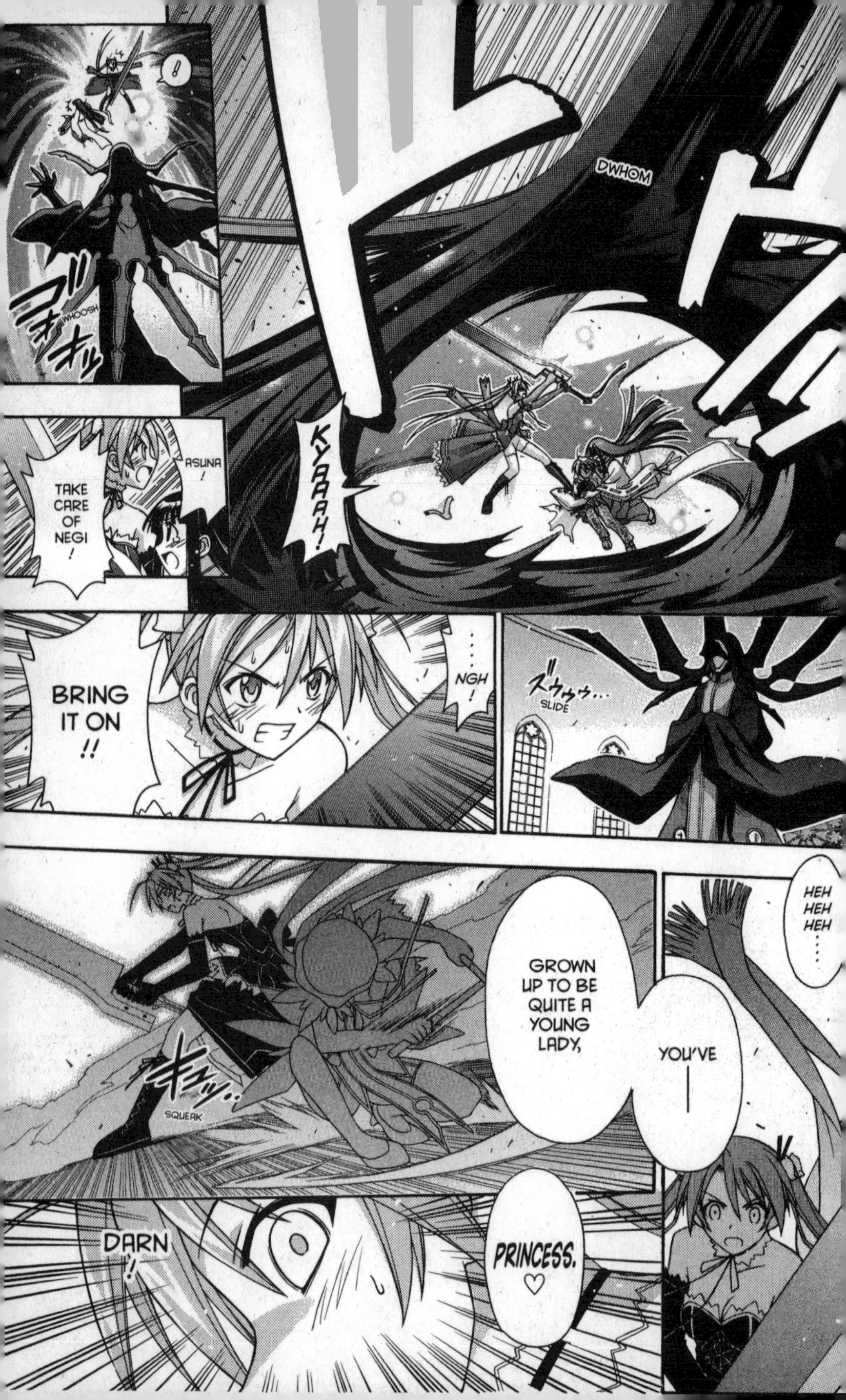
DWHOM
KYAAAH!
!
WHOOSH
ASUNA!
TAKE CARE OF NEGI!
SLIDE
...... NGH!
BRING IT ON!!
HEH HEH HEH....
YOU'VE —
GROWN UP TO BE QUITE A YOUNG LADY,
PRINCESS. ♡
SQUEAK
DARN!

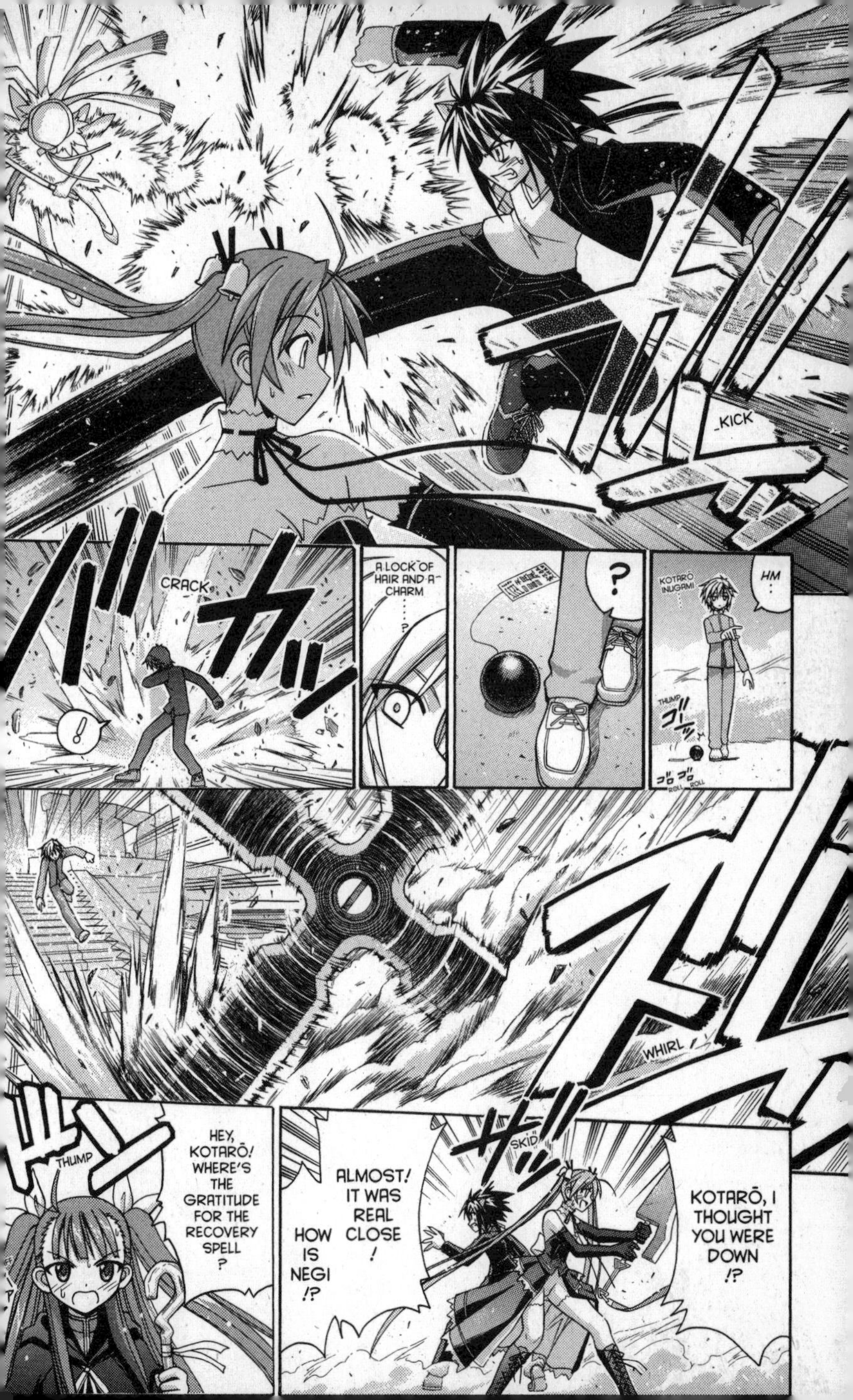
KICK
HM ...
KOTARŌ INUGAMI ...
THUMP
ROLL ROLL
?
A LOCK OF HAIR AND A CHARM ......?
CRACK
!
WHIRL
SKID
KOTARŌ, I THOUGHT YOU WERE DOWN !?
ALMOST! IT WAS REAL CLOSE !
HOW IS NEGI !?
THUMP
HEY, KOTARŌ! WHERE'S THE GRATITUDE FOR THE RECOVERY SPELL ?

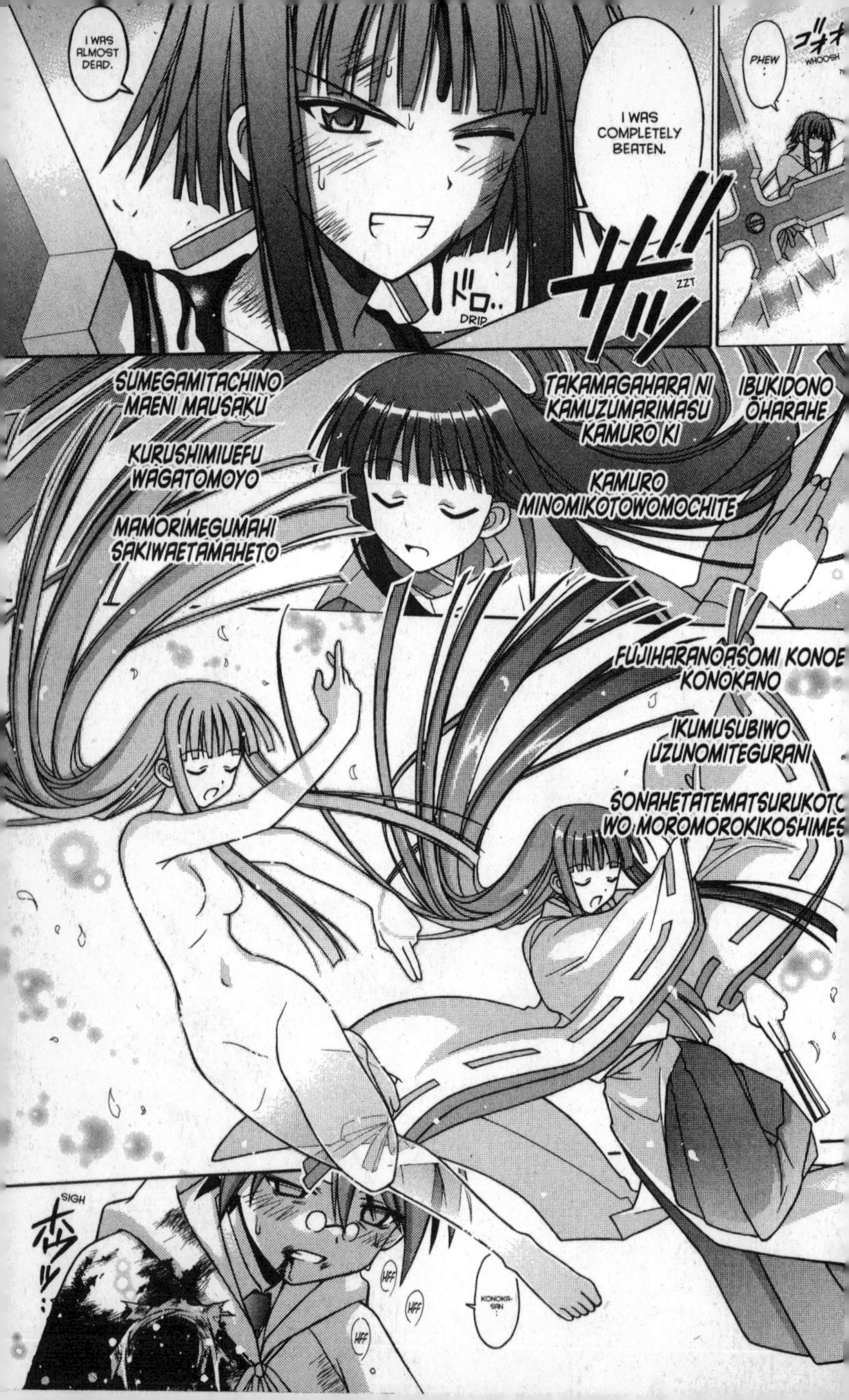
ゴォオ
WHOOSH
PHEW
:
I WAS COMPLETELY BEATEN.
I WAS ALMOST DEAD.
ザッ
ZZT
ドロ..
DRIP
IBUKIDONO ŌHARAHE
TAKAMAGAHARA NI KAMUZUMARIMASU KAMURO KI
KAMURO MINOMIKOTOWOMOCHITE
SUMEGAMITACHINO MAENI MAUSAKU
KURUSHIMIUEFU WAGATOMOYO
MAMORIMEGUMAHI SAKIWAETAMAHETO
FUJIHARANOASOMI KONOE KONOKANO
IKUMUSUBIWO UZUNOMITEGURANI
SONAHETATEMATSURUKOTO WO MOROMOROKIKOSHIMES
KONOKA-SAN
:
HFF
HFF
HFF
SIGH
ホッ

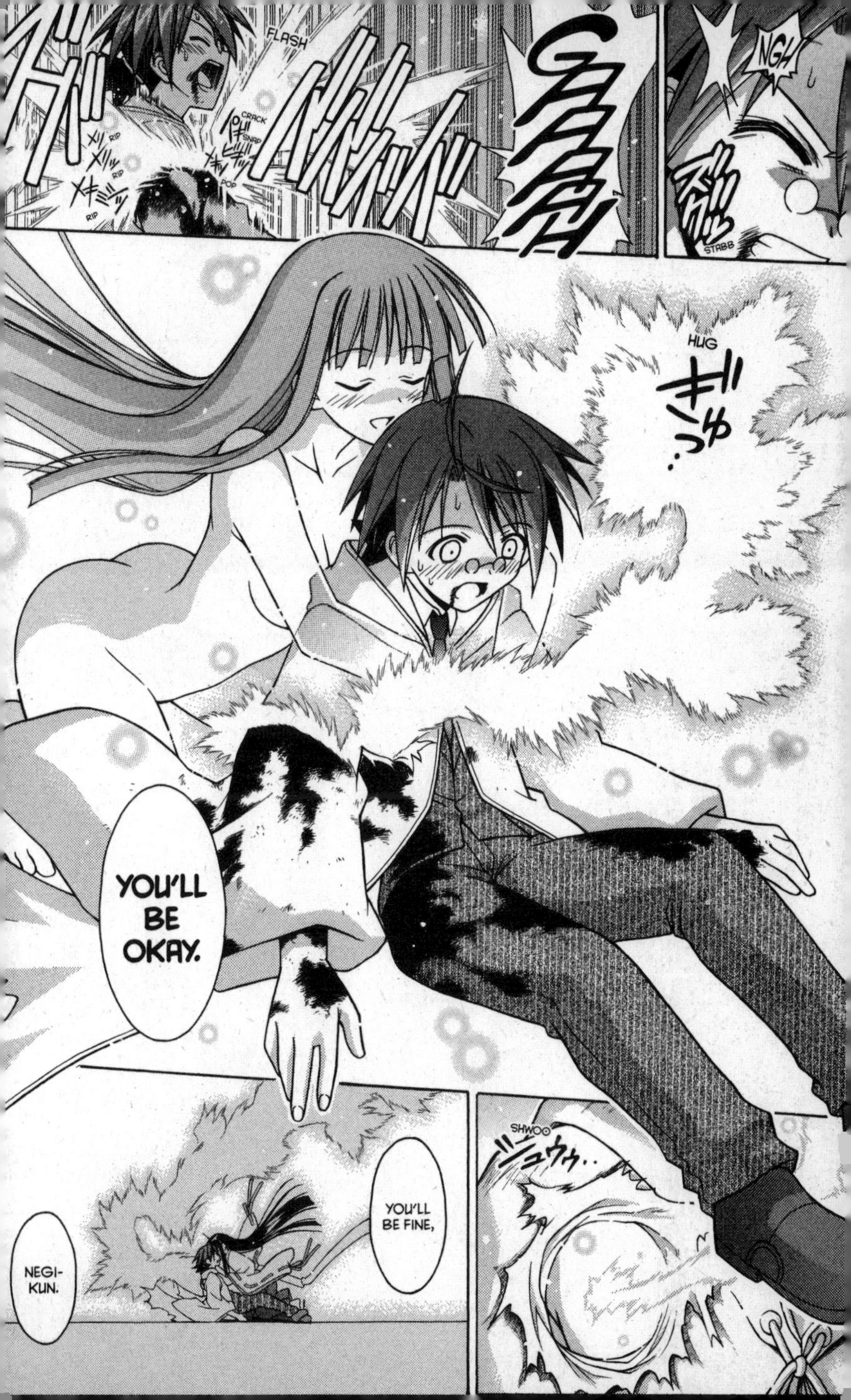
NGH
STABB
FLASH
RIP
RIP
RIP
CRACK
SNAP
POP
HUG
ぎゅっ…
YOU'LL BE OKAY.
SHWOO
シュウゥ…
YOU'LL BE FINE,
NEGI-KUN.

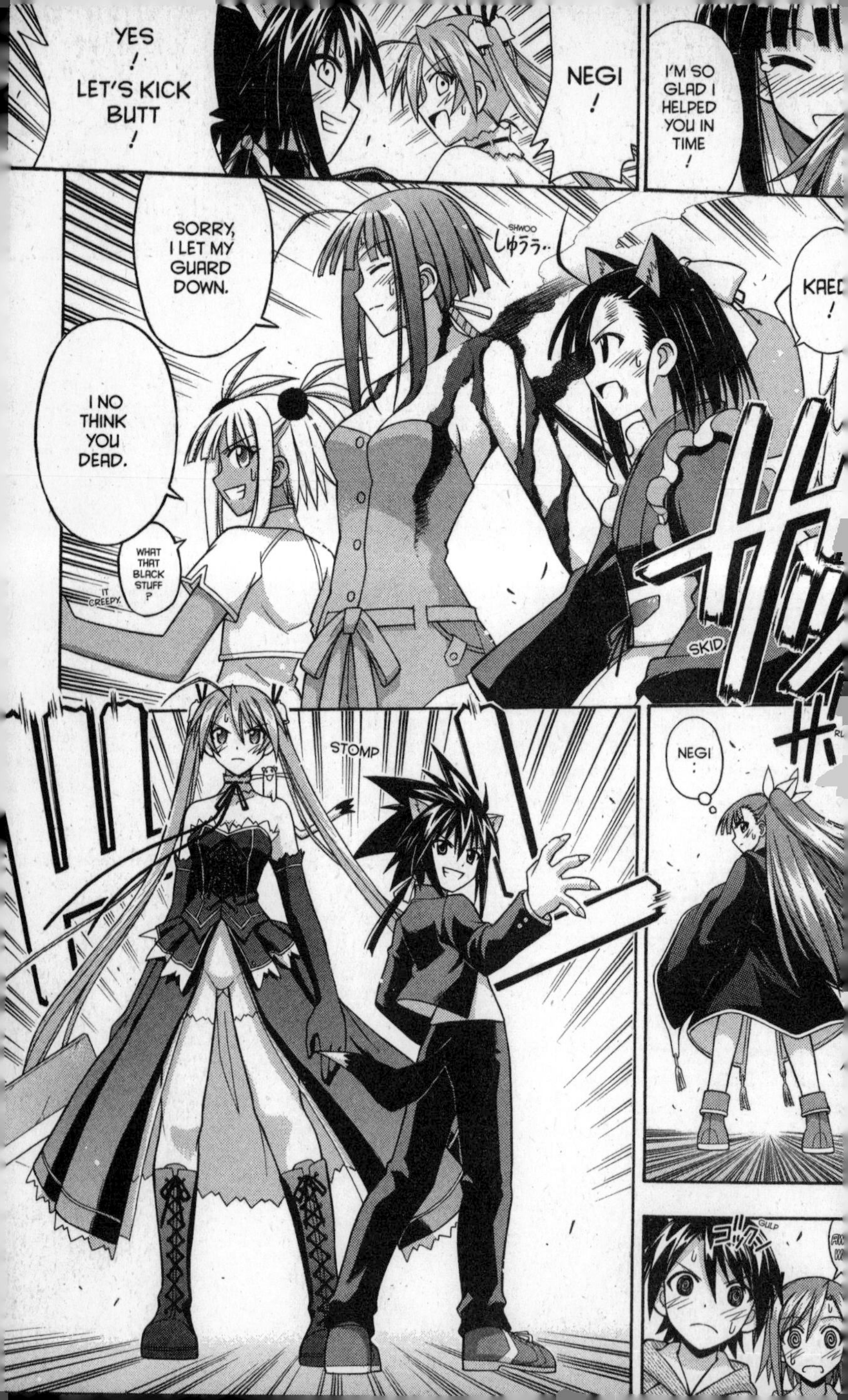
I'M SO GLAD I HELPED YOU IN TIME !
NEGI !
YES ! LET'S KICK BUTT !
KAED !
SHWOO
しゅうう..
SORRY, I LET MY GUARD DOWN.
I NO THINK YOU DEAD.
WHAT THAT BLACK STUFF ?
IT CREEPY.
SKID
NEGI :
GULP
STOMP

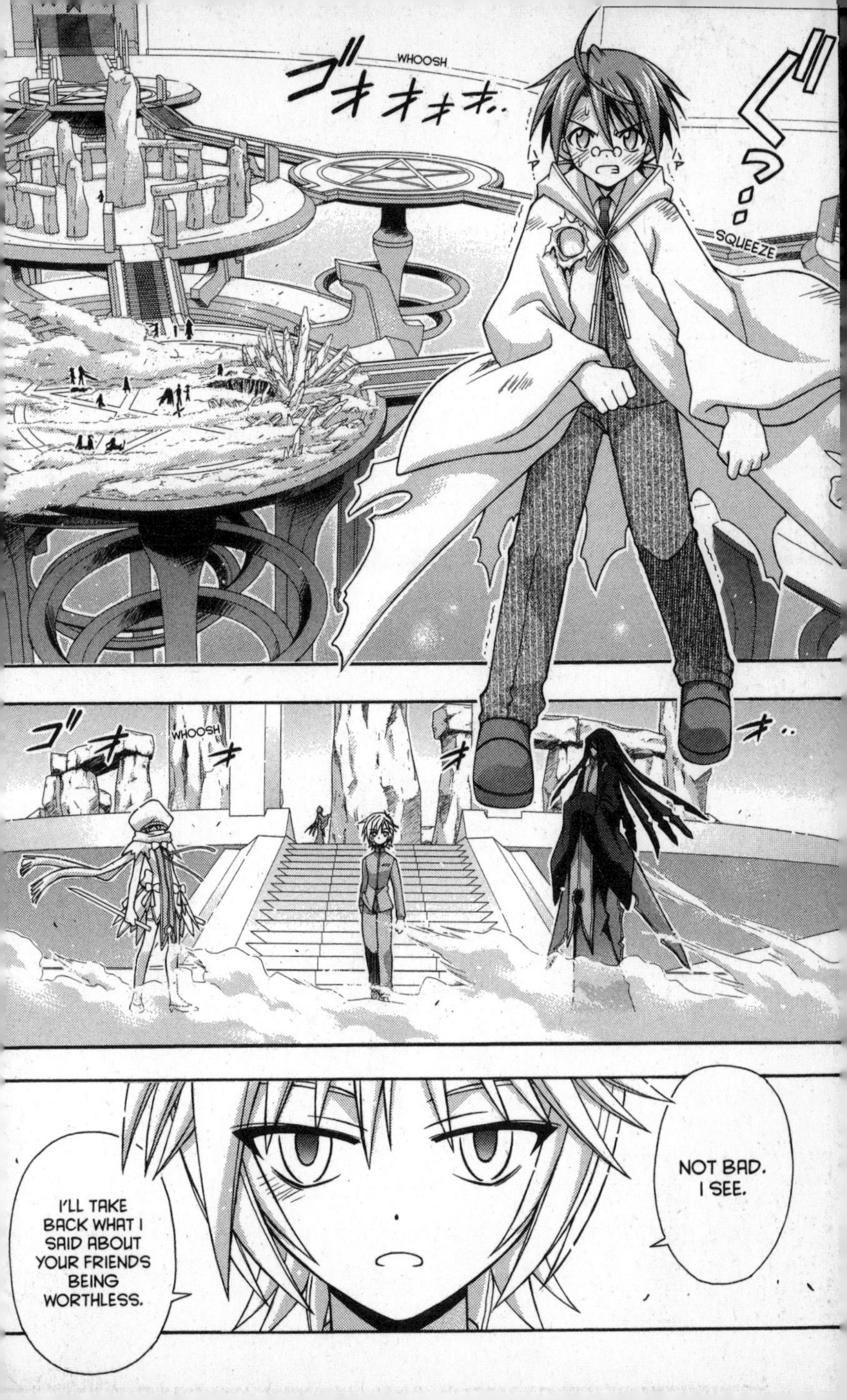
WHOOSH
SQUEEZE
WHOOSH
NOT BAD. I SEE.
I'LL TAKE BACK WHAT I SAID ABOUT YOUR FRIENDS BEING WORTHLESS.

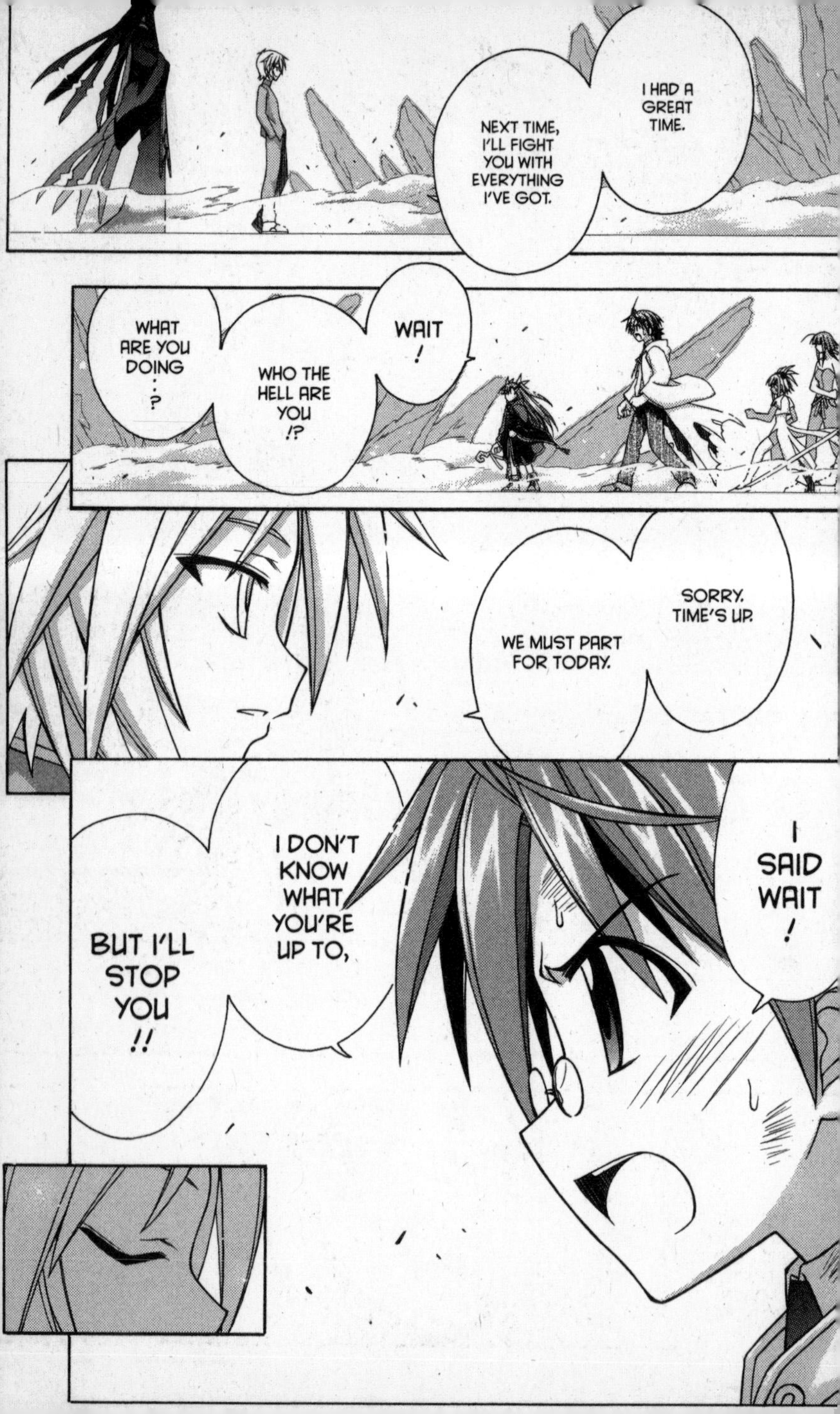
I HAD A GREAT TIME.
NEXT TIME, I'LL FIGHT YOU WITH EVERYTHING I'VE GOT.
WAIT!
WHO THE HELL ARE YOU!?
WHAT ARE YOU DOING...?
SORRY. TIME'S UP.
WE MUST PART FOR TODAY.
I SAID WAIT!
I DON'T KNOW WHAT YOU'RE UP TO,
BUT I'LL STOP YOU!!

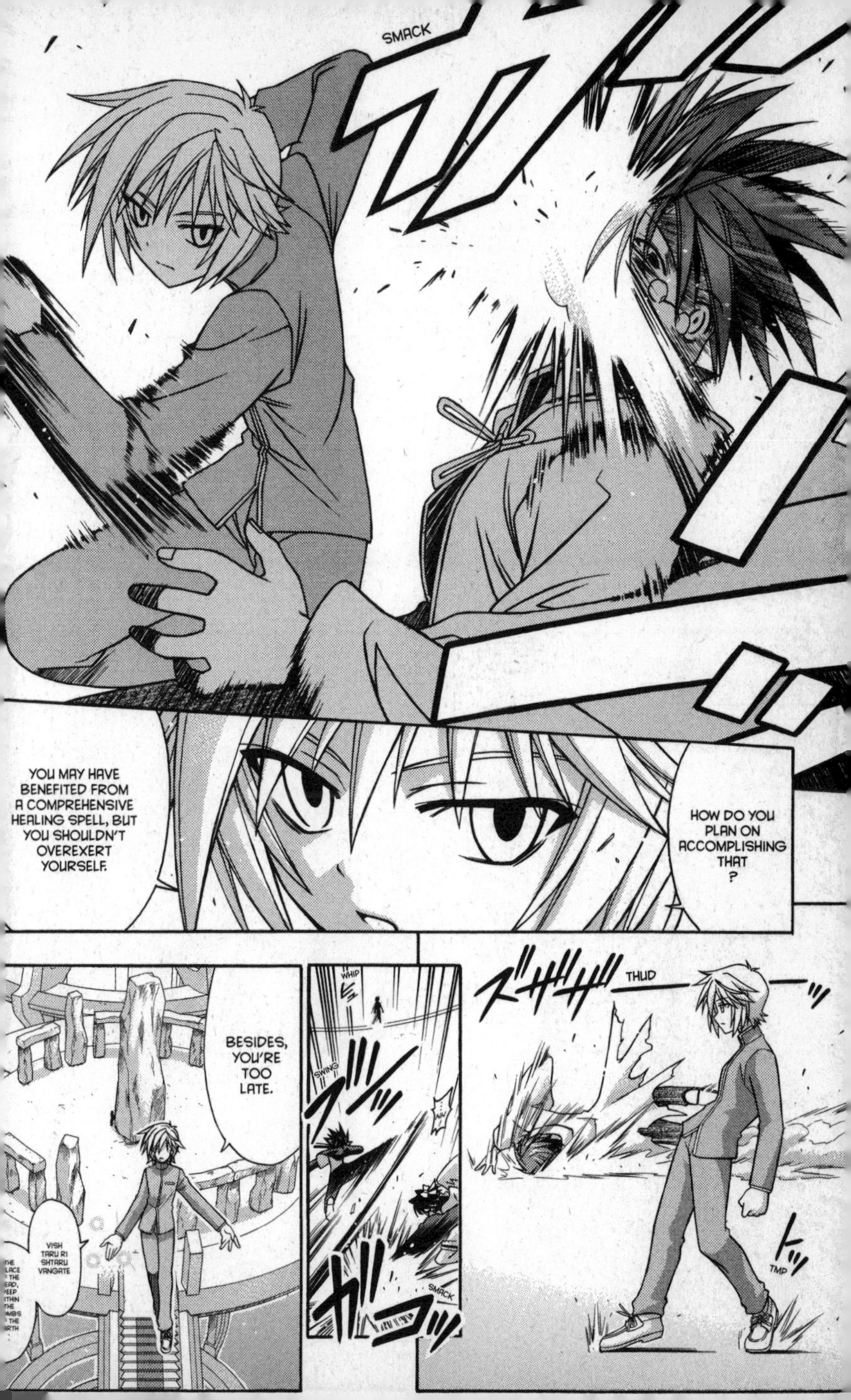
SMACK
HOW DO YOU PLAN ON ACCOMPLISHING THAT?
YOU MAY HAVE BENEFITED FROM A COMPREHENSIVE HEALING SPELL, BUT YOU SHOULDN'T OVEREXERT YOURSELF.
THUD
TMP
WHIP
SWING
SMACK
BESIDES, YOU'RE TOO LATE.
VISH TARU RI SHTARU VANGATE

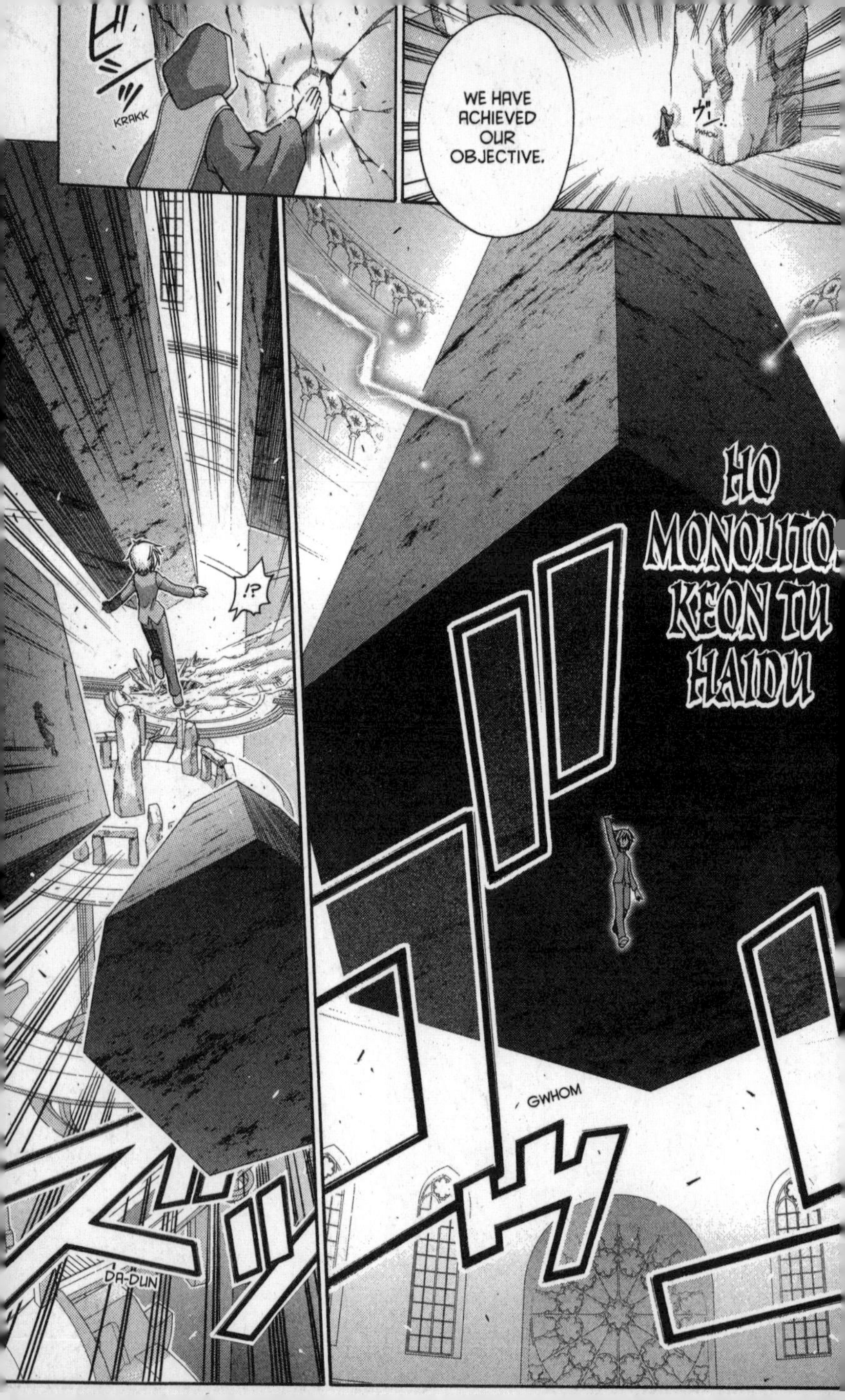
ヴー
VWHOM
WE HAVE ACHIEVED OUR OBJECTIVE.
KRAKK
HO MONOLITO KEON TU HAIDU
GWHOM
!?
DA-DUN

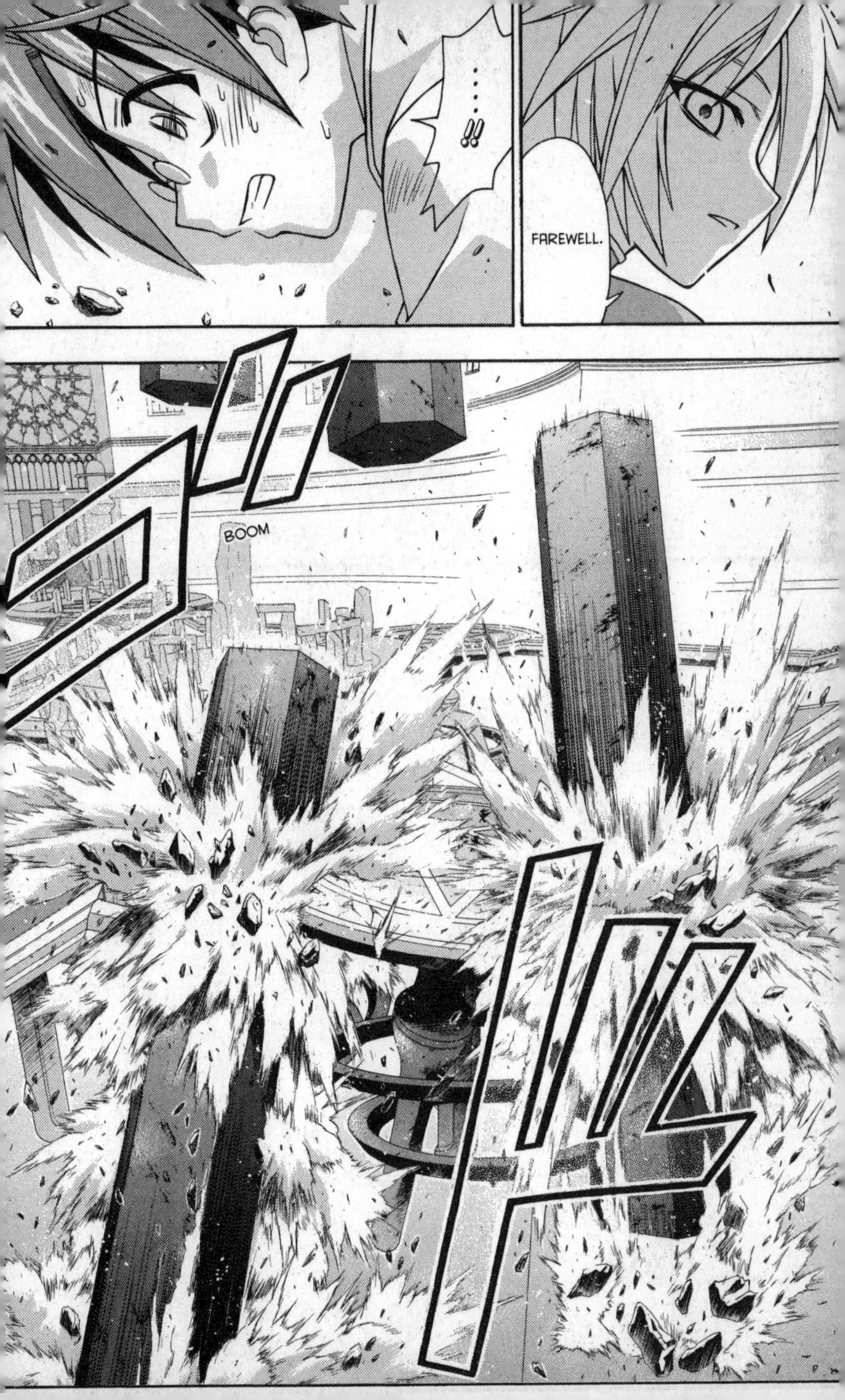
FAREWELL.
...!!
BOOM

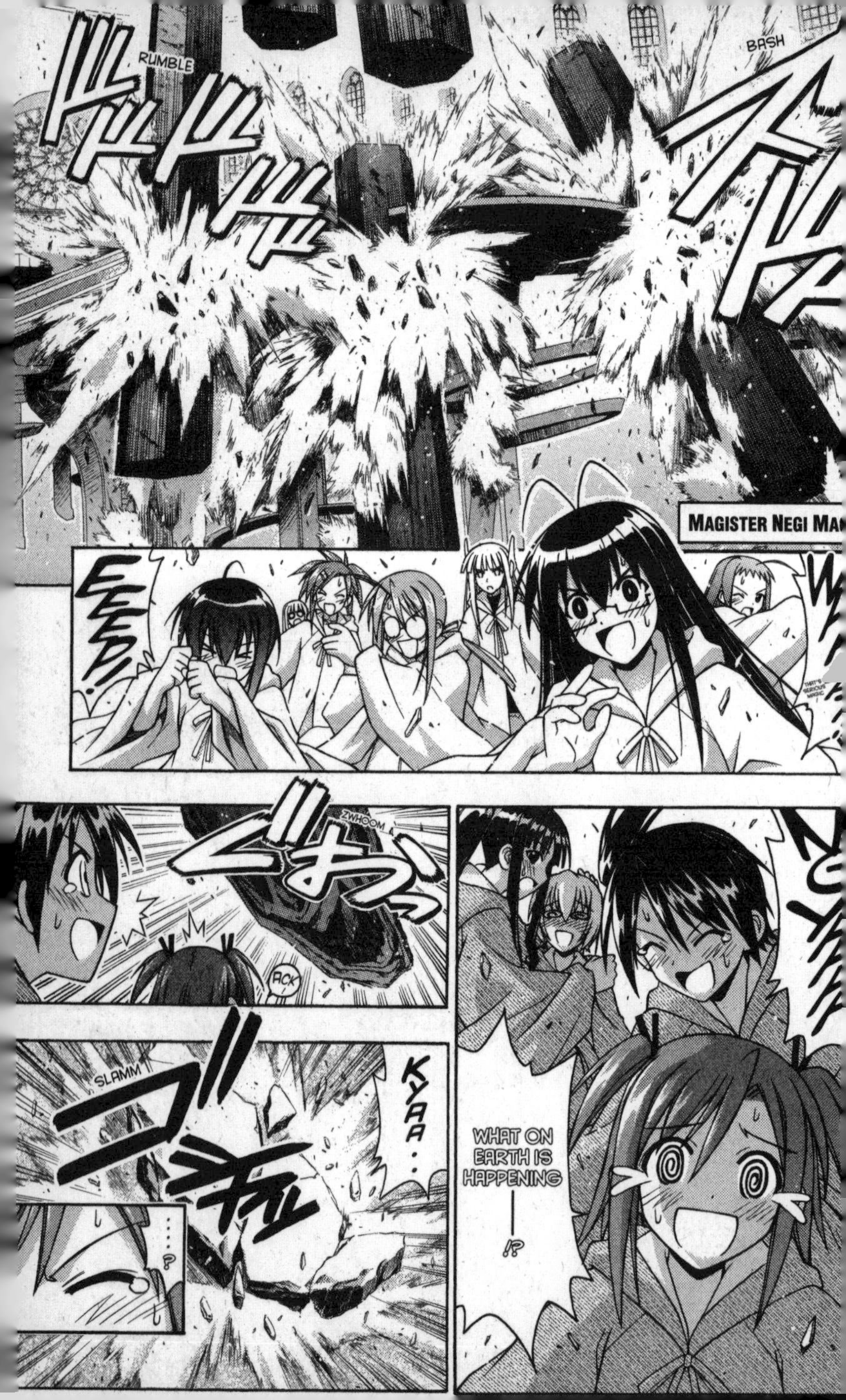
BASH
RUMBLE
MAGISTER NEGI MAG
THAT'S SERIOUS MAGIC
EEEEP!!
WHAT ON EARTH IS HAPPENING —!?
ZWHOOM
ACK
KYAA..
SLAMM
....?

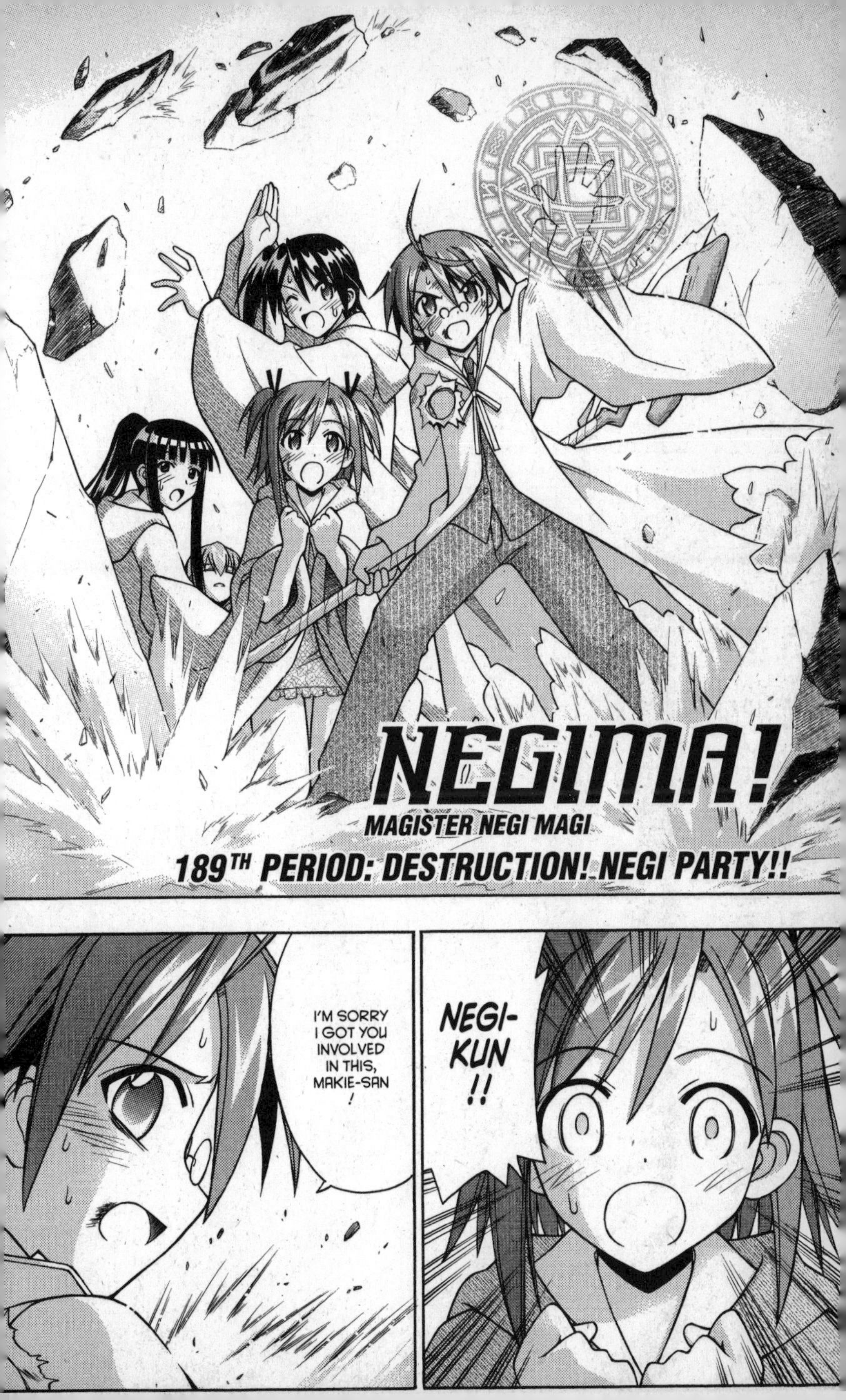
NEGIMA!
MAGISTER NEGI MAGI
189TH PERIOD: DESTRUCTION! NEGI PARTY!!
NEGI-KUN!!
I'M SORRY I GOT YOU INVOLVED IN THIS, MAKIE-SAN!

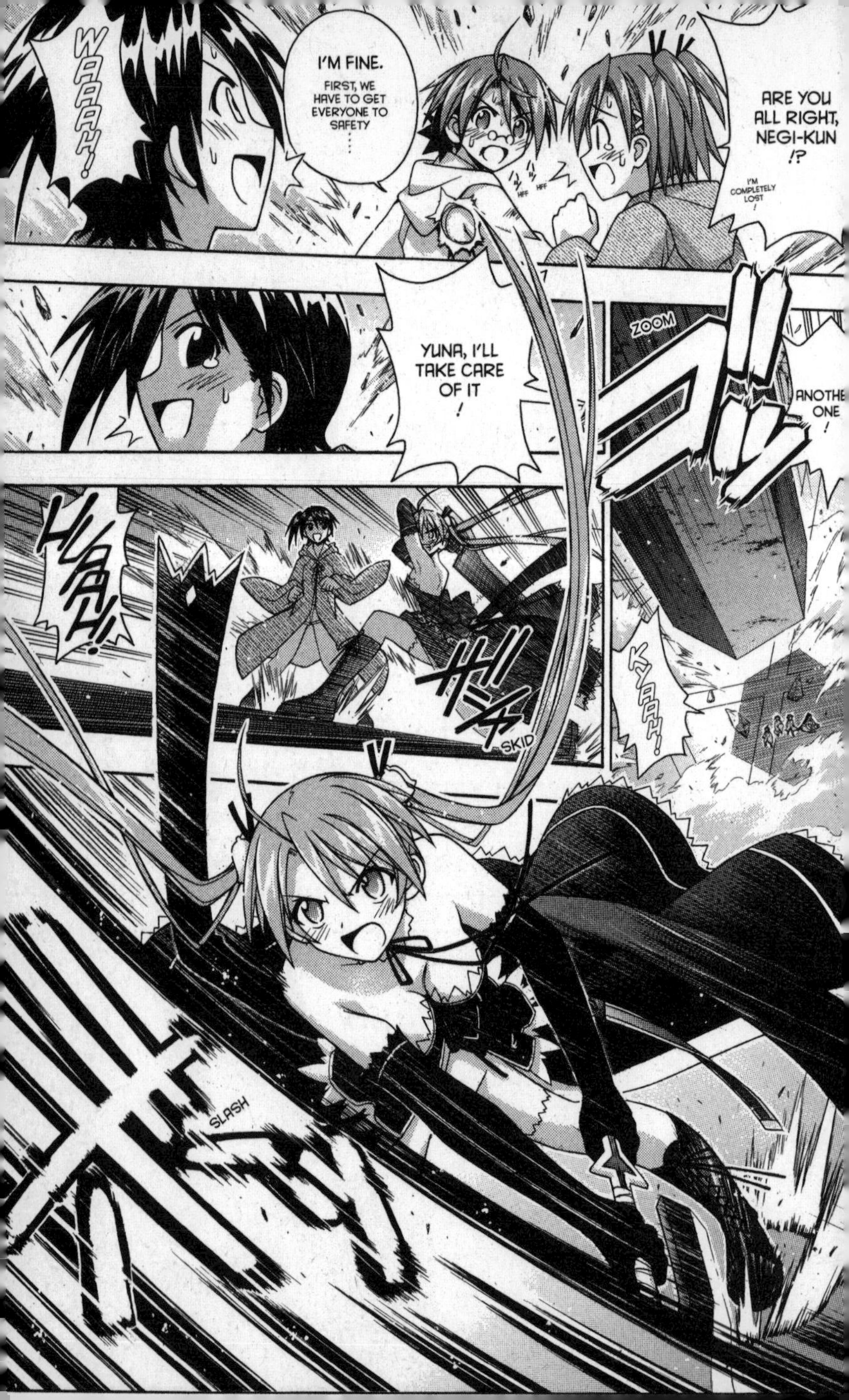
ARE YOU ALL RIGHT, NEGI-KUN!?
I'M COMPLETELY LOST!
HFF HFF
I'M FINE.
FIRST, WE HAVE TO GET EVERYONE TO SAFETY...
WAAAAH!
ZOOM
ANOTHE ONE!
YUNA, I'LL TAKE CARE OF IT!
KYAAAH!
SKID
HUAAH!
SLASH

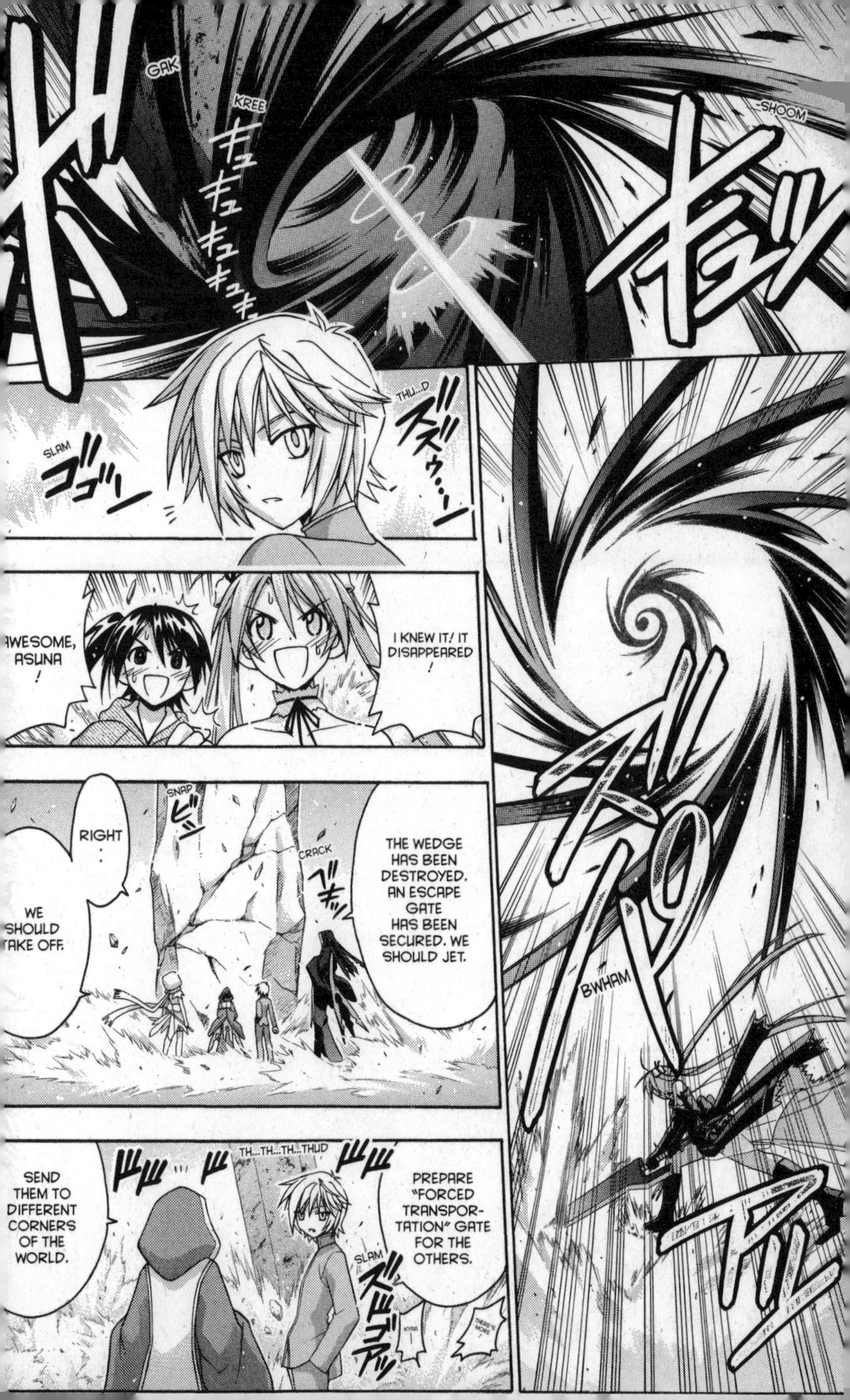
-SHOOM
KREE
GAK
BWHAM
THU...D
SLAM
I KNEW IT! IT DISAPPEARED!
AWESOME, ASUNA!
THE WEDGE HAS BEEN DESTROYED. AN ESCAPE GATE HAS BEEN SECURED. WE SHOULD JET.
CRACK
SNAP
RIGHT...
WE SHOULD TAKE OFF.
TH...TH...TH...THUD
PREPARE "FORCED TRANSPORTATION" GATE FOR THE OTHERS.
SEND THEM TO DIFFERENT CORNERS OF THE WORLD.
THERE'S MORE!
SLAM
KYAA!

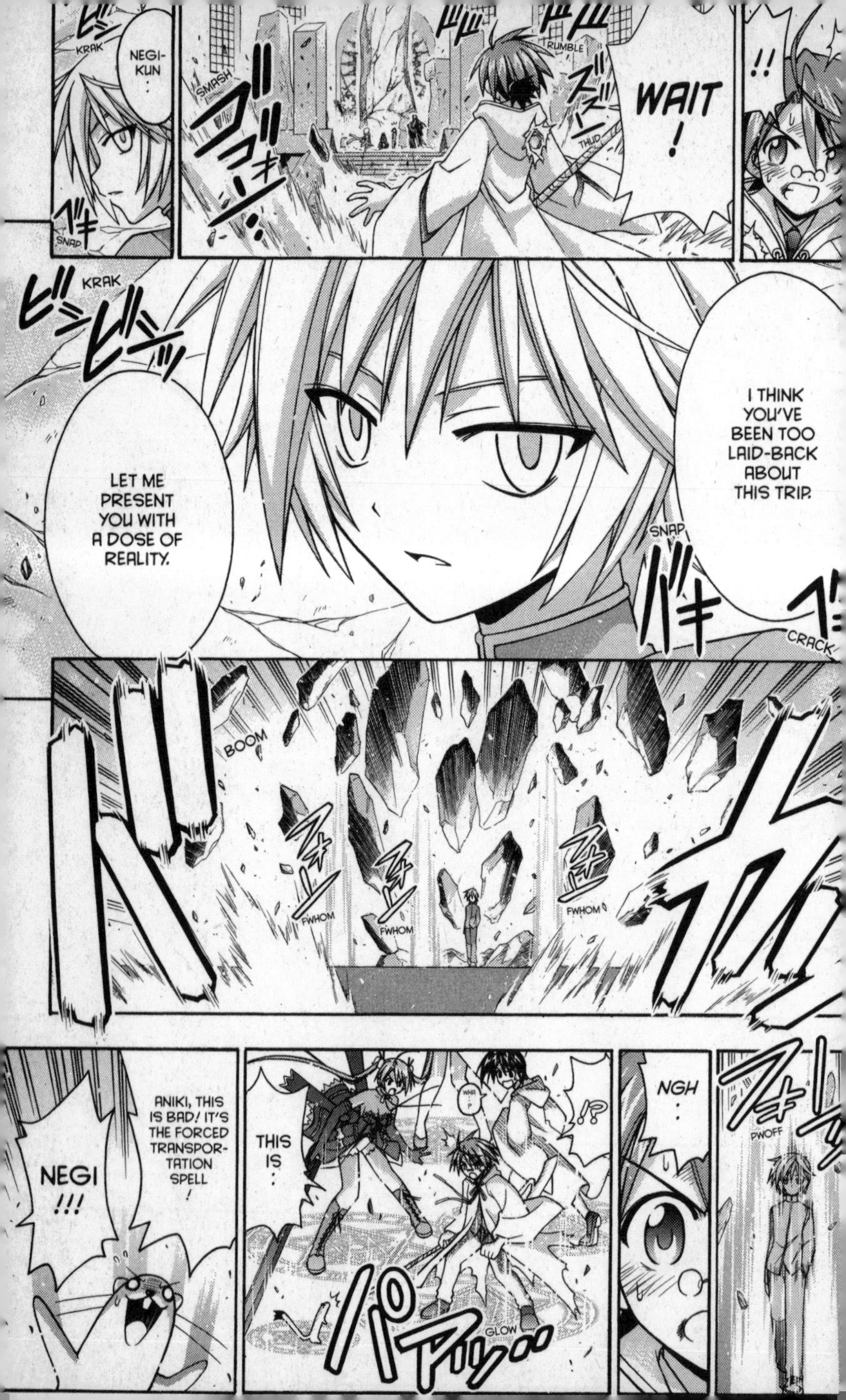
!!
WAIT!
RUMBLE
THUD
SMASH
KRAK
NEGI-KUN...
SNAP
I THINK YOU'VE BEEN TOO LAID-BACK ABOUT THIS TRIP.
SNAP
CRACK
LET ME PRESENT YOU WITH A DOSE OF REALITY.
KRAK
BOOM
FWHOM
FWHOM
FWHOM
PWOFF
NGH...
!?
WHA...?
THIS IS
GLOW
ANIKI, THIS IS BAD! IT'S THE FORCED TRANSPORTATION SPELL!
NEGI!!!

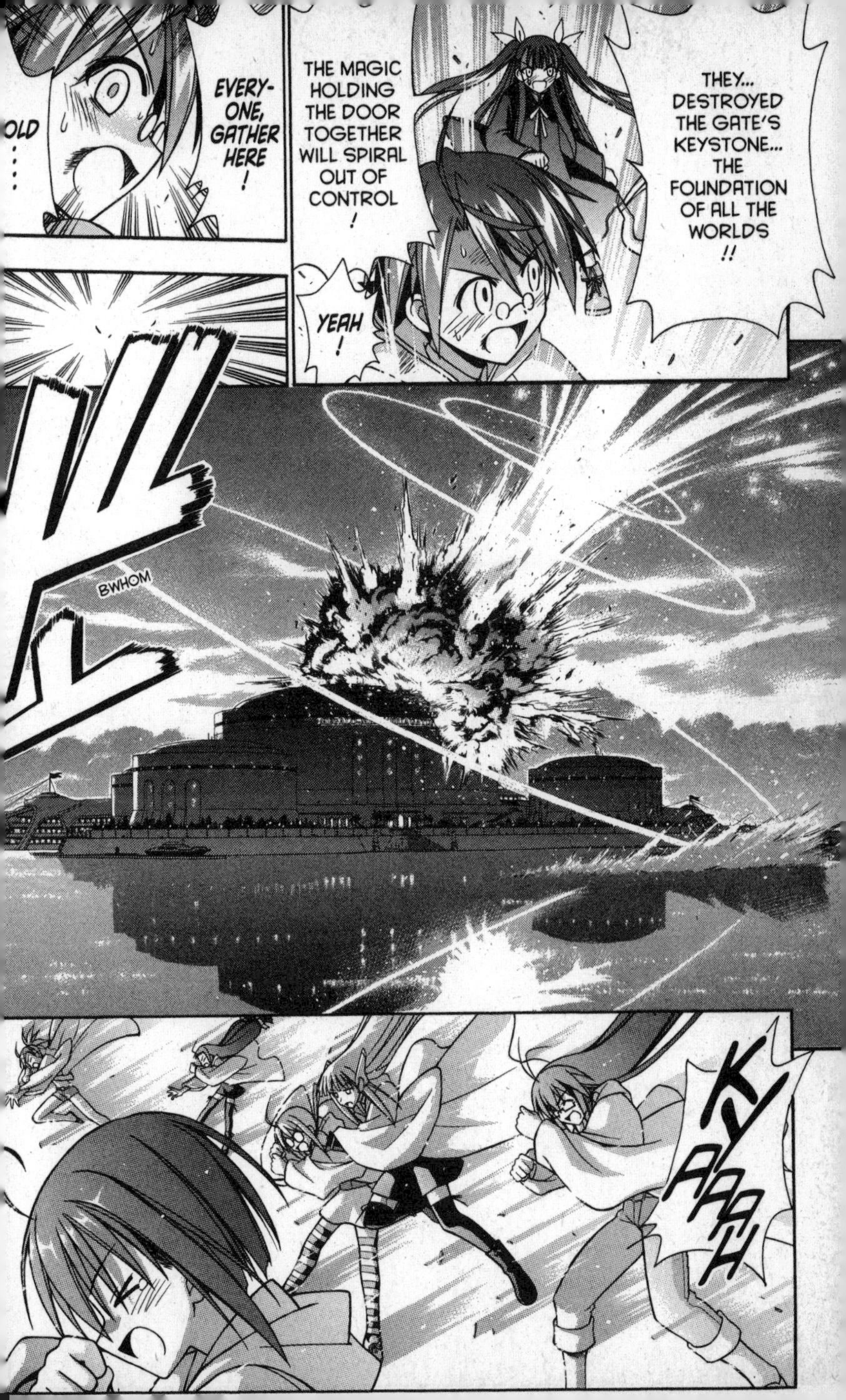
THEY... DESTROYED THE GATE'S KEYSTONE... THE FOUNDATION OF ALL THE WORLDS!!
THE MAGIC HOLDING THE DOOR TOGETHER WILL SPIRAL OUT OF CONTROL!
YEAH!
EVERY-ONE, GATHER HERE!
OLD...
BWHOM
KYAAAH

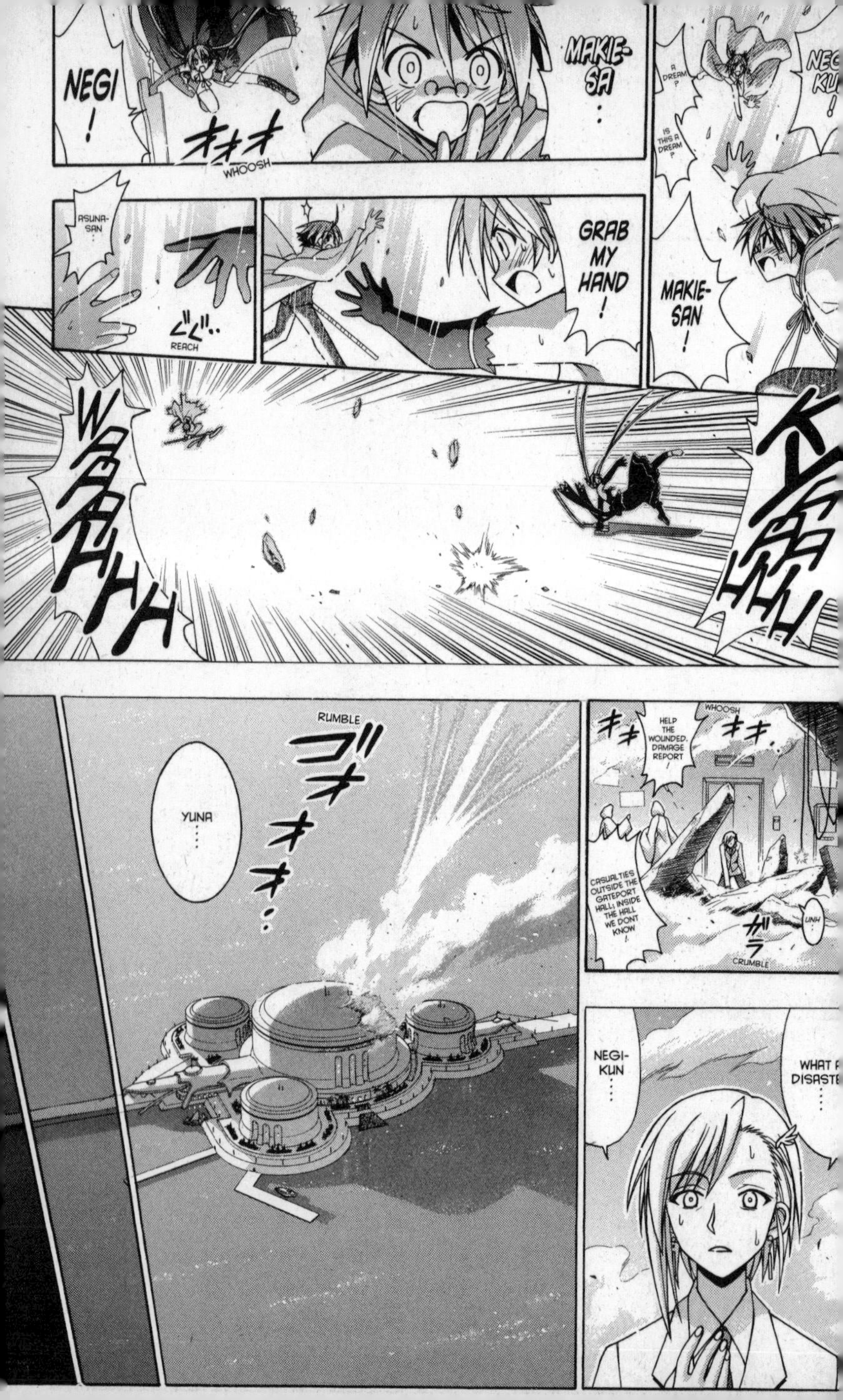
NEGI-KUN!
A DREAM?
IS THIS A DREAM?
MAKIE-SAN!
MAKIE-SAN...
NEGI!
オオオ
WHOOSH
GRAB MY HAND!
ASUNA-SAN...
ぐぐ…
REACH
KYAAAHHH
WAAAHHH
キキ
WHOOSH
HELP THE WOUNDED. DAMAGE REPORT!
キキ
CASUALTIES OUTSIDE THE GATEPORT HALL; INSIDE THE HALL WE DONT KNOW!
UNH...
ガラ
CRUMBLE
WHAT A DISASTE...
NEGI-KUN...
RUMBLE
ゴオオオ..
YUNA...

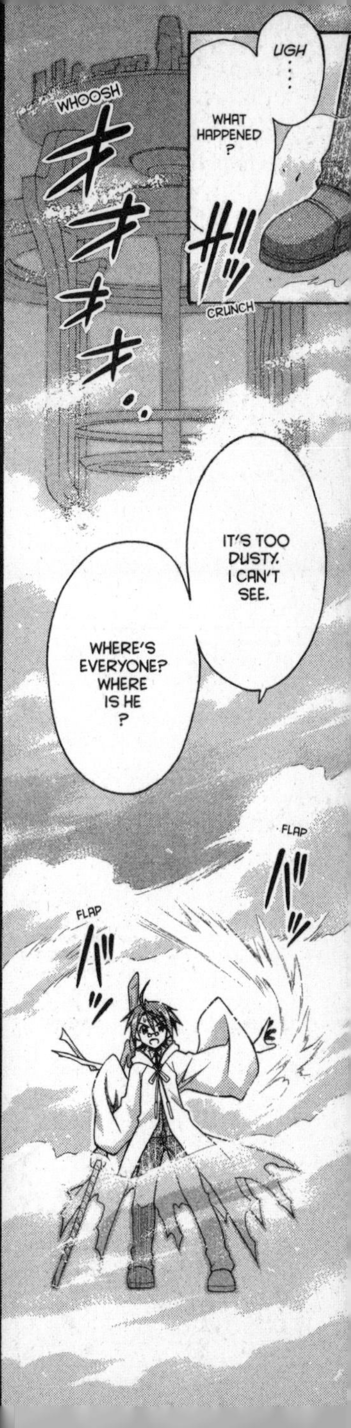
UGH ...
WHAT HAPPENED ?
CRUNCH
WHOOSH
IT'S TOO DUSTY. I CAN'T SEE.
WHERE'S EVERYONE? WHERE IS HE ?
FLAP
FLAP

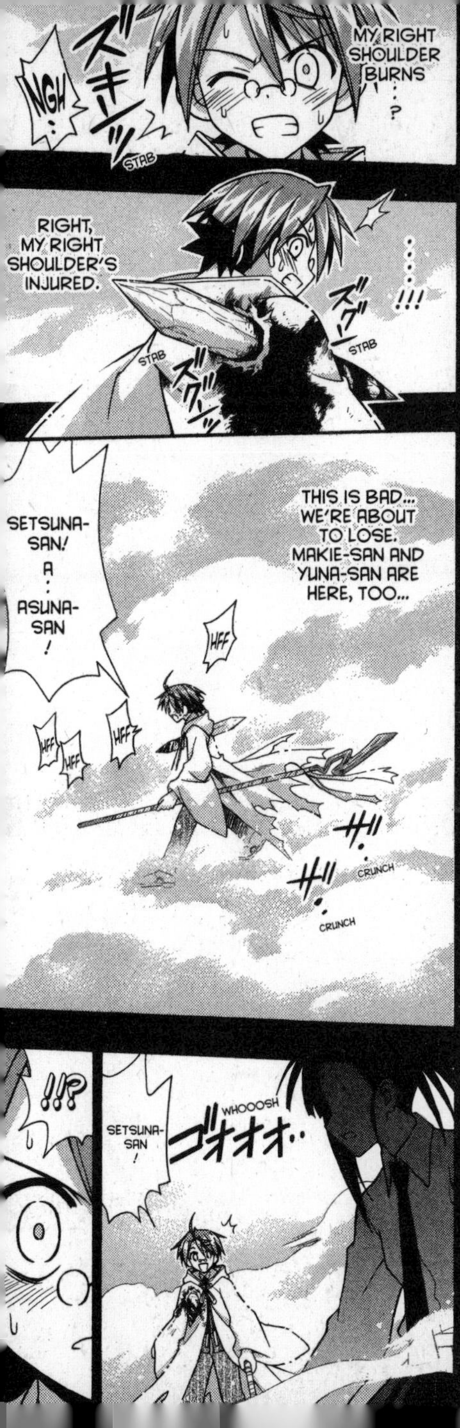
MY RIGHT SHOULDER BURNS ... ?
NGH ...
STAB
... !!!
STAB
STAB
RIGHT, MY RIGHT SHOULDER'S INJURED.
THIS IS BAD... WE'RE ABOUT TO LOSE. MAKIE-SAN AND YUNA-SAN ARE HERE, TOO...
SETSUNA-SAN! A... ASUNA-SAN!
HFF
HFF
HFF
HFF
CRUNCH
CRUNCH
WHOOOSH
SETSUNA-SAN!
!!?

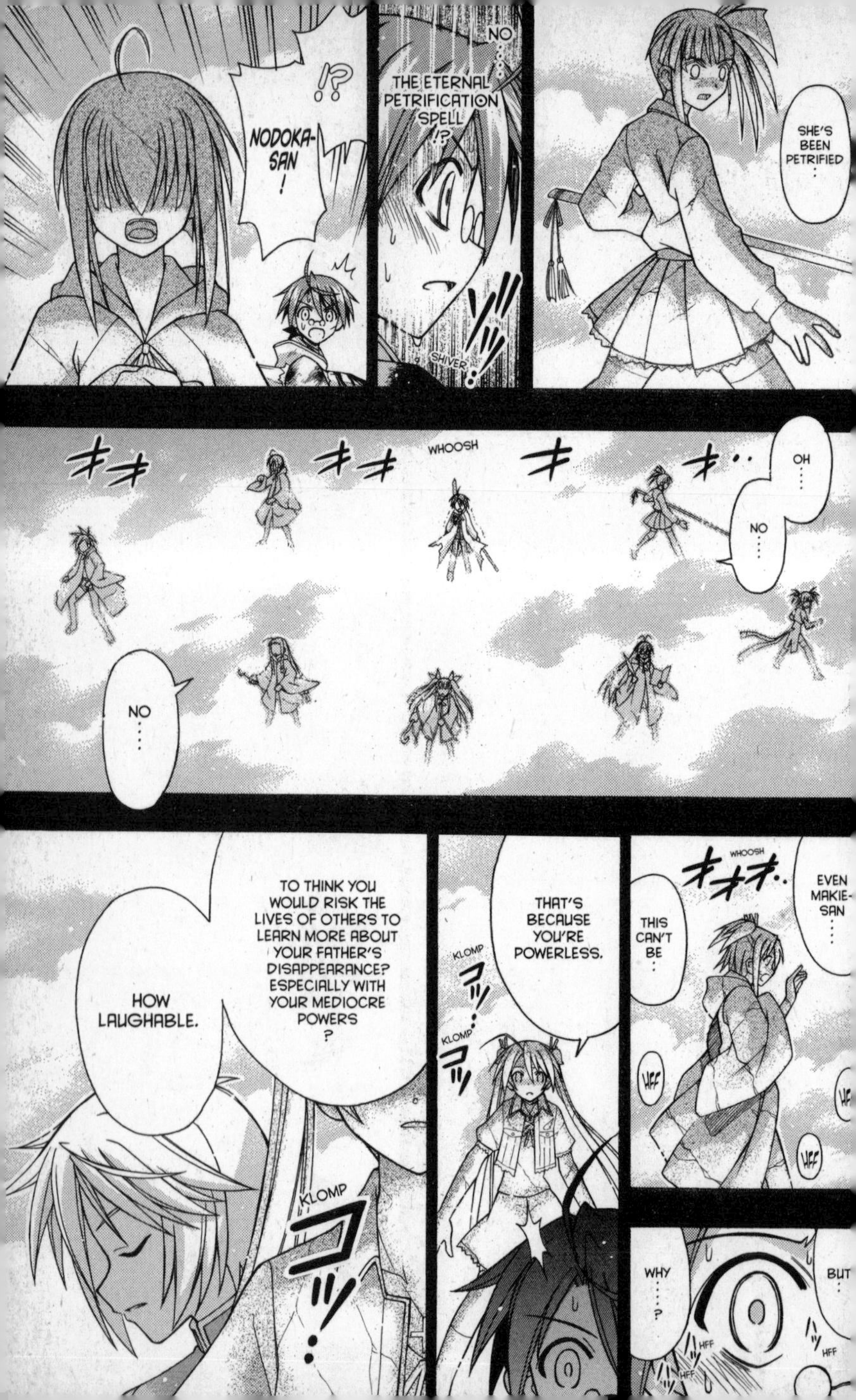
SHE'S BEEN PETRIFIED...
NO....
THE ETERNAL PETRIFICATION SPELL!?
SHIVER
!?
NODOKA-SAN!
OH....
NO....
WHOOSH
NO....
EVEN MAKIE-SAN....
WHOOSH
THIS CAN'T BE...
HFF
HFF
BUT
WHY....?
HFF
HFF
HFF
THAT'S BECAUSE YOU'RE POWERLESS.
KLOMP
KLOMP
TO THINK YOU WOULD RISK THE LIVES OF OTHERS TO LEARN MORE ABOUT YOUR FATHER'S DISAPPEARANCE? ESPECIALLY WITH YOUR MEDIOCRE POWERS?
HOW LAUGHABLE.
KLOMP

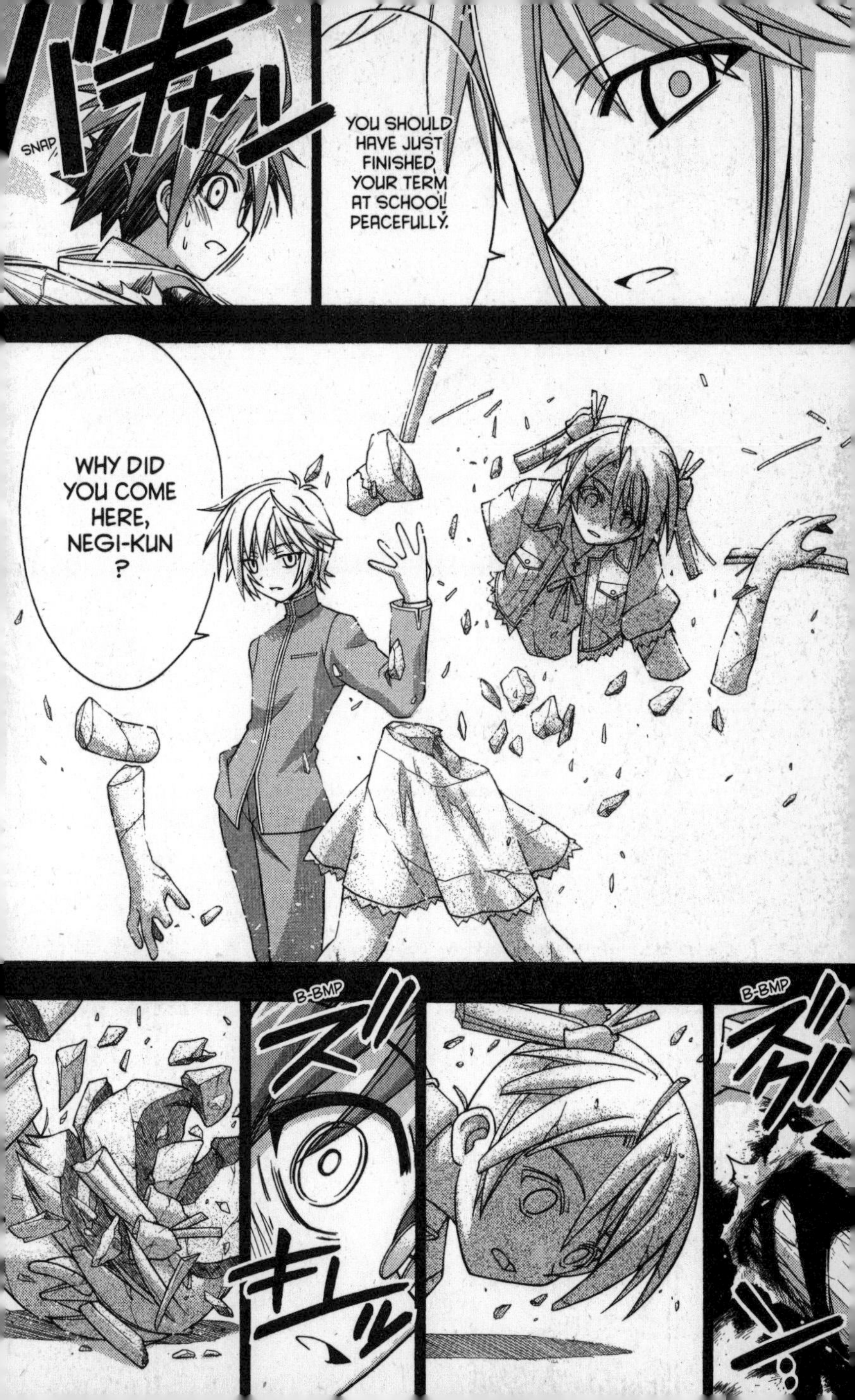
YOU SHOULD HAVE JUST FINISHED YOUR TERM AT SCHOOL PEACEFULLY.
SNAP
WHY DID YOU COME HERE, NEGI-KUN ?
B-BMP
B-BMP

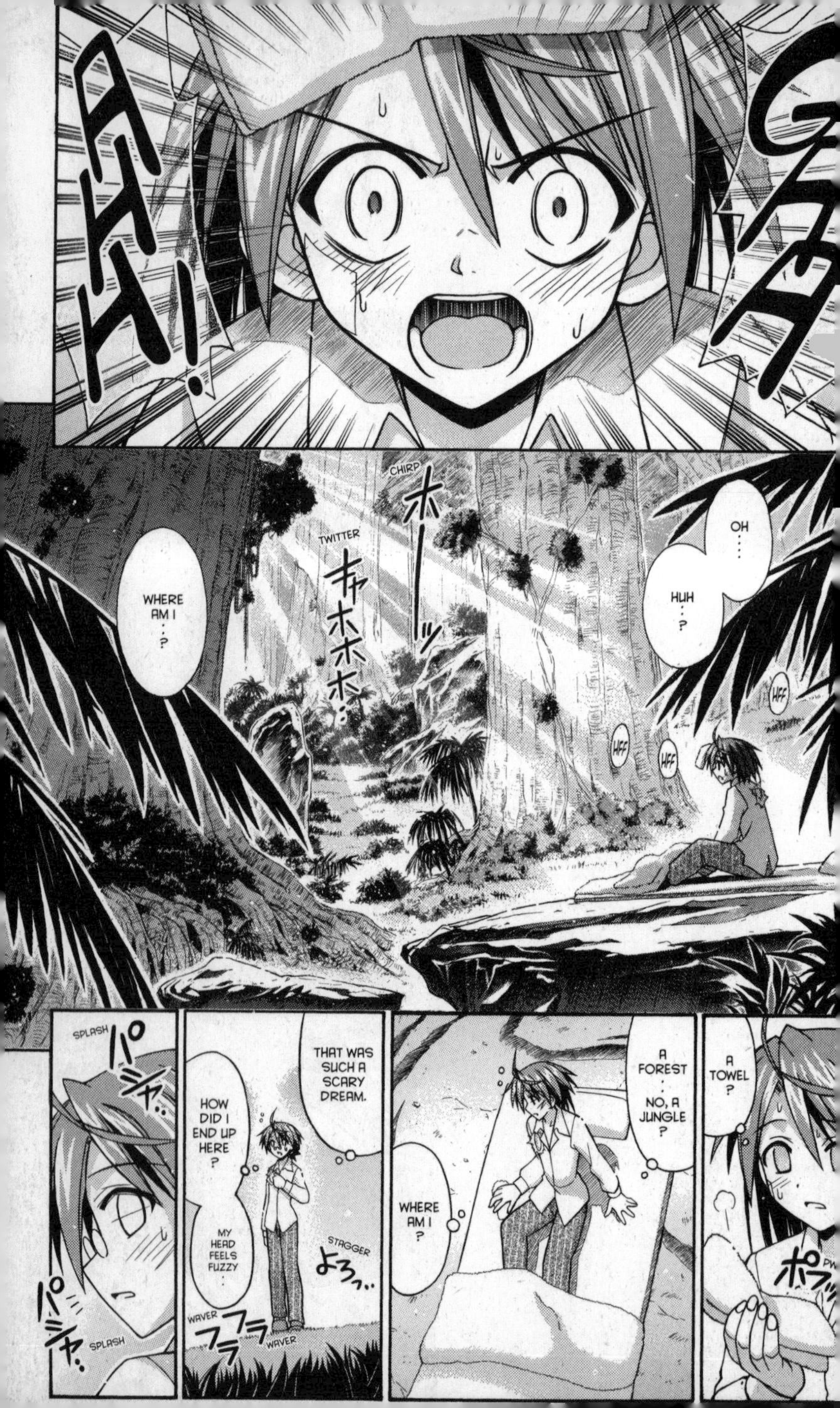
GYAA
AAH!
CHIRP
ホーッ
TWITTER
キャホホホ…
OH.....
HUH...?
HFF
HFF
HFF
HFF
WHERE AM I...?
A TOWEL?
PW
ポフッ
A FOREST... NO, A JUNGLE?
WHERE AM I?
THAT WAS SUCH A SCARY DREAM.
HOW DID I END UP HERE?
MY HEAD FEELS FUZZY...
STAGGER
よろっ…
WAVER
フラフラ
WAVER
SPLASH
パシャ…
パシャ…
SPLASH

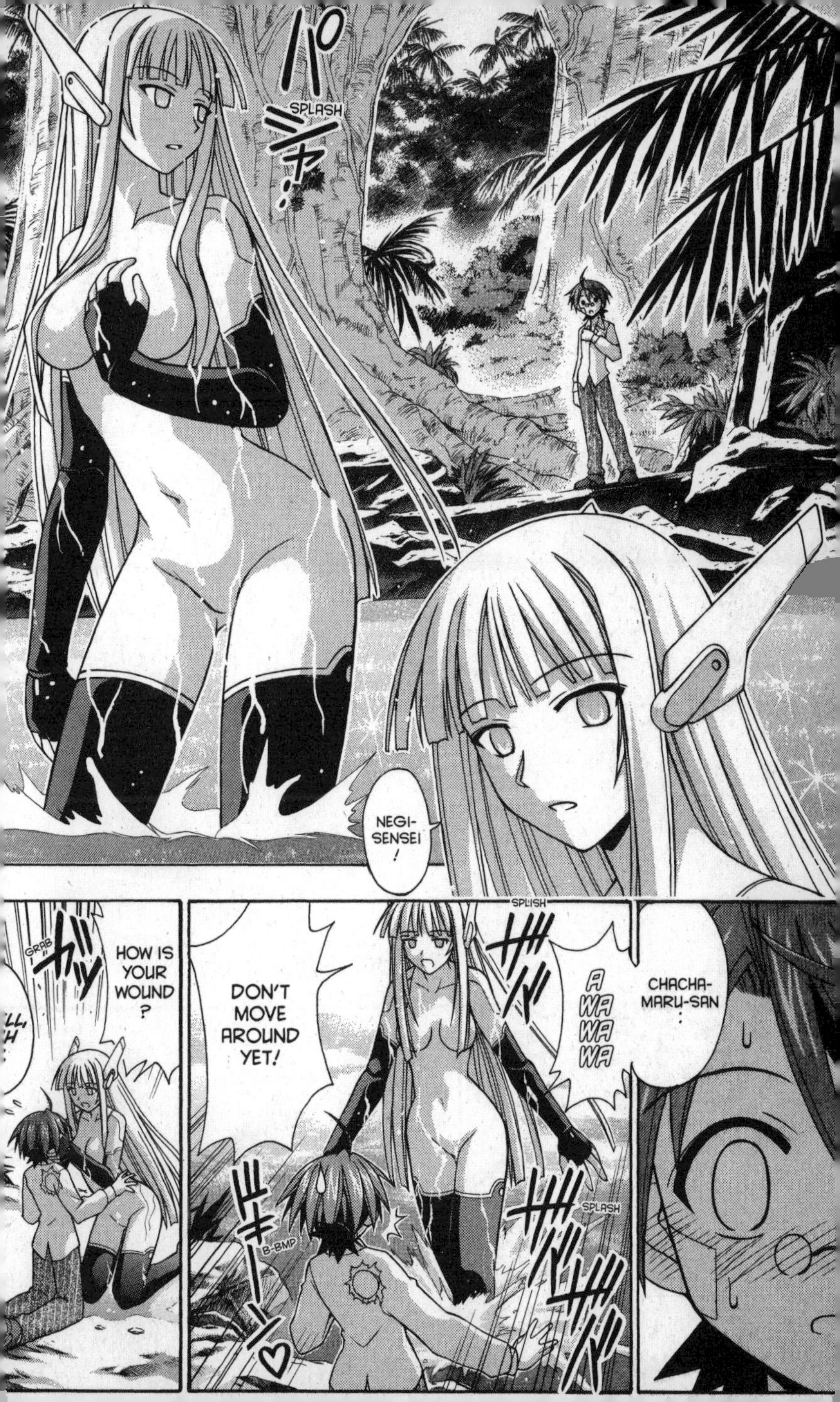

パシャ!!
SPLASH
NEGI-SENSEI!
CHACHA-MARU-SAN...
AWAWAWA
SPLASH
DON'T MOVE AROUND YET!
B-BMP
SPLASH
GRAB
HOW IS YOUR WOUND?

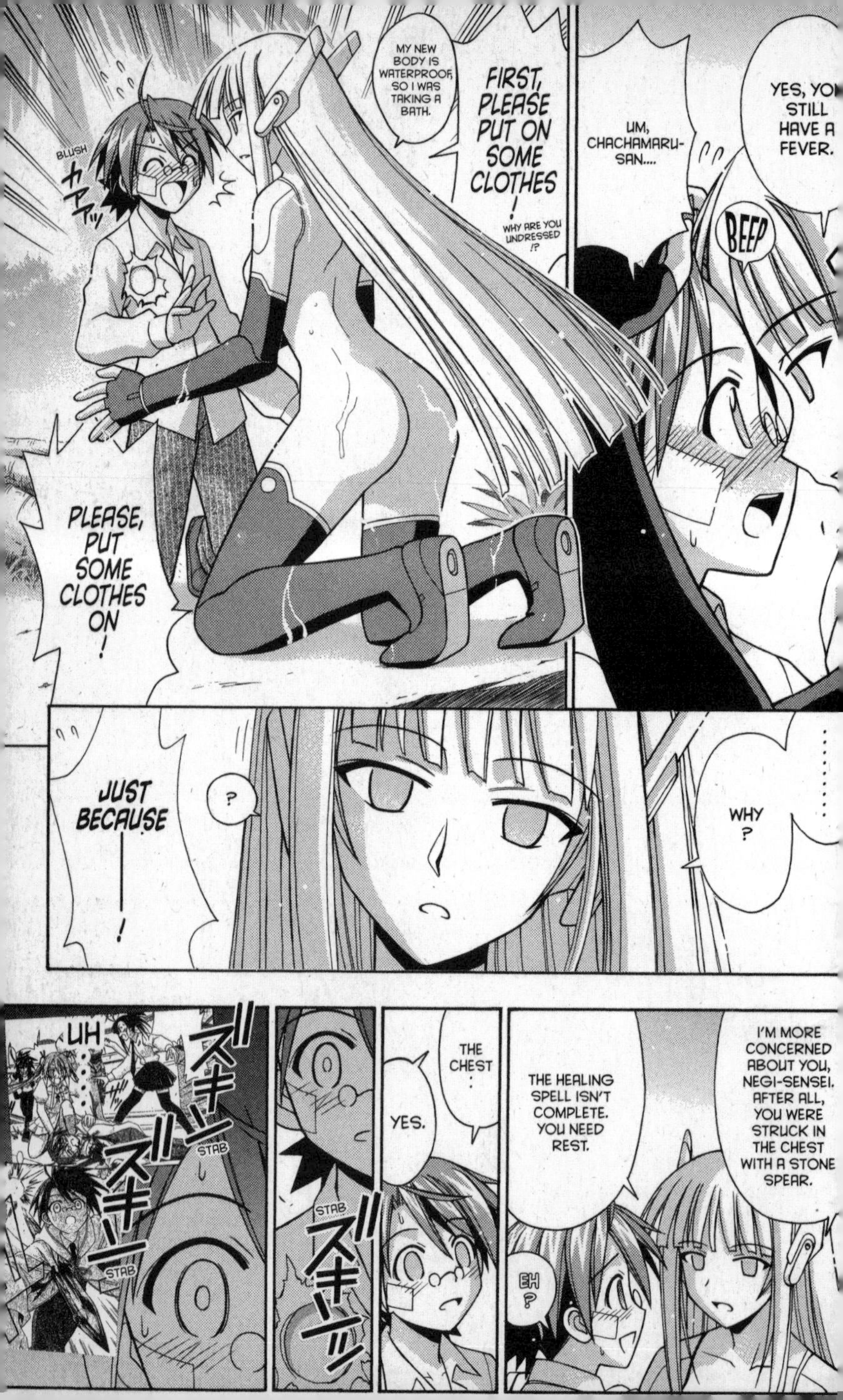
YES, YO STILL HAVE A FEVER.
BEEP
UM, CHACHAMARU-SAN....
FIRST, PLEASE PUT ON SOME CLOTHES!
WHY ARE YOU UNDRESSED!?
MY NEW BODY IS WATERPROOF, SO I WAS TAKING A BATH.
BLUSH
PLEASE, PUT SOME CLOTHES ON!
......
WHY?
?
JUST BECAUSE—!
I'M MORE CONCERNED ABOUT YOU, NEGI-SENSEI. AFTER ALL, YOU WERE STRUCK IN THE CHEST WITH A STONE SPEAR.
EH?
THE HEALING SPELL ISN'T COMPLETE. YOU NEED REST.
THE CHEST:
YES.
STAB
UH...
STAB
STAB

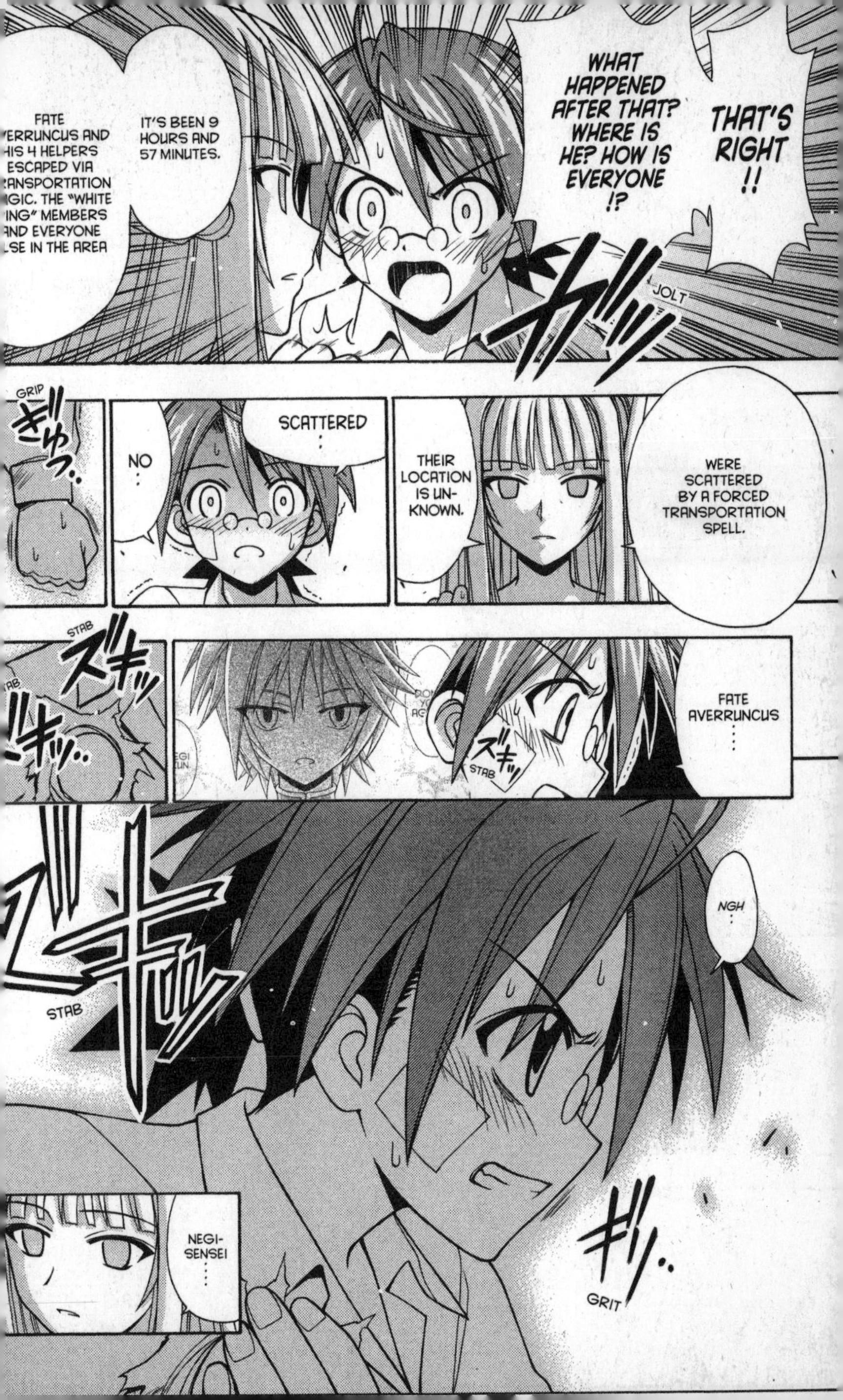
THAT'S RIGHT !!
WHAT HAPPENED AFTER THAT? WHERE IS HE? HOW IS EVERYONE !?
JOLT
IT'S BEEN 9 HOURS AND 57 MINUTES.
FATE VERRUNCUS AND HIS 4 HELPERS ESCAPED VIA RANSPORTATION AGIC. THE "WHITE ING" MEMBERS AND EVERYONE LSE IN THE AREA
WERE SCATTERED BY A FORCED TRANSPORTATION SPELL.
THEIR LOCATION IS UN-KNOWN.
SCATTERED ...
NO ...
GRIP
FATE AVERRUNCUS ....
STAB
STAB
STAB
NGH ...
STAB
GRIT
NEGI-SENSEI ....

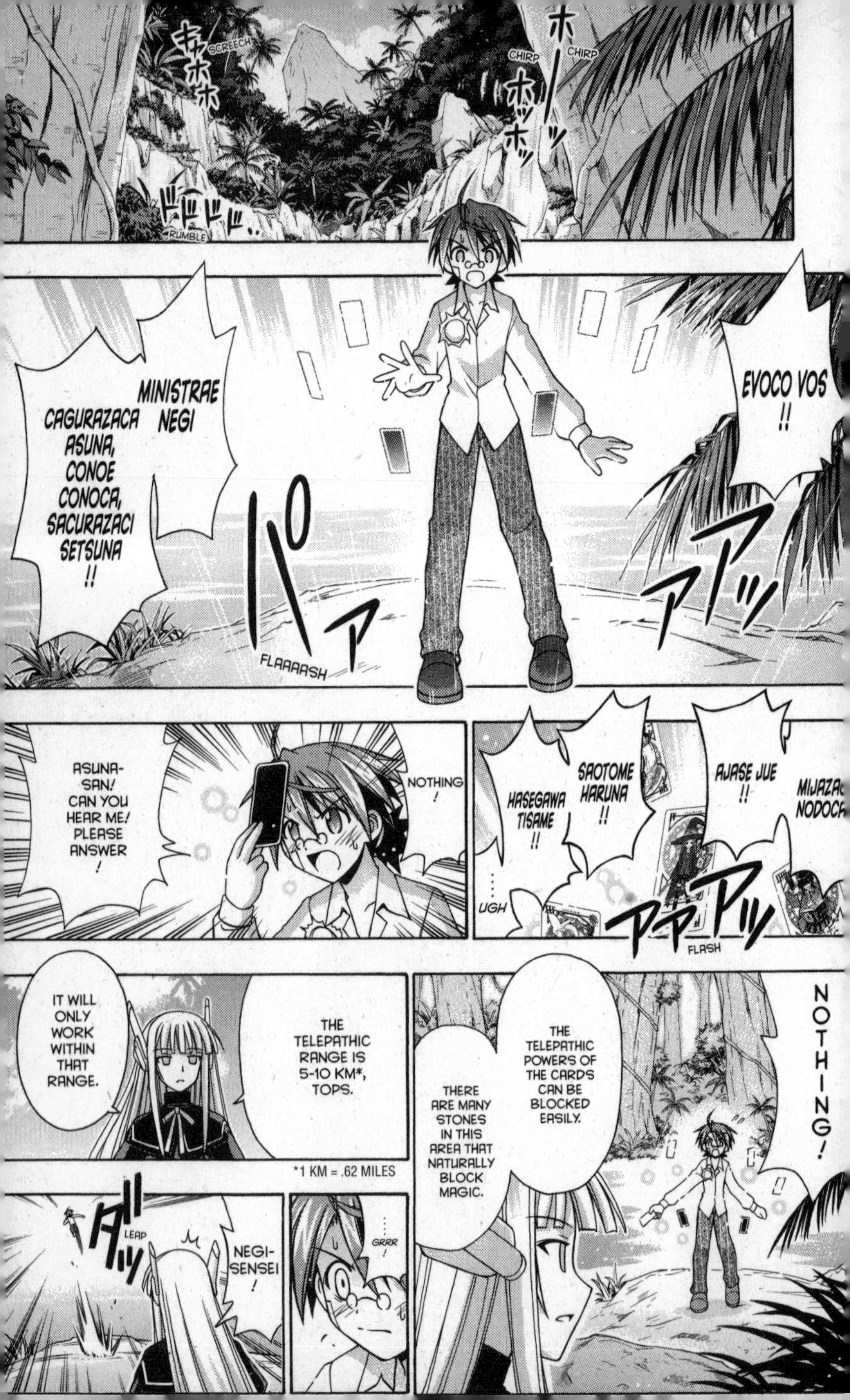
ホーッ ホッホッ
CHIRP CHIRP
キャホホ
SCREECH
ドドドド..
RUMBLE
EVOCO VOS !!
MINISTRAE NEGI
CAGURAZACA ASUNA, CONOE CONOCA, SACURAZACI SETSUNA !!
パァアッ
FLAAAASH
MIJAZAC NODOCA
AJASE JUE !!
SAOTOME HARUNA !!
HASEGAWA TISAME !!
... UGH
アァアッ
FLASH
NOTHING!
ASUNA-SAN! CAN YOU HEAR ME! PLEASE ANSWER!
NOTHING!
THE TELEPATHIC POWERS OF THE CARDS CAN BE BLOCKED EASILY.
THERE ARE MANY STONES IN THIS AREA THAT NATURALLY BLOCK MAGIC.
THE TELEPATHIC RANGE IS 5-10 KM*, TOPS.
IT WILL ONLY WORK WITHIN THAT RANGE.
*1 KM = .62 MILES
... GRRR!
NEGI-SENSEI!
ダッ
LEAP

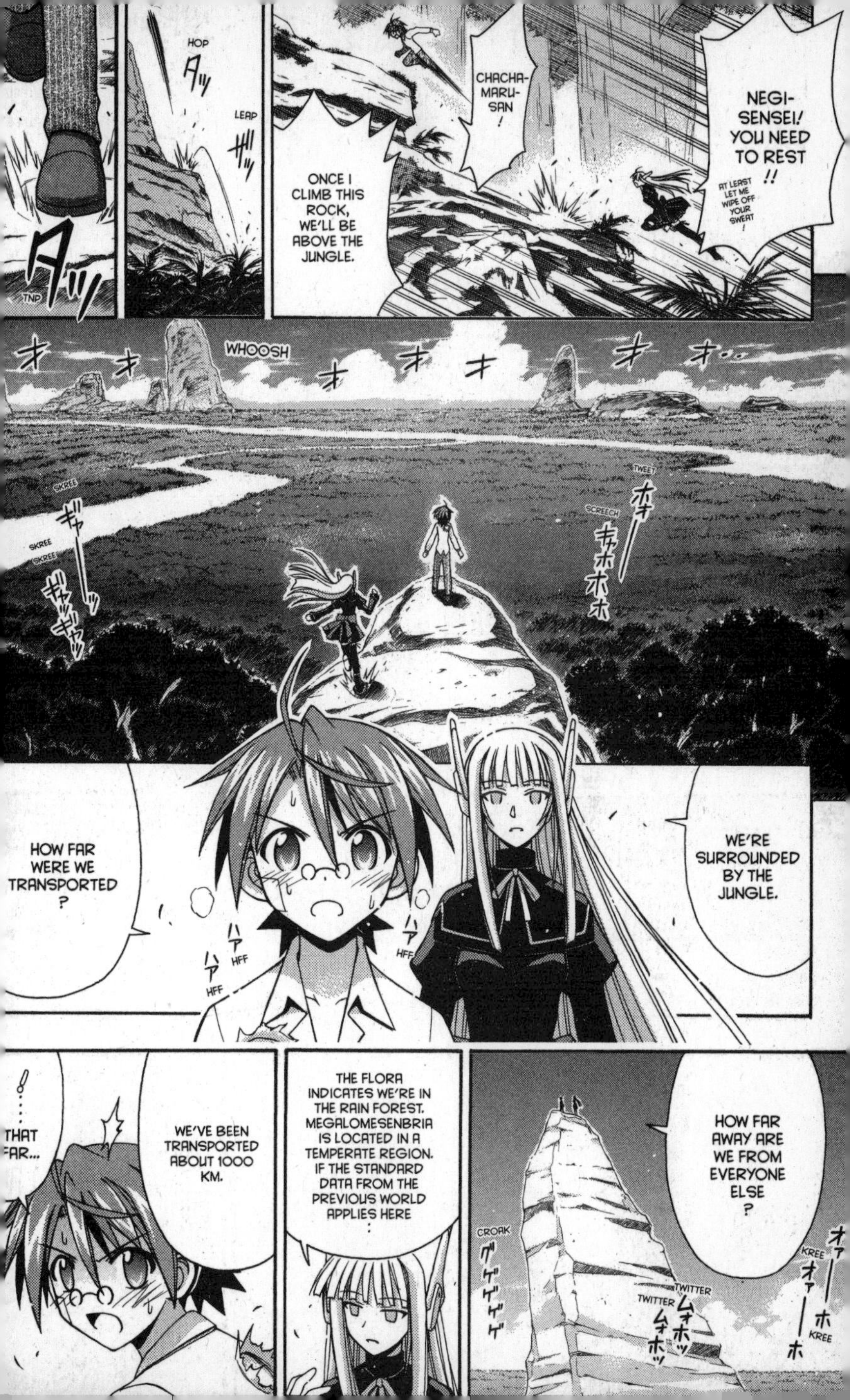
NEGI-SENSEI! YOU NEED TO REST!!
AT LEAST LET ME WIPE OFF YOUR SWEAT!
CHACHAMARU-SAN!
ONCE I CLIMB THIS ROCK, WE'LL BE ABOVE THE JUNGLE.
HOP
LEAP
TNP
WHOOSH
TWEET
SCREECH
SKREE
SKREE
SKREE
WE'RE SURROUNDED BY THE JUNGLE.
HOW FAR WERE WE TRANSPORTED?
HFF
HFF
HFF
HOW FAR AWAY ARE WE FROM EVERYONE ELSE?
KREE
KREE
TWITTER
TWITTER
CROAK
THE FLORA INDICATES WE'RE IN THE RAIN FOREST. MEGALOMESENBRIA IS LOCATED IN A TEMPERATE REGION. IF THE STANDARD DATA FROM THE PREVIOUS WORLD APPLIES HERE...
WE'VE BEEN TRANSPORTED ABOUT 1000 KM.
!... THAT FAR...

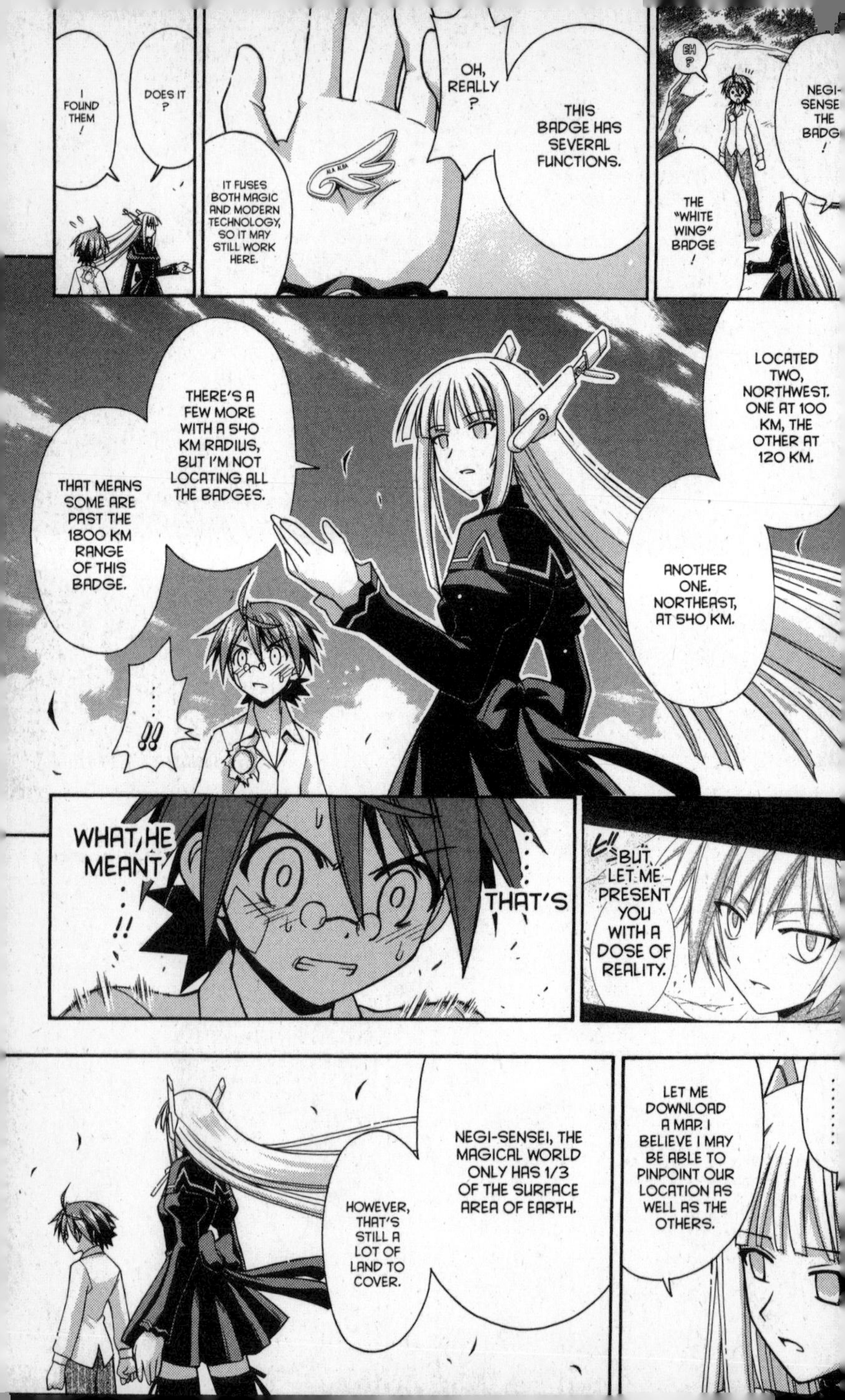
NEGI-SENSE THE BADG !
EH ?
THE "WHITE WING" BADGE !
THIS BADGE HAS SEVERAL FUNCTIONS.
OH, REALLY ?
ALA ALBA
IT FUSES BOTH MAGIC AND MODERN TECHNOLOGY, SO IT MAY STILL WORK HERE.
DOES IT ?
I FOUND THEM !
LOCATED TWO, NORTHWEST. ONE AT 100 KM, THE OTHER AT 120 KM.
ANOTHER ONE. NORTHEAST, AT 540 KM.
THERE'S A FEW MORE WITH A 540 KM RADIUS, BUT I'M NOT LOCATING ALL THE BADGES.
THAT MEANS SOME ARE PAST THE 1800 KM RANGE OF THIS BADGE.
......!!
BUT LET ME PRESENT YOU WITH A DOSE OF REALITY.
THAT'S ...
WHAT HE MEANT ...!!
LET ME DOWNLOAD A MAP. I BELIEVE I MAY BE ABLE TO PINPOINT OUR LOCATION AS WELL AS THE OTHERS.
NEGI-SENSEI, THE MAGICAL WORLD ONLY HAS 1/3 OF THE SURFACE AREA OF EARTH.
HOWEVER, THAT'S STILL A LOT OF LAND TO COVER.

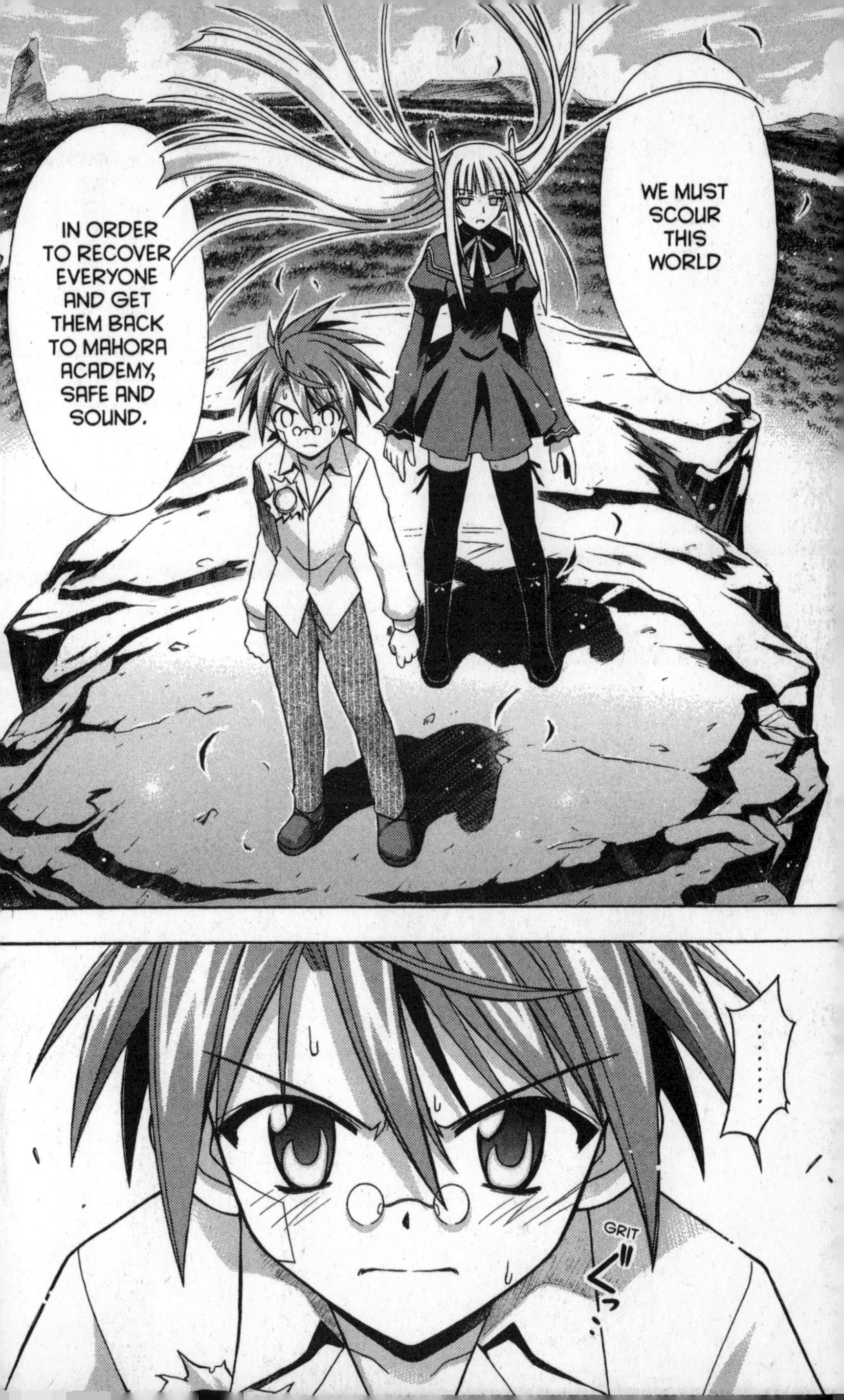
WE MUST SCOUR THIS WORLD
IN ORDER TO RECOVER EVERYONE AND GET THEM BACK TO MAHORA ACADEMY, SAFE AND SOUND.
......
GRIT

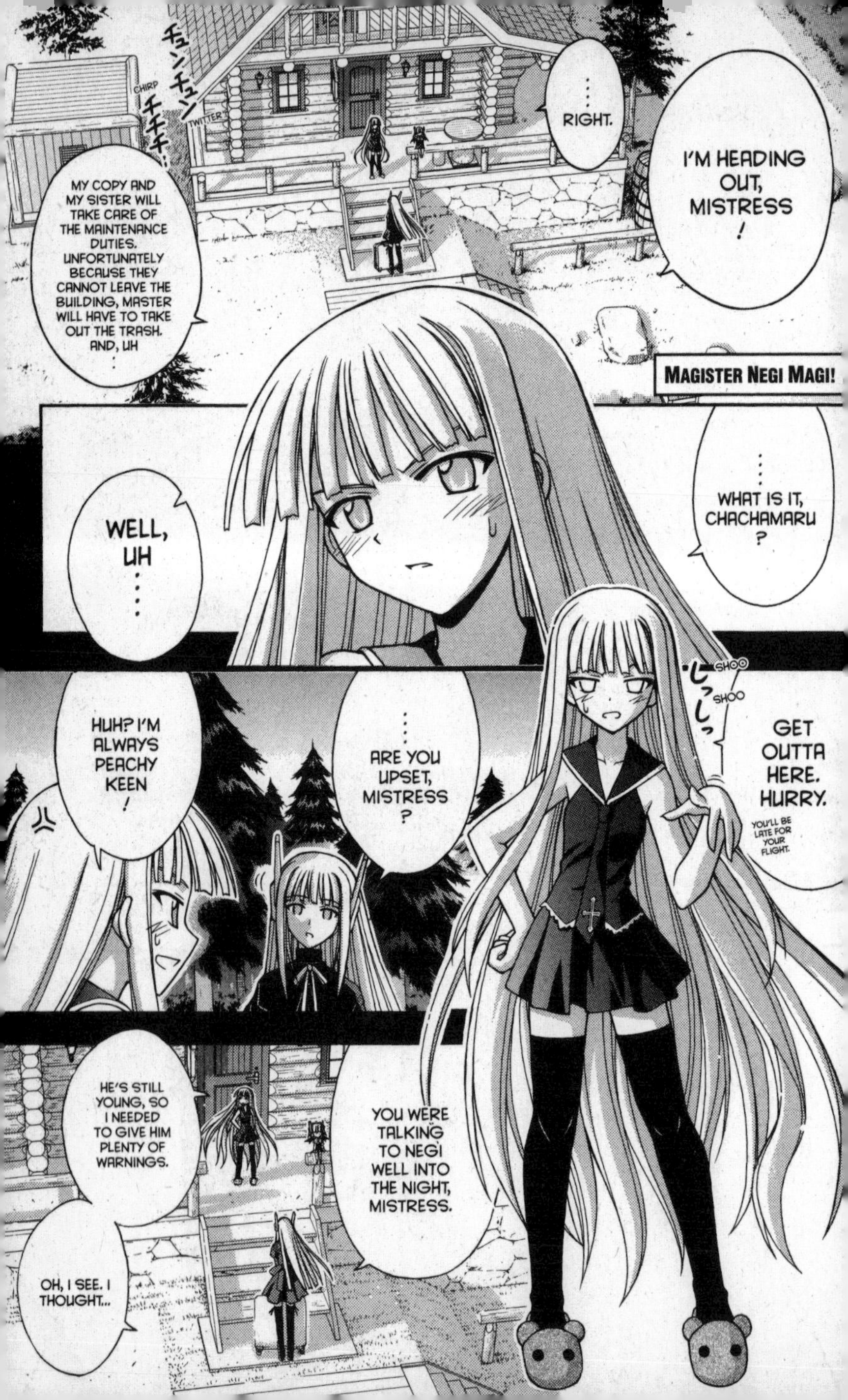
MAGISTER NEGI MAGI!
I'M HEADING OUT, MISTRESS!
...RIGHT.
チュンチュン
CHIRP
チチチ
TWITTER
MY COPY AND MY SISTER WILL TAKE CARE OF THE MAINTENANCE DUTIES. UNFORTUNATELY BECAUSE THEY CANNOT LEAVE THE BUILDING, MASTER WILL HAVE TO TAKE OUT THE TRASH. AND, UH...
...WHAT IS IT, CHACHAMARU?
WELL, UH...
しっしっ
SHOO SHOO
GET OUTTA HERE. HURRY.
YOU'LL BE LATE FOR YOUR FLIGHT.
...ARE YOU UPSET, MISTRESS?
HUH? I'M ALWAYS PEACHY KEEN!
YOU WERE TALKING TO NEGI WELL INTO THE NIGHT, MISTRESS.
HE'S STILL YOUNG, SO I NEEDED TO GIVE HIM PLENTY OF WARNINGS.
OH, I SEE. I THOUGHT...

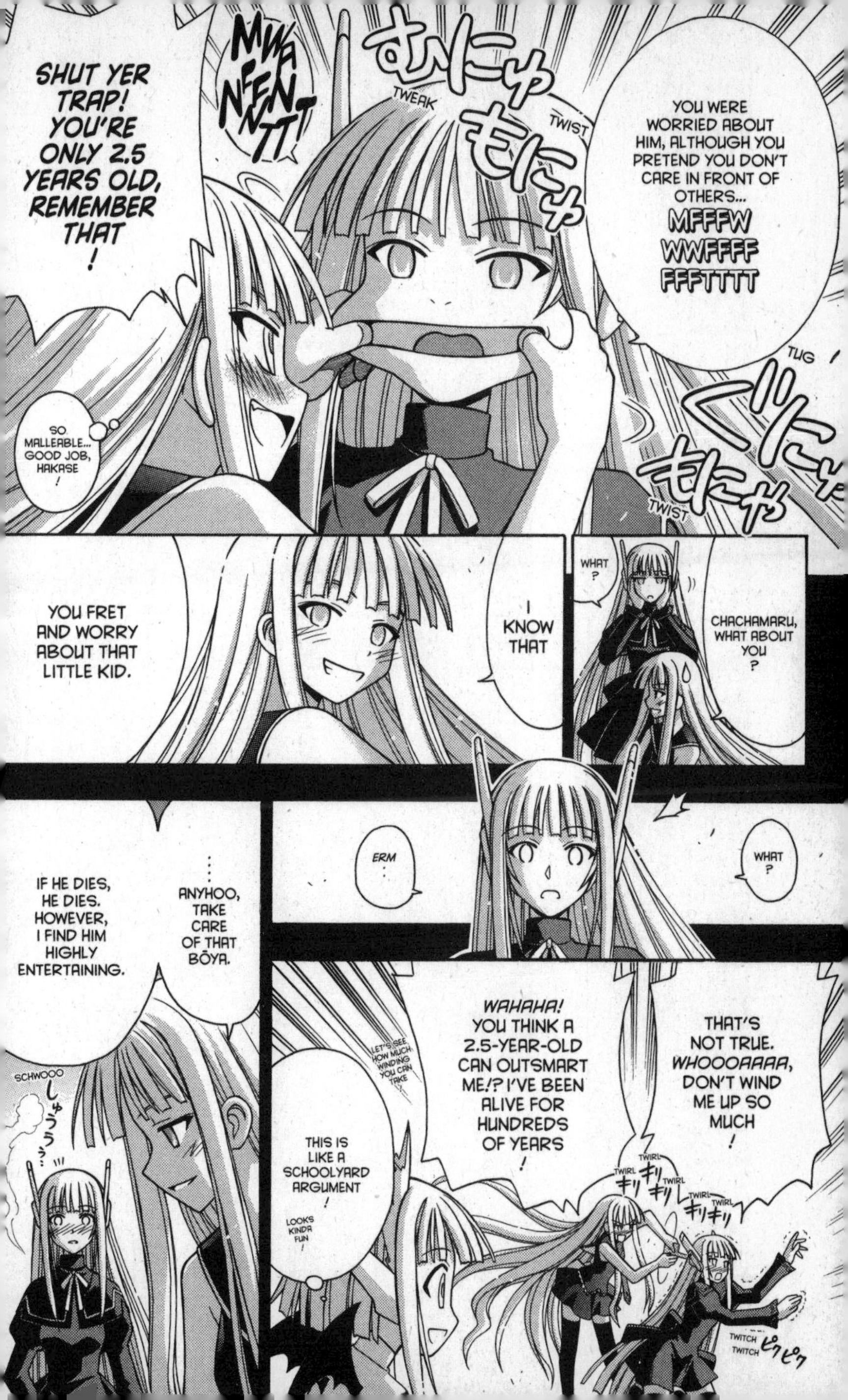
YOU WERE WORRIED ABOUT HIM, ALTHOUGH YOU PRETEND YOU DON'T CARE IN FRONT OF OTHERS... MFFFW WWFFFF FFFTTTT
むにゅ TWEAK
もにゅ TWIST
MWANFENNTTT
SHUT YER TRAP! YOU'RE ONLY 2.5 YEARS OLD, REMEMBER THAT!
TUG くりにゅ
もにゅ TWIST
SO MALLEABLE... GOOD JOB, HAKASE!
WHAT?
CHACHAMARU, WHAT ABOUT YOU?
I KNOW THAT
YOU FRET AND WORRY ABOUT THAT LITTLE KID.
WHAT?
ERM...
... ANYHOO, TAKE CARE OF THAT BŌYA.
IF HE DIES, HE DIES. HOWEVER, I FIND HIM HIGHLY ENTERTAINING.
THAT'S NOT TRUE. WHOOOAAAA, DON'T WIND ME UP SO MUCH!
WAHAHA! YOU THINK A 2.5-YEAR-OLD CAN OUTSMART ME!? I'VE BEEN ALIVE FOR HUNDREDS OF YEARS!
TWIRL キリ TWIRL キリ TWIRL キリ TWIRL キリ TWIRL キリ
TWITCH TWITCH ピクピク
LET'S SEE HOW MUCH WINDING YOU CAN TAKE!
THIS IS LIKE A SCHOOLYARD ARGUMENT!
LOOKS KINDA FUN!
SCHWOOO しゅううう

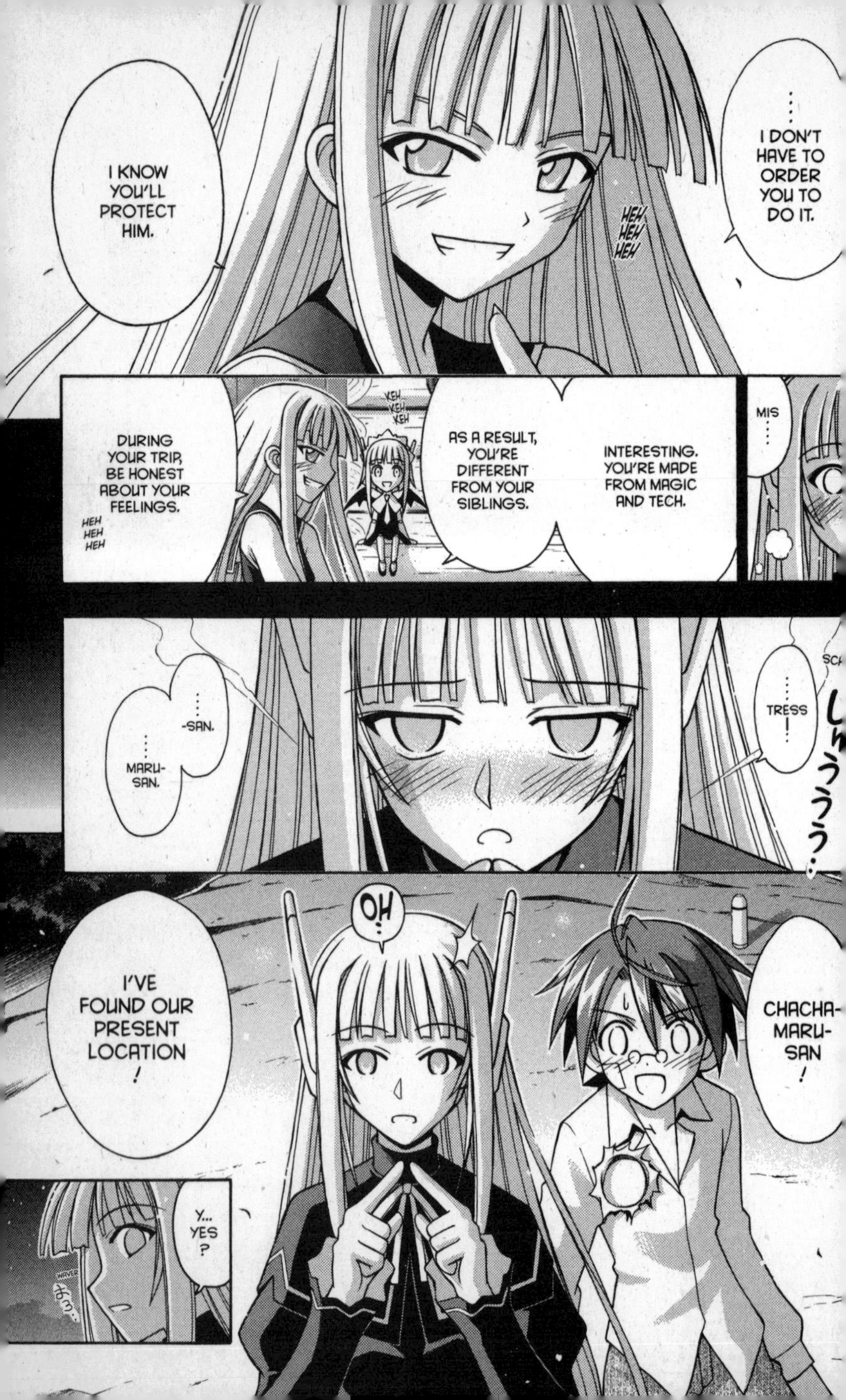

...... I DON'T HAVE TO ORDER YOU TO DO IT.
HEH HEH HEH
I KNOW YOU'LL PROTECT HIM.
MIS ......
INTERESTING. YOU'RE MADE FROM MAGIC AND TECH.
AS A RESULT, YOU'RE DIFFERENT FROM YOUR SIBLINGS.
KEH KEH KEH
DURING YOUR TRIP, BE HONEST ABOUT YOUR FEELINGS.
HEH HEH HEH
SCH
...... TRESS !
...... -SAN.
...... MARU-SAN.
CHACHA-MARU-SAN !
OH
I'VE FOUND OUR PRESENT LOCATION !
Y... YES ?
WAVER

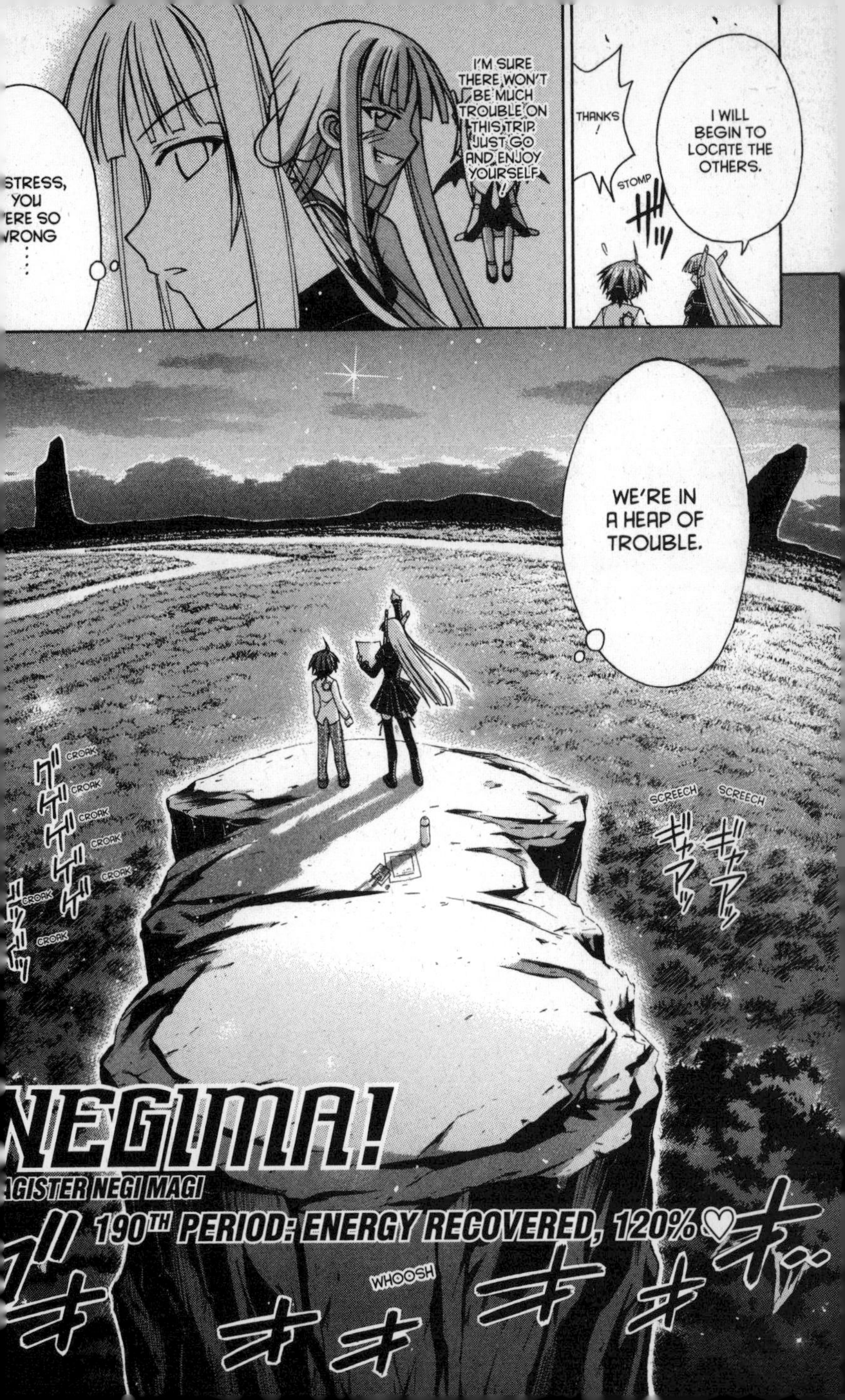
I WILL BEGIN TO LOCATE THE OTHERS.
THANKS!
STOMP
I'M SURE THERE WON'T BE MUCH TROUBLE ON THIS TRIP. JUST GO AND ENJOY YOURSELF!
STRESS, YOU ERE SO RONG ......
WE'RE IN A HEAP OF TROUBLE.
SCREECH
SCREECH
CROAK
CROAK
CROAK
CROAK
CROAK
CROAK
CROAK
NEGIMA!
AGISTER NEGI MAGI
190TH PERIOD: ENERGY RECOVERED, 120%♡
WHOOSH

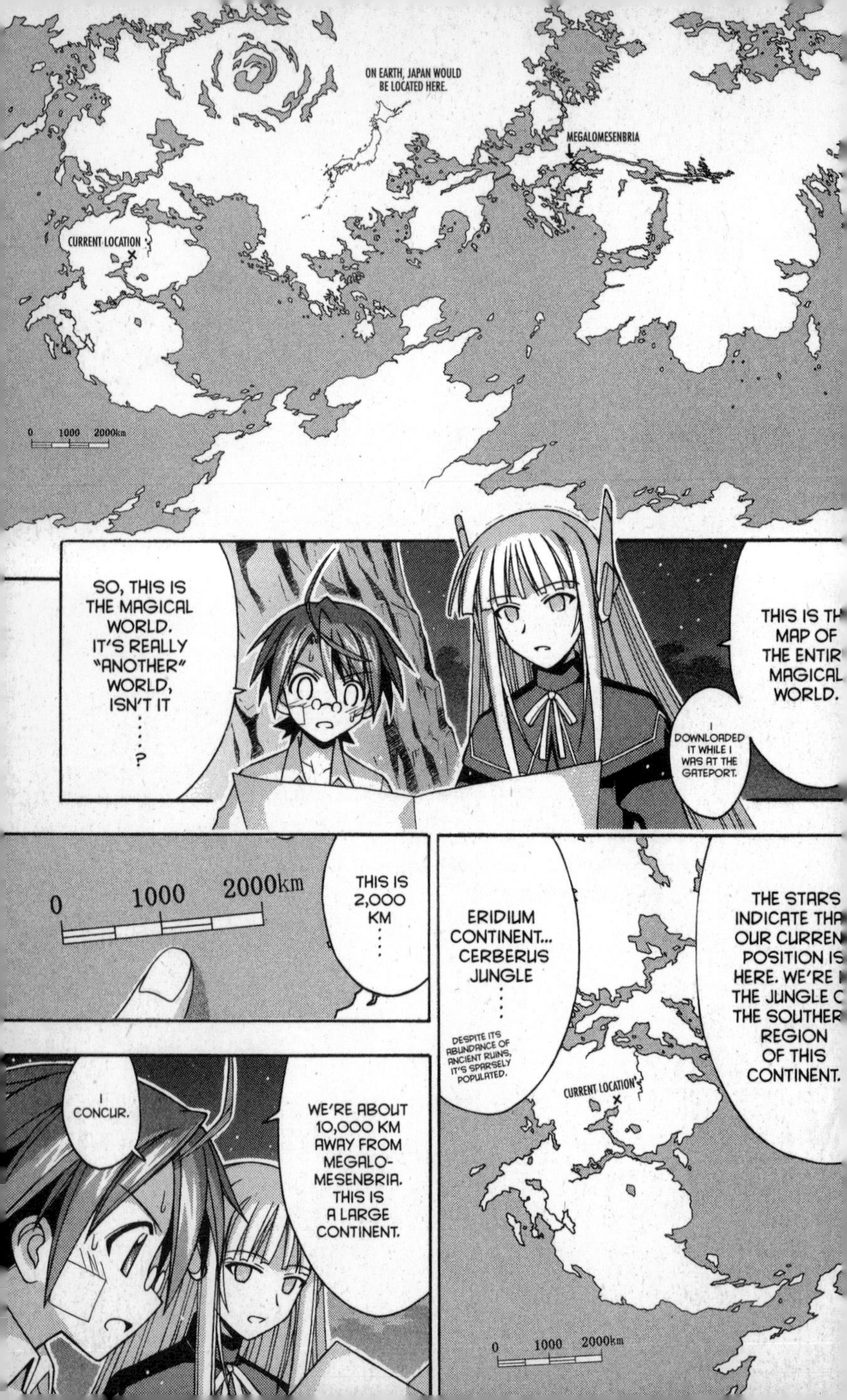
ON EARTH, JAPAN WOULD BE LOCATED HERE.
MEGALOMESENBRIA
CURRENT LOCATION
0 1000 2000km
THIS IS TH MAP OF THE ENTIR MAGICAL WORLD.
I DOWNLOADED IT WHILE I WAS AT THE GATEPORT.
SO, THIS IS THE MAGICAL WORLD. IT'S REALLY "ANOTHER" WORLD, ISN'T IT ....?
THE STARS INDICATE THA OUR CURREN POSITION IS HERE. WE'RE I THE JUNGLE C THE SOUTHER REGION OF THIS CONTINENT.
ERIDIUM CONTINENT... CERBERUS JUNGLE ...
DESPITE ITS ABUNDANCE OF ANCIENT RUINS, IT'S SPARSELY POPULATED.
CURRENT LOCATION
0 1000 2000km
0 1000 2000km
THIS IS 2,000 KM ....
WE'RE ABOUT 10,000 KM AWAY FROM MEGALO-MESENBRIA. THIS IS A LARGE CONTINENT.
I CONCUR.

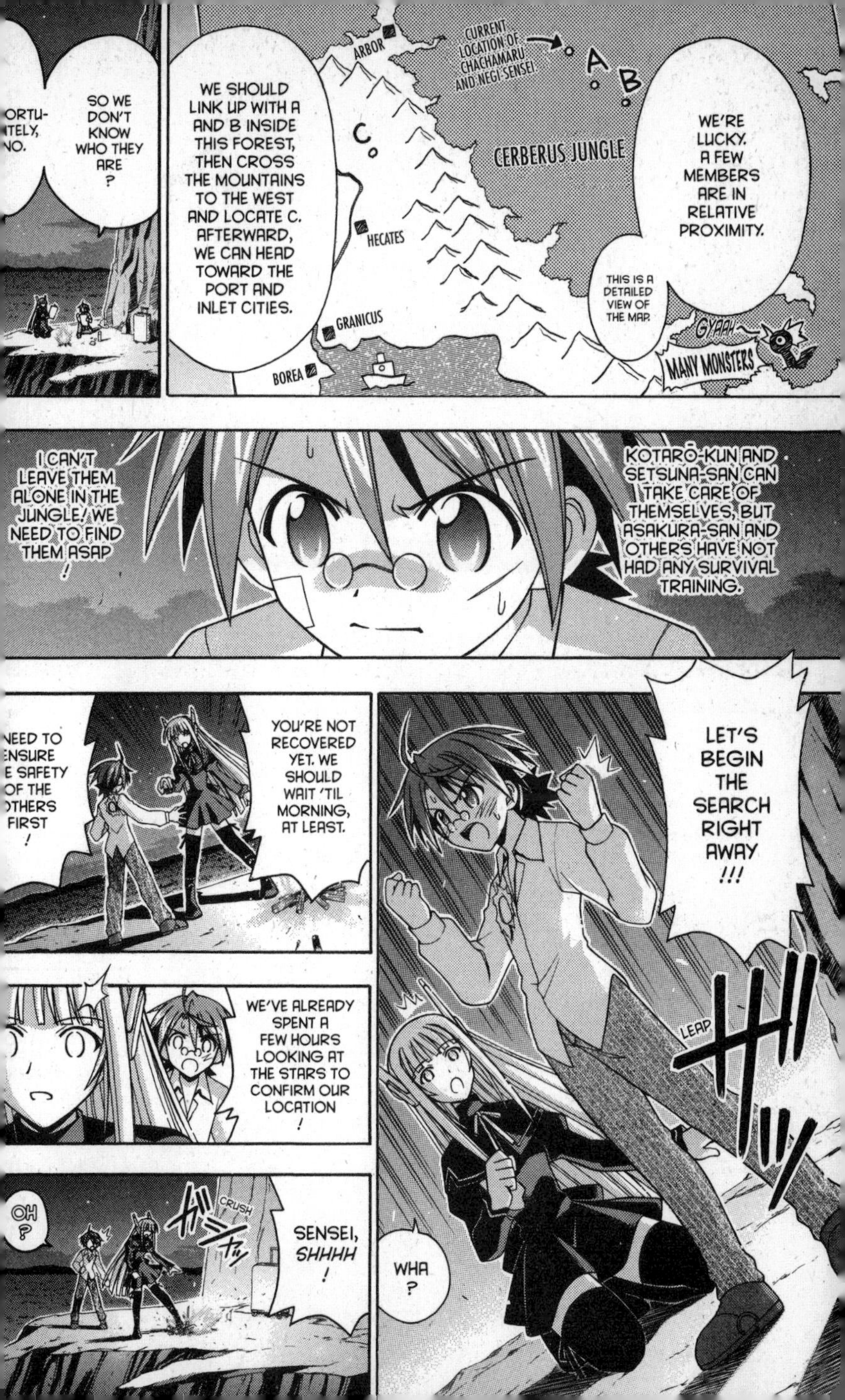
WE'RE LUCKY. A FEW MEMBERS ARE IN RELATIVE PROXIMITY.
THIS IS A DETAILED VIEW OF THE MAP.
CURRENT LOCATION OF CHACHAMARU AND NEGI-SENSEI
A
B
CERBERUS JUNGLE
GYAAH
MANY MONSTERS
ARBOR
C
HECATES
GRANICUS
BOREA
WE SHOULD LINK UP WITH A AND B INSIDE THIS FOREST, THEN CROSS THE MOUNTAINS TO THE WEST AND LOCATE C. AFTERWARD, WE CAN HEAD TOWARD THE PORT AND INLET CITIES.
SO WE DON'T KNOW WHO THEY ARE?
ORTU- ITELY, NO.
KOTARŌ-KUN AND SETSUNA-SAN CAN TAKE CARE OF THEMSELVES, BUT ASAKURA-SAN AND OTHERS HAVE NOT HAD ANY SURVIVAL TRAINING.
I CAN'T LEAVE THEM ALONE IN THE JUNGLE! WE NEED TO FIND THEM ASAP!
LET'S BEGIN THE SEARCH RIGHT AWAY!!!
LEAP
WHA?
YOU'RE NOT RECOVERED YET. WE SHOULD WAIT 'TIL MORNING, AT LEAST.
NEED TO ENSURE E SAFETY OF THE OTHERS FIRST!
WE'VE ALREADY SPENT A FEW HOURS LOOKING AT THE STARS TO CONFIRM OUR LOCATION!
SENSEI, SHHHH!
CRUSH
OH?

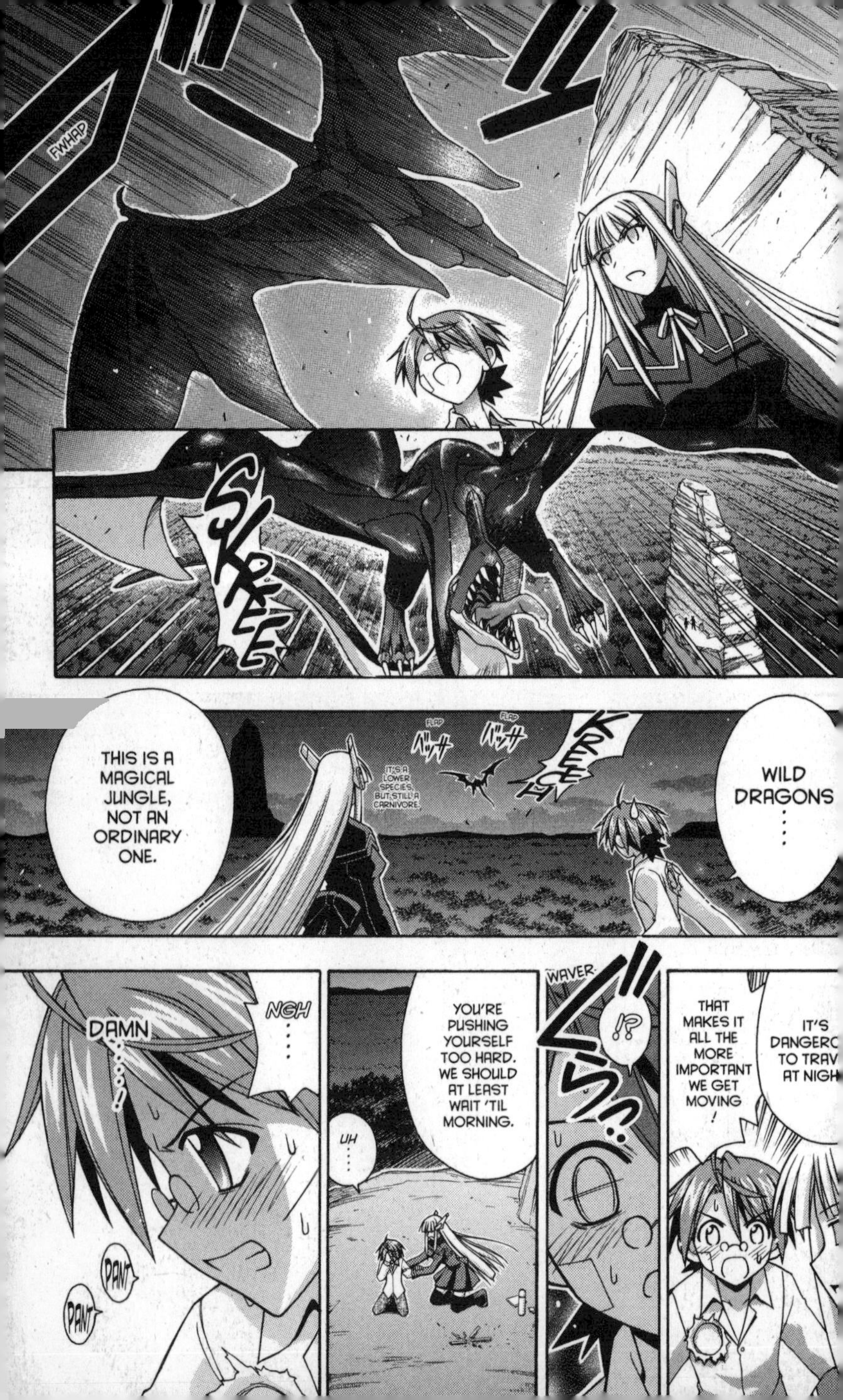

FWHAP
SKREE
WILD DRAGONS ....
KREEEH
FLAP
FLAP
IT'S A LOWER SPECIES, BUT STILL A CARNIVORE.
THIS IS A MAGICAL JUNGLE, NOT AN ORDINARY ONE.
IT'S DANGERO TO TRAV AT NIGH
THAT MAKES IT ALL THE MORE IMPORTANT WE GET MOVING!
WAVER
!?
YOU'RE PUSHING YOURSELF TOO HARD. WE SHOULD AT LEAST WAIT 'TIL MORNING.
UH ....
NGH ....
DAMN ......!
PANT
PANT

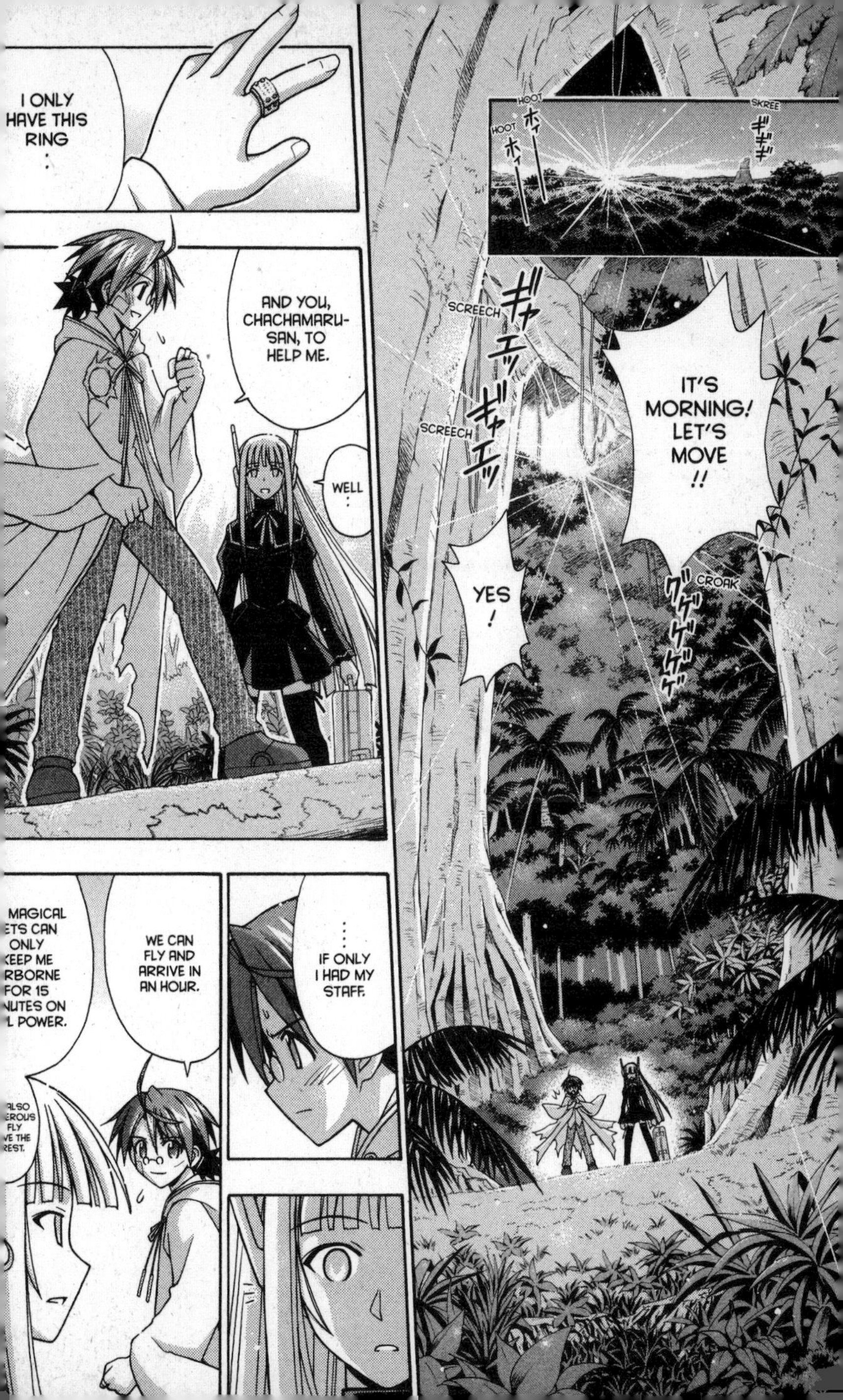
HOOT
HOOT
SKREE
SCREECH
SCREECH
IT'S MORNING! LET'S MOVE!!
YES!
CROAK
I ONLY HAVE THIS RING...
AND YOU, CHACHAMARU-SAN, TO HELP ME.
WELL...
...IF ONLY I HAD MY STAFF.
WE CAN FLY AND ARRIVE IN AN HOUR.
MAGICAL ETS CAN ONLY KEEP ME RBORNE FOR 15 NUTES ON L POWER.
ALSO EROUS FLY VE THE REST.

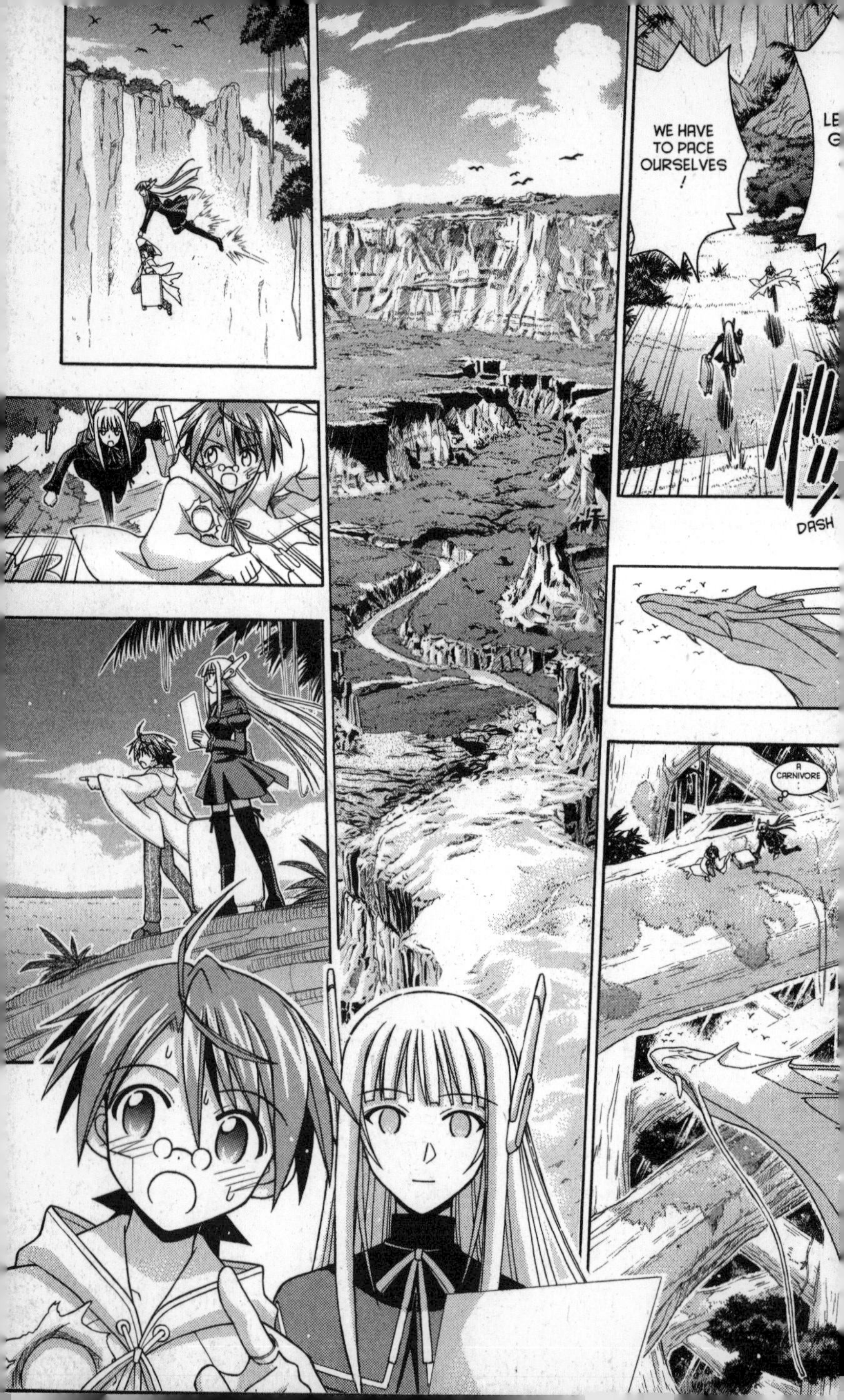
WE HAVE TO PACE OURSELVES!
DASH
A CARNIVORE...

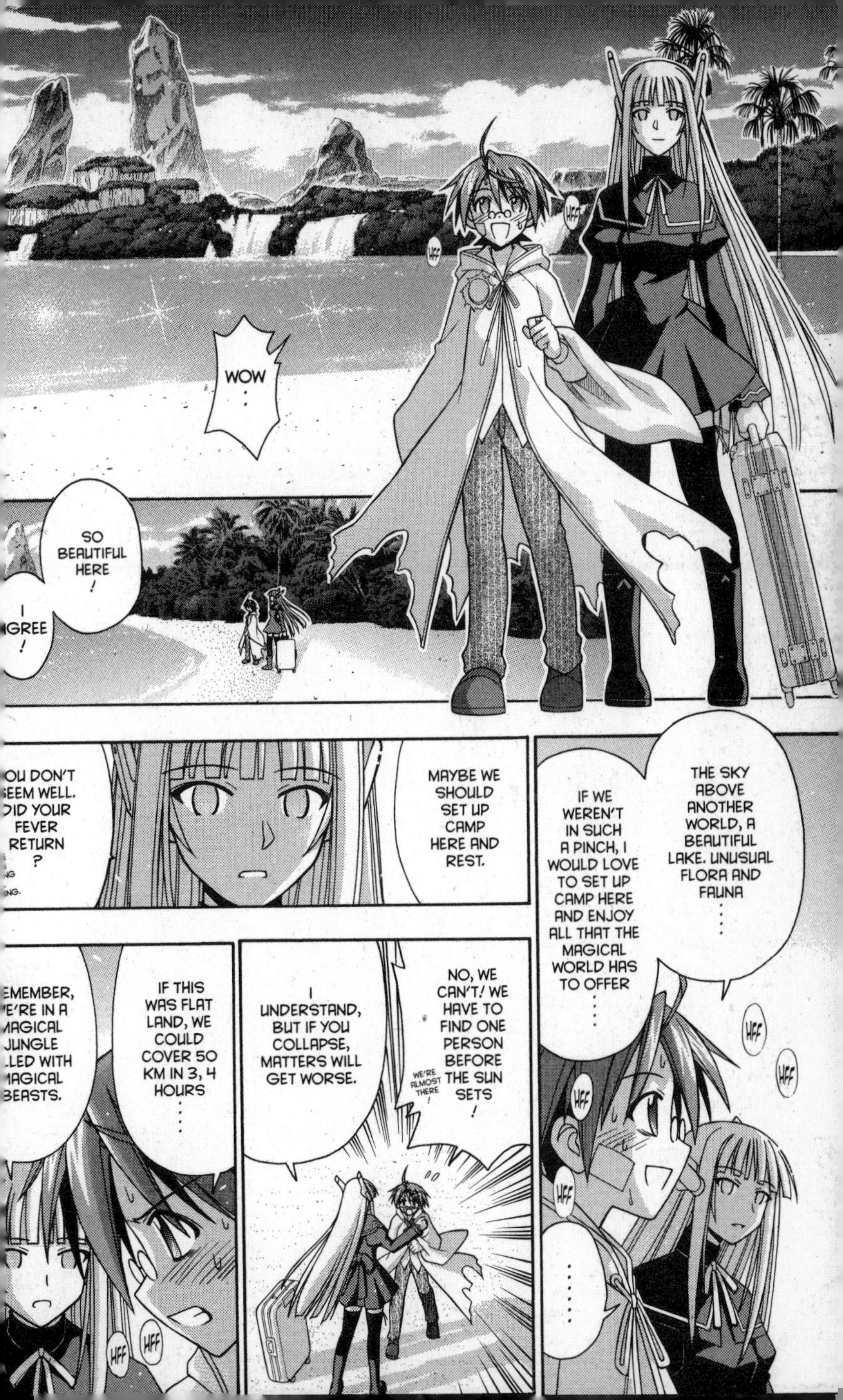
HFF
HFF
WOW ...
SO BEAUTIFUL HERE!
I GREE!
THE SKY ABOVE ANOTHER WORLD, A BEAUTIFUL LAKE. UNUSUAL FLORA AND FAUNA ....
IF WE WEREN'T IN SUCH A PINCH, I WOULD LOVE TO SET UP CAMP HERE AND ENJOY ALL THAT THE MAGICAL WORLD HAS TO OFFER ....
HFF
HFF
HFF
HFF
....
MAYBE WE SHOULD SET UP CAMP HERE AND REST.
OU DON'T SEEM WELL. DID YOUR FEVER RETURN?
NO, WE CAN'T! WE HAVE TO FIND ONE PERSON BEFORE THE SUN SETS!
WE'RE ALMOST THERE!
I UNDERSTAND, BUT IF YOU COLLAPSE, MATTERS WILL GET WORSE.
IF THIS WAS FLAT LAND, WE COULD COVER 50 KM IN 3, 4 HOURS ....
EMEMBER, E'RE IN A AGICAL JUNGLE LLED WITH AGICAL BEASTS.
HFF
HFF

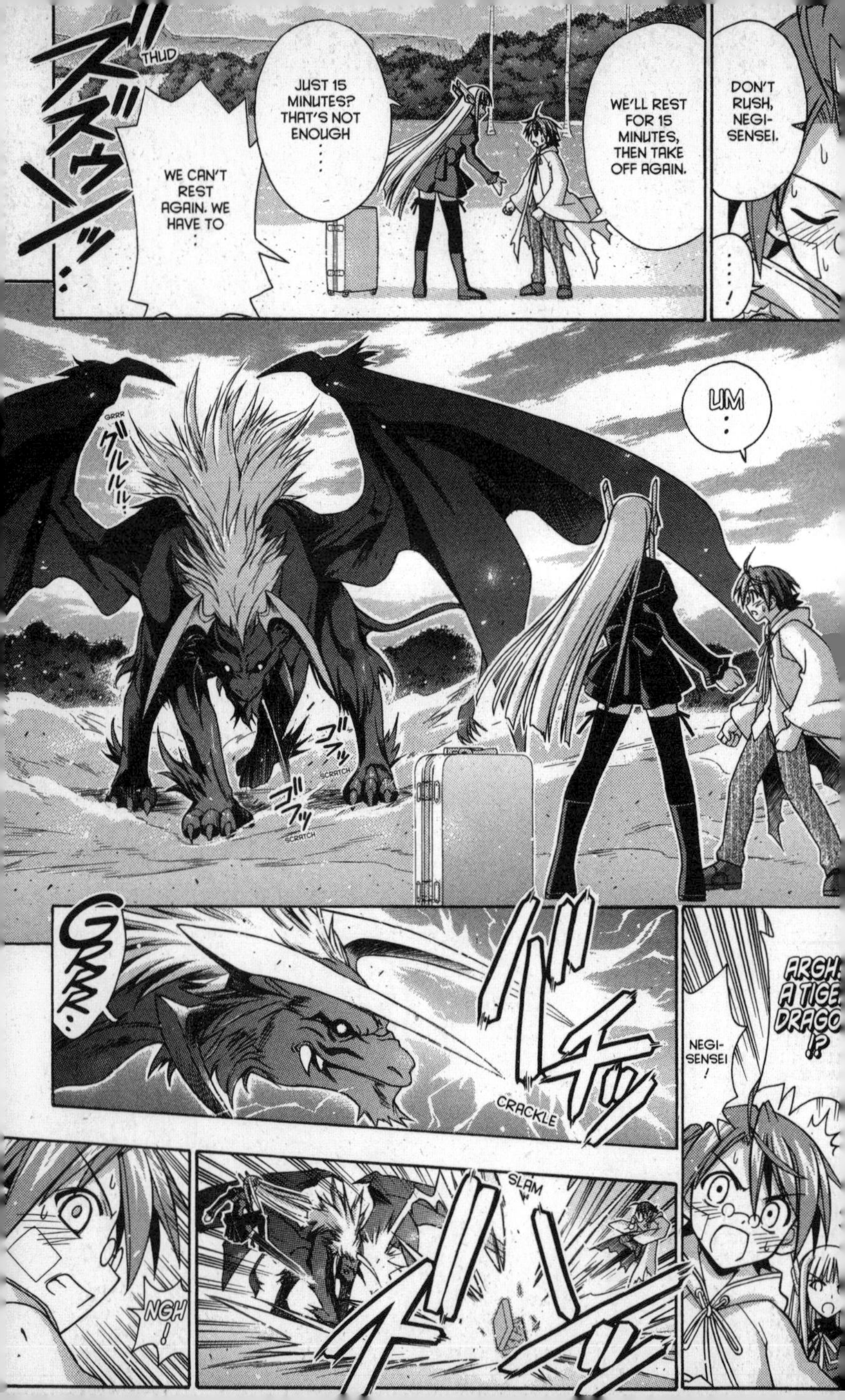
DON'T RUSH, NEGI-SENSEI.
.....!
WE'LL REST FOR 15 MINUTES, THEN TAKE OFF AGAIN.
JUST 15 MINUTES? THAT'S NOT ENOUGH ....
WE CAN'T REST AGAIN. WE HAVE TO ...
THUD
UM ..
GRRR
SCRATCH
SCRATCH
ARGH. A TIGE DRAGO !?
NEGI-SENSEI !
GRRR..
CRACKLE
SLAM
NGH !

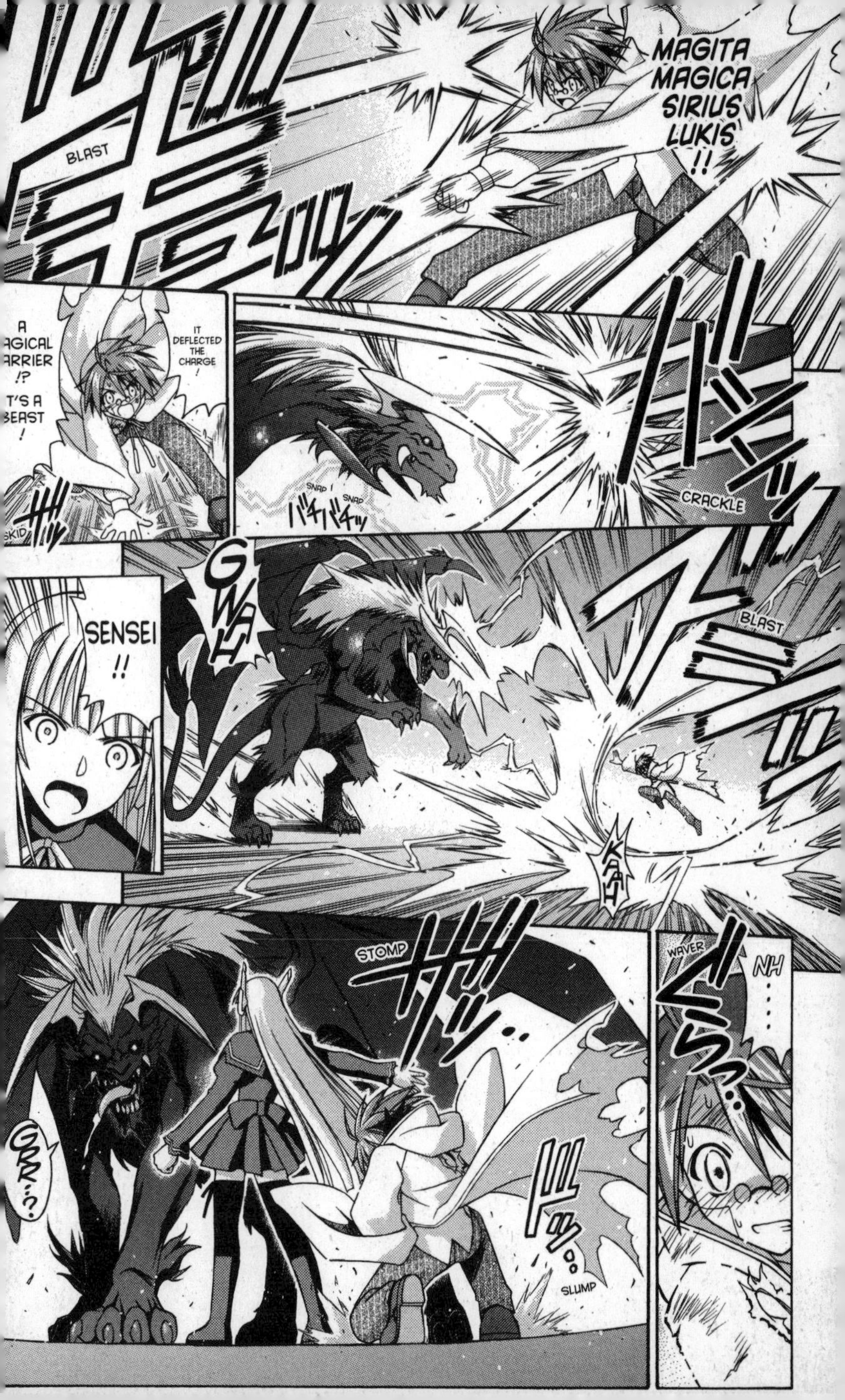
MAGITA MAGICA SIRIUS LUKIS !!
BLAST
CRACKLE
SNAP SNAP
IT DEFLECTED THE CHARGE !
A AGICAL ARRIER !?
T'S A EAST !
SKID
BLAST
KAH
GWAH
SENSEI !!
WAVER
NH ...
STOMP
SLUMP
GRR..?

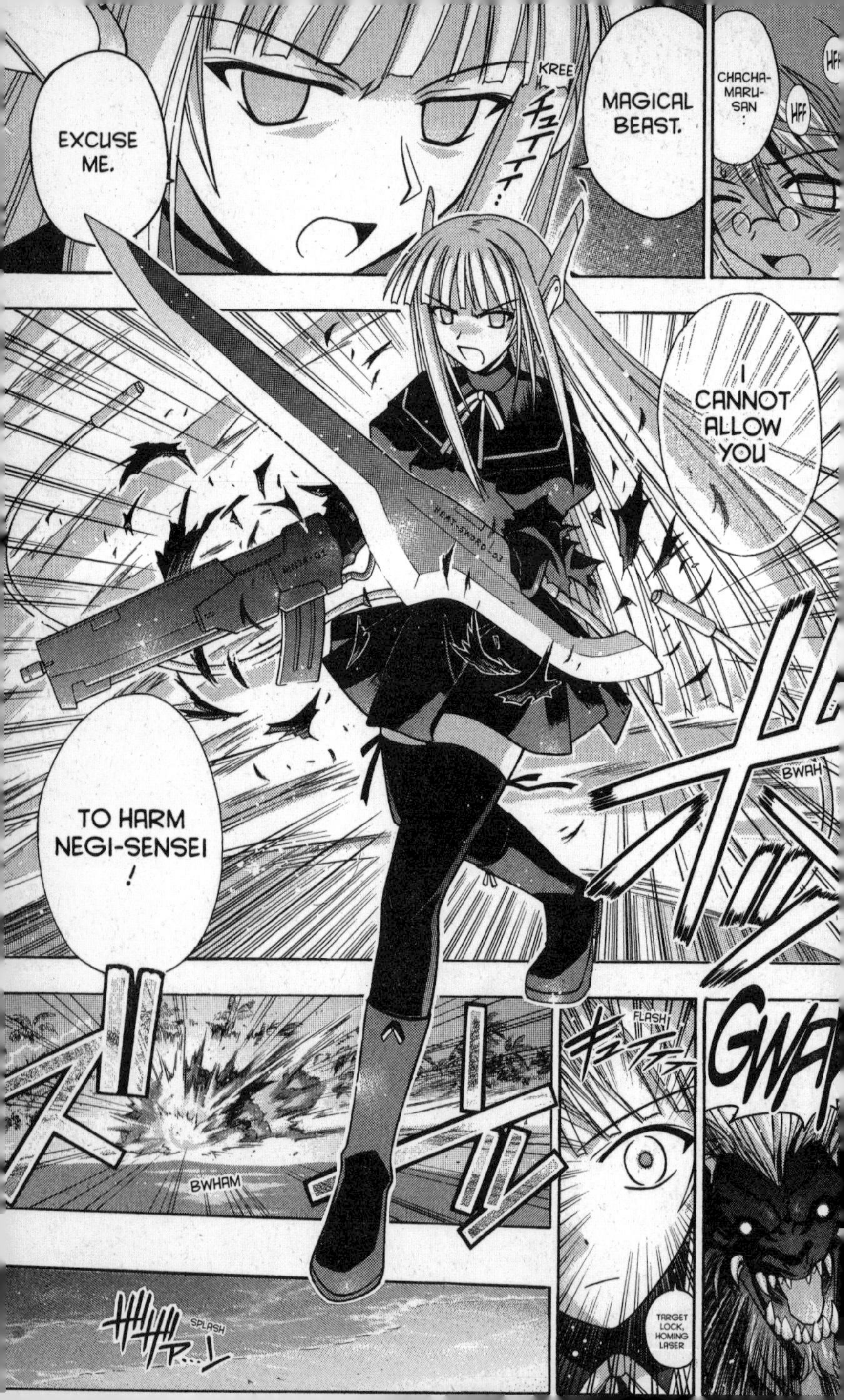

HFF
HFF
CHACHAMARU-SAN...
MAGICAL BEAST.
KREE
EXCUSE ME.
I CANNOT ALLOW YOU
TO HARM NEGI-SENSEI!
BWAH
GWA
FLASH
TARGET LOCK, HOMING LASER
BWHAM
SPLASH

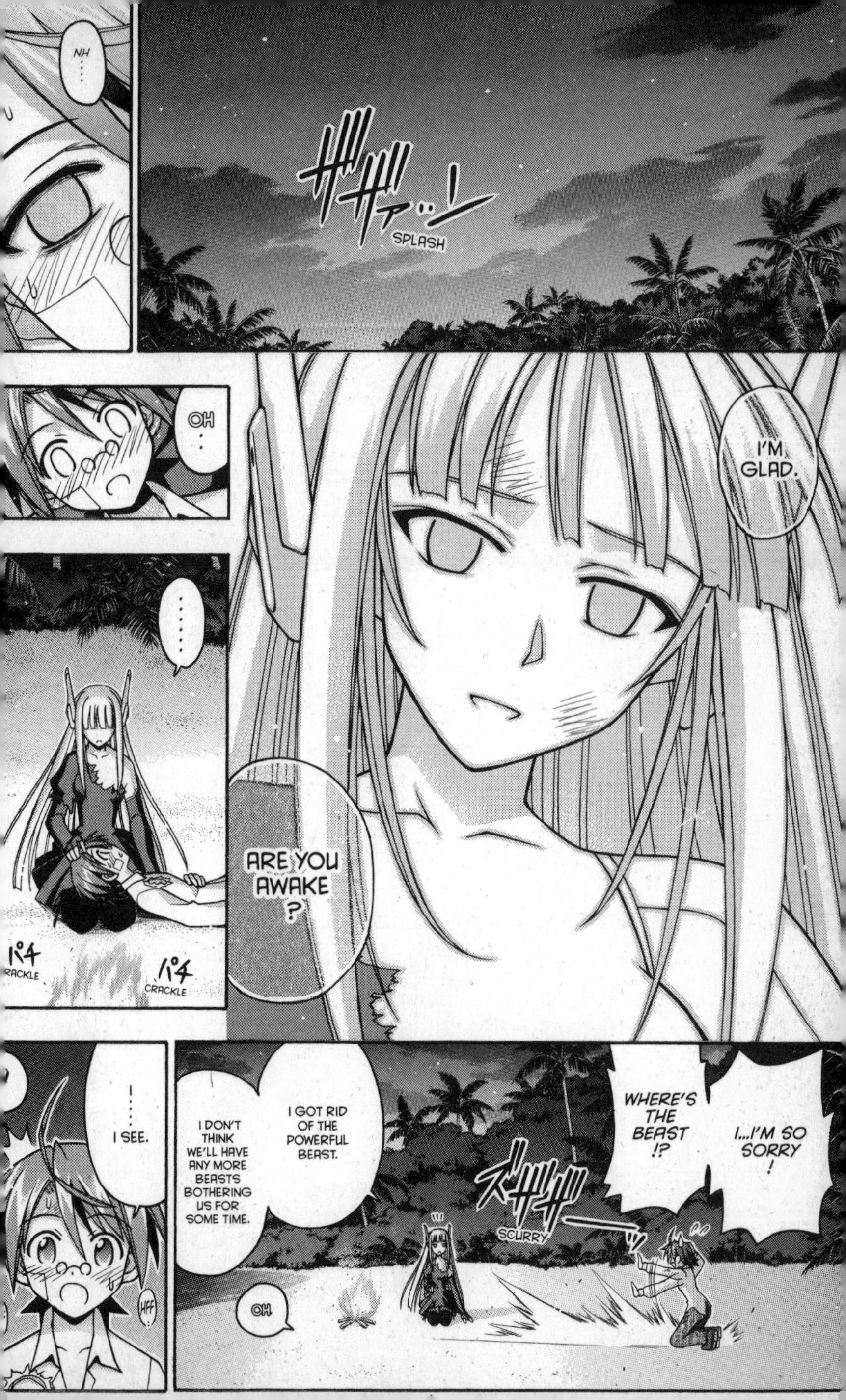
SPLASH
NH.....
I'M GLAD.
ARE YOU AWAKE?
OH...
......
CRACKLE
CRACKLE
I...I'M SO SORRY!
WHERE'S THE BEAST!?
SCURRY
I GOT RID OF THE POWERFUL BEAST.
I DON'T THINK WE'LL HAVE ANY MORE BEASTS BOTHERING US FOR SOME TIME.
OH
!... I SEE.
HFF

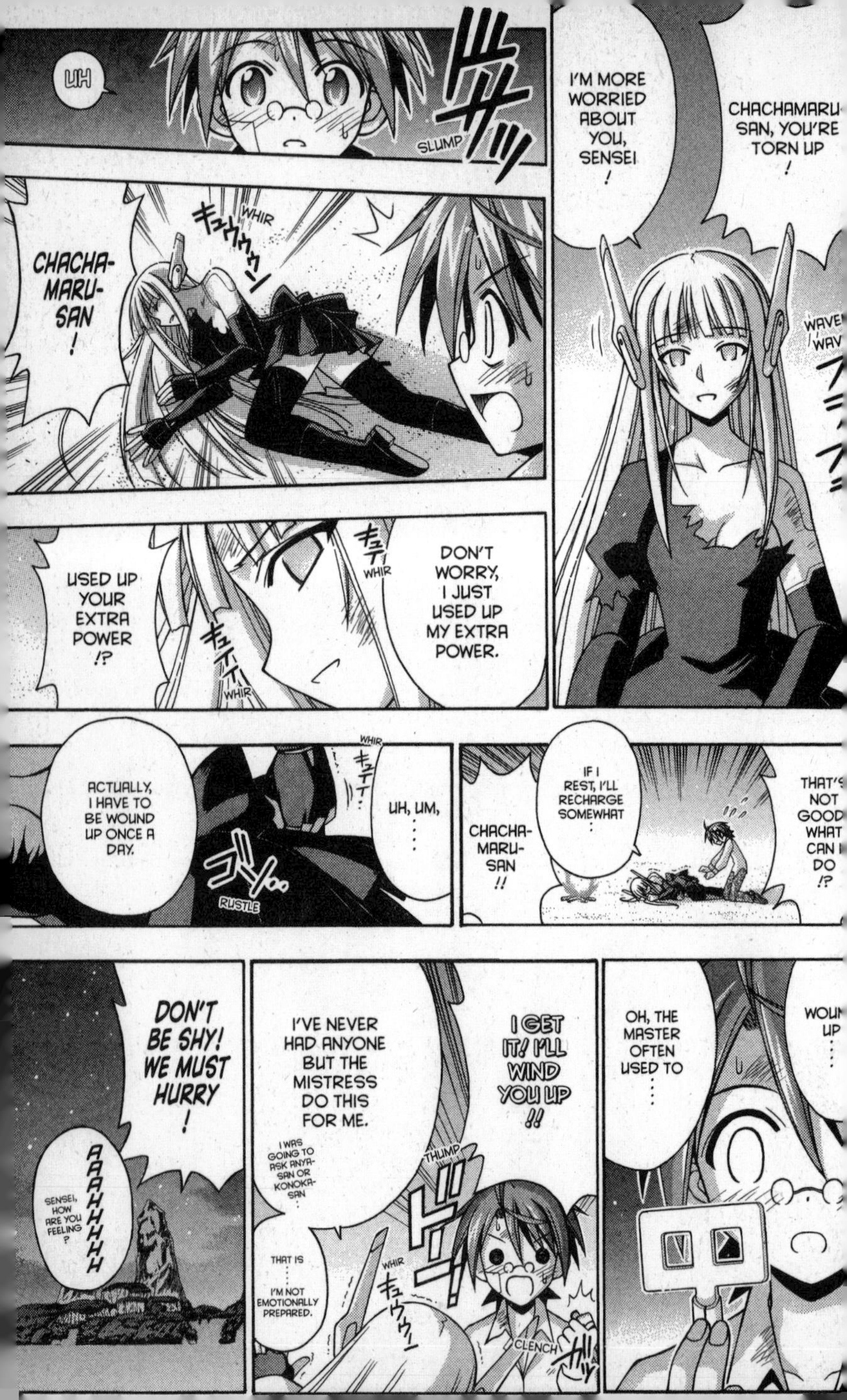
CHACHAMARU-SAN, YOU'RE TORN UP!
I'M MORE WORRIED ABOUT YOU, SENSEI!
WAVE WAV
UH
SLUMP
WHIR
CHACHA-MARU-SAN!
DON'T WORRY, I JUST USED UP MY EXTRA POWER.
WHIR
WHIR
USED UP YOUR EXTRA POWER!?
THAT'S NOT GOOD WHAT CAN I DO!?
IF I REST, I'LL RECHARGE SOMEWHAT...
CHACHA-MARU-SAN!!
WHIR
UH, UM, ...
ACTUALLY, I HAVE TO BE WOUND UP ONCE A DAY.
RUSTLE
WOUN UP...
OH, THE MASTER OFTEN USED TO...
I GET IT! I'LL WIND YOU UP!!
THUMP
I'VE NEVER HAD ANYONE BUT THE MISTRESS DO THIS FOR ME.
I WAS GOING TO ASK ANYA-SAN OR KONOKA-SAN
THAT IS... I'M NOT EMOTIONALLY PREPARED.
WHIR
CLENCH
DON'T BE SHY! WE MUST HURRY!
AAAHHHHHH
SENSEI, HOW ARE YOU FEELING?

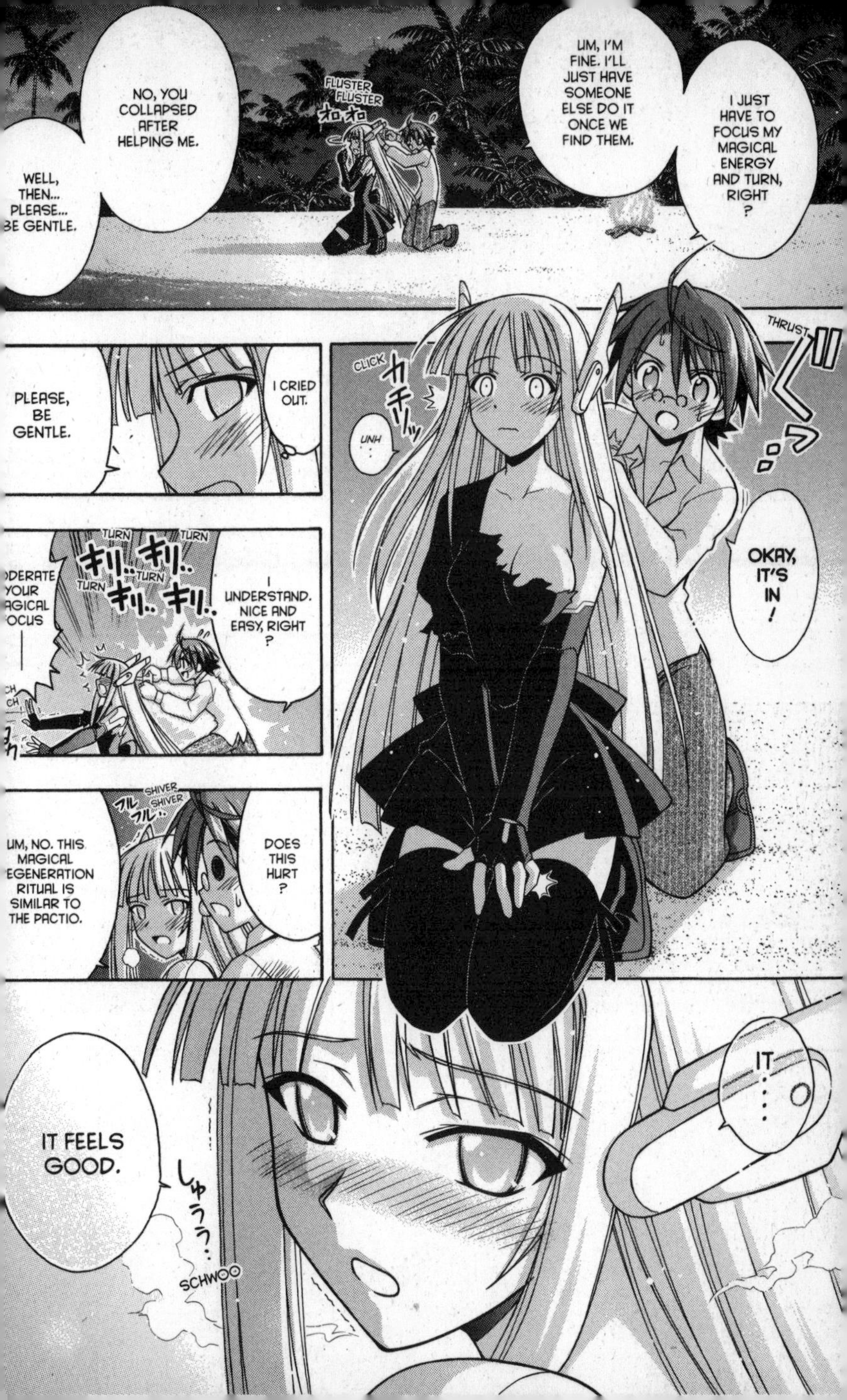

UM, I'M FINE. I'LL JUST HAVE SOMEONE ELSE DO IT ONCE WE FIND THEM.
NO, YOU COLLAPSED AFTER HELPING ME.
FLUSTER FLUSTER
WELL, THEN... PLEASE... BE GENTLE.
I JUST HAVE TO FOCUS MY MAGICAL ENERGY AND TURN, RIGHT?
THRUST
CLICK
UNH
OKAY, IT'S IN!
I CRIED OUT.
PLEASE, BE GENTLE.
TURN TURN TURN TURN
I UNDERSTAND. NICE AND EASY, RIGHT?
ODERATE YOUR AGICAL FOCUS —
DOES THIS HURT?
SHIVER SHIVER
UM, NO. THIS MAGICAL EGENERATION RITUAL IS SIMILAR TO THE PACTIO.
IT...
IT FEELS GOOD.
SCHWOO

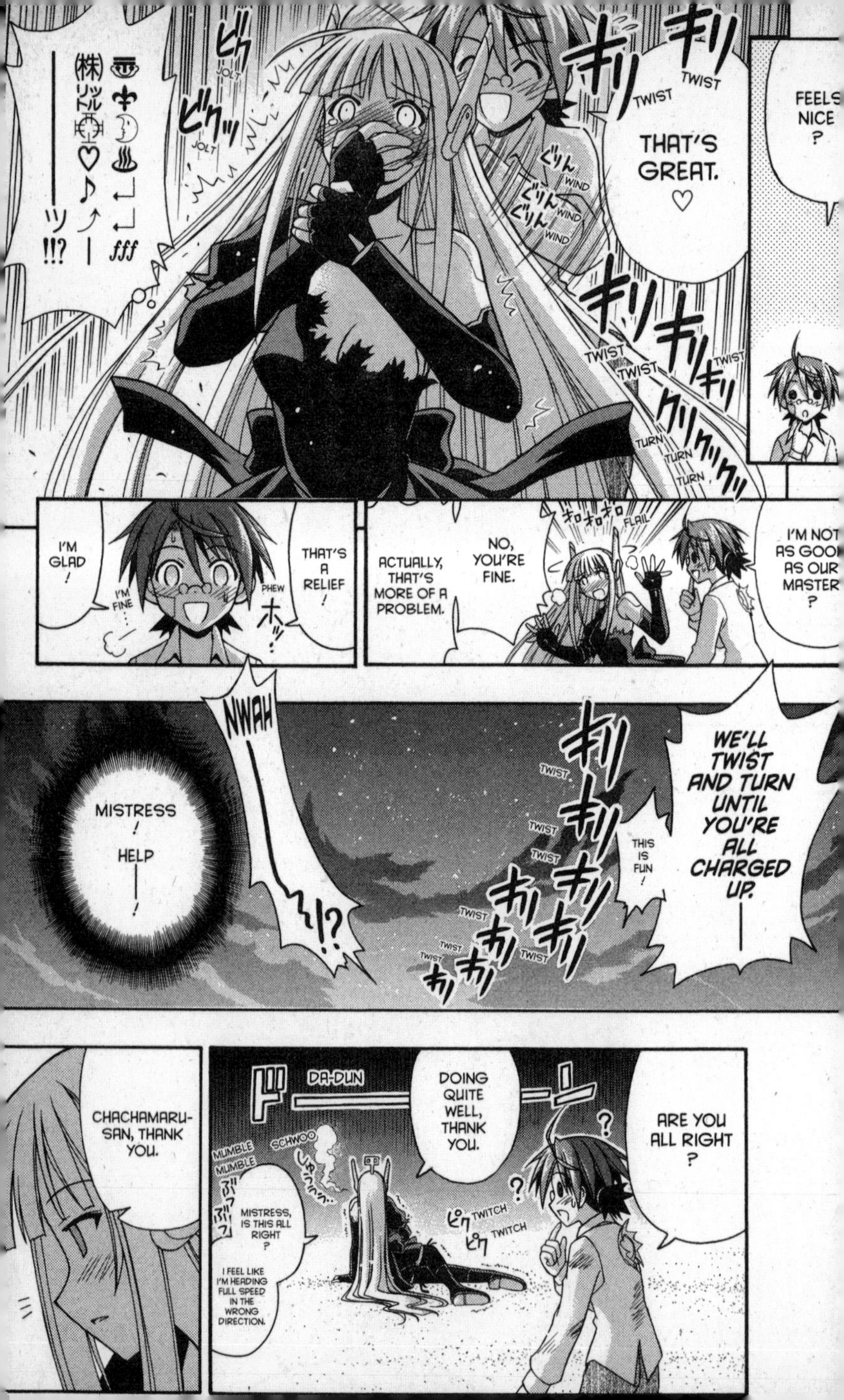
FEELS NICE?
TWIST TWIST
THAT'S GREAT. ♡
TWIST
WIND WIND WIND
JOLT JOLT
TWIST TWIST TWIST
TURN TURN TURN
I'M NOT AS GOOD AS OUR MASTER?
FLAIL
NO, YOU'RE FINE.
ACTUALLY, THAT'S MORE OF A PROBLEM.
THAT'S A RELIEF!
PHEW
I'M GLAD!
I'M FINE...
WE'LL TWIST AND TURN UNTIL YOU'RE ALL CHARGED UP.—
THIS IS FUN!
TWIST TWIST TWIST TWIST TWIST TWIST TWIST
NWAH—!?
MISTRESS! HELP—!
ARE YOU ALL RIGHT?
DOING QUITE WELL, THANK YOU.
DA-DUN
TWITCH TWITCH
SCHWOO
MUMBLE MUMBLE
MISTRESS, IS THIS ALL RIGHT?
I FEEL LIKE I'M HEADING FULL SPEED IN THE WRONG DIRECTION.
CHACHAMARU-SAN, THANK YOU.

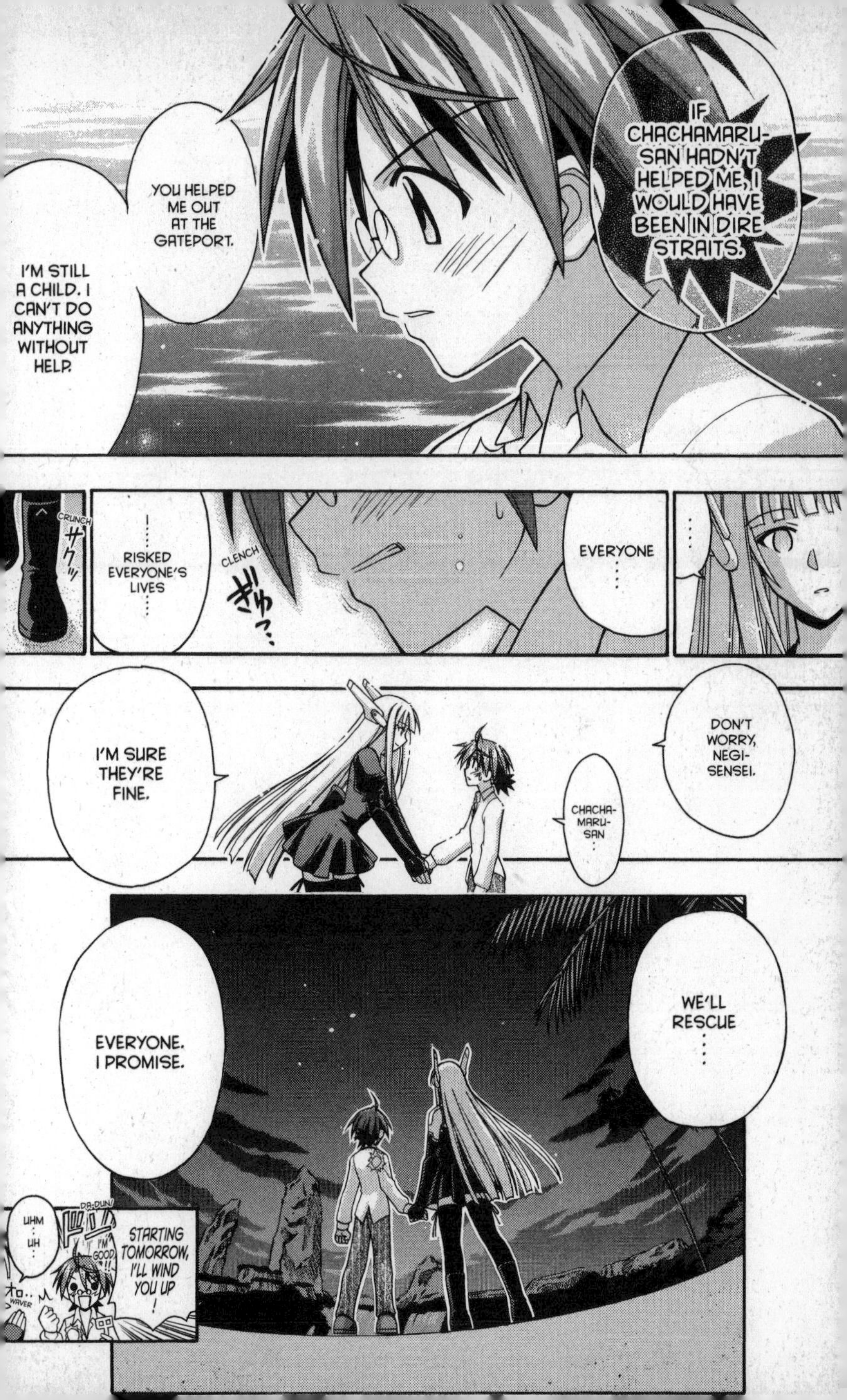
IF CHACHAMARU-SAN HADN'T HELPED ME, I WOULD HAVE BEEN IN DIRE STRAITS.
YOU HELPED ME OUT AT THE GATEPORT.
I'M STILL A CHILD. I CAN'T DO ANYTHING WITHOUT HELP.
. . .
EVERYONE . . .
CLENCH
ぎゅっ
I . . . RISKED EVERYONE'S LIVES . . .
CRUNCH
ザクッ
DON'T WORRY, NEGI-SENSEI.
CHACHA-MARU-SAN . . .
I'M SURE THEY'RE FINE.
WE'LL RESCUE . . .
EVERYONE. I PROMISE.
DA-DUN!
I'M GOOD!!
STARTING TOMORROW, I'LL WIND YOU UP!
UHM . . . UH
オロ..
WAVER

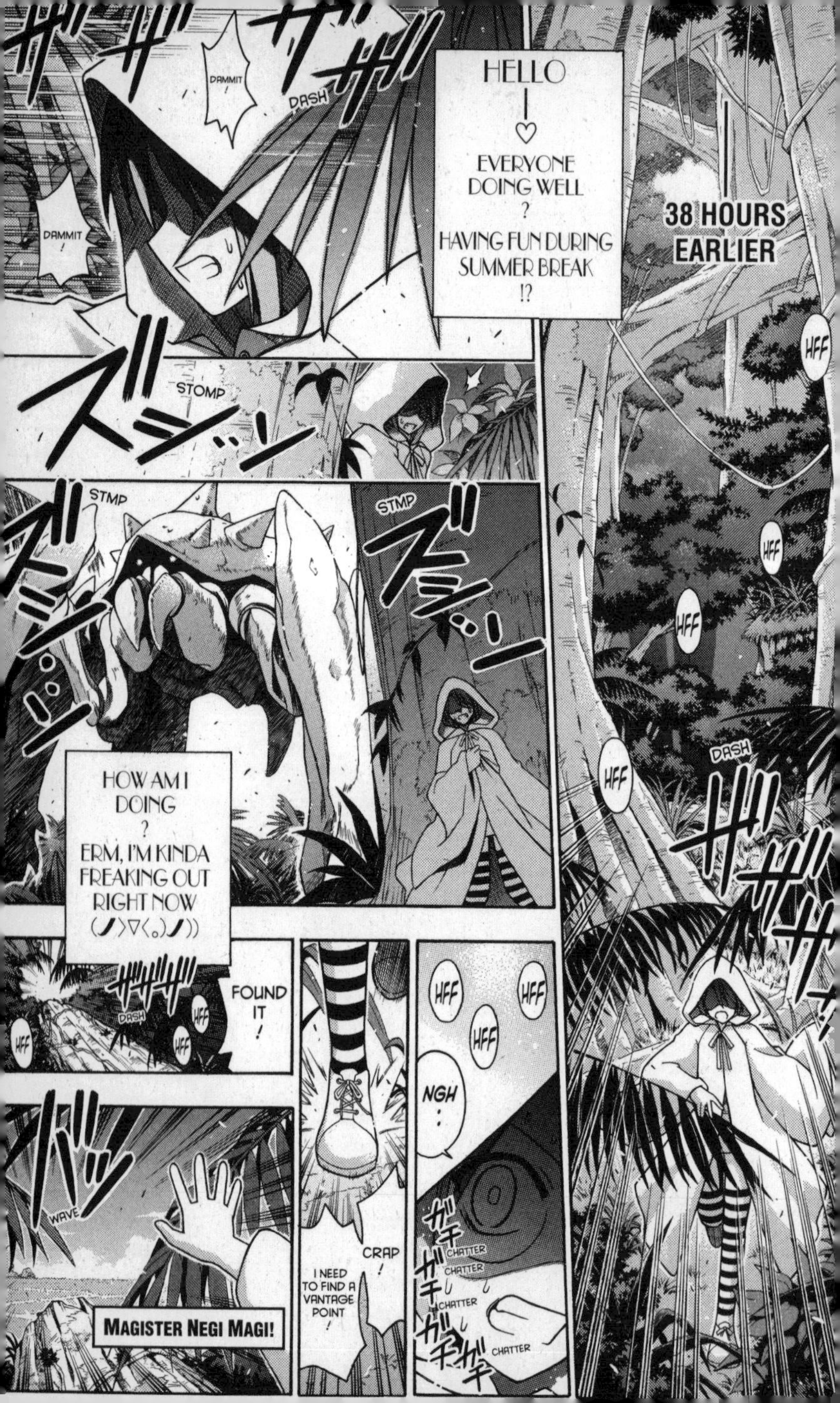
38 HOURS EARLIER
HFF
HFF
HFF
HFF
DASH
DAMMIT!
HELLO
♡
EVERYONE DOING WELL?
HAVING FUN DURING SUMMER BREAK!?
DASH
DAMMIT!
STOMP
STMP
STMP
HOW AM I DOING?
ERM, I'M KINDA FREAKING OUT RIGHT NOW
(ノ>▽<。)ノ))
HFF
HFF
HFF
NGH:
CHATTER
CHATTER
CHATTER
CHATTER
CRAP!
I NEED TO FIND A VANTAGE POINT!
FOUND IT!
DASH
HFF
HFF
HFF
WAVE
MAGISTER NEGI MAGI!

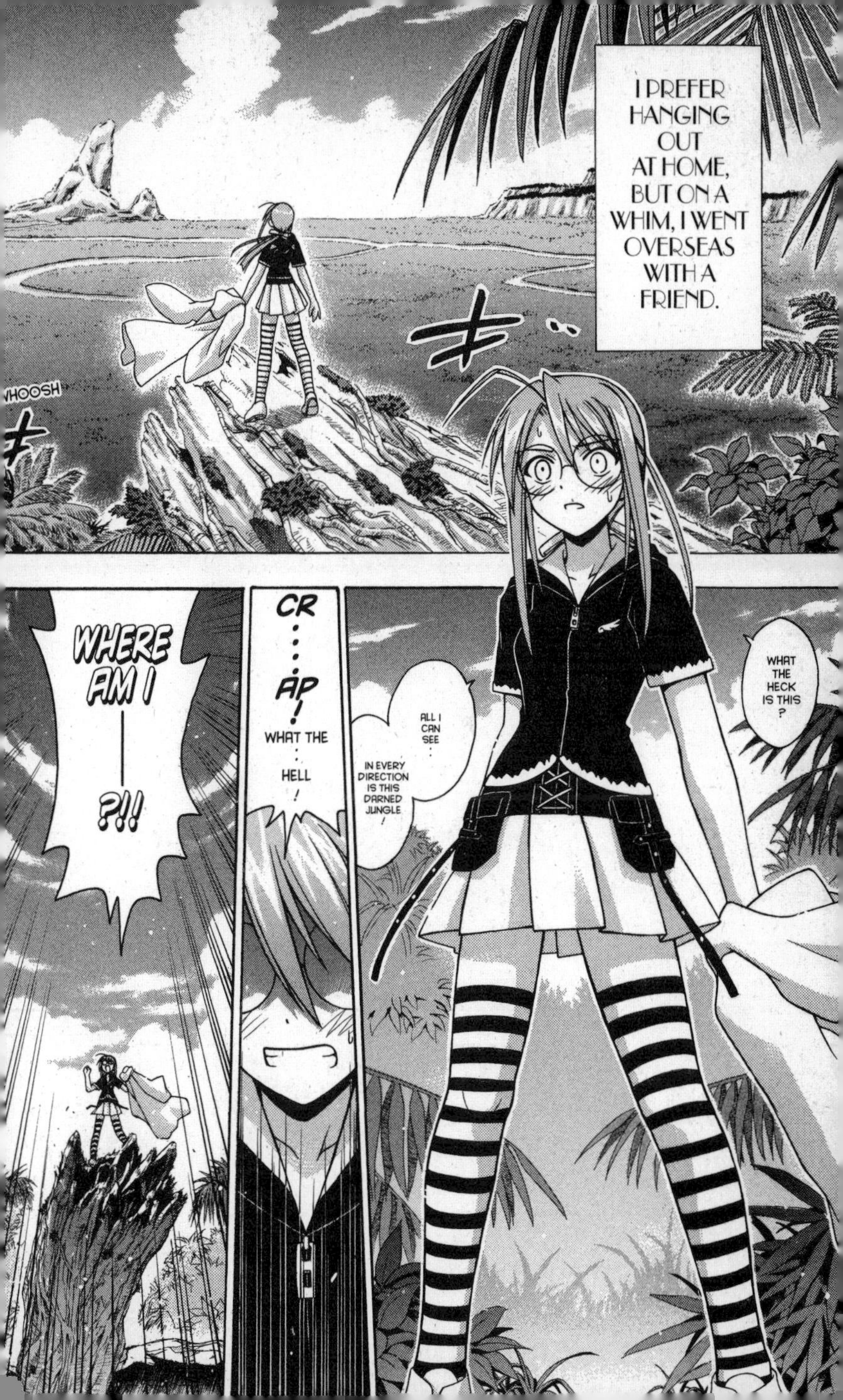
I PREFER HANGING OUT AT HOME, BUT ON A WHIM, I WENT OVERSEAS WITH A FRIEND.
WHOOSH
WHAT THE HECK IS THIS?
ALL I CAN SEE...
IN EVERY DIRECTION IS THIS DARNED JUNGLE!
CR...AP!
WHAT THE... HELL!
WHERE AM I——?!!

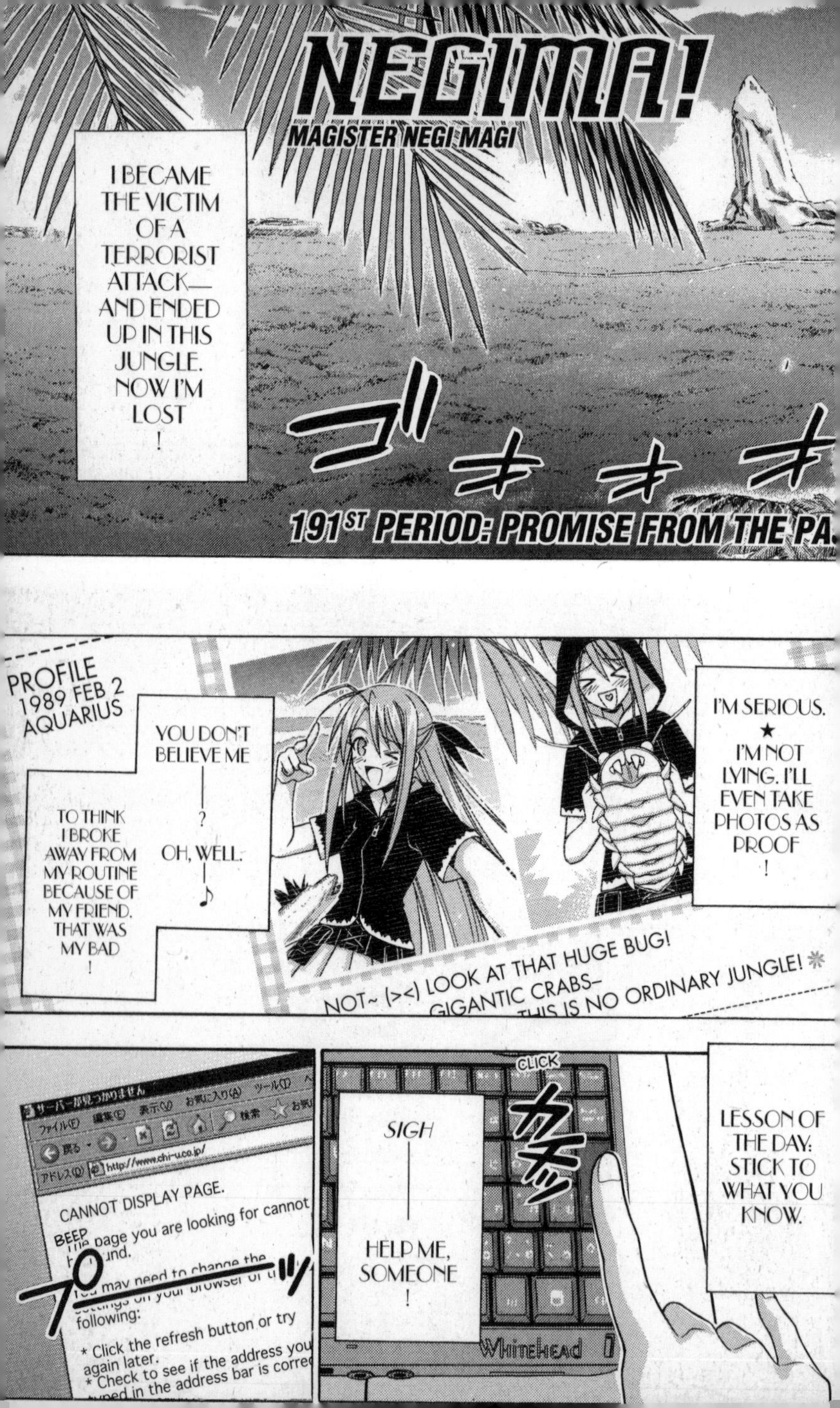

NEGIMA!
MAGISTER NEGI MAGI
I BECAME THE VICTIM OF A TERRORIST ATTACK— AND ENDED UP IN THIS JUNGLE. NOW I'M LOST !
191ST PERIOD: PROMISE FROM THE PA
I'M SERIOUS. ★ I'M NOT LYING. I'LL EVEN TAKE PHOTOS AS PROOF !
YOU DON'T BELIEVE ME —? OH, WELL. —♪
TO THINK I BROKE AWAY FROM MY ROUTINE BECAUSE OF MY FRIEND. THAT WAS MY BAD !
PROFILE 1989 FEB 2 AQUARIUS
NOT~ (><) LOOK AT THAT HUGE BUG! GIGANTIC CRABS– THIS IS NO ORDINARY JUNGLE!
LESSON OF THE DAY: STICK TO WHAT YOU KNOW.
CLICK
SIGH — HELP ME, SOMEONE !
Whitehead
http://www.chi-u.co.jp/
CANNOT DISPLAY PAGE.
The page you are looking for cannot be found.
You may need to change the settings on your browser or try the following:
* Click the refresh button or try again later.
* Check to see if the address you typed in the address bar is correct
BEEP

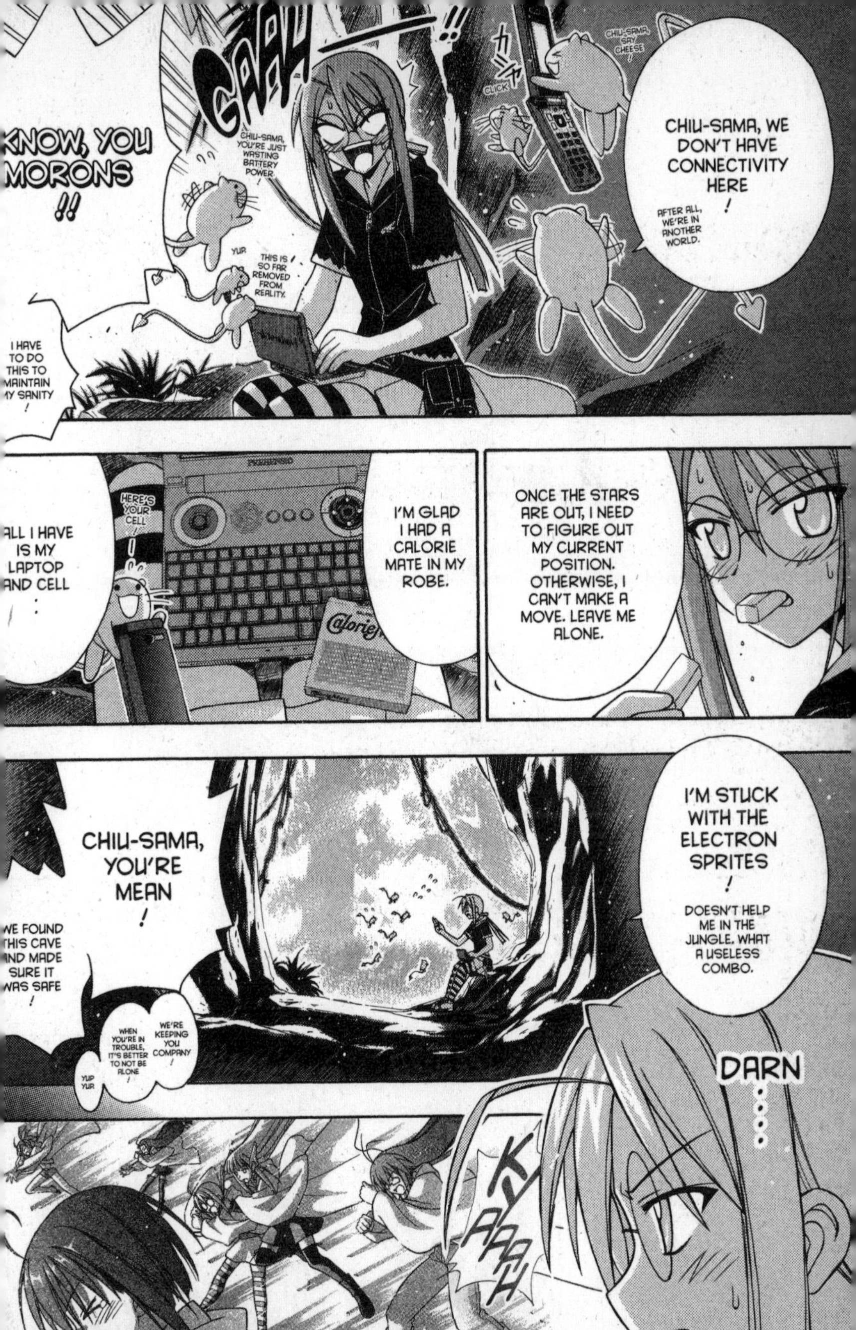
CHIU-SAMA, SAY CHEESE
CLICK
CHIU-SAMA, WE DON'T HAVE CONNECTIVITY HERE!
AFTER ALL, WE'RE IN ANOTHER WORLD.
CHIU-SAMA, YOU'RE JUST WASTING BATTERY POWER!
THIS IS SO FAR REMOVED FROM REALITY!
YUR
KNOW, YOU MORONS!!
I HAVE TO DO THIS TO MAINTAIN MY SANITY!
ONCE THE STARS ARE OUT, I NEED TO FIGURE OUT MY CURRENT POSITION. OTHERWISE, I CAN'T MAKE A MOVE. LEAVE ME ALONE.
I'M GLAD I HAD A CALORIE MATE IN MY ROBE.
HERE'S YOUR CELL!
ALL I HAVE IS MY LAPTOP AND CELL:
I'M STUCK WITH THE ELECTRON SPRITES!
DOESN'T HELP ME IN THE JUNGLE. WHAT A USELESS COMBO.
DARN....
CHIU-SAMA, YOU'RE MEAN!
WE FOUND THIS CAVE AND MADE SURE IT WAS SAFE!
WE'RE KEEPING YOU COMPANY!
WHEN YOU'RE IN TROUBLE, IT'S BETTER TO NOT BE ALONE!
YUP YUR.
KYAAAH

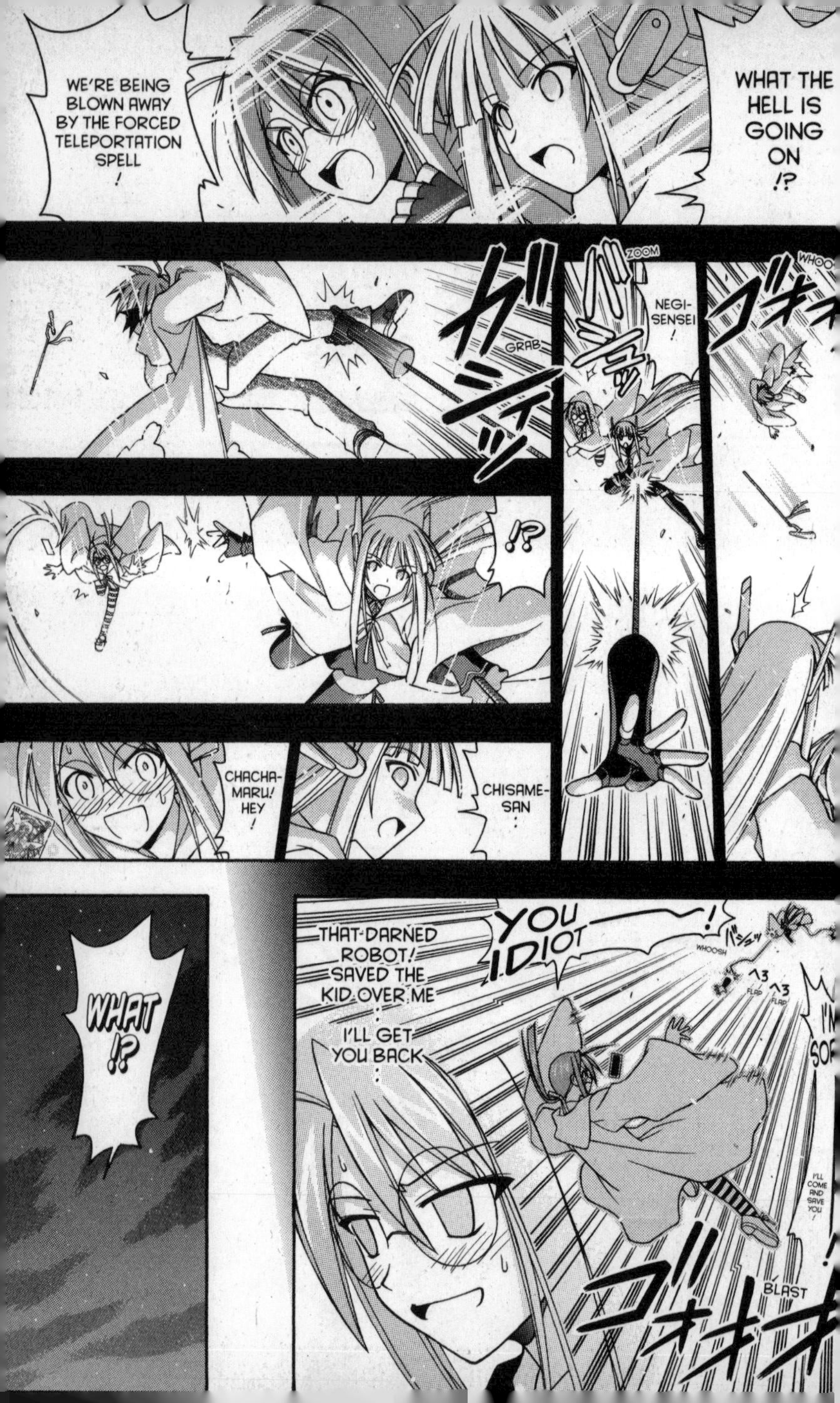
WHAT THE HELL IS GOING ON !?
WE'RE BEING BLOWN AWAY BY THE FORCED TELEPORTATION SPELL !
WHOO
ZOOM
NEGI-SENSEI !
GRAB
!?
CHISAME-SAN ...
CHACHAMARU! HEY !
YOU I.D.IOT——!
WHOOSH
FLAP
FLAP
I'M SOR
THAT DARNED ROBOT! SAVED THE KID OVER ME ...
I'LL GET YOU BACK ...
I'LL COME AND SAVE YOU
BLAST
WHAT !?

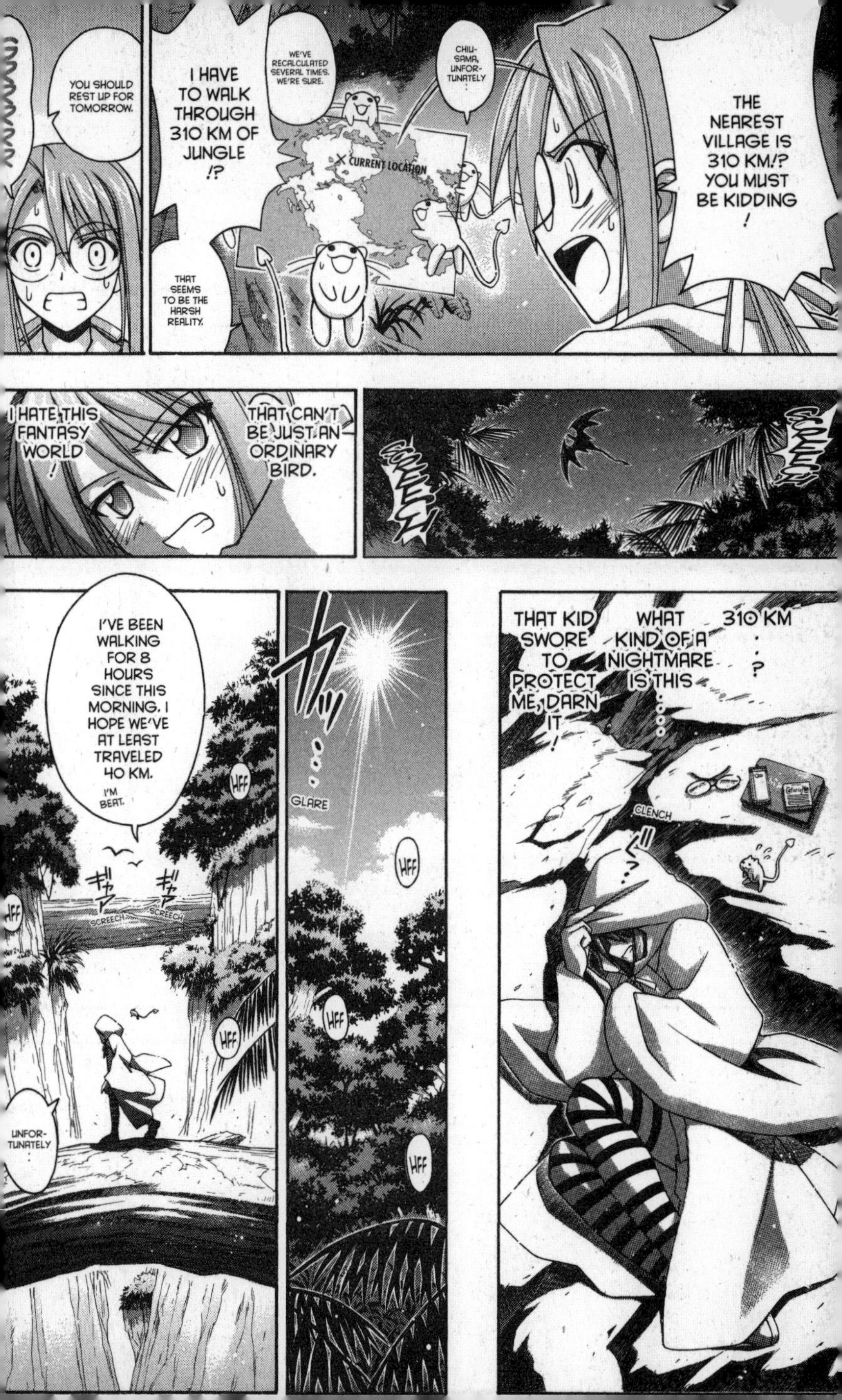
THE NEAREST VILLAGE IS 310 KM!? YOU MUST BE KIDDING!
CHIU-SAMA, UNFOR-TUNATELY...
WE'VE RECALCULATED SEVERAL TIMES. WE'RE SURE.
× CURRENT LOCATION
THAT SEEMS TO BE THE HARSH REALITY.
I HAVE TO WALK THROUGH 310 KM OF JUNGLE!?
YOU SHOULD REST UP FOR TOMORROW.
THAT CAN'T BE JUST AN ORDINARY BIRD.
I HATE THIS FANTASY WORLD!
310 KM...?
WHAT KIND OF A NIGHTMARE IS THIS....
THAT KID SWORE TO PROTECT ME, DARN IT!
CLENCH
GLARE
HFF
HFF
HFF
I'VE BEEN WALKING FOR 8 HOURS SINCE THIS MORNING. I HOPE WE'VE AT LEAST TRAVELED 40 KM.
I'M BEAT.
SCREECH
SCREECH
HFF
HFF
UNFOR-TUNATELY...

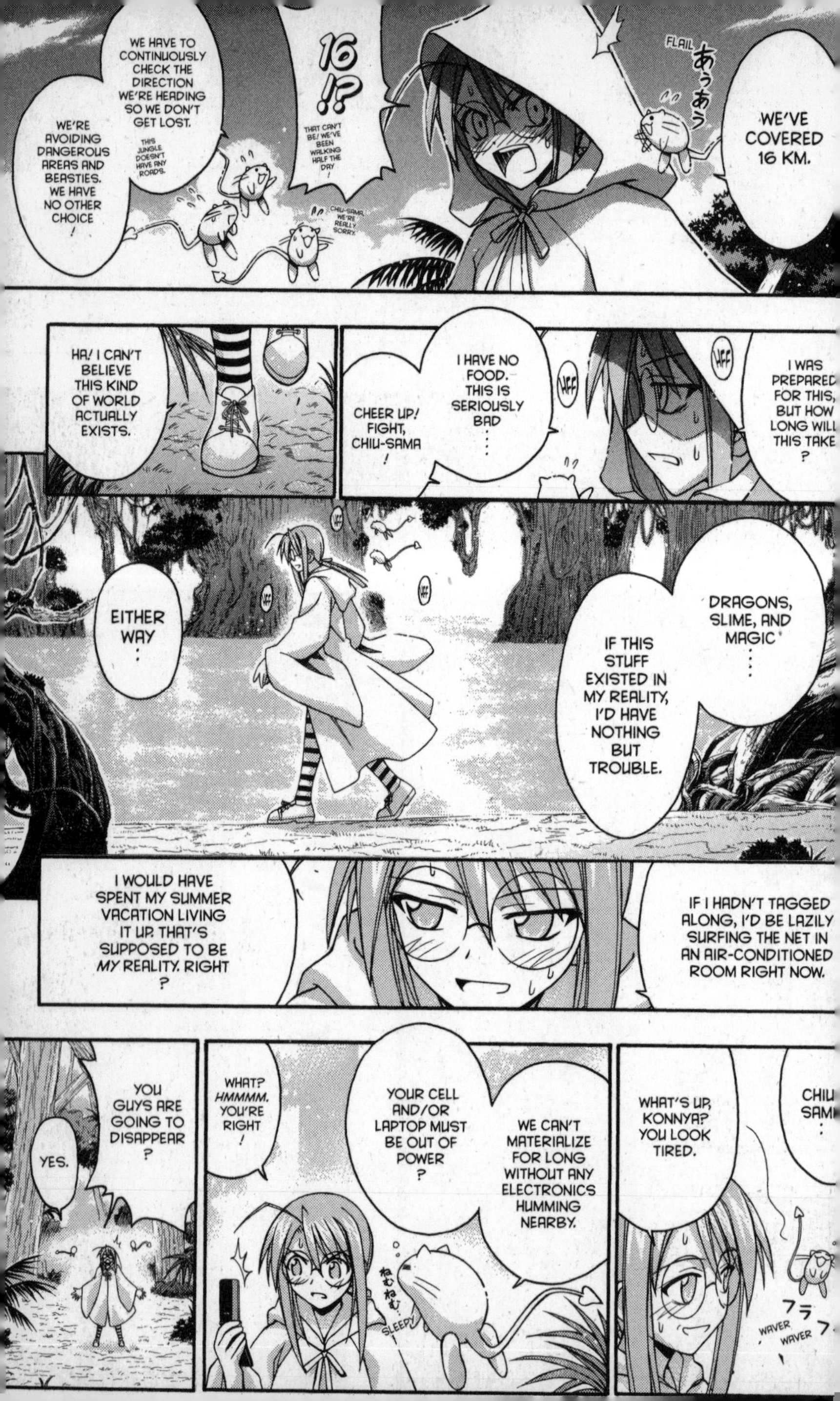

WE'VE COVERED 16 KM.
FLAIL あうあう
16 !?
THAT CAN'T BE! WE'VE BEEN WALKING HALF THE DAY!
CHIU-SAMA, WE'RE REALLY SORRY.
WE HAVE TO CONTINUOUSLY CHECK THE DIRECTION WE'RE HEADING SO WE DON'T GET LOST.
THIS JUNGLE DOESN'T HAVE ANY ROADS.
WE'RE AVOIDING DANGEROUS AREAS AND BEASTIES. WE HAVE NO OTHER CHOICE!
I WAS PREPARED FOR THIS, BUT HOW LONG WILL THIS TAKE?
HFF
HFF
I HAVE NO FOOD. THIS IS SERIOUSLY BAD...
CHEER UP! FIGHT, CHIU-SAMA!
HA! I CAN'T BELIEVE THIS KIND OF WORLD ACTUALLY EXISTS.
DRAGONS, SLIME, AND MAGIC...
IF THIS STUFF EXISTED IN MY REALITY, I'D HAVE NOTHING BUT TROUBLE.
EITHER WAY...
IF I HADN'T TAGGED ALONG, I'D BE LAZILY SURFING THE NET IN AN AIR-CONDITIONED ROOM RIGHT NOW.
I WOULD HAVE SPENT MY SUMMER VACATION LIVING IT UP. THAT'S SUPPOSED TO BE *MY* REALITY. RIGHT?
CHIU SAM...
WHAT'S UP, KONNYA? YOU LOOK TIRED.
フラフ
WAVER WAVER
WE CAN'T MATERIALIZE FOR LONG WITHOUT ANY ELECTRONICS HUMMING NEARBY.
YOUR CELL AND/OR LAPTOP MUST BE OUT OF POWER?
WHAT? *HMMMM.* YOU'RE RIGHT!
ねむねむ
SLEEPY
YOU GUYS ARE GOING TO DISAPPEAR?
YES.

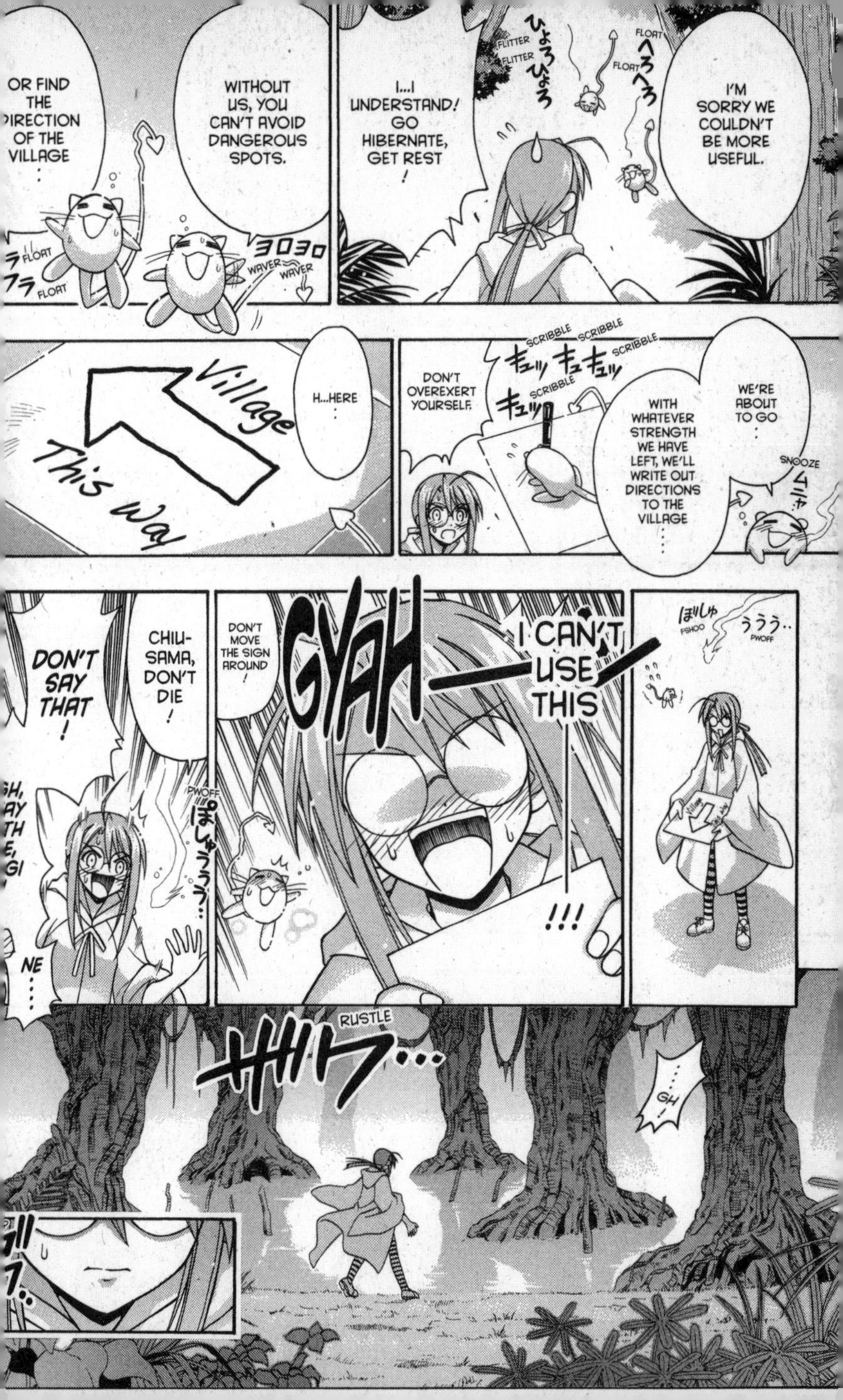
FLOAT へろへろ FLOAT
I'M SORRY WE COULDN'T BE MORE USEFUL.
FLITTER ひょろひょろ FLITTER
I...I UNDERSTAND! GO HIBERNATE, GET REST!
WITHOUT US, YOU CAN'T AVOID DANGEROUS SPOTS.
ヨロヨロ WAVER WAVER
OR FIND THE DIRECTION OF THE VILLAGE...
フラフラ FLOAT FLOAT
WE'RE ABOUT TO GO...
SNOOZE ムニャ
WITH WHATEVER STRENGTH WE HAVE LEFT, WE'LL WRITE OUT DIRECTIONS TO THE VILLAGE...
SCRIBBLE キュッ キュキュッ SCRIBBLE SCRIBBLE キュッ SCRIBBLE
DON'T OVEREXERT YOURSELF.
H...HERE...
Village
This way
ぽしゅ FSHOO
ううう.. PWOFF
I CAN'T USE THIS
GYAH
DON'T MOVE THE SIGN AROUND!
!!!
PWOFF ぽしゅううう...
CHIU-SAMA, DON'T DIE!
DON'T SAY THAT!
NE....
RUSTLE ザッ...
...GH!

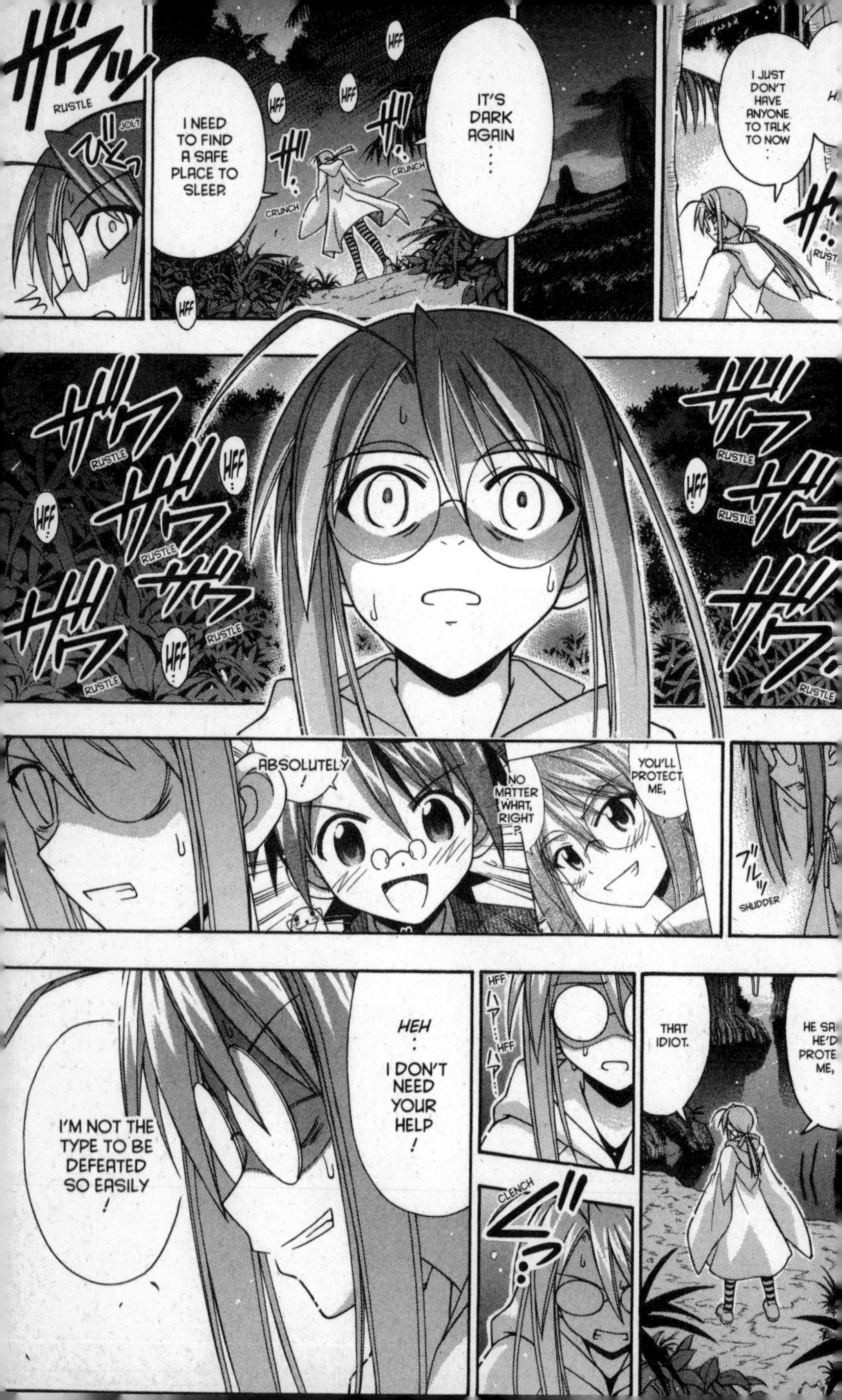

I JUST DON'T HAVE ANYONE TO TALK TO NOW...
H
RUST
IT'S DARK AGAIN......
HFF
HFF
HFF
CRUNCH
I NEED TO FIND A SAFE PLACE TO SLEEP.
CRUNCH
HFF
RUSTLE
JOLT
RUSTLE
HFF
RUSTLE
RUSTLE
RUSTLE
RUSTLE
HFF
RUSTLE
HFF
RUSTLE
HFF
RUSTLE
SHUDDER
YOU'LL PROTECT ME,
NO MATTER WHAT, RIGHT...?
ABSOLUTELY!
HE SA HE'D PROTE ME,
THAT IDIOT.
HFF HFF
CLENCH
HEH... I DON'T NEED YOUR HELP!
I'M NOT THE TYPE TO BE DEFEATED SO EASILY!

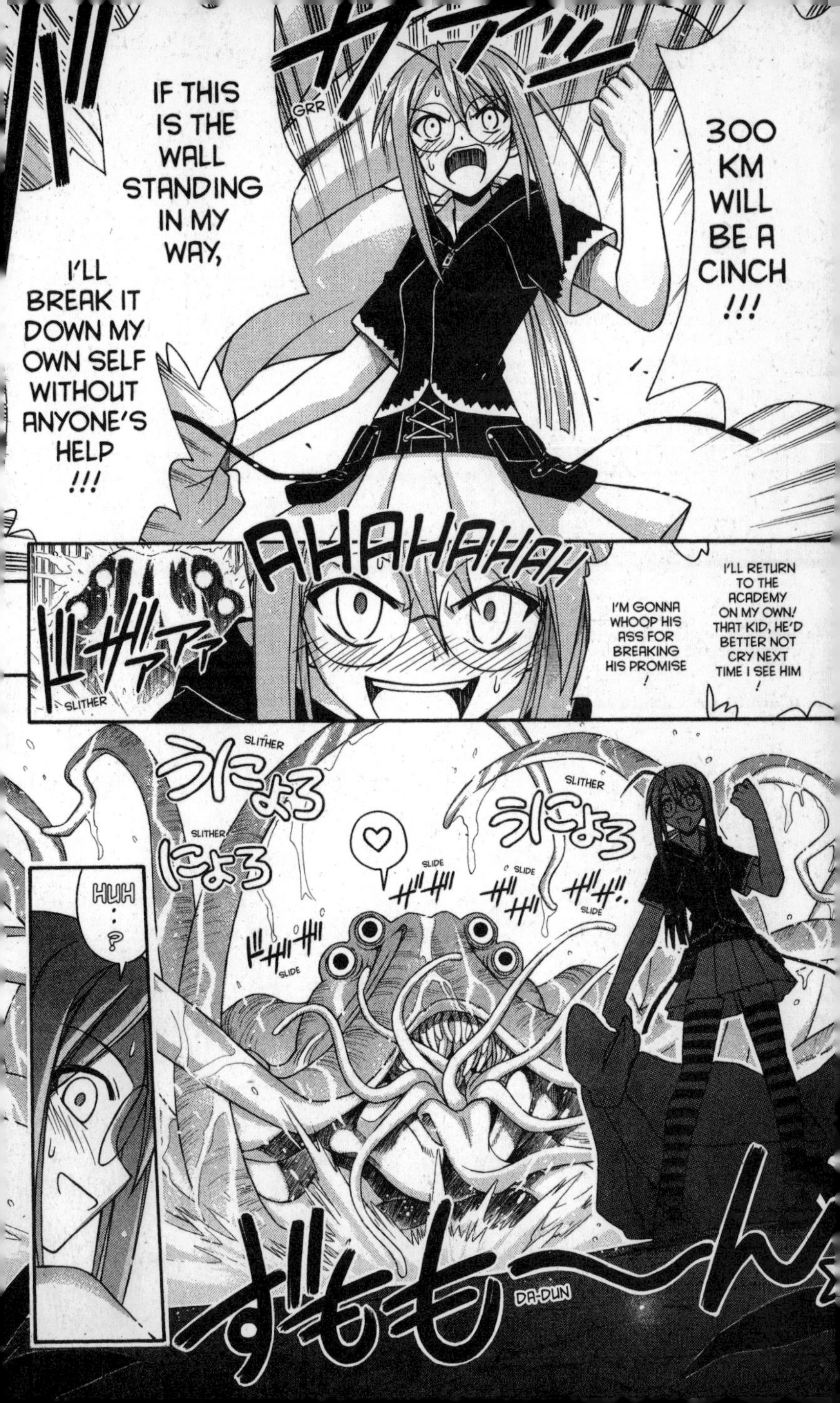

300 KM WILL BE A CINCH !!!
GRR
IF THIS IS THE WALL STANDING IN MY WAY,
I'LL BREAK IT DOWN MY OWN SELF WITHOUT ANYONE'S HELP !!!
I'LL RETURN TO THE ACADEMY ON MY OWN! THAT KID, HE'D BETTER NOT CRY NEXT TIME I SEE HIM !
I'M GONNA WHOOP HIS ASS FOR BREAKING HIS PROMISE !
AHAHAHAHAH
SLITHER
SLITHER
SLIDE
SLIDE
♡
SLITHER
SLITHER
SLIDE
HUH ...?
DA-DUN

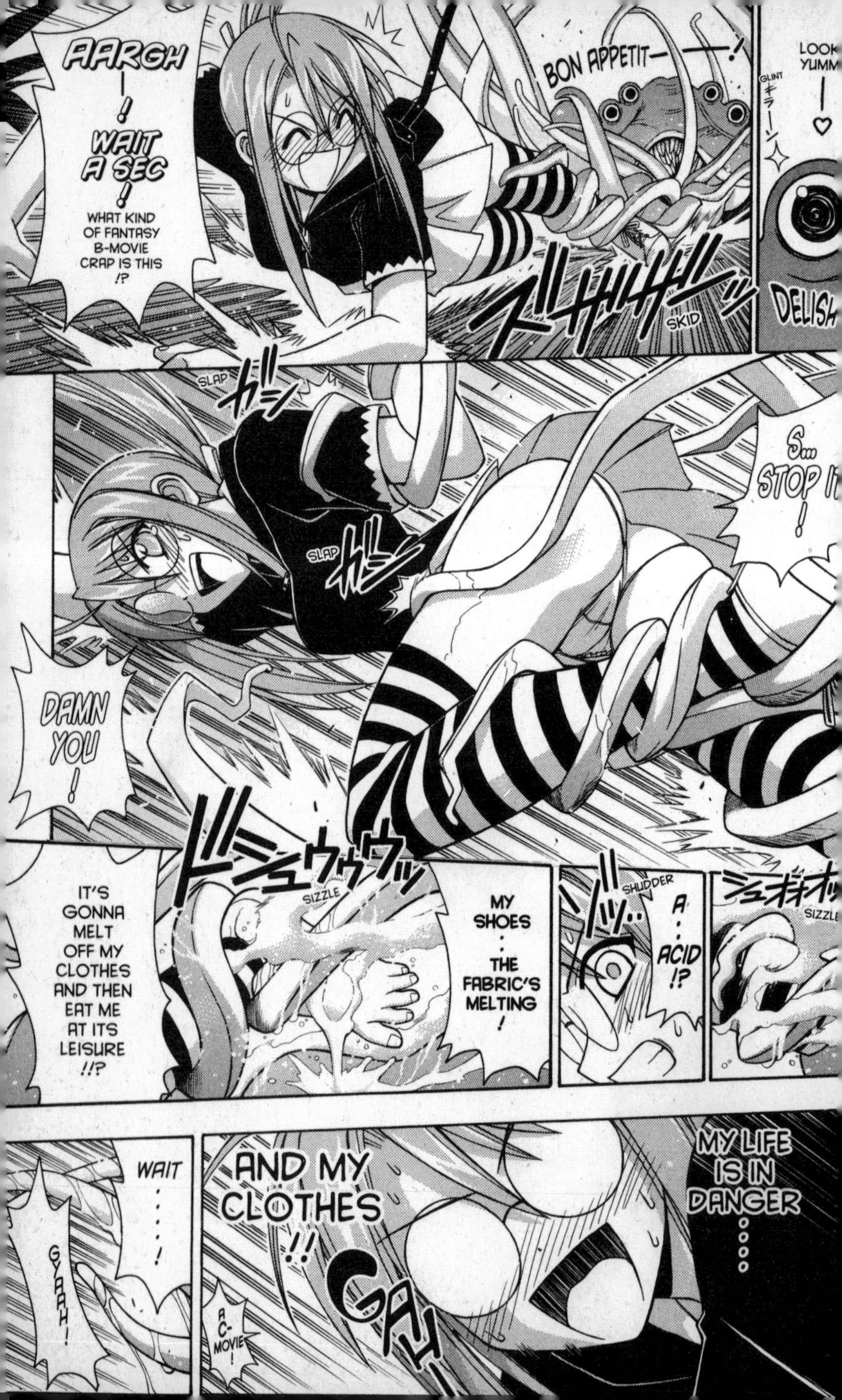
LOOK YUMM— ♡
GLINT
DELISH
BON APPETIT——!
SKID
AARGH—! WAIT A SEC! WHAT KIND OF FANTASY B-MOVIE CRAP IS THIS!?
SLAP
S... STOP IT!
SLAP
DAMN YOU!
SIZZLE
SHUDDER
A... ACID!?
SIZZLE
MY SHOES... THE FABRIC'S MELTING!
IT'S GONNA MELT OFF MY CLOTHES AND THEN EAT ME AT ITS LEISURE!!?
MY LIFE IS IN DANGER.....
AND MY CLOTHES!!
GAH
A C-MOVIE!
WAIT...!
GYAAH!

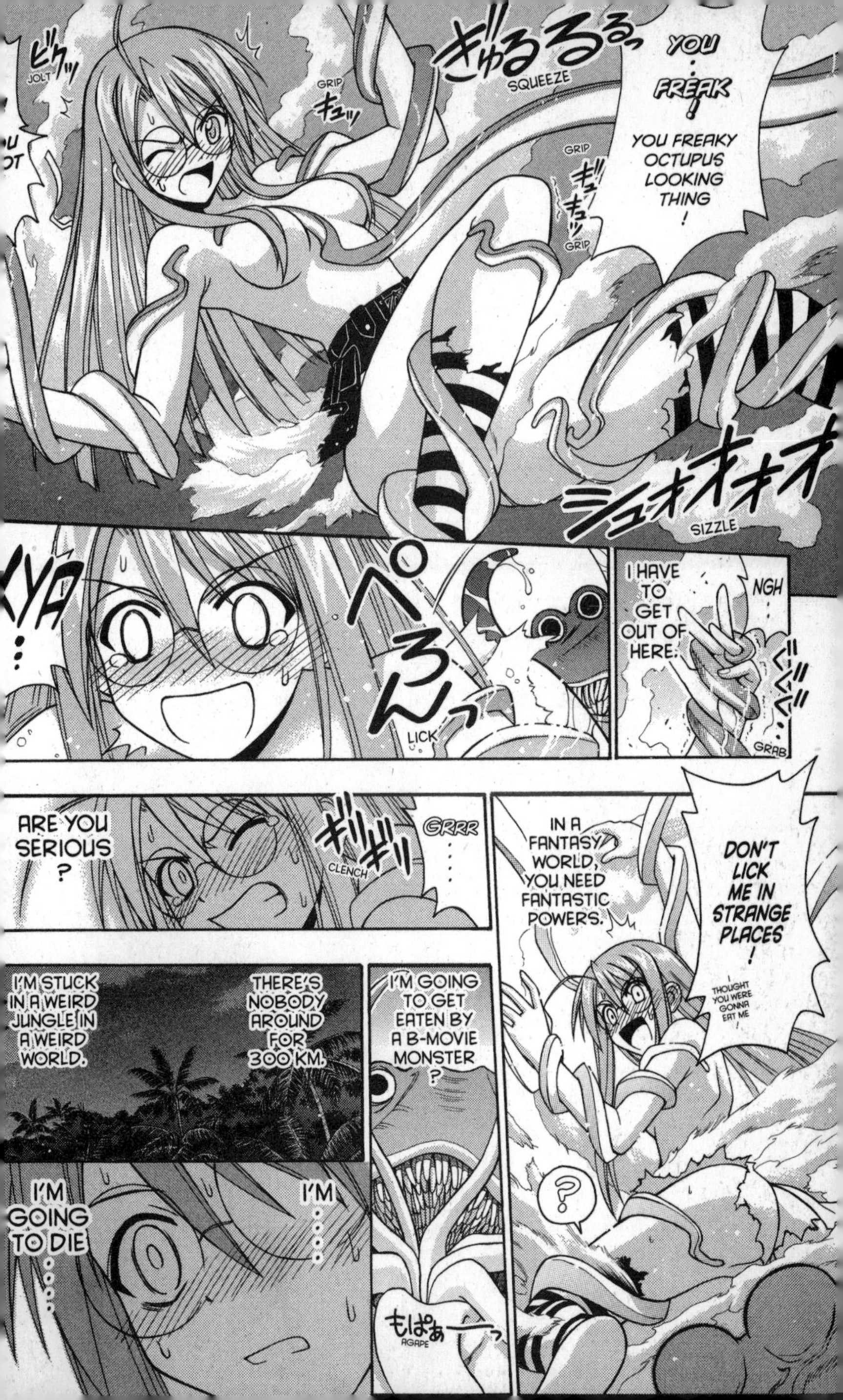

きゅるるるっ
SQUEEZE
YOU... FREAK!
YOU FREAKY OCTUPUS LOOKING THING!
GRIP
ギュギュッ
GRIP
GRIP
ギュッ
ビクッ
JOLT
シュオオオオ
SIZZLE
I HAVE TO GET OUT OF HERE.
NGH
じじじ…
GRAB
ぺろんっ
LICK
KYA...
DON'T LICK ME IN STRANGE PLACES!
I THOUGHT YOU WERE GONNA EAT ME!
IN A FANTASY WORLD, YOU NEED FANTASTIC POWERS.
?
GRRR....
ギリギリ
CLENCH
ARE YOU SERIOUS?
I'M GOING TO GET EATEN BY A B-MOVIE MONSTER?
もぱぁーっ
AGAPE
THERE'S NOBODY AROUND FOR 300 KM.
I'M STUCK IN A WEIRD JUNGLE IN A WEIRD WORLD.
I'M.....
I'M GOING TO DIE.....

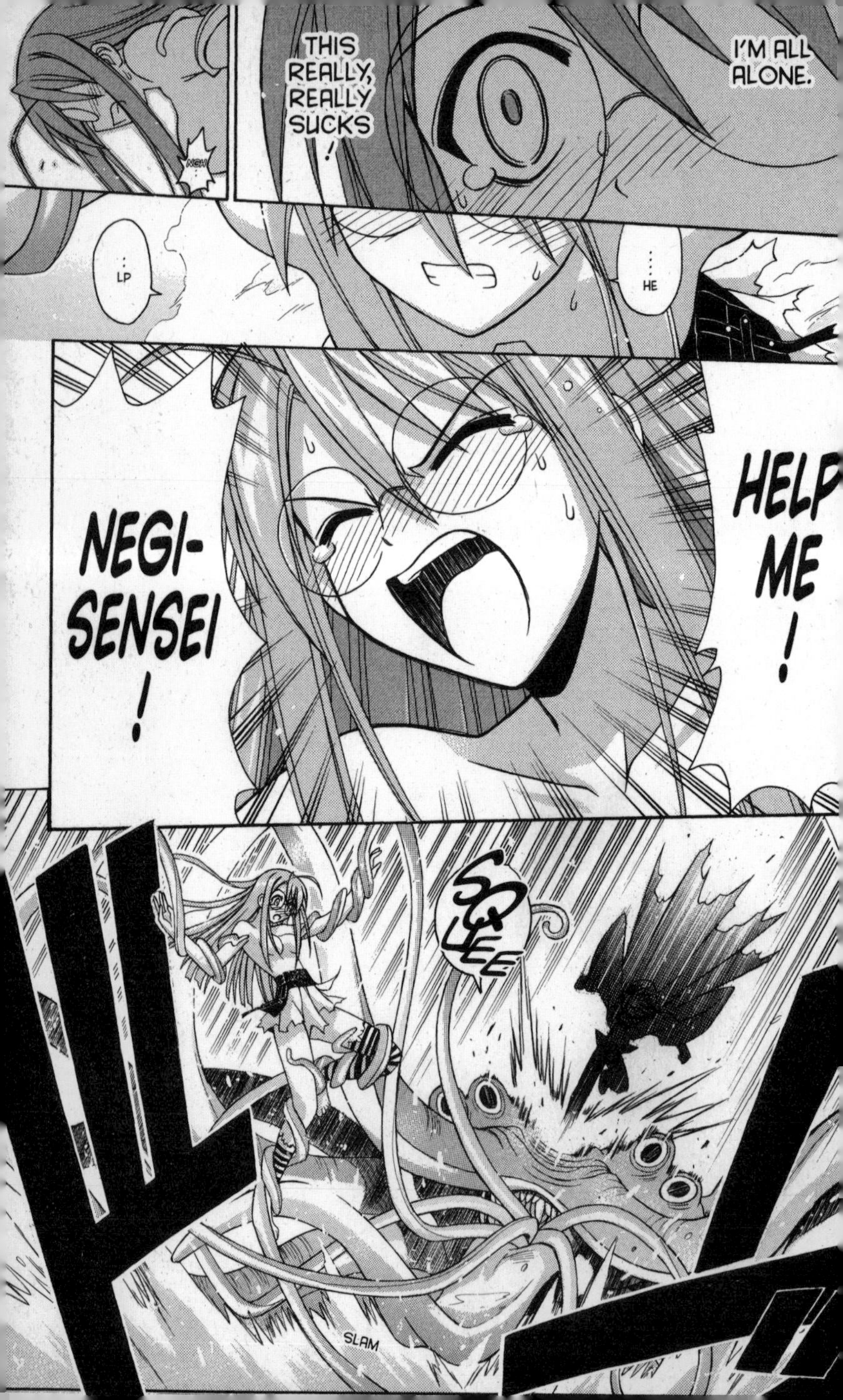
I'M ALL ALONE.
THIS REALLY, REALLY SUCKS!
NGH
...HE
...LP
HELP ME!
NEGI-SENSEI!
SQUEE
SLAM

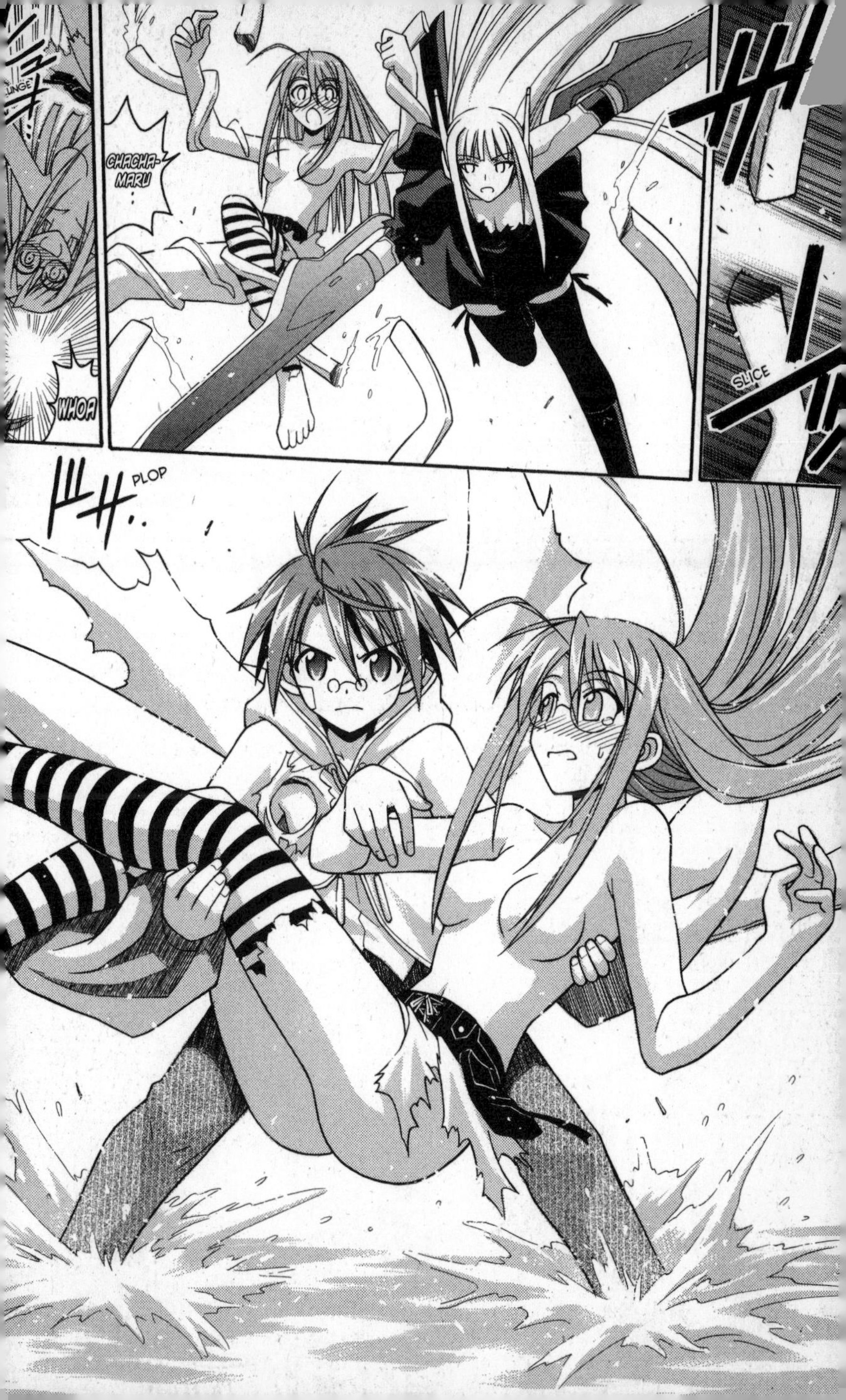
SLICE
CHACHA-MARU...!
LUNGE
WHOA
PLOP

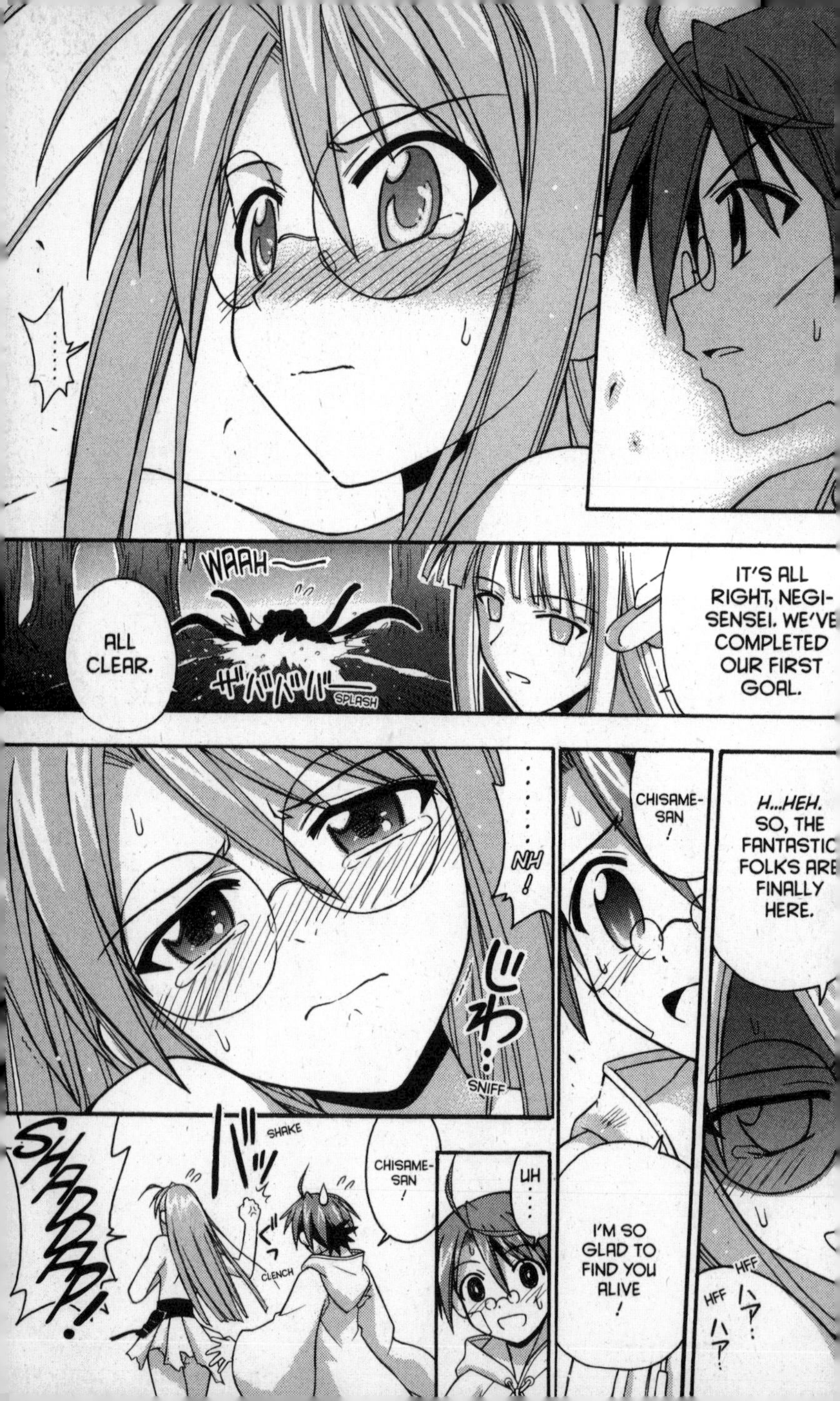
......!
IT'S ALL RIGHT, NEGI-SENSEI. WE'VE COMPLETED OUR FIRST GOAL.
WAAH—
ALL CLEAR.
SPLASH
H...HEH. SO, THE FANTASTIC FOLKS ARE FINALLY HERE.
HFF
HFF
CHISAME-SAN!
......NH!
SNIFF
I'M SO GLAD TO FIND YOU ALIVE!
UH......
CHISAME-SAN!
SHAKE
CLENCH
SHAAAP!

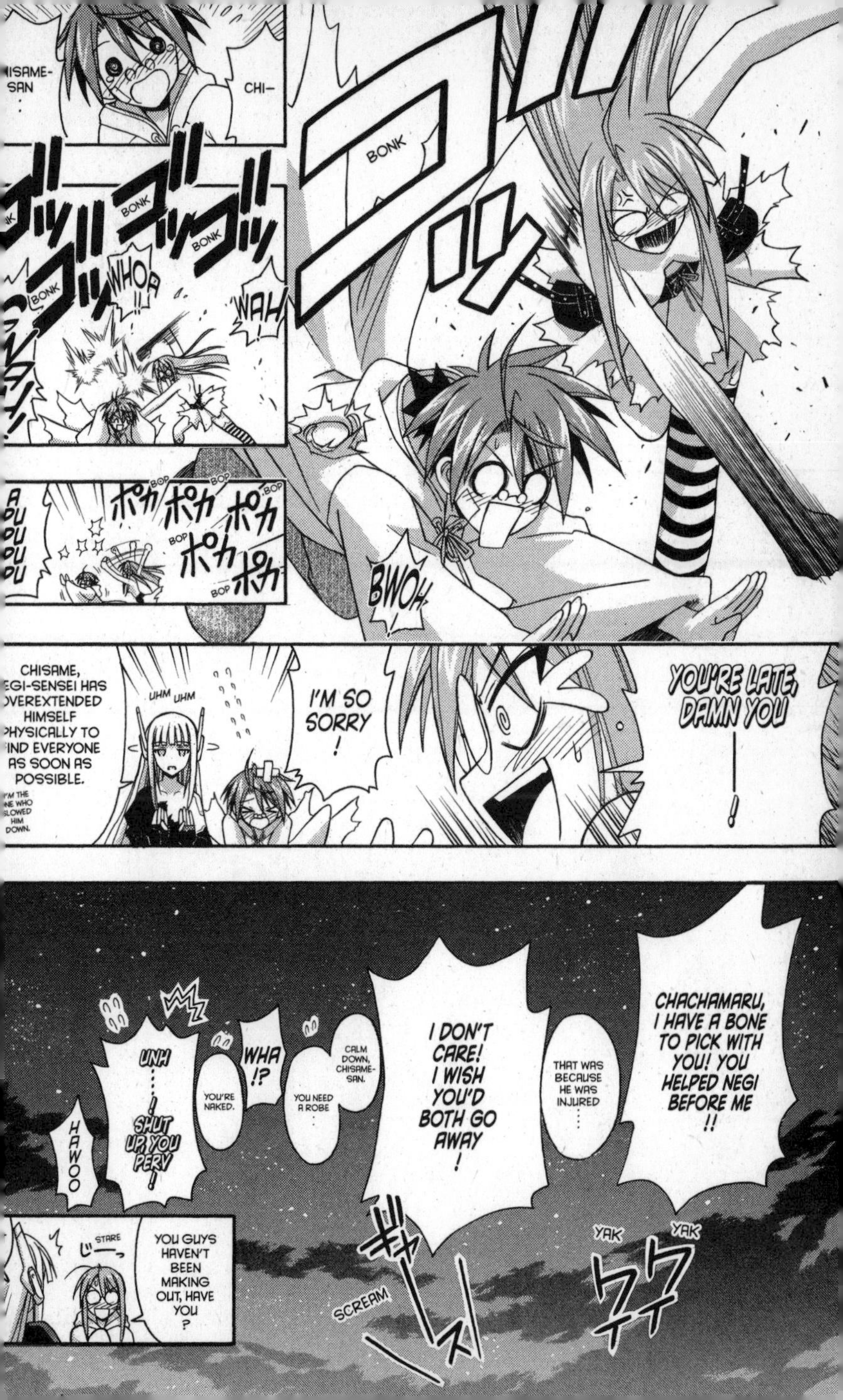
BONK
BWOH!
ISAME-SAN...
CHI—
BONK
BONK
BONK
NK
WHOA!!
WAH!
BOP
BOP
BOP
BOP
BOP
ADUDUDUDU
YOU'RE LATE, DAMN YOU—!
I'M SO SORRY!
UHM UHM
CHISAME, EGI-SENSEI HAS OVEREXTENDED HIMSELF PHYSICALLY TO FIND EVERYONE AS SOON AS POSSIBLE.
'M THE NE WHO SLOWED HIM DOWN.
CHACHAMARU, I HAVE A BONE TO PICK WITH YOU! YOU HELPED NEGI BEFORE ME!!
THAT WAS BECAUSE HE WAS INJURED...
I DON'T CARE! I WISH YOU'D BOTH GO AWAY!
CALM DOWN, CHISAME-SAN.
YOU NEED A ROBE
WHA!?
YOU'RE NAKED.
UNH...! SHUT UP YOU PERV!
HAWOO
YAK
YAK
SCREAM
STARE
YOU GUYS HAVEN'T BEEN MAKING OUT, HAVE YOU?

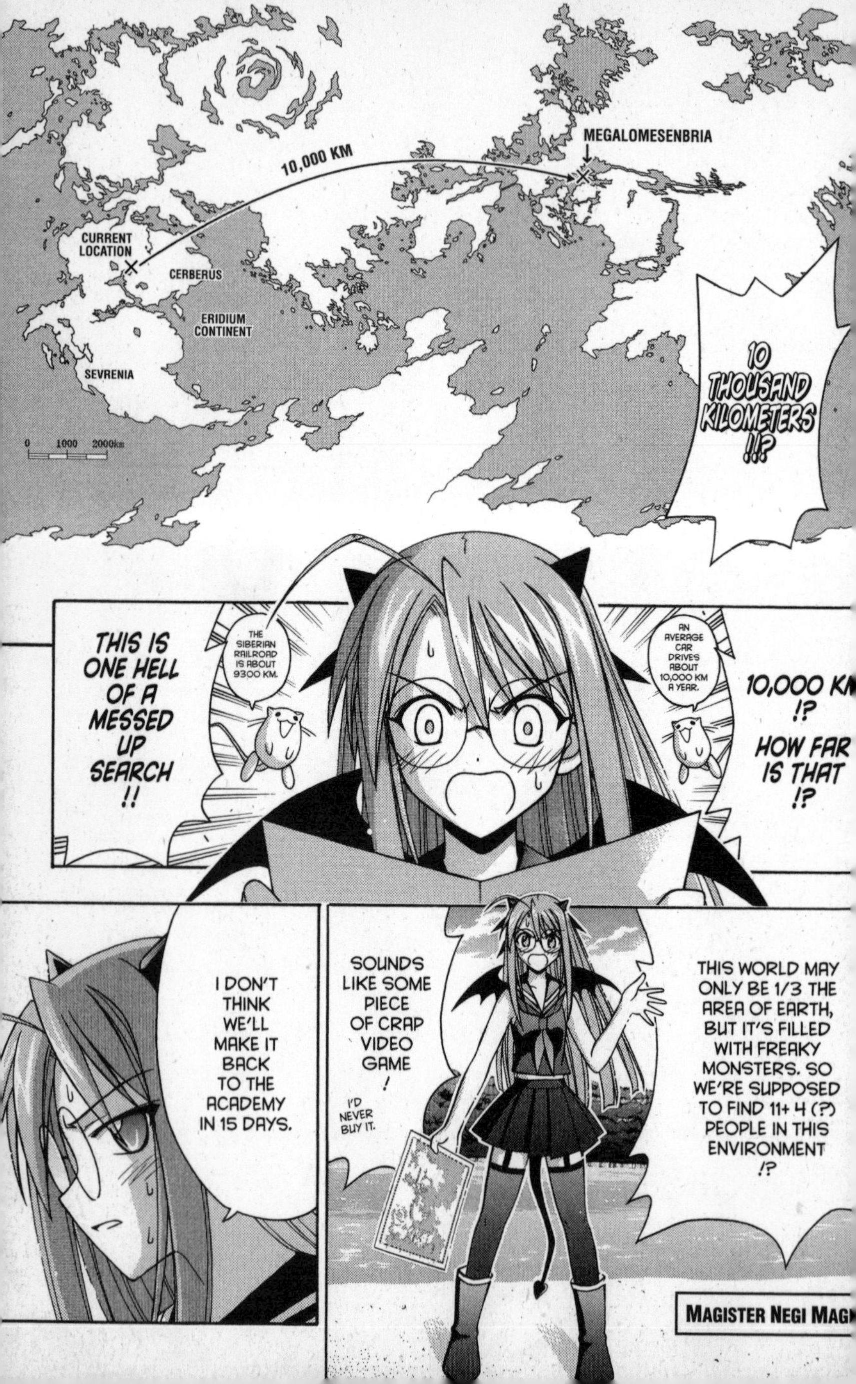

MEGALOMESENBRIA
10,000 KM
CURRENT LOCATION
CERBERUS
ERIDIUM CONTINENT
SEVRENIA
0 1000 2000km
10 THOUSAND KILOMETERS !!?
10,000 K !? HOW FAR IS THAT !?
AN AVERAGE CAR DRIVES ABOUT 10,000 KM A YEAR.
THE SIBERIAN RAILROAD IS ABOUT 9300 KM.
THIS IS ONE HELL OF A MESSED UP SEARCH !!
THIS WORLD MAY ONLY BE 1/3 THE AREA OF EARTH, BUT IT'S FILLED WITH FREAKY MONSTERS. SO WE'RE SUPPOSED TO FIND 11+ 4 (?) PEOPLE IN THIS ENVIRONMENT !?
SOUNDS LIKE SOME PIECE OF CRAP VIDEO GAME !
I'D NEVER BUY IT.
I DON'T THINK WE'LL MAKE IT BACK TO THE ACADEMY IN 15 DAYS.
MAGISTER NEGI MAG

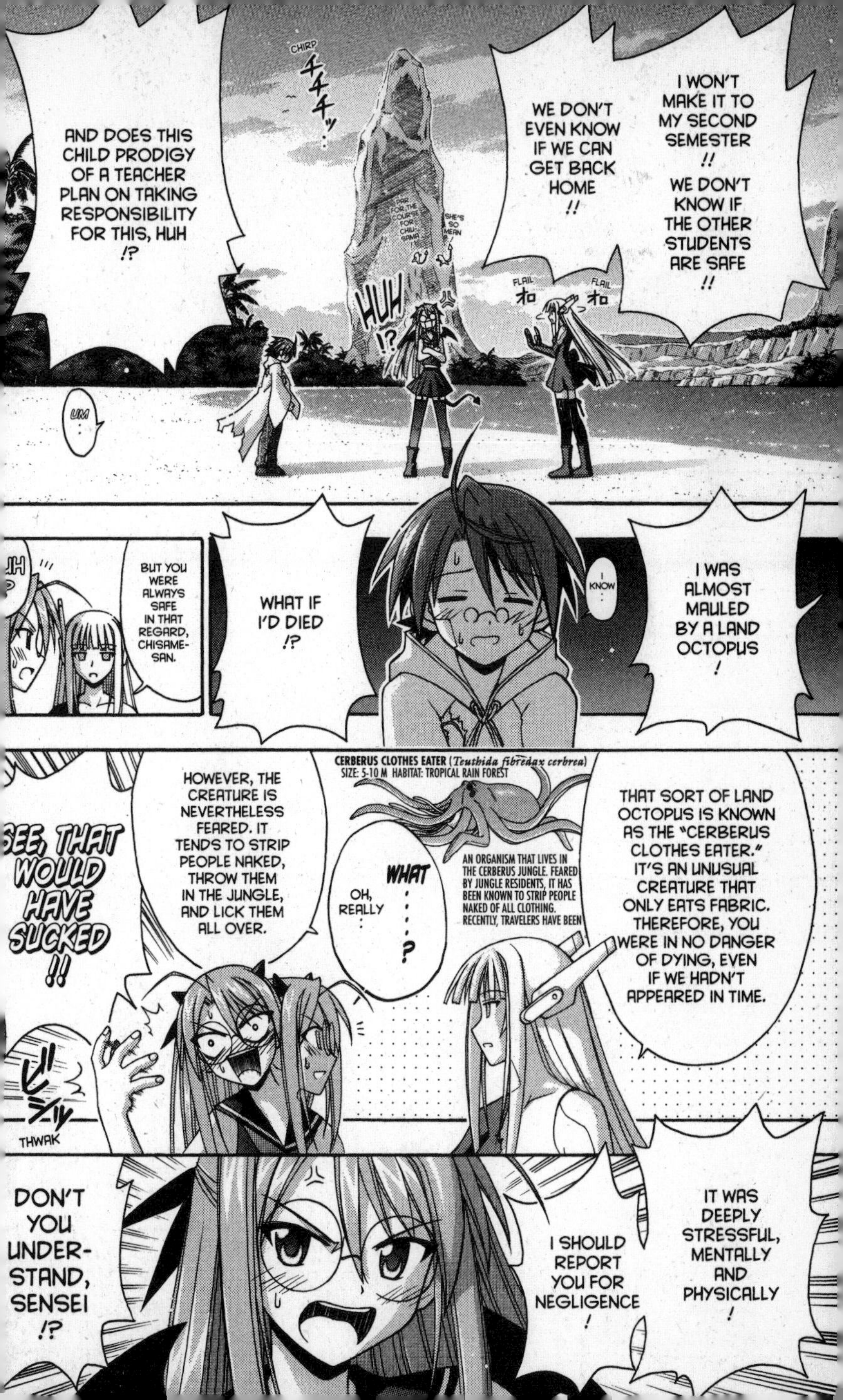
I WON'T MAKE IT TO MY SECOND SEMESTER!! WE DON'T KNOW IF THE OTHER STUDENTS ARE SAFE!!
WE DON'T EVEN KNOW IF WE CAN GET BACK HOME!!
CHIRP
SHE'S SO MEAN!
PAR FOR THE COURSE FOR CHIU-SAMA!
FLAIL FLAIL
HUH!?
AND DOES THIS CHILD PRODIGY OF A TEACHER PLAN ON TAKING RESPONSIBILITY FOR THIS, HUH!?
UM...
I WAS ALMOST MAULED BY A LAND OCTOPUS!
I KNOW...
WHAT IF I'D DIED!?
BUT YOU WERE ALWAYS SAFE IN THAT REGARD, CHISAME-SAN.
THAT SORT OF LAND OCTOPUS IS KNOWN AS THE "CERBERUS CLOTHES EATER." IT'S AN UNUSUAL CREATURE THAT ONLY EATS FABRIC. THEREFORE, YOU WERE IN NO DANGER OF DYING, EVEN IF WE HADN'T APPEARED IN TIME.
CERBERUS CLOTHES EATER (Teuthida fibredax cerbrea)
SIZE: 5-10 M HABITAT: TROPICAL RAIN FOREST
AN ORGANISM THAT LIVES IN THE CERBERUS JUNGLE. FEARED BY JUNGLE RESIDENTS, IT HAS BEEN KNOWN TO STRIP PEOPLE NAKED OF ALL CLOTHING. RECENTLY, TRAVELERS HAVE BEEN
WHAT...?
OH, REALLY...
HOWEVER, THE CREATURE IS NEVERTHELESS FEARED. IT TENDS TO STRIP PEOPLE NAKED, THROW THEM IN THE JUNGLE, AND LICK THEM ALL OVER.
SEE, THAT WOULD HAVE SUCKED!!
THWAK
IT WAS DEEPLY STRESSFUL, MENTALLY AND PHYSICALLY!
I SHOULD REPORT YOU FOR NEGLIGENCE!
DON'T YOU UNDERSTAND, SENSEI!?

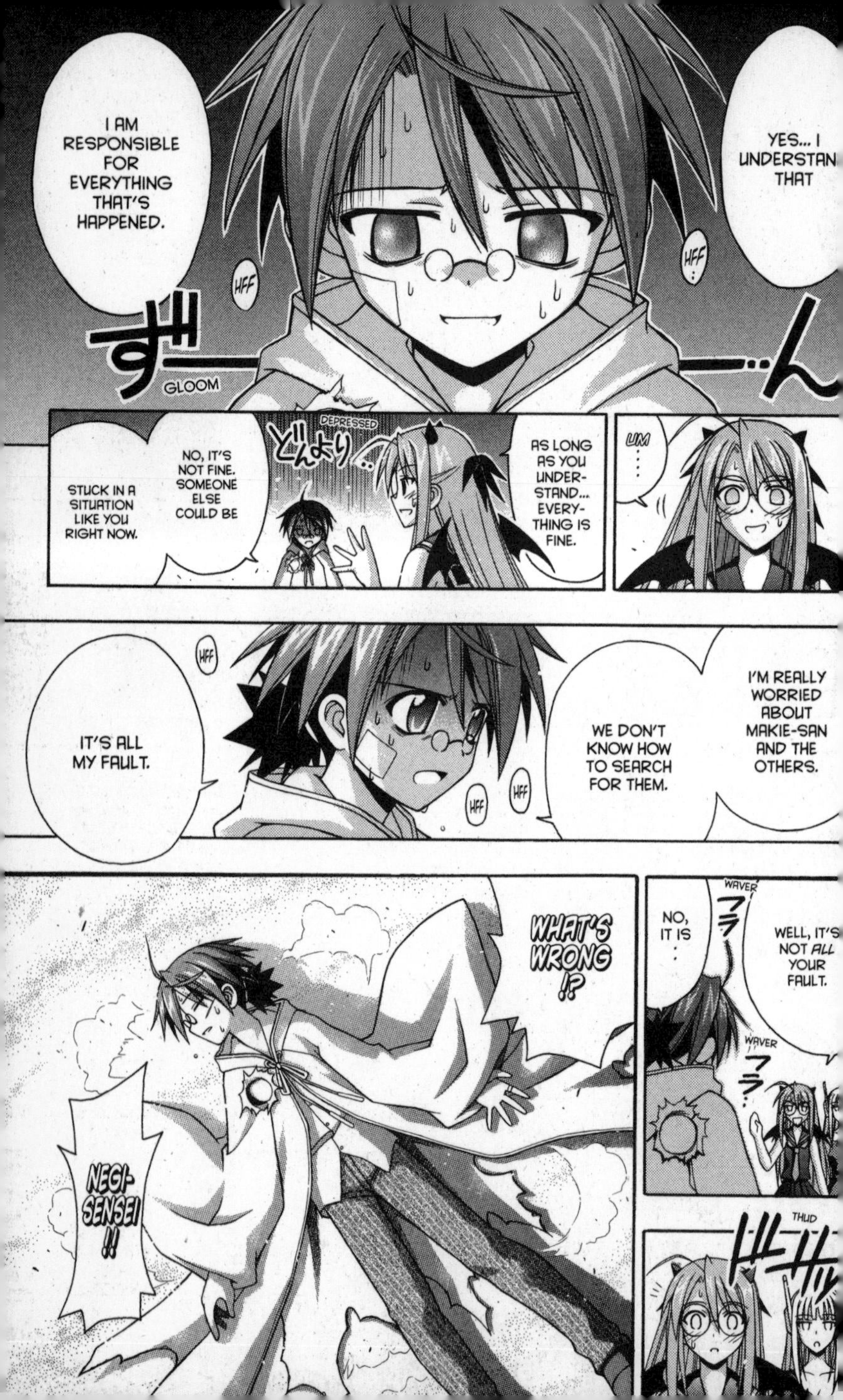
YES... I UNDERSTAN THAT
HFF...
I AM RESPONSIBLE FOR EVERYTHING THAT'S HAPPENED.
HFF
ずーーーん
GLOOM
UM...
AS LONG AS YOU UNDERSTAND... EVERYTHING IS FINE.
どんより...
DEPRESSED
NO, IT'S NOT FINE. SOMEONE ELSE COULD BE
STUCK IN A SITUATION LIKE YOU RIGHT NOW.
I'M REALLY WORRIED ABOUT MAKIE-SAN AND THE OTHERS.
WE DON'T KNOW HOW TO SEARCH FOR THEM.
HFF
HFF
IT'S ALL MY FAULT.
HFF
WELL, IT'S NOT *ALL* YOUR FAULT.
フラ
WAVER
NO, IT IS...
フラ
WAVER
THUD
WHAT'S WRONG!?
NEGI-SENSEI!!

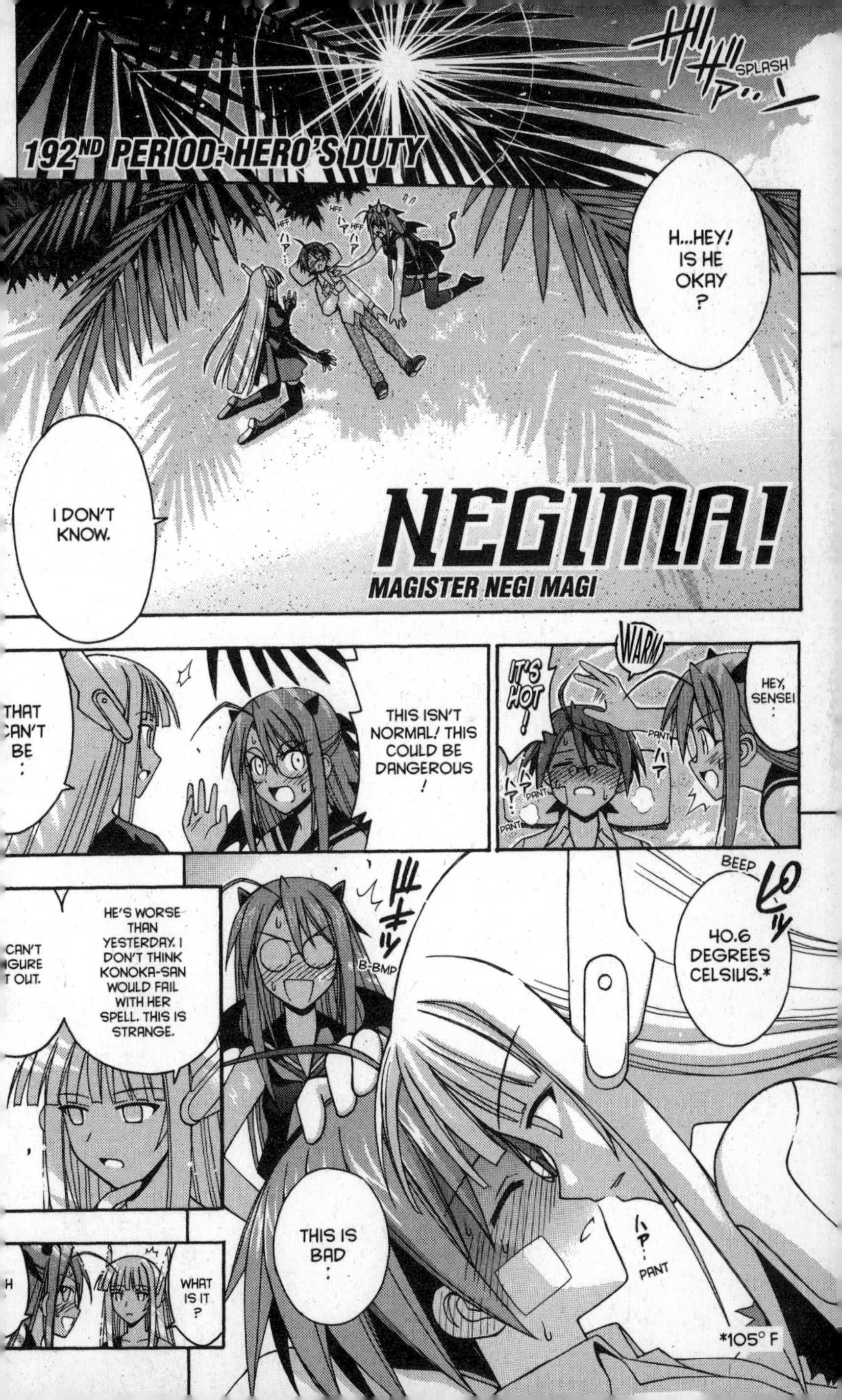
SPLASH
192ND PERIOD: HERO'S DUTY
HFF
HFF
HFF
H...HEY! IS HE OKAY?
I DON'T KNOW.
NEGIMA!
MAGISTER NEGI MAGI
HEY, SENSEI
WARM
IT'S HOT!
PANT
PANT
PANT
THIS ISN'T NORMAL! THIS COULD BE DANGEROUS!
THAT CAN'T BE
BEEP
40.6 DEGREES CELSIUS.*
B-BMP
HE'S WORSE THAN YESTERDAY. I DON'T THINK KONOKA-SAN WOULD FAIL WITH HER SPELL. THIS IS STRANGE.
CAN'T IGURE T OUT.
THIS IS BAD
PANT
WHAT IS IT?
H
*105° F

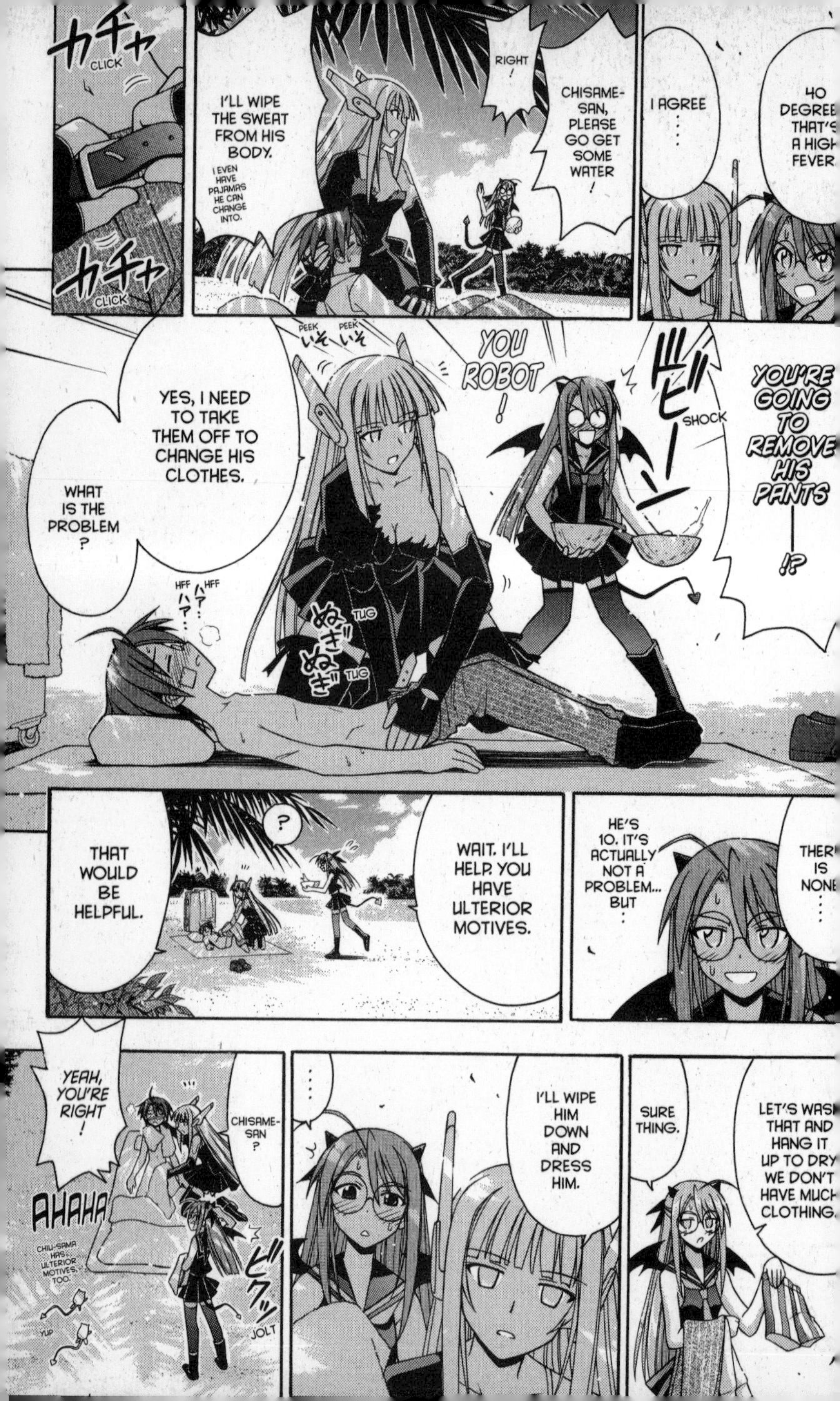
40 DEGREE THAT'S A HIGH FEVER
I AGREE ...
RIGHT!
CHISAME-SAN, PLEASE GO GET SOME WATER!
I'LL WIPE THE SWEAT FROM HIS BODY.
I EVEN HAVE PAJAMAS HE CAN CHANGE INTO.
カチャ CLICK
カチャ CLICK
YOU'RE GOING TO REMOVE HIS PANTS—!?
ビビー SHOCK
YOU ROBOT!
いそ PEEK いそ PEEK
YES, I NEED TO TAKE THEM OFF TO CHANGE HIS CLOTHES.
WHAT IS THE PROBLEM?
ハア HFF ハア HFF
ぬぎ TUG ぬぎ TUG
THER IS NONE ...
HE'S 10. IT'S ACTUALLY NOT A PROBLEM... BUT...
WAIT. I'LL HELP. YOU HAVE ULTERIOR MOTIVES.
?
THAT WOULD BE HELPFUL.
LET'S WAS THAT AND HANG IT UP TO DRY WE DON'T HAVE MUCH CLOTHING.
SURE THING.
I'LL WIPE HIM DOWN AND DRESS HIM.
...
CHISAME-SAN?
YEAH, YOU'RE RIGHT!
AHAHA
CHIU-SAMA HAS ULTERIOR MOTIVES, TOO.
YUP
ビクッ JOLT

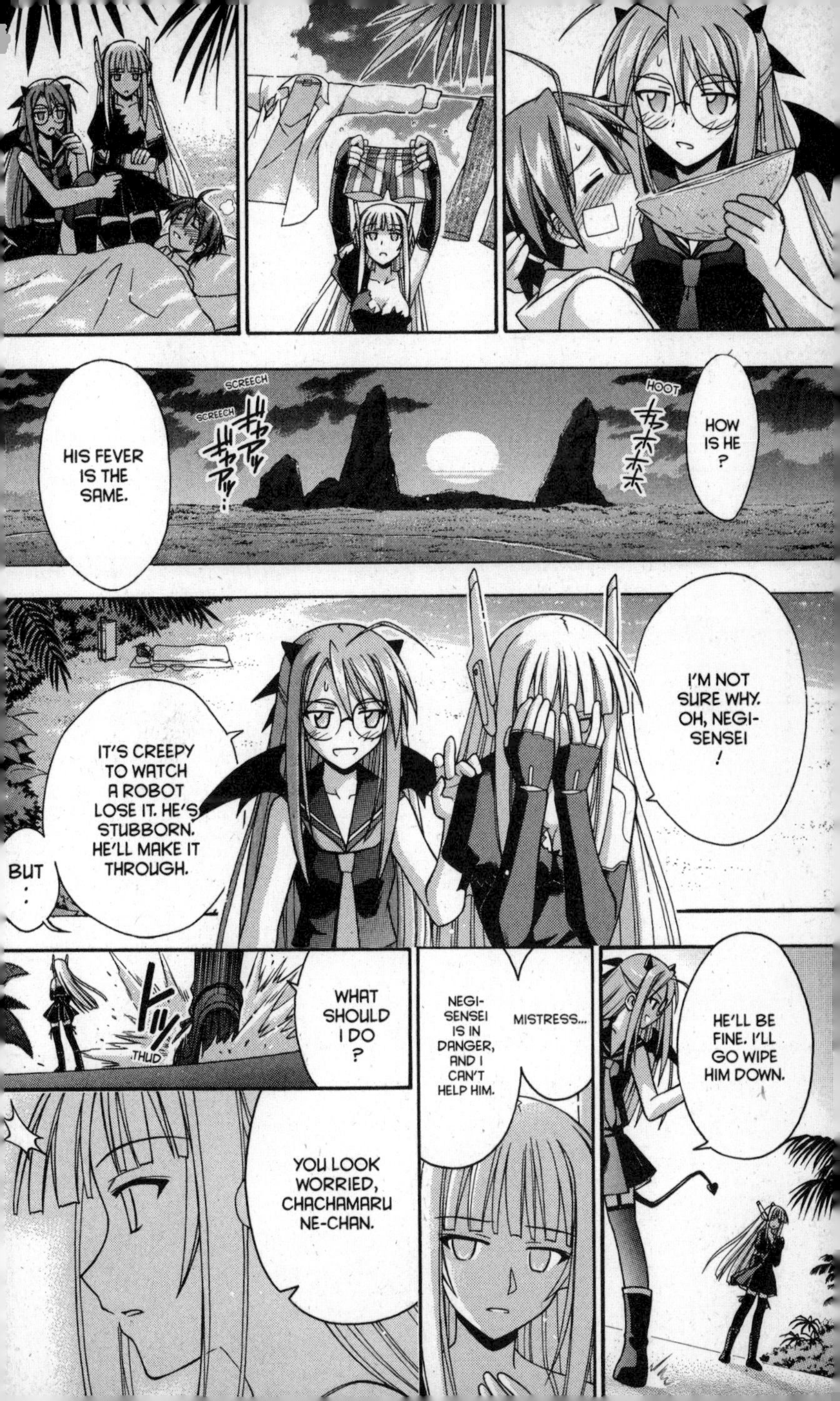
HOOT
HOW IS HE ?
SCREECH
SCREECH
HIS FEVER IS THE SAME.
I'M NOT SURE WHY. OH, NEGI-SENSEI !
IT'S CREEPY TO WATCH A ROBOT LOSE IT. HE'S STUBBORN. HE'LL MAKE IT THROUGH.
BUT :
HE'LL BE FINE. I'LL GO WIPE HIM DOWN.
MISTRESS...
NEGI-SENSEI IS IN DANGER, AND I CAN'T HELP HIM.
WHAT SHOULD I DO ?
THUD
YOU LOOK WORRIED, CHACHAMARU NE-CHAN.

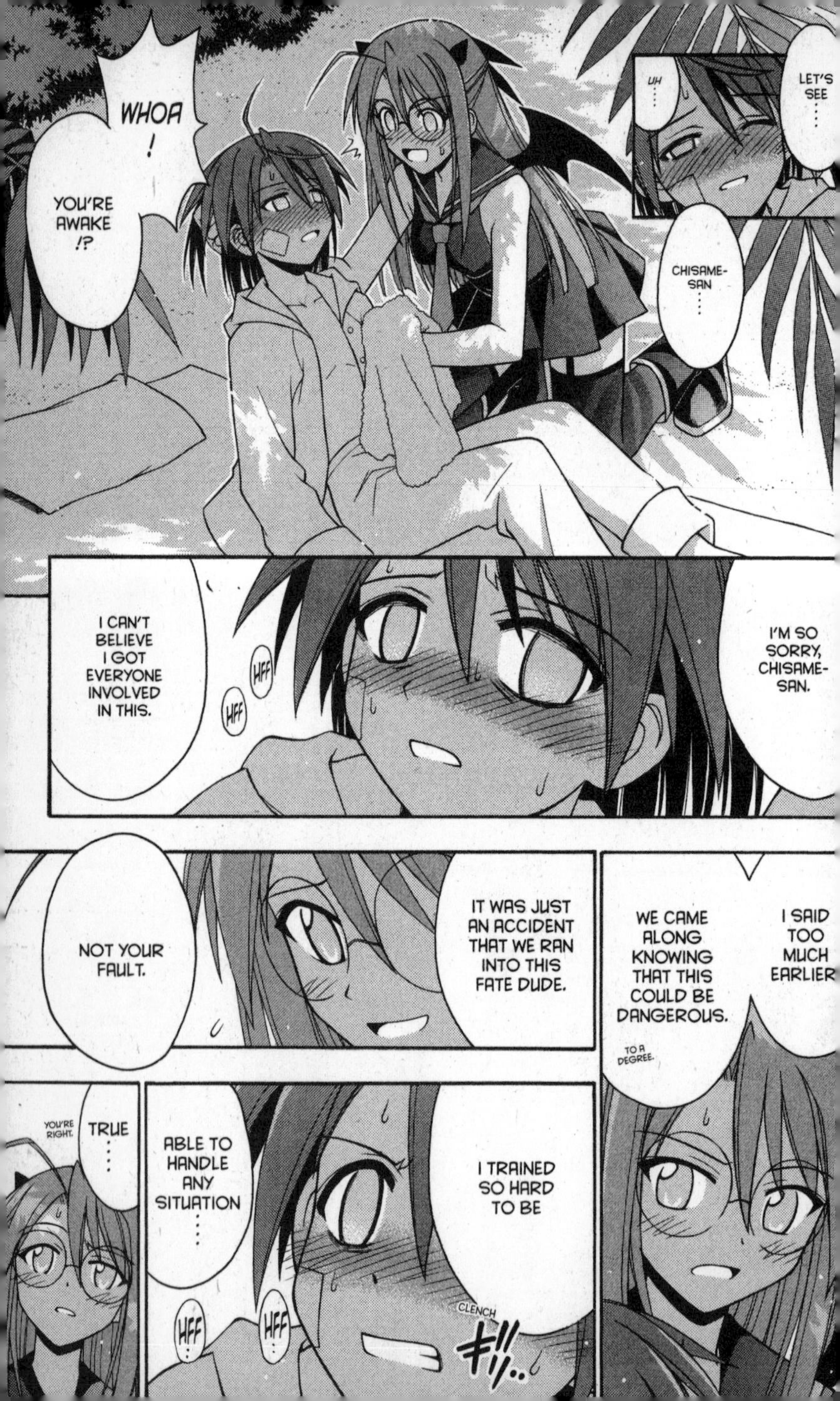
LET'S SEE ......
UH ......
CHISAME-SAN ......
WHOA !
YOU'RE AWAKE !?
I'M SO SORRY, CHISAME-SAN.
I CAN'T BELIEVE I GOT EVERYONE INVOLVED IN THIS.
HFF
HFF
I SAID TOO MUCH EARLIER
WE CAME ALONG KNOWING THAT THIS COULD BE DANGEROUS.
TO A DEGREE.
IT WAS JUST AN ACCIDENT THAT WE RAN INTO THIS FATE DUDE.
NOT YOUR FAULT.
I TRAINED SO HARD TO BE
ABLE TO HANDLE ANY SITUATION ......
HFF
HFF
CLENCH
TRUE ......
YOU'RE RIGHT.

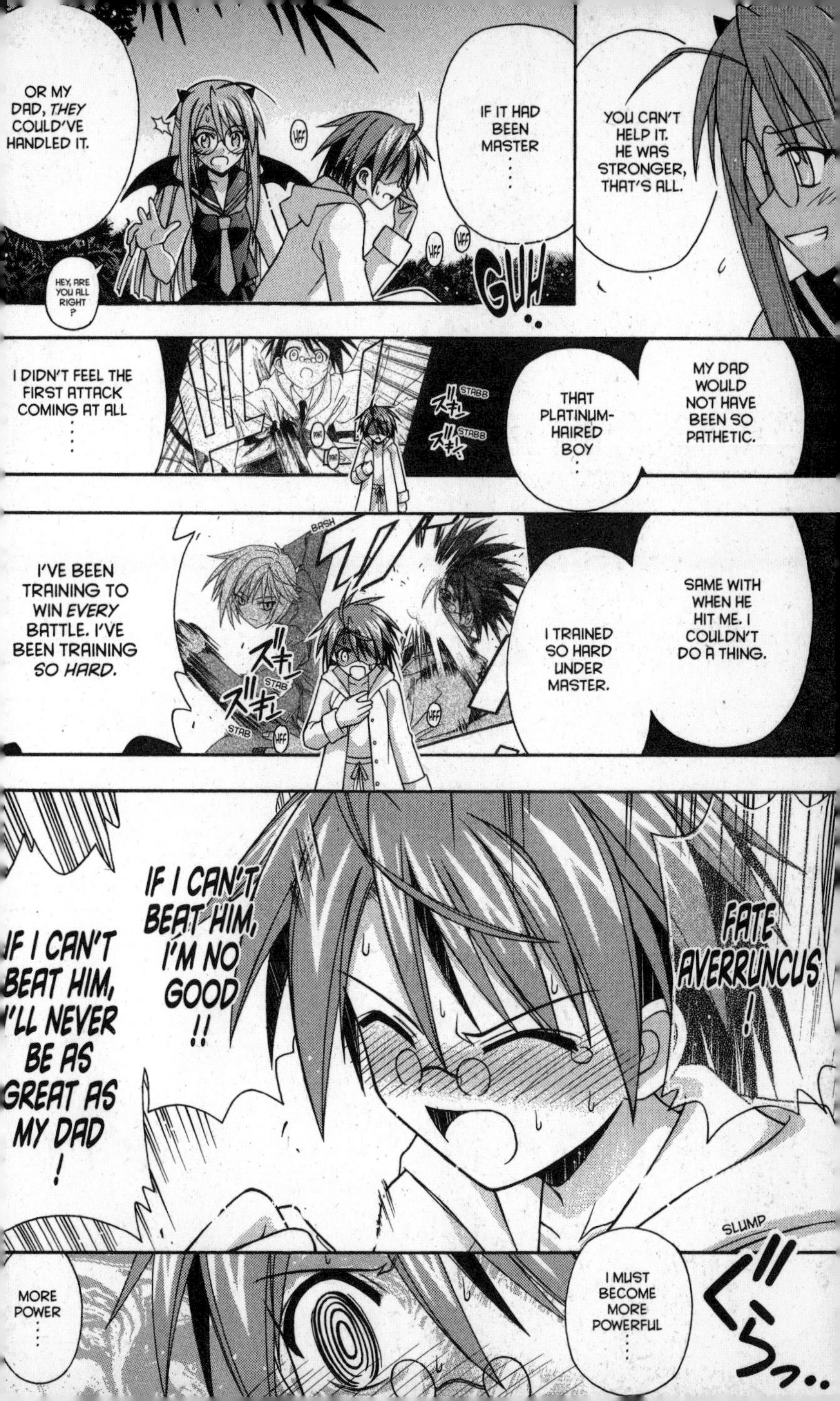
YOU CAN'T HELP IT. HE WAS STRONGER, THAT'S ALL.
IF IT HAD BEEN MASTER ....
GUH..
HUFF
HUFF
HUFF
OR MY DAD, *THEY* COULD'VE HANDLED IT.
HEY, ARE YOU ALL RIGHT?
MY DAD WOULD NOT HAVE BEEN SO PATHETIC.
THAT PLATINUM-HAIRED BOY ...
STABB
STABB
PANT
PANT
I DIDN'T FEEL THE FIRST ATTACK COMING AT ALL ....
SAME WITH WHEN HE HIT ME. I COULDN'T DO A THING.
I TRAINED SO HARD UNDER MASTER.
BASH
STAB
STAB
HUFF
HUFF
I'VE BEEN TRAINING TO WIN *EVERY* BATTLE. I'VE BEEN TRAINING *SO HARD.*
FATE AVERRUNCUS!
IF I CAN'T BEAT HIM, I'M NO GOOD!!
IF I CAN'T BEAT HIM, I'LL NEVER BE AS GREAT AS MY DAD!
SLUMP
I MUST BECOME MORE POWERFUL ....
MORE POWER ....

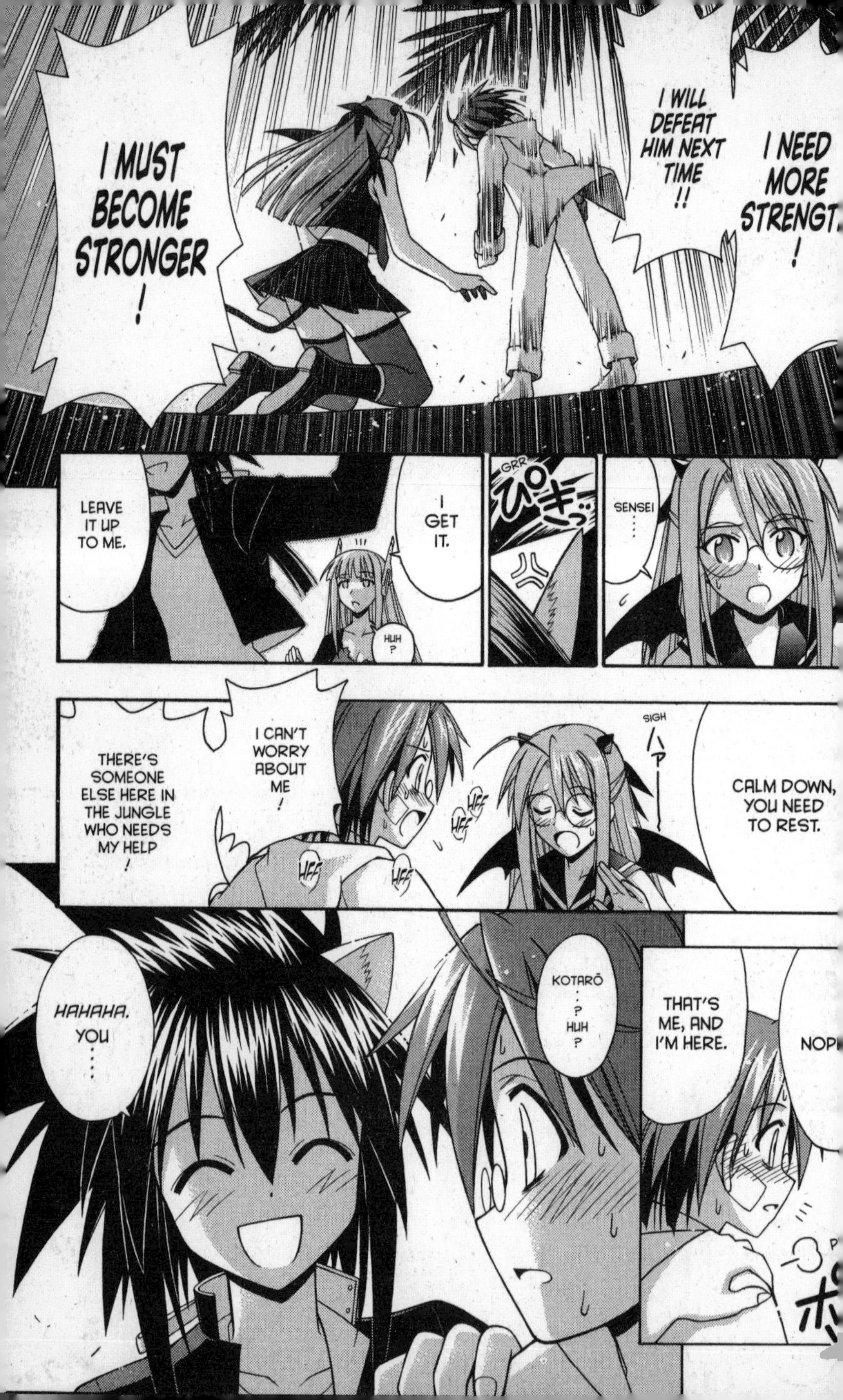
I NEED MORE STRENGT !
I WILL DEFEAT HIM NEXT TIME !!
I MUST BECOME STRONGER !
SENSEI ...
GRR
ひきっ
I GET IT.
HUH ?
LEAVE IT UP TO ME.
CALM DOWN, YOU NEED TO REST.
SIGH
ハァー
HFF
HFF
I CAN'T WORRY ABOUT ME !
THERE'S SOMEONE ELSE HERE IN THE JUNGLE WHO NEEDS MY HELP !
HFF
HFF
NOP
THAT'S ME, AND I'M HERE.
KOTARŌ ... ? HUH ?
HAHAHA. YOU ....

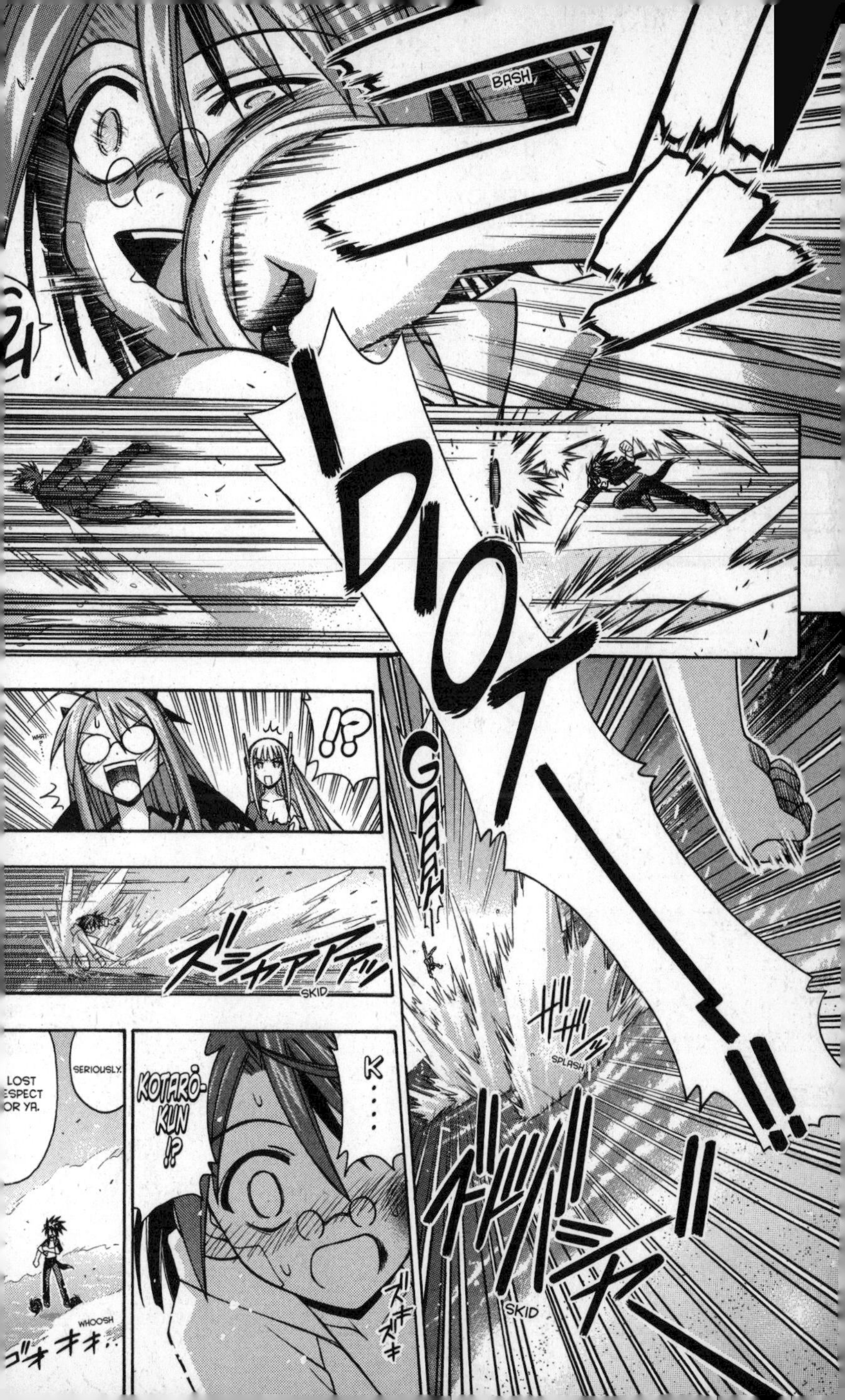

BASH
IDIOT———!!
GAAAAH!!
ザザッ
SPLASH
ズザザーッ
SKID
ズキズキ
WHAT?...
!?
ズシャアアッ
SKID
K....
KOTARŌ-KUN!?
SERIOUSLY.
LOST
ESPECT
OR YA.
ゴオオオ...
WHOOSH

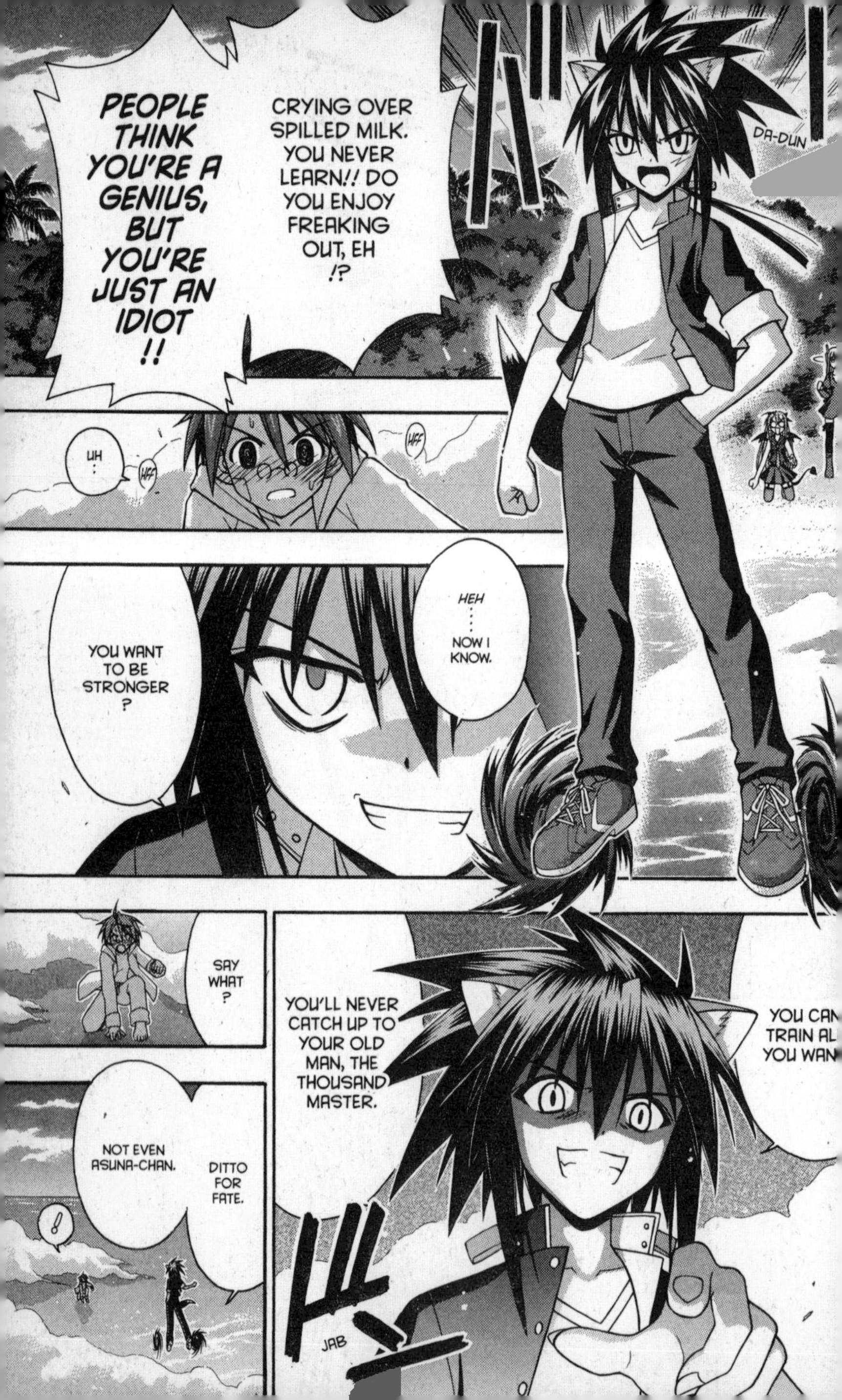
DA-DUN
CRYING OVER SPILLED MILK. YOU NEVER LEARN!! DO YOU ENJOY FREAKING OUT, EH !?
PEOPLE THINK YOU'RE A GENIUS, BUT YOU'RE JUST AN IDIOT !!
HFF
HFF
UH...
HEH... NOW I KNOW.
YOU WANT TO BE STRONGER ?
YOU CAN TRAIN AL YOU WAN
YOU'LL NEVER CATCH UP TO YOUR OLD MAN, THE THOUSAND MASTER.
JAB
SAY WHAT ?
DITTO FOR FATE.
NOT EVEN ASUNA-CHAN.
!

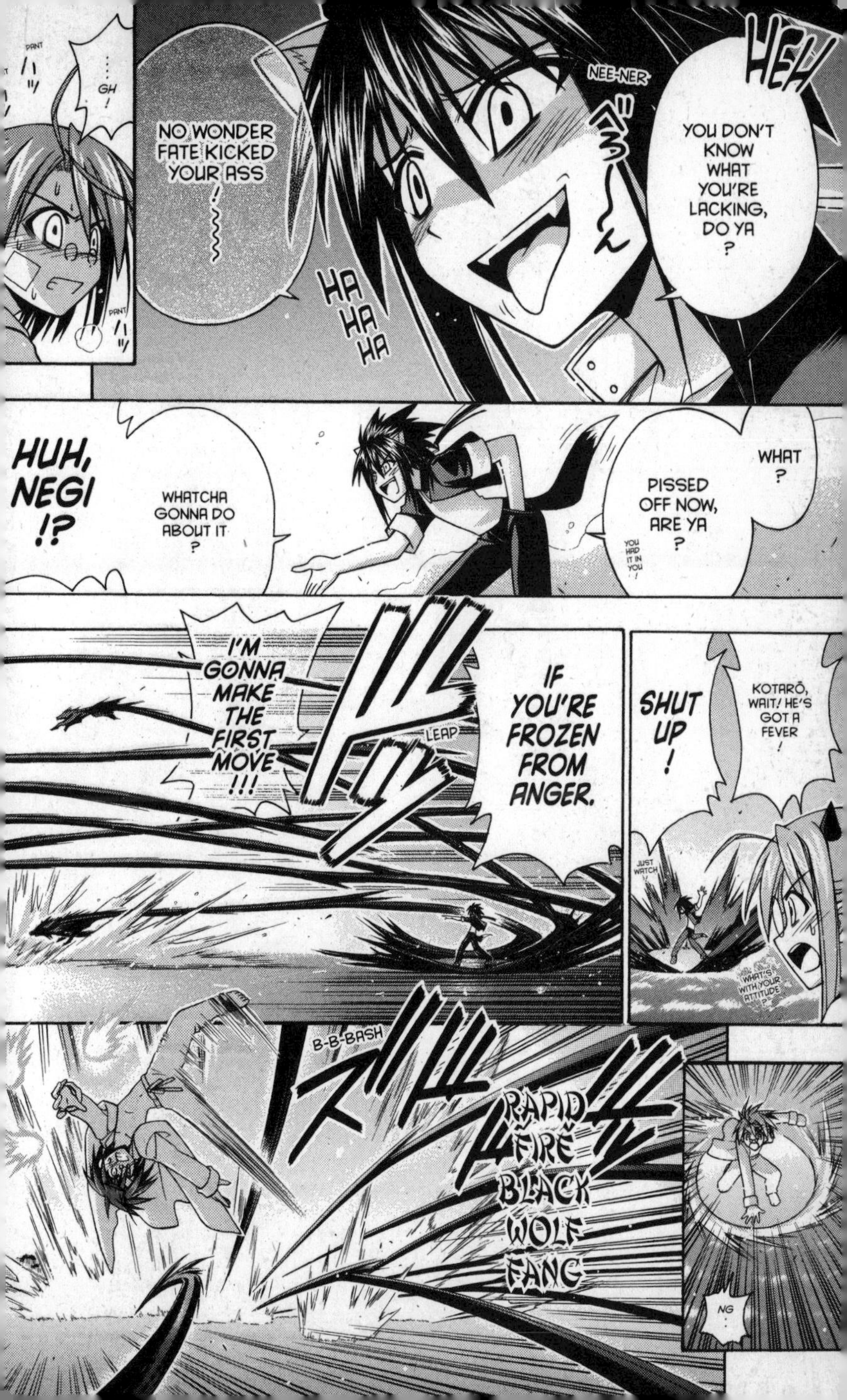
HEH
YOU DON'T KNOW WHAT YOU'RE LACKING, DO YA?
NEE-NER
HA HA HA
NO WONDER FATE KICKED YOUR ASS!
PANT
...GH!
PANT
WHAT?
PISSED OFF NOW, ARE YA?
YOU HAD IT IN YOU!
WHATCHA GONNA DO ABOUT IT?
HUH, NEGI!?
KOTARŌ, WAIT! HE'S GOT A FEVER!
SHUT UP!
JUST WATCH
WHAT'S WITH YOUR ATTITUDE?
IF YOU'RE FROZEN FROM ANGER.
LEAP
I'M GONNA MAKE THE FIRST MOVE!!!
NG...
RAPID-FIRE BLACK WOLF FANG
B-B-BASH

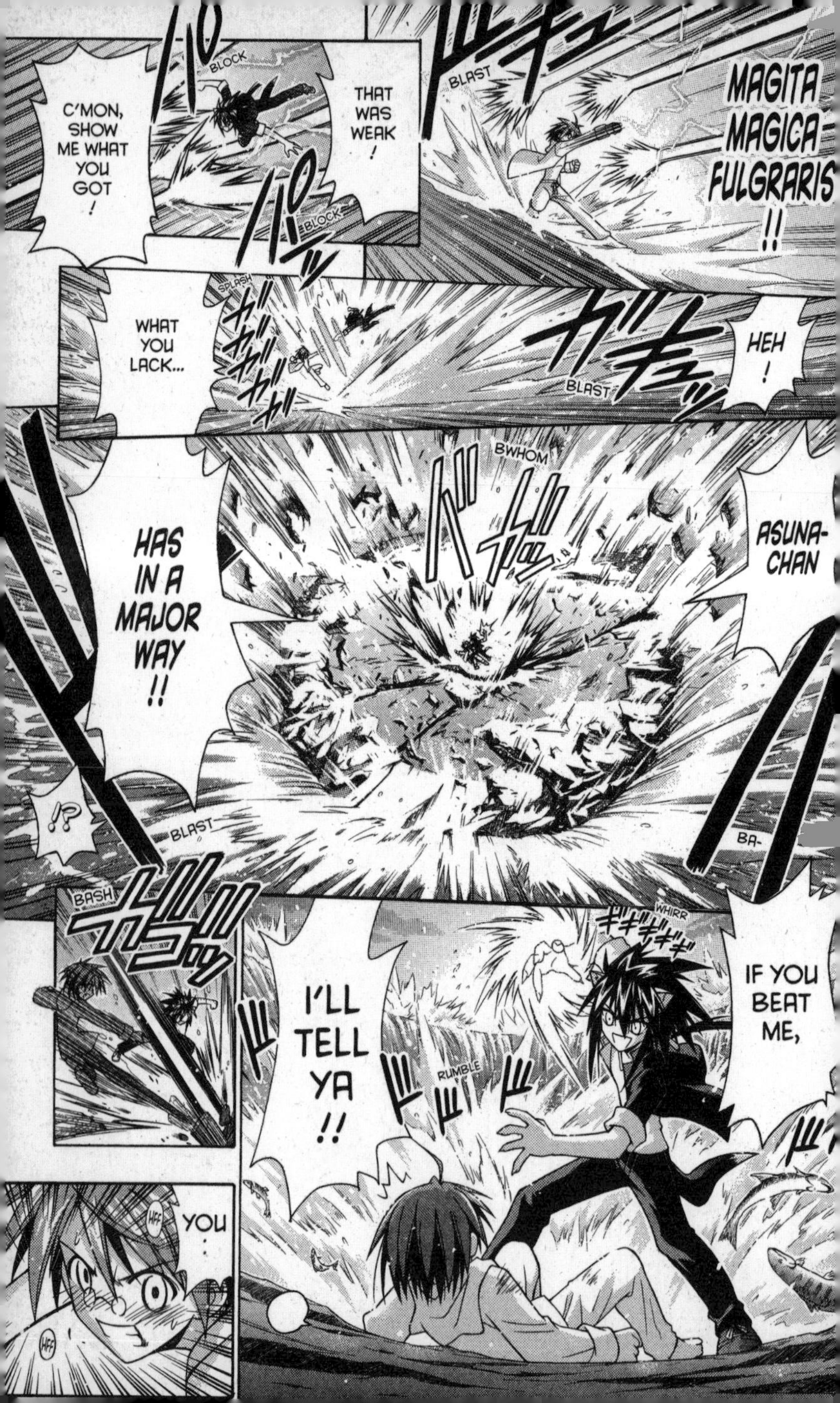
MAGITA MAGICA FULGRARIS!!
BLAST
BLOCK
THAT WAS WEAK!
BLOCK
C'MON, SHOW ME WHAT YOU GOT!
HEH!
BLAST
WHAT YOU LACK...
SPLASH
ASUNA-CHAN
BWHOM
HAS IN A MAJOR WAY!!
BA-
BLAST
!?
IF YOU BEAT ME,
WHIRR
I'LL TELL YA!!
RUMBLE
BASH
YOU...
HFF
HFF

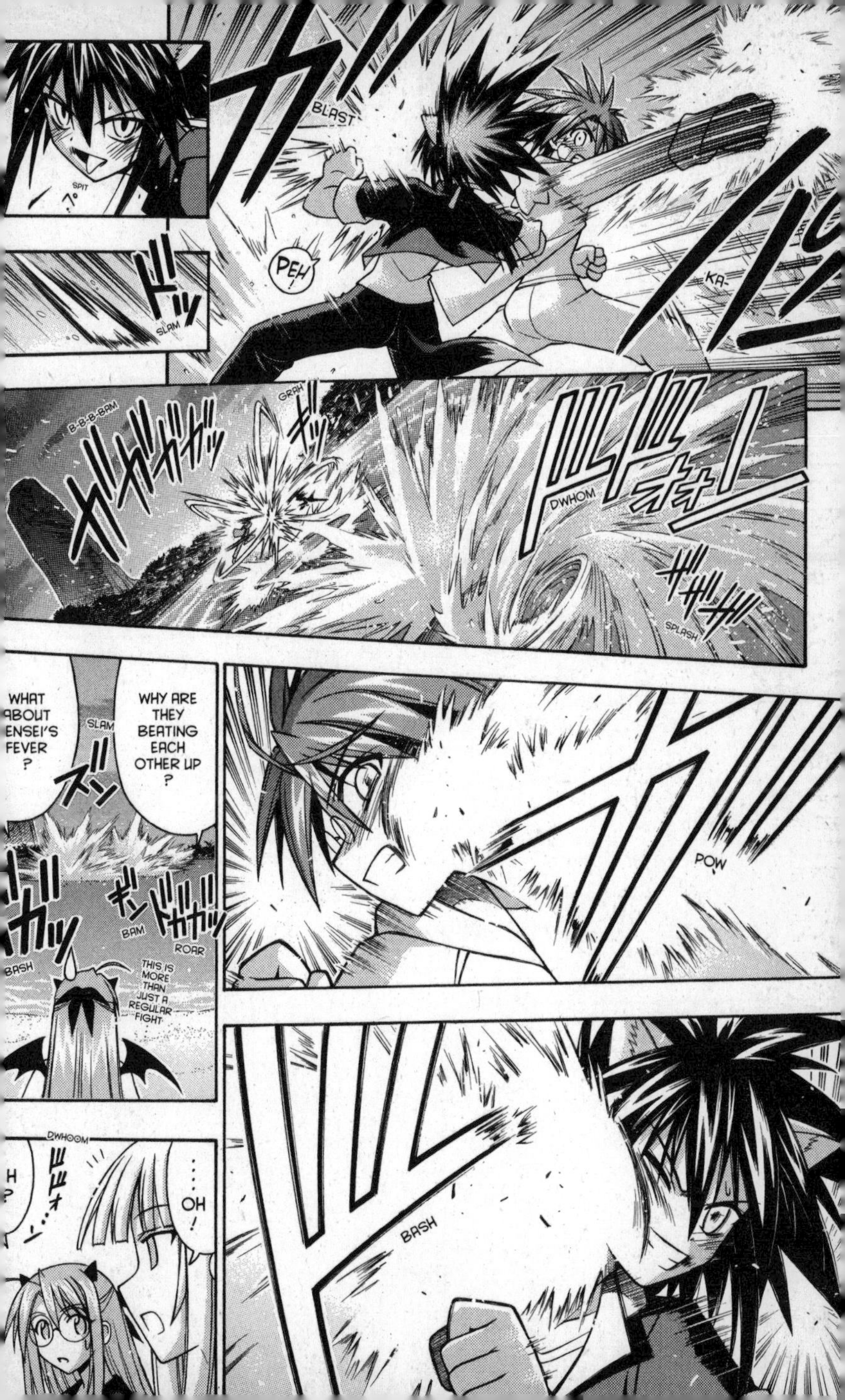

BLAST
KA-
PEH!
SPIT
SLAM
DWHOM
SPLASH
GRAH
B-B-B-BAM
POW
WHY ARE THEY BEATING EACH OTHER UP?
WHAT ABOUT ENSEI'S FEVER?
SLAM
ROAR
BAM
BASH
THIS IS MORE THAN JUST A REGULAR FIGHT...
BASH
DWHOOM
...OH!

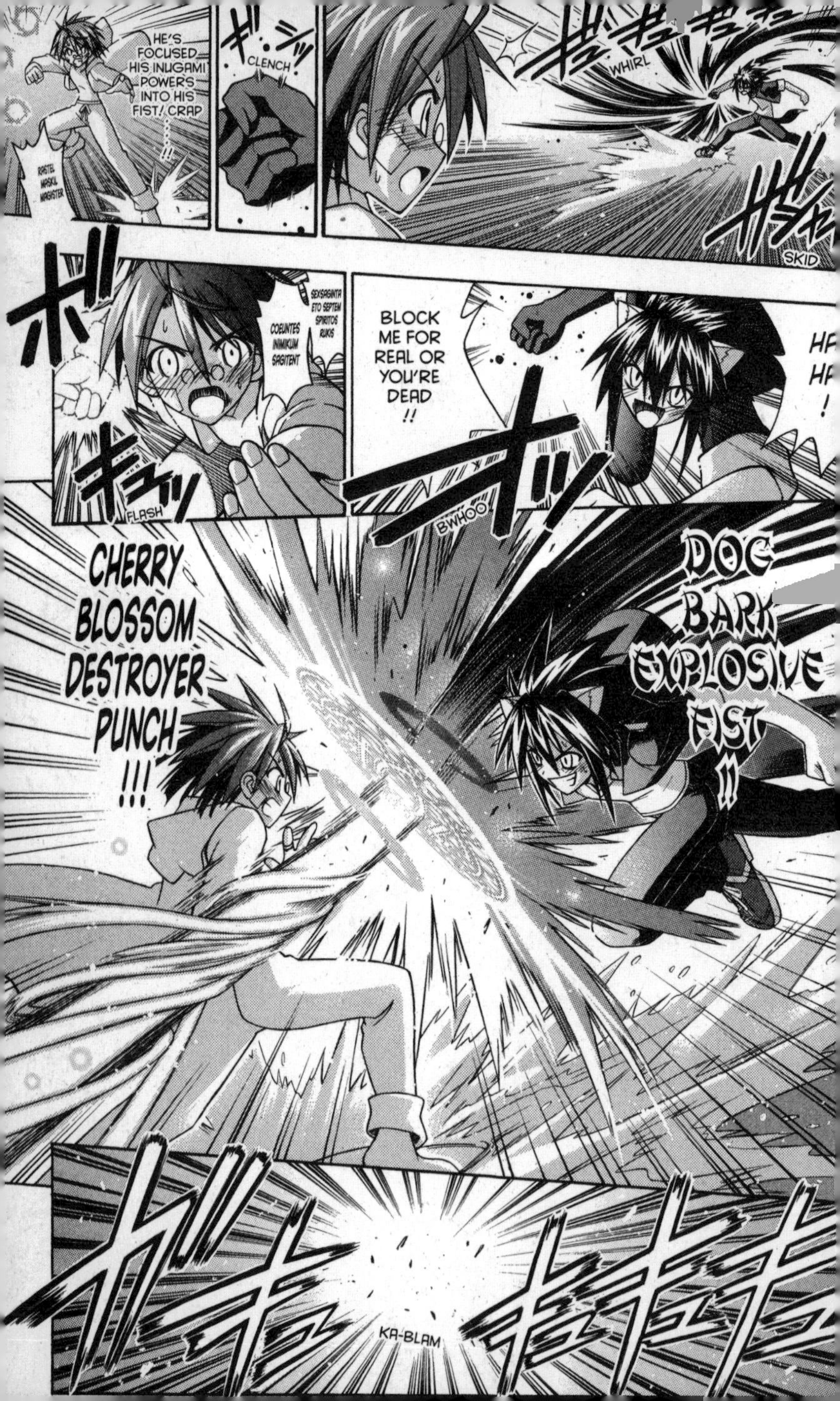
WHIRL
SKID
CLENCH
HE'S FOCUSED HIS INUGAMI POWERS INTO HIS FIST! CRAP
......!!
RASTEL MASKIL MAGISTER
BLOCK ME FOR REAL OR YOU'RE DEAD!!
HF HF!
BWHOO
SEXSAGINTA ETO SEPTEM SPIRITOS RUKIS
COEUNTES INIMIKUM SAGITENT
FLASH
DOG BARK EXPLOSIVE FIST!!
CHERRY BLOSSOM DESTROYER PUNCH!!!
KA-BLAM

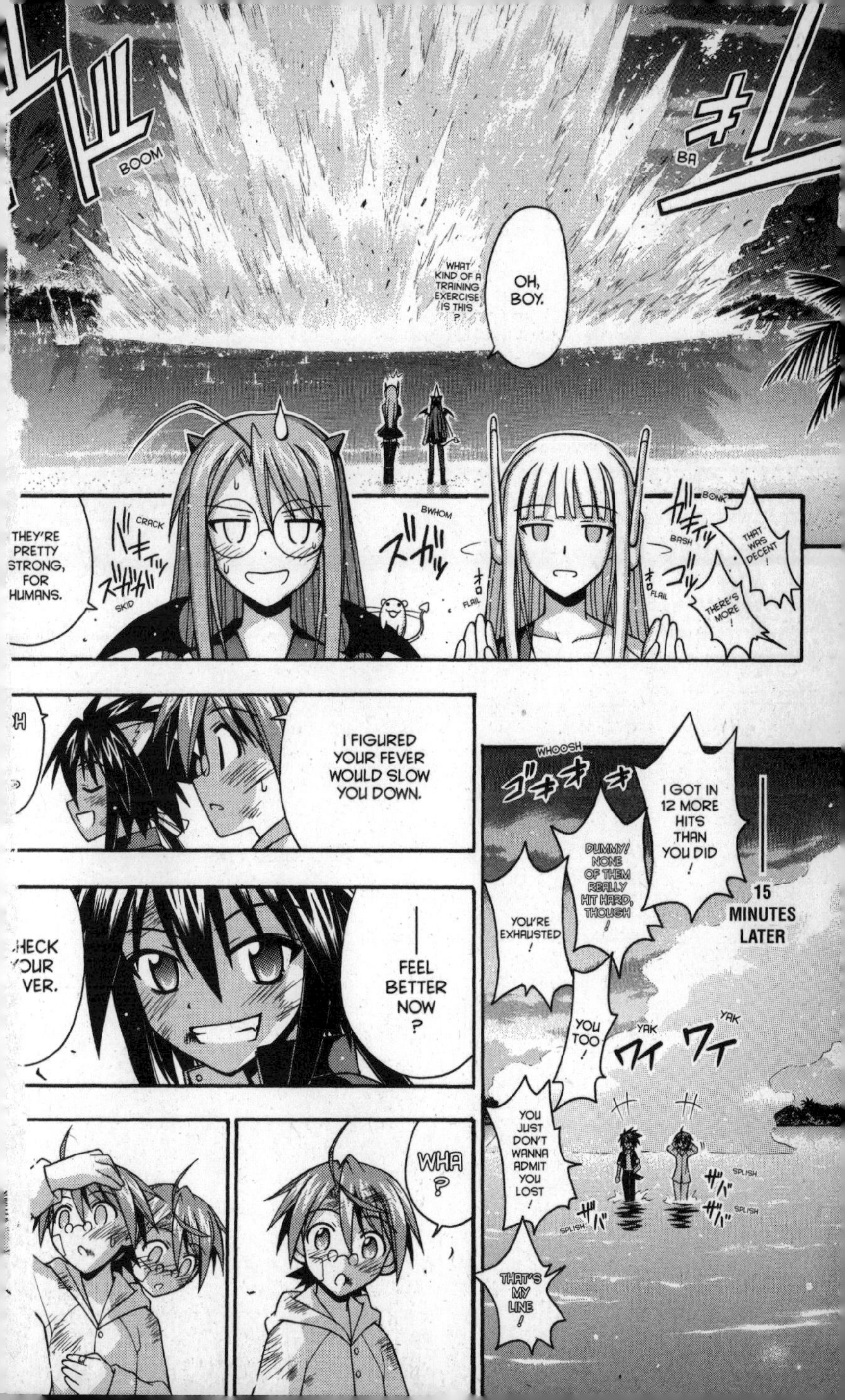
BA
OH, BOY.
WHAT KIND OF A TRAINING EXERCISE IS THIS?
BOOM
BONK
THAT WAS DECENT!
BASH
THERE'S MORE!
FLAIL
BWHOM
FLAIL
CRACK
SKID
THEY'RE PRETTY STRONG, FOR HUMANS.
15 MINUTES LATER
I GOT IN 12 MORE HITS THAN YOU DID!
WHOOSH
DUMMY! NONE OF THEM REALLY HIT HARD, THOUGH!
YOU'RE EXHAUSTED!
YOU TOO!
YAK
YAK
YOU JUST DON'T WANNA ADMIT YOU LOST!
SPLISH
SPLISH
SPLISH
THAT'S MY LINE!
I FIGURED YOUR FEVER WOULD SLOW YOU DOWN.
FEEL BETTER NOW?
WHA?

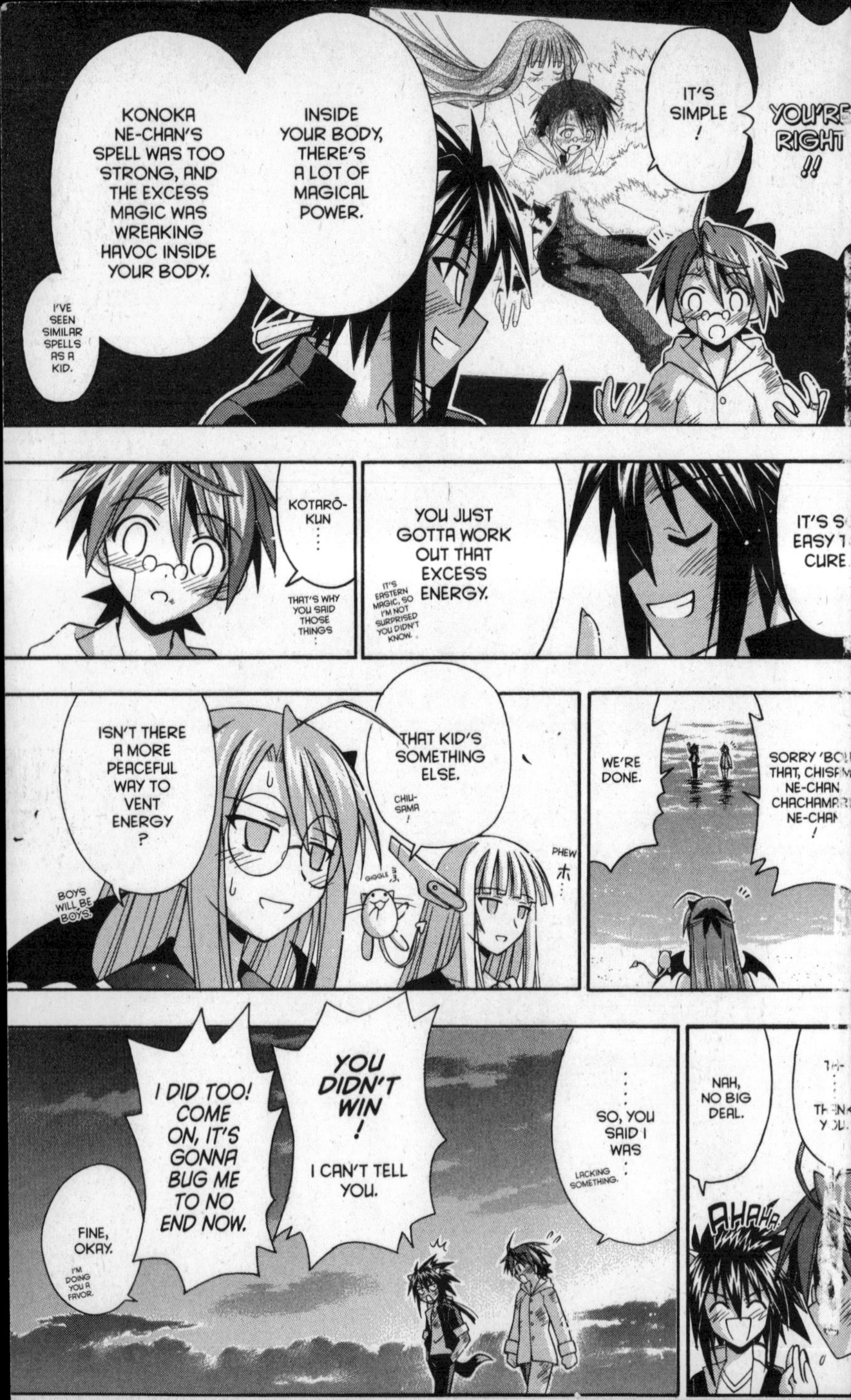
YOU'RE RIGHT!!
IT'S SIMPLE!
INSIDE YOUR BODY, THERE'S A LOT OF MAGICAL POWER.
KONOKA NE-CHAN'S SPELL WAS TOO STRONG, AND THE EXCESS MAGIC WAS WREAKING HAVOC INSIDE YOUR BODY.
I'VE SEEN SIMILAR SPELLS AS A KID.
IT'S S EASY T CURE.
YOU JUST GOTTA WORK OUT THAT EXCESS ENERGY.
IT'S EASTERN MAGIC, SO I'M NOT SURPRISED YOU DIDN'T KNOW.
KOTARŌ-KUN...
THAT'S WHY YOU SAID THOSE THINGS...
SORRY 'BO THAT, CHISA NE-CHAN CHACHAM NE-CHAN!
WE'RE DONE.
PHEW
ホ...
THAT KID'S SOMETHING ELSE.
CHIU-SAMA!
GIGGLE
ISN'T THERE A MORE PEACEFUL WAY TO VENT ENERGY?
BOYS WILL BE BOYS.
NAH, NO BIG DEAL.
AHAHA
SO, YOU SAID I WAS...
LACKING SOMETHING.
YOU DIDN'T WIN!
I CAN'T TELL YOU.
I DID TOO! COME ON, IT'S GONNA BUG ME TO NO END NOW.
FINE, OKAY.
I'M DOING YOU A FAVOR.

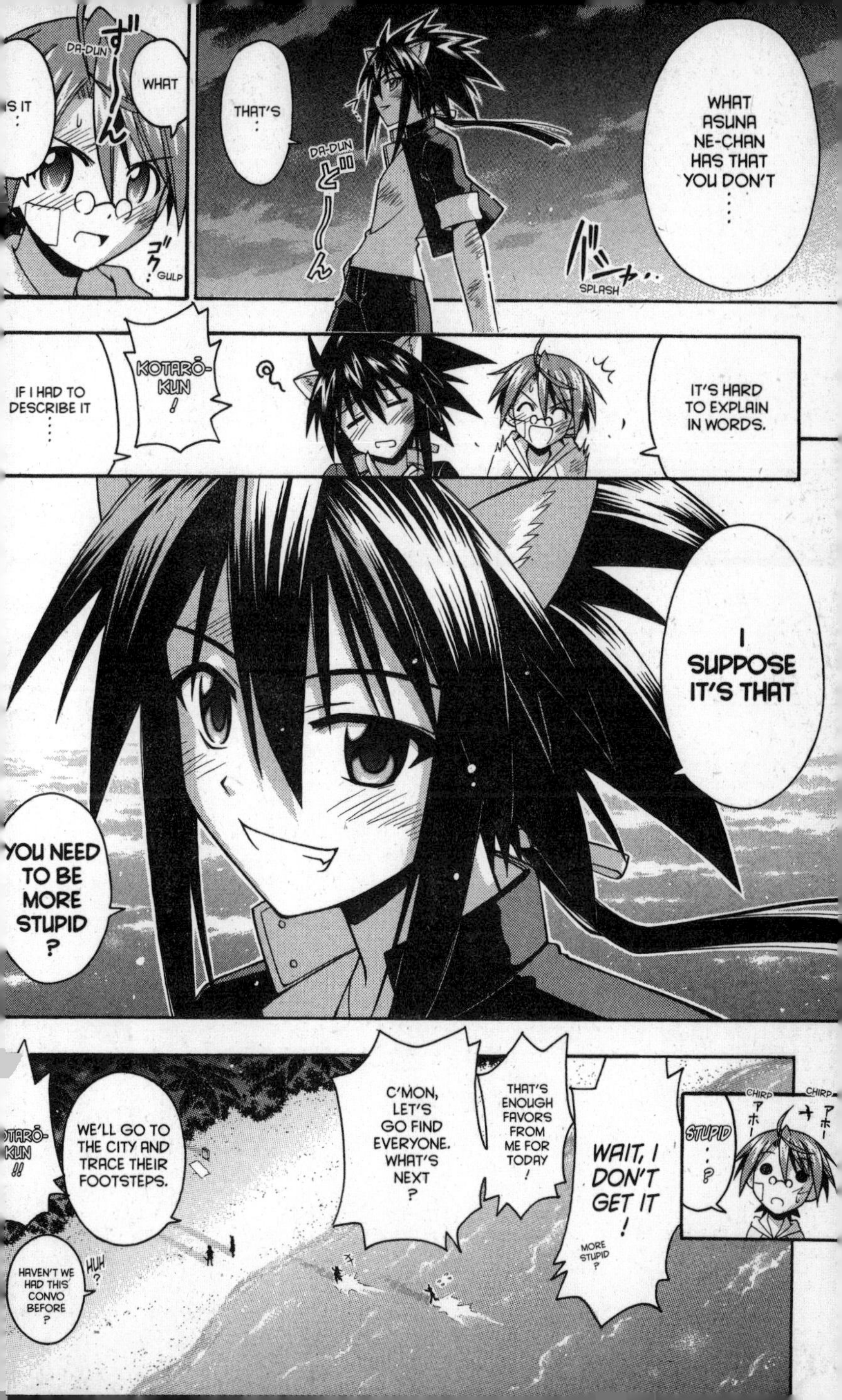

WHAT ASUNA NE-CHAN HAS THAT YOU DON'T ...
SPLASH
THAT'S ...
DA-DUN
WHAT
IS IT ...
DA-DUN
GULP
IT'S HARD TO EXPLAIN IN WORDS.
KOTARŌ-KUN!
IF I HAD TO DESCRIBE IT ...
I SUPPOSE IT'S THAT
YOU NEED TO BE MORE STUPID?
CHIRP
CHIRP
STUPID ...?
WAIT, I DON'T GET IT!
MORE STUPID?
THAT'S ENOUGH FAVORS FROM ME FOR TODAY!
C'MON, LET'S GO FIND EVERYONE. WHAT'S NEXT?
WE'LL GO TO THE CITY AND TRACE THEIR FOOTSTEPS.
KOTARŌ-KUN!!
HUH?
HAVEN'T WE HAD THIS CONVO BEFORE?

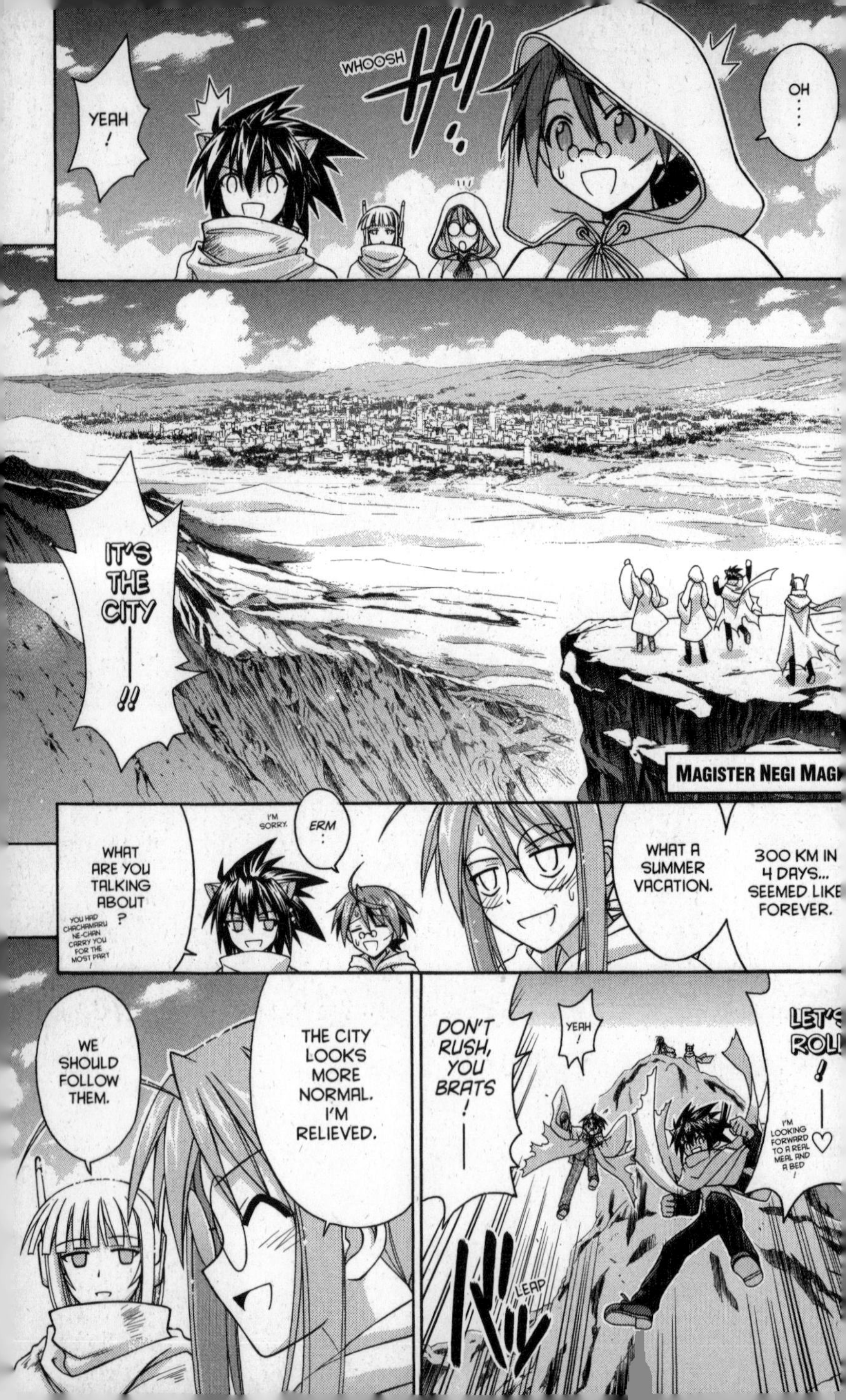

OH......
WHOOSH
YEAH!
IT'S THE CITY——!!
MAGISTER NEGI MAGI
300 KM IN 4 DAYS... SEEMED LIKE FOREVER.
WHAT A SUMMER VACATION.
ERM:
I'M SORRY.
WHAT ARE YOU TALKING ABOUT?
YOU HAD CHACHAMARU NE-CHAN CARRY YOU FOR THE MOST PART!
LET'S ROLL!——♡
I'M LOOKING FORWARD TO A REAL MEAL AND A BED!
YEAH!
DON'T RUSH, YOU BRATS!——
LEAP
THE CITY LOOKS MORE NORMAL. I'M RELIEVED.
WE SHOULD FOLLOW THEM.

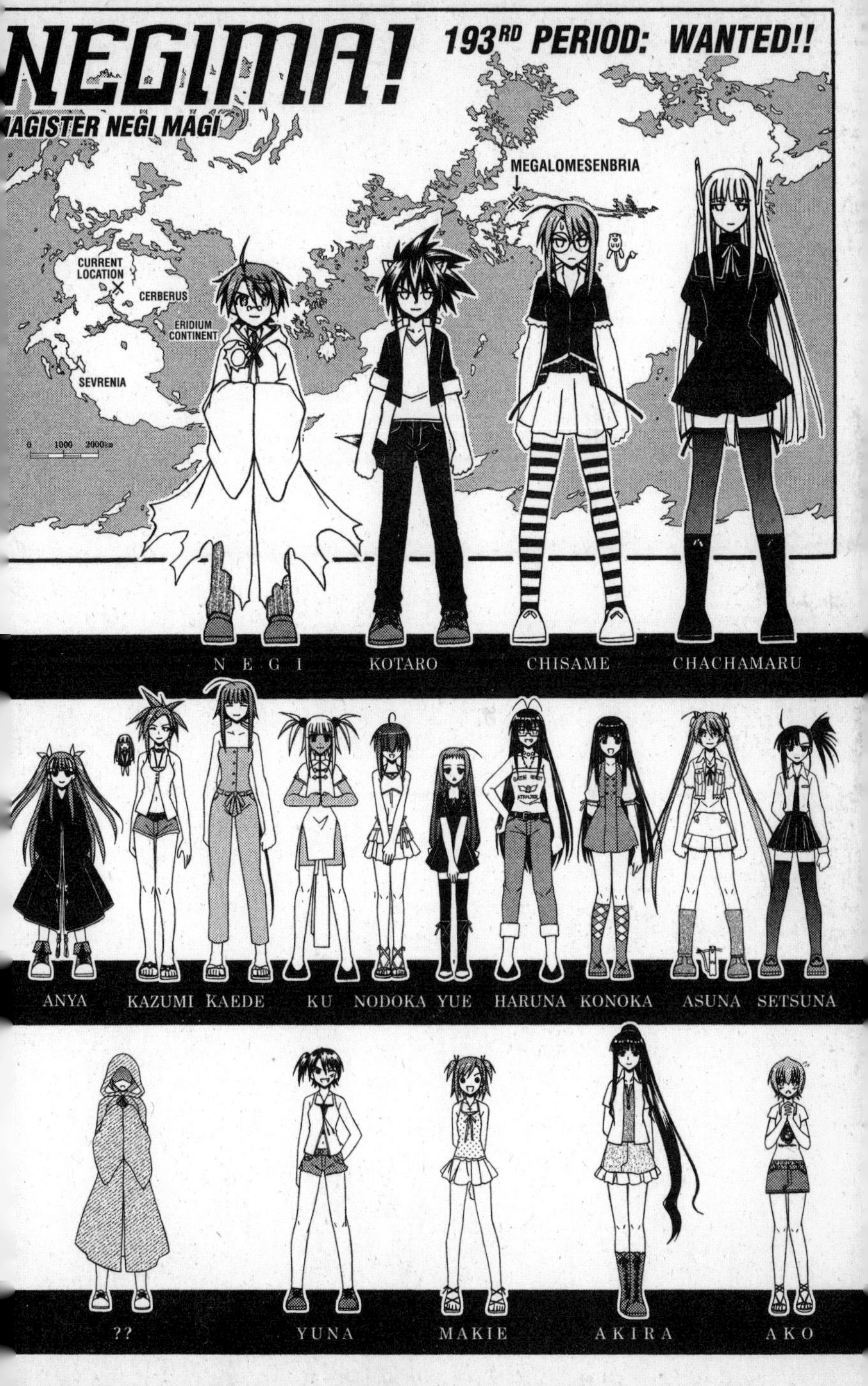
NEGIMA!
193RD PERIOD: WANTED!!
AGISTER NEGI MAGI
MEGALOMESENBRIA
CURRENT LOCATION
CERBERUS
ERIDIUM CONTINENT
SEVRENIA
0 1000 2000km
N E G I
KOTARO
CHISAME
CHACHAMARU
ANYA
KAZUMI
KAEDE
KU
NODOKA
YUE
HARUNA
KONOKA
ASUNA
SETSUNA
??
YUNA
MAKIE
AKIRA
AKO

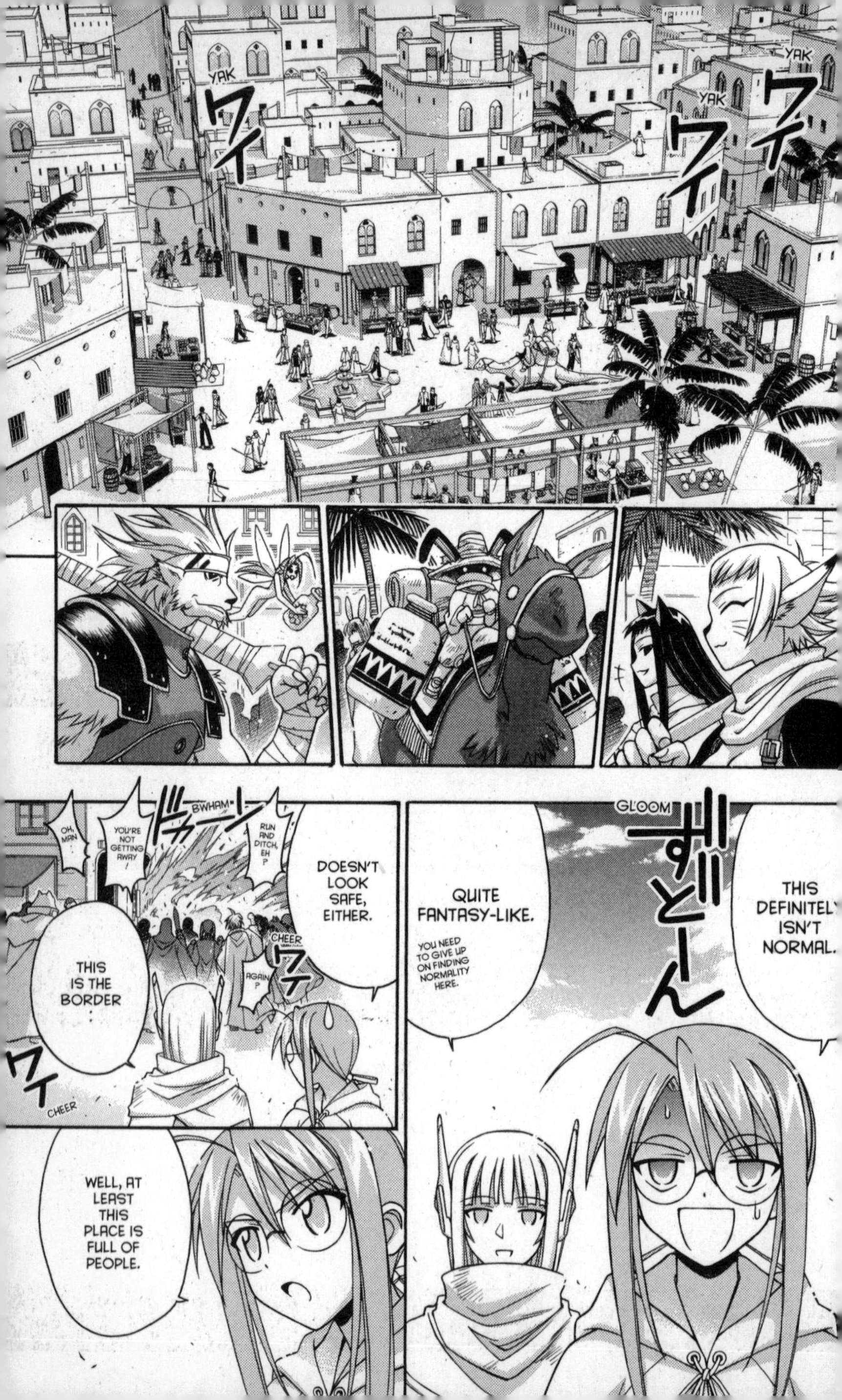
YAK
ワイ
YAK
ワイ
YAK
ワイ
GLOOM
ずどーん
THIS DEFINITEL ISN'T NORMAL.
QUITE FANTASY-LIKE.
YOU NEED TO GIVE UP ON FINDING NORMALITY HERE.
BWHAM
ドカーン
RUN AND DITCH, EH?
YOU'RE NOT GETTING AWAY!
OH, MAN
DOESN'T LOOK SAFE, EITHER.
CHEER
ワイ
AGAIN?
THIS IS THE BORDER
ワイ
CHEER
WELL, AT LEAST THIS PLACE IS FULL OF PEOPLE.

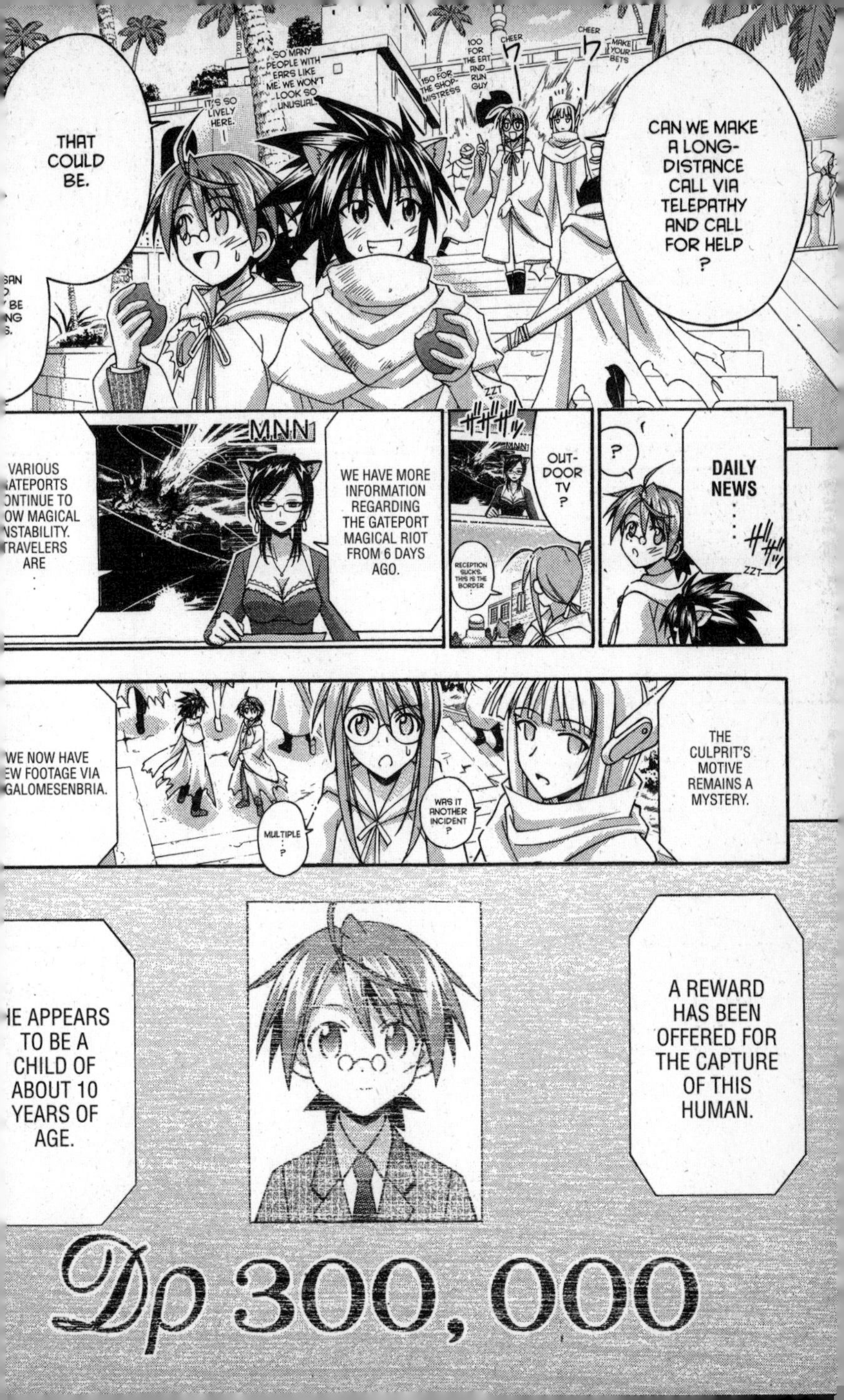
CAN WE MAKE A LONG-DISTANCE CALL VIA TELEPATHY AND CALL FOR HELP?
MAKE YOUR BETS
CHEER
CHEER
100 FOR THE EAT AND RUN GUY
150 FOR THE SHOP-MISTRESS
SO MANY PEOPLE WITH EARS LIKE ME; WE WON'T LOOK SO UNUSUAL.
IT'S SO LIVELY HERE.
THAT COULD BE.
DAILY NEWS...
?
ZZT
OUT-DOOR TV?
ZZT
MNN
RECEPTION SUCKS. THIS IS THE BORDER.
WE HAVE MORE INFORMATION REGARDING THE GATEPORT MAGICAL RIOT FROM 6 DAYS AGO.
MNN
VARIOUS ATEPORTS ONTINUE TO OW MAGICAL NSTABILITY. TRAVELERS ARE...
THE CULPRIT'S MOTIVE REMAINS A MYSTERY.
WAS IT ANOTHER INCIDENT?
MULTIPLE...?
WE NOW HAVE EW FOOTAGE VIA GALOMESENBRIA.
A REWARD HAS BEEN OFFERED FOR THE CAPTURE OF THIS HUMAN.
IE APPEARS TO BE A CHILD OF ABOUT 10 YEARS OF AGE.
Dp 300,000

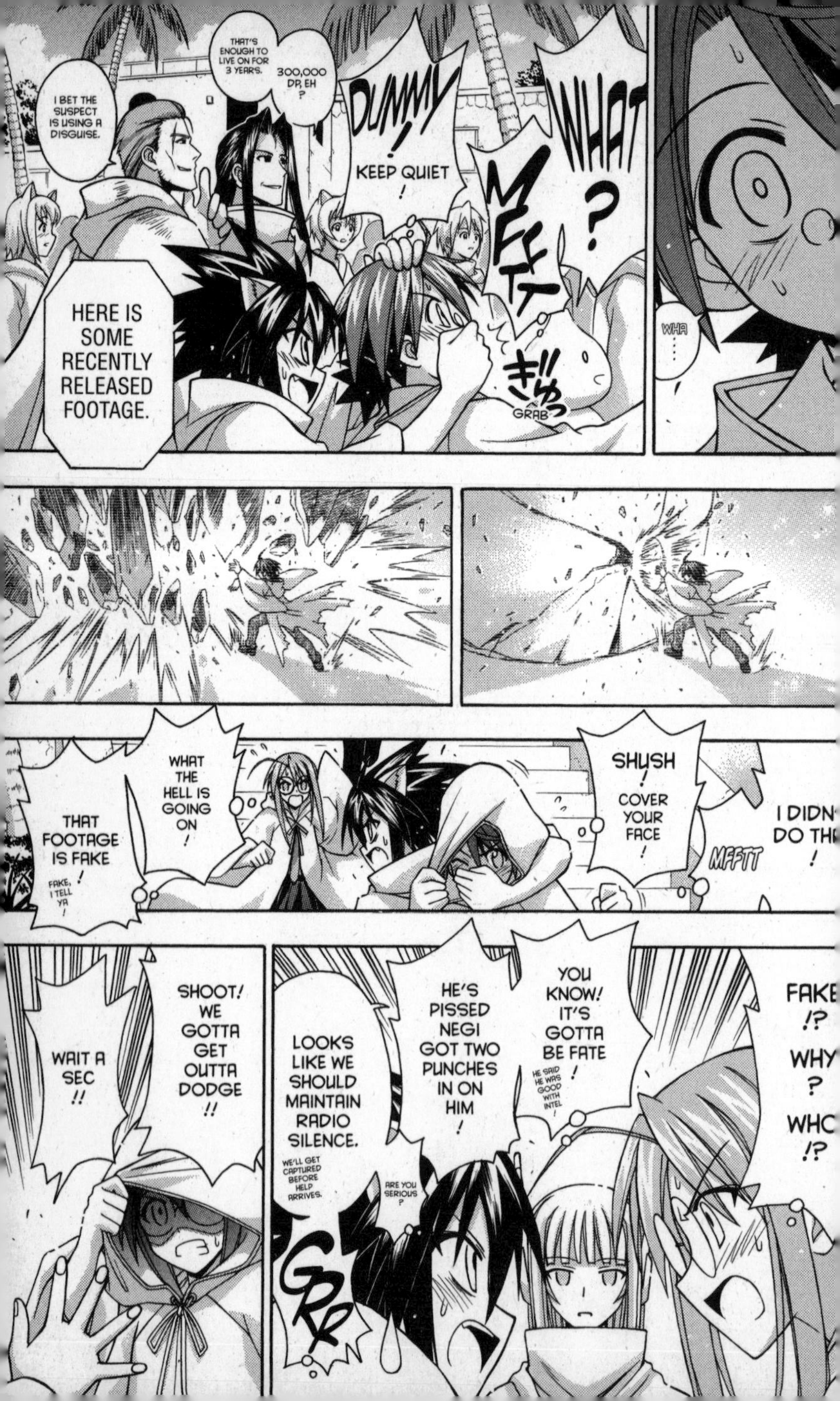

WHA......
WHAT?
MFFTT
ぎゅっ
GRAB
DUMMY! KEEP QUIET!
300,000 DP, EH?
THAT'S ENOUGH TO LIVE ON FOR 3 YEARS.
I BET THE SUSPECT IS USING A DISGUISE.
HERE IS SOME RECENTLY RELEASED FOOTAGE.
I DIDN DO TH!
MFFTT
SHUSH! COVER YOUR FACE!
WHAT THE HELL IS GOING ON!
THAT FOOTAGE IS FAKE
FAKE, I TELL YA!
FAKE!? WHY? WHO!?
YOU KNOW! IT'S GOTTA BE FATE!
HE SAID HE WAS GOOD WITH INTEL!
HE'S PISSED NEGI GOT TWO PUNCHES IN ON HIM!
ARE YOU SERIOUS?
LOOKS LIKE WE SHOULD MAINTAIN RADIO SILENCE.
WE'LL GET CAPTURED BEFORE HELP ARRIVES.
GRR
SHOOT! WE GOTTA GET OUTTA DODGE!!
WAIT A SEC!!

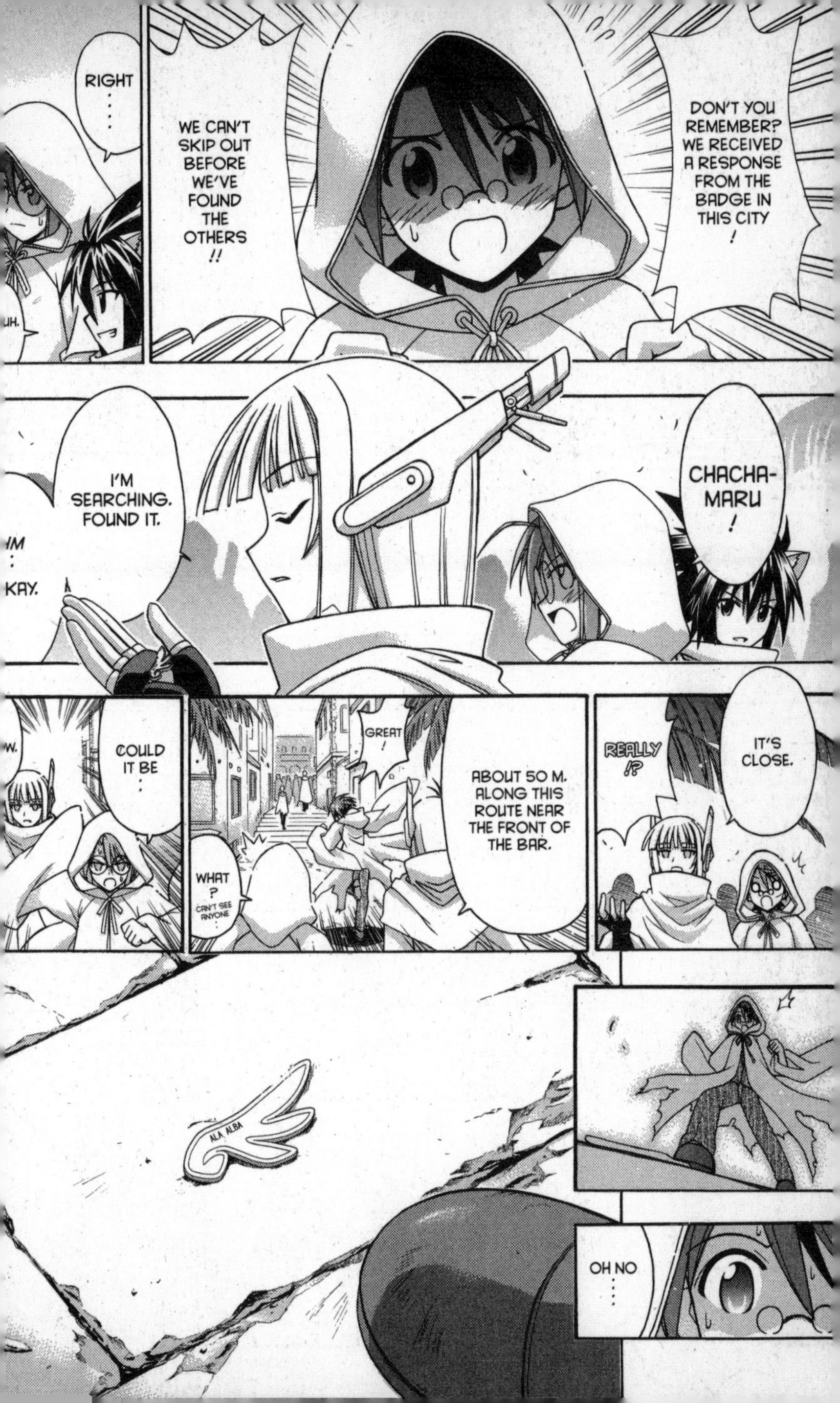
DON'T YOU REMEMBER? WE RECEIVED A RESPONSE FROM THE BADGE IN THIS CITY!
WE CAN'T SKIP OUT BEFORE WE'VE FOUND THE OTHERS!!
RIGHT...
UH.
CHACHA-MARU!
I'M SEARCHING. FOUND IT.
KAY.
IT'S CLOSE.
REALLY!?
ABOUT 50 M. ALONG THIS ROUTE NEAR THE FRONT OF THE BAR.
GREAT!
WHAT?
CAN'T SEE ANYONE...
COULD IT BE...
ALA ALBA
OH NO...

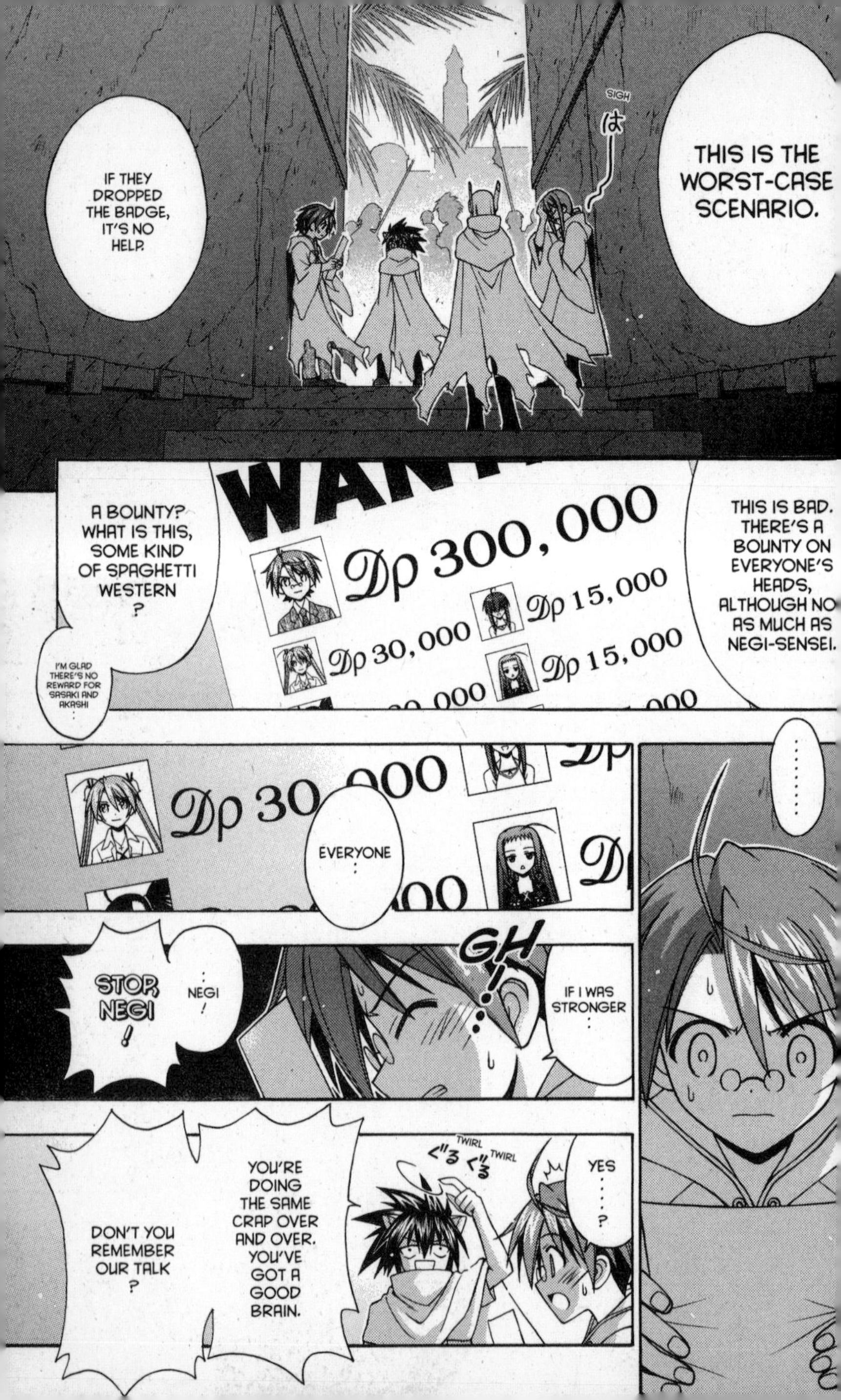
THIS IS THE WORST-CASE SCENARIO.
SIGH
は
IF THEY DROPPED THE BADGE, IT'S NO HELP.
THIS IS BAD. THERE'S A BOUNTY ON EVERYONE'S HEADS, ALTHOUGH NO AS MUCH AS NEGI-SENSEI.
Dp 300,000
Dp 15,000
Dp 30,000
Dp 15,000
A BOUNTY? WHAT IS THIS, SOME KIND OF SPAGHETTI WESTERN?
I'M GLAD THERE'S NO REWARD FOR SASAKI AND AKASHI...
......
Dp 30,000
EVERYONE...
IF I WAS STRONGER...
GH!...
NEGI!
STOP, NEGI!
YES.....?
TWIRL TWIRL
ぐるぐる
YOU'RE DOING THE SAME CRAP OVER AND OVER. YOU'VE GOT A GOOD BRAIN.
DON'T YOU REMEMBER OUR TALK?

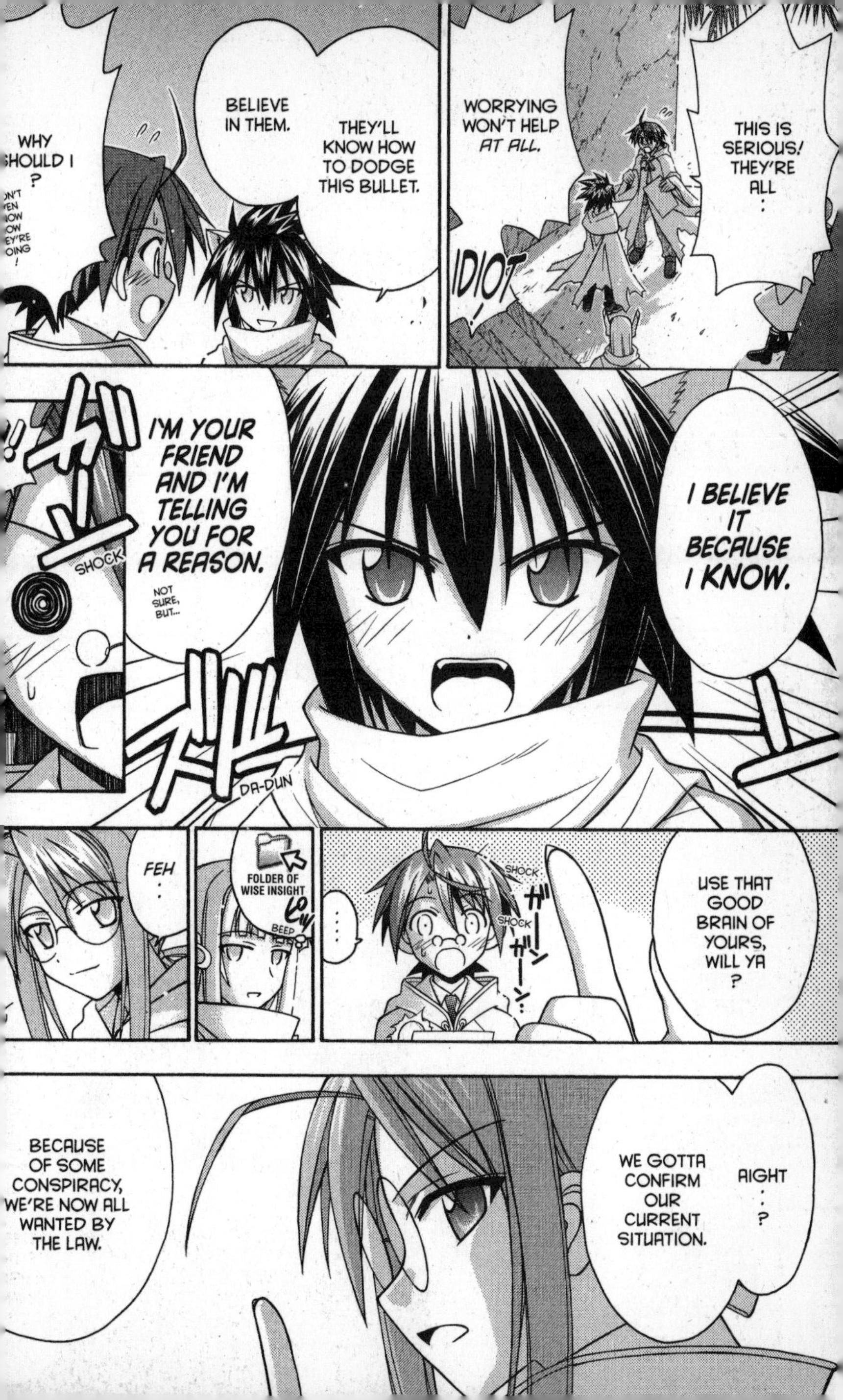
THIS IS SERIOUS! THEY'RE ALL . . .
WORRYING WON'T HELP AT ALL.
IDIOT
BELIEVE IN THEM. THEY'LL KNOW HOW TO DODGE THIS BULLET.
WHY SHOULD I ?
I BELIEVE IT BECAUSE I KNOW.
I'M YOUR FRIEND AND I'M TELLING YOU FOR A REASON.
NOT SURE, BUT...
DA-DUN
SHOCK
USE THAT GOOD BRAIN OF YOURS, WILL YA ?
SHOCK
SHOCK
. . . .
FOLDER OF WISE INSIGHT
BEEP
FEH . .
AIGHT . . ?
WE GOTTA CONFIRM OUR CURRENT SITUATION.
BECAUSE OF SOME CONSPIRACY, WE'RE NOW ALL WANTED BY THE LAW.

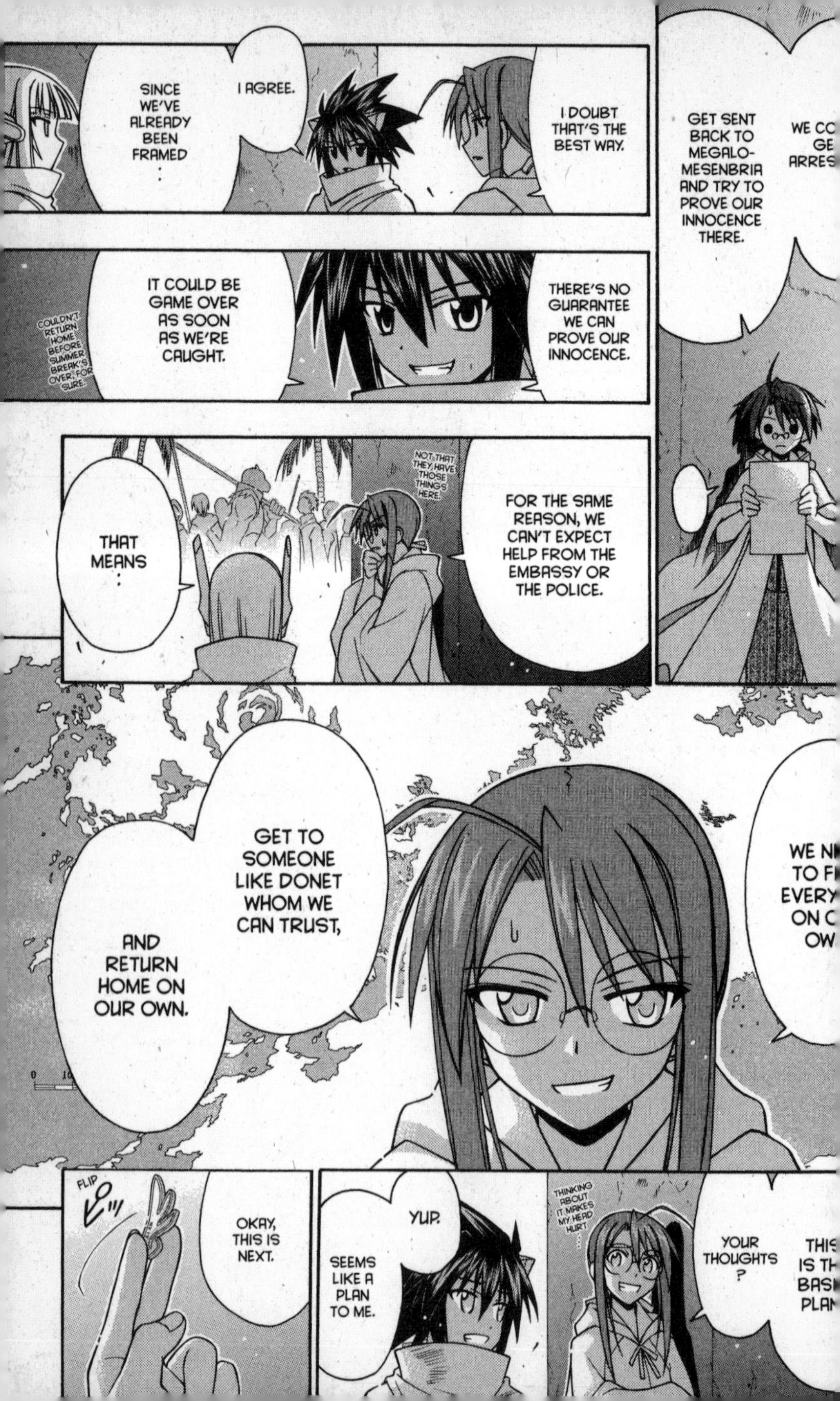

WE CO GE ARRES
GET SENT BACK TO MEGALO-MESENBRIA AND TRY TO PROVE OUR INNOCENCE THERE.
I DOUBT THAT'S THE BEST WAY.
I AGREE.
SINCE WE'VE ALREADY BEEN FRAMED...
THERE'S NO GUARANTEE WE CAN PROVE OUR INNOCENCE.
IT COULD BE GAME OVER AS SOON AS WE'RE CAUGHT.
COULDN'T RETURN HOME BEFORE SUMMER BREAK'S OVER, FOR SURE.
FOR THE SAME REASON, WE CAN'T EXPECT HELP FROM THE EMBASSY OR THE POLICE.
NOT THAT THEY HAVE THOSE THINGS HERE.
THAT MEANS...
WE N TO F EVERY ON O OW
GET TO SOMEONE LIKE DONET WHOM WE CAN TRUST,
AND RETURN HOME ON OUR OWN.
THIS IS TH BAS PLAN
YOUR THOUGHTS?
THINKING ABOUT IT MAKES MY HEAD HURT...
YUP.
SEEMS LIKE A PLAN TO ME.
OKAY, THIS IS NEXT.
FLIP

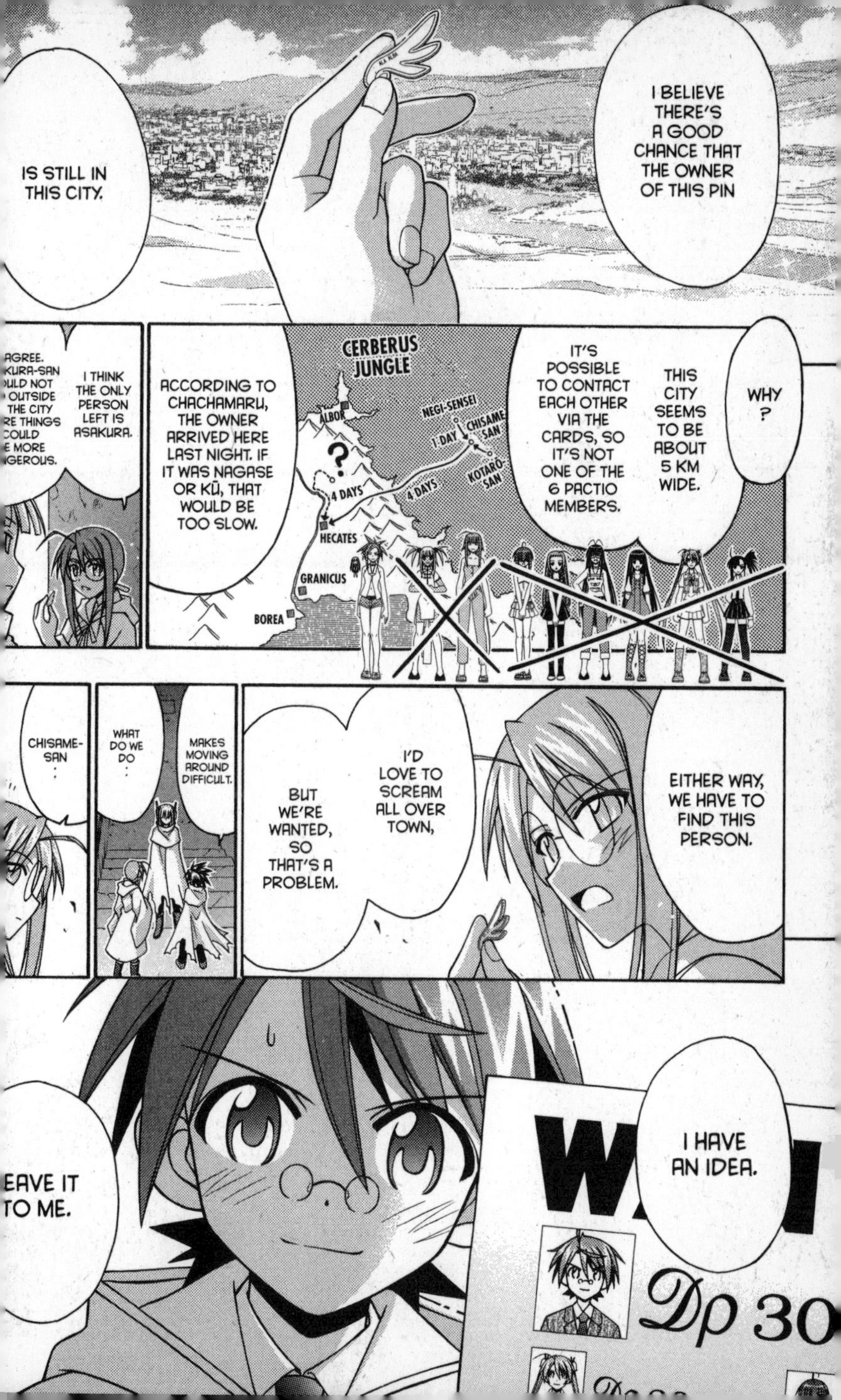
I BELIEVE THERE'S A GOOD CHANCE THAT THE OWNER OF THIS PIN
IS STILL IN THIS CITY.
WHY?
THIS CITY SEEMS TO BE ABOUT 5 KM WIDE.
IT'S POSSIBLE TO CONTACT EACH OTHER VIA THE CARDS, SO IT'S NOT ONE OF THE 6 PACTIO MEMBERS.
CERBERUS JUNGLE
NEGI-SENSEI
CHISAME SAN
1 DAY
KOTARO-SAN
ALBOR
?
4 DAYS
4 DAYS
HECATES
GRANICUS
BOREA
ACCORDING TO CHACHAMARU, THE OWNER ARRIVED HERE LAST NIGHT. IF IT WAS NAGASE OR KŪ, THAT WOULD BE TOO SLOW.
I THINK THE ONLY PERSON LEFT IS ASAKURA.
AGREE. KURA-SAN ULD NOT OUTSIDE THE CITY RE THINGS COULD E MORE GEROUS.
EITHER WAY, WE HAVE TO FIND THIS PERSON.
I'D LOVE TO SCREAM ALL OVER TOWN,
BUT WE'RE WANTED, SO THAT'S A PROBLEM.
MAKES MOVING AROUND DIFFICULT.
WHAT DO WE DO...
CHISAME-SAN...
I HAVE AN IDEA.
EAVE IT TO ME.
Dp 30

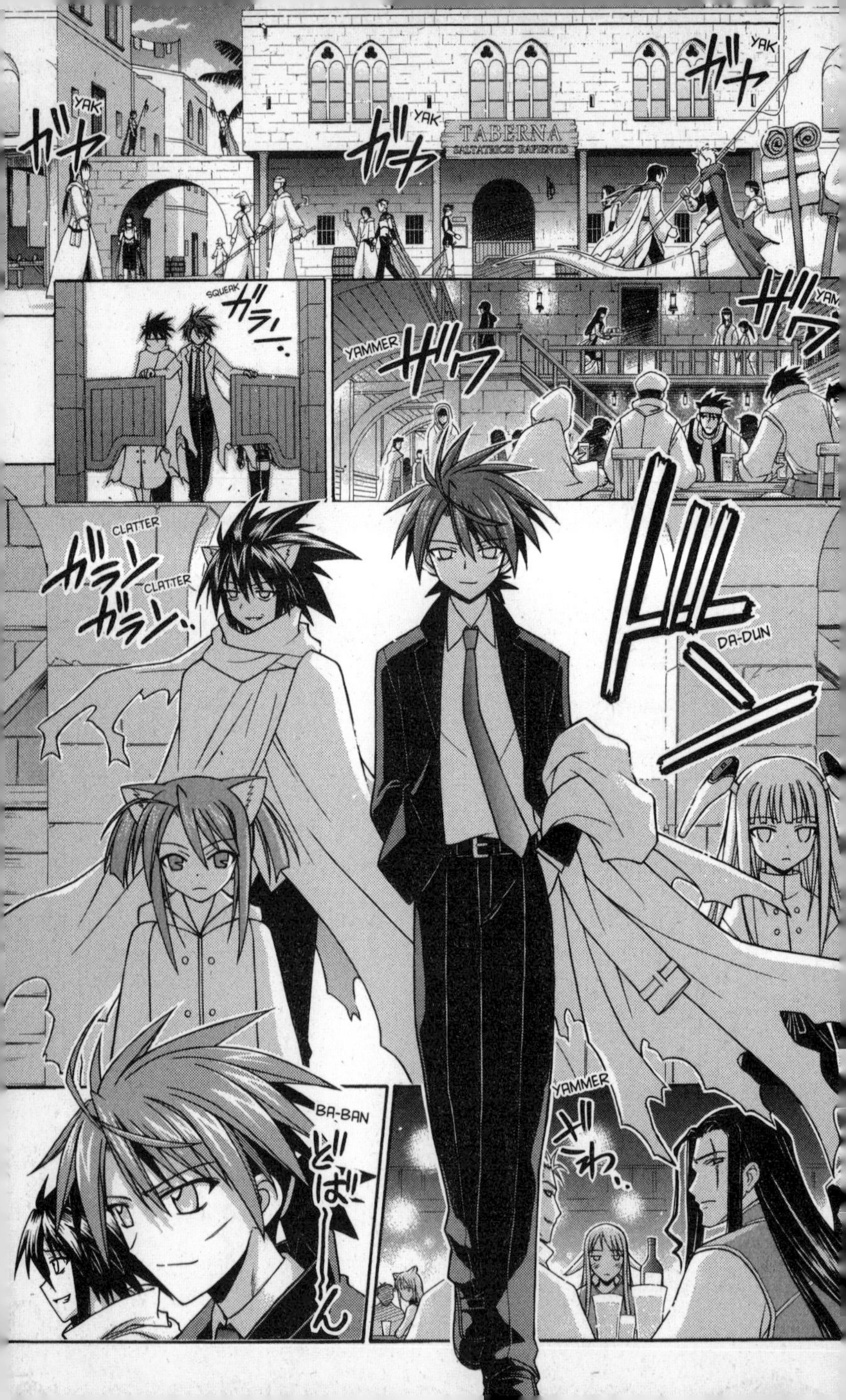

YAK
ガヤ
TABERNA
SALTATRICES RAPIENTIS
YAK
ガヤ
YAK
ガヤ
YAM
ザワ
YAMMER
ザワ
SQUEAK
ガラン
DA-DUN
CLATTER
ガラン
CLATTER
ガラン
YAMMER
ざわ..
BA-BAN
どばーん

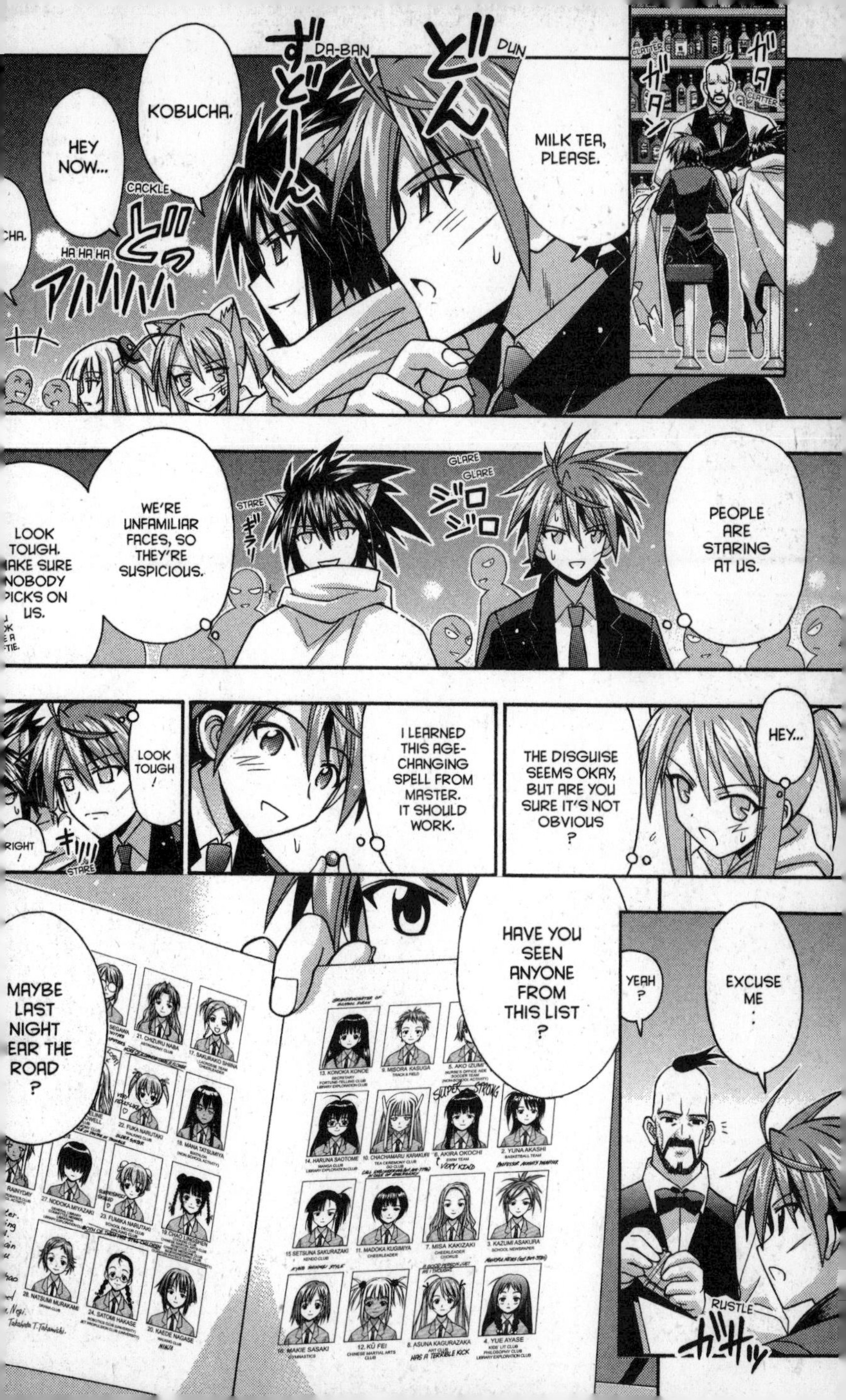
CLATTER
ガタ
CLATTER
ガタン
DUN
どん
DA-BAN
ずどーん
MILK TEA, PLEASE.
KOBUCHA.
HEY NOW...
CACKLE
どっ
HA HA HA
アハハハ
CHA.
PEOPLE ARE STARING AT US.
GLARE GLARE
ジロジロ
STARE
ギラ
WE'RE UNFAMILIAR FACES, SO THEY'RE SUSPICIOUS.
LOOK TOUGH. AKE SURE NOBODY PICKS ON US.
HEY...
THE DISGUISE SEEMS OKAY, BUT ARE YOU SURE IT'S NOT OBVIOUS?
I LEARNED THIS AGE-CHANGING SPELL FROM MASTER. IT SHOULD WORK.
LOOK TOUGH!
RIGHT!
STARE
ギリ
EXCUSE ME:
YEAH?
RUSTLE
ガサッ
HAVE YOU SEEN ANYONE FROM THIS LIST?
MAYBE LAST NIGHT EAR THE ROAD?
13. KONOKA KONOE
9. MISORA KASUGA
5. AKO IZUMI
14. HARUNA SAOTOME
10. CHACHAMARU KARAKURI
6. AKIRA OKOCHI
2. YUNA AKASHI
15. SETSUNA SAKURAZAKI
11. MADOKA KUGIMIYA
7. MISA KAKIZAKI
3. KAZUMI ASAKURA
16. MAKIE SASAKI
12. KŪ FEI
8. ASUNA KAGURAZAKA
4. YUE AYASE
21. CHIZURU NABA
17. SAKURAKO SHIINA
22. FUKA NARUTAKI
18. MANA TATSUMIYA
27. NODOKA MIYAZAKI
23. FUMIKA NARUTAKI
19. CHAO LINGSHEN
28. NATSUMI MURAKAMI
24. SATOMI HAKASE
20. KAEDE NAGASE

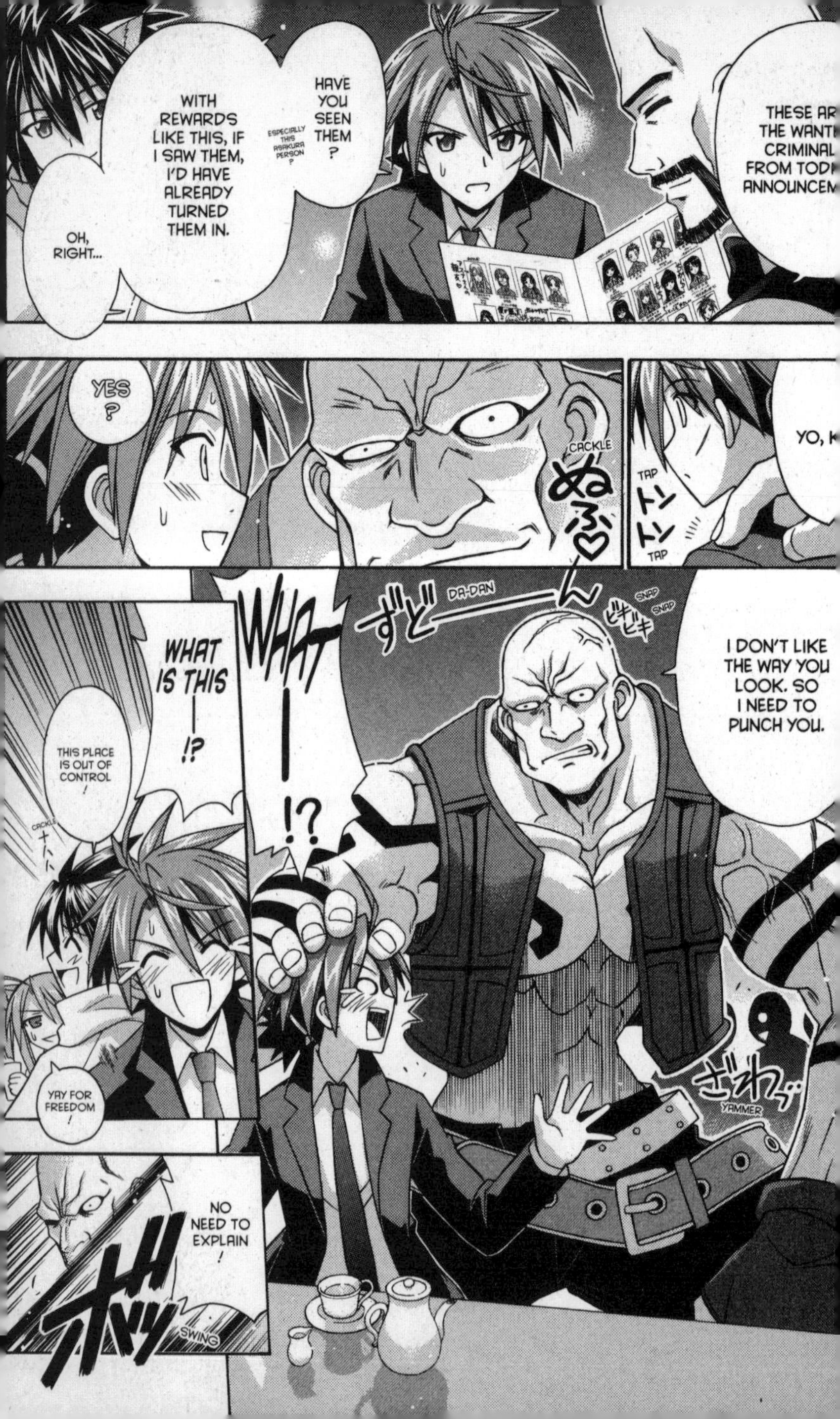
THESE AR THE WANT CRIMINAL FROM TOD ANNOUNCEM
HAVE YOU SEEN THEM?
ESPECIALLY THIS ASAKURA PERSON?
WITH REWARDS LIKE THIS, IF I SAW THEM, I'D HAVE ALREADY TURNED THEM IN.
OH, RIGHT...
YO, K
TAP トントン TAP
CACKLE ぬふ♡ん
YES?
ずど———ん DA-DAN
SNAP ビキビキ SNAP
I DON'T LIKE THE WAY YOU LOOK. SO I NEED TO PUNCH YOU.
WHAT——!?
ざわっ YAMMER
WHAT IS THIS——!?
THIS PLACE IS OUT OF CONTROL!
CACKLE ナハハ
YAY FOR FREEDOM!
NO NEED TO EXPLAIN!
SWING

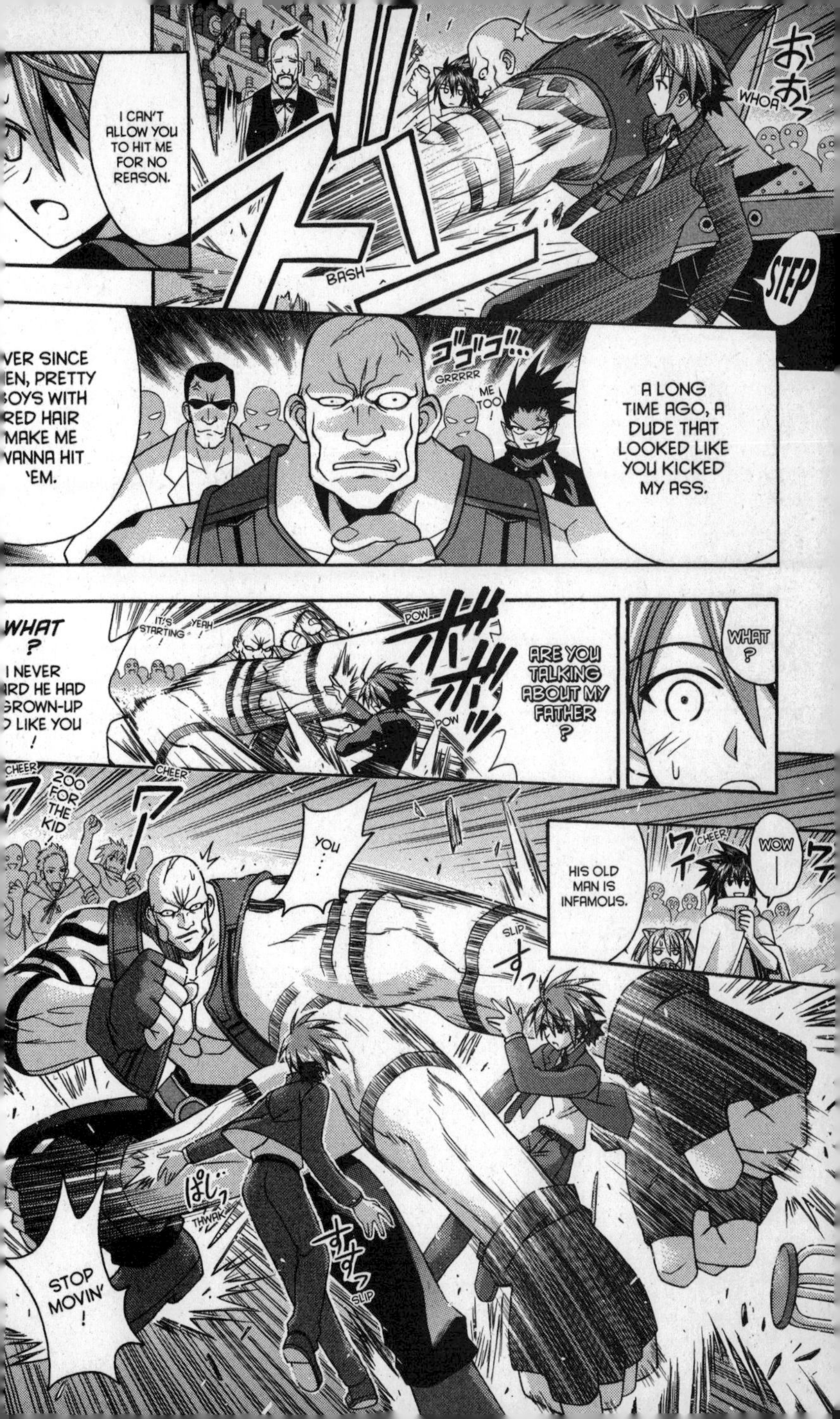
おおっ
WHOA
STEP
BASH
I CAN'T ALLOW YOU TO HIT ME FOR NO REASON.
A LONG TIME AGO, A DUDE THAT LOOKED LIKE YOU KICKED MY ASS.
ME TOO!
ゴゴゴ!!...
GRRRRR
VER SINCE EN, PRETTY OYS WITH RED HAIR MAKE ME VANNA HIT 'EM.
WHAT?
ARE YOU TALKING ABOUT MY FATHER?
POW
POW
YEAH!
IT'S STARTING!
WHAT? I NEVER RD HE HAD GROWN-UP D LIKE YOU!
WOW—
CHEER
HIS OLD MAN IS INFAMOUS.
SLIP
すっ
YOU...
CHEER
200 FOR THE KID
CHEER
ぱしっ
THWAK
すすっ
SLIP
STOP MOVIN'!

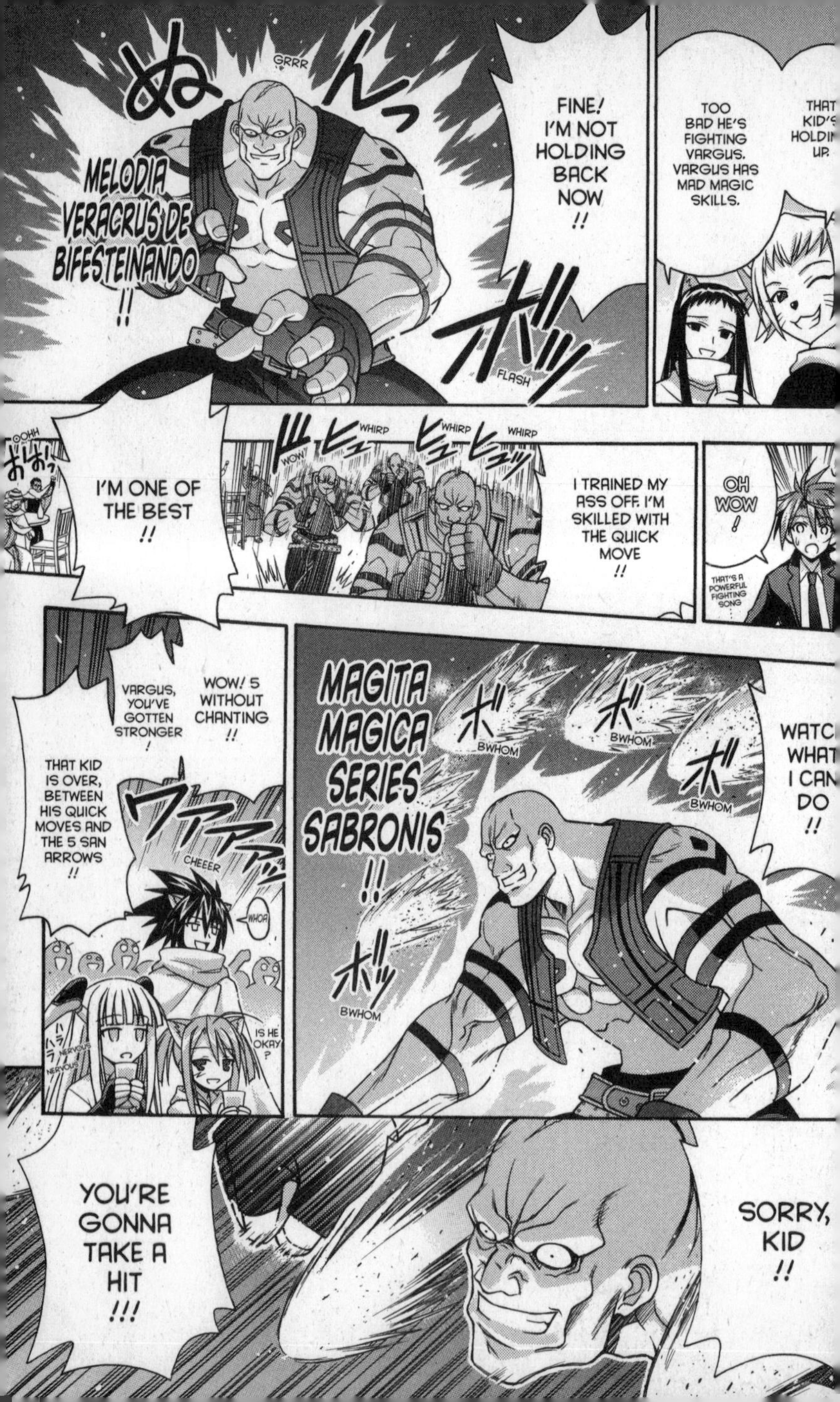
THAT KID'S HOLDIN UP.
TOO BAD HE'S FIGHTING VARGUS. VARGUS HAS MAD MAGIC SKILLS.
FINE! I'M NOT HOLDING BACK NOW !!
ぬんっ
GRRR
MELODIA VERACRUS DE BIFESTEINANDO !!
ボッ
FLASH
OH WOW !
THAT'S A POWERFUL FIGHTING SONG ...
I TRAINED MY ASS OFF. I'M SKILLED WITH THE QUICK MOVE !!
ドヒュ ヒュ ヒュ ヒュッ
WOW
WHIRP
WHIRP
WHIRP
I'M ONE OF THE BEST !!
おおっ
OOHH
WATC WHAT I CAN DO !!
MAGITA MAGICA SERIES SABRONIS !!
ボ
BWHOM
ボ
BWHOM
ボ
BWHOM
ボッ
BWHOM
WOW! 5 WITHOUT CHANTING !!
VARGUS, YOU'VE GOTTEN STRONGER !
THAT KID IS OVER, BETWEEN HIS QUICK MOVES AND THE 5 SAN ARROWS !!
ワァァァッ
CHEEER
WHOA
IS HE OKAY ?
ハラハラ
NERVOUS
NERVOUS
SORRY, KID !!
YOU'RE GONNA TAKE A HIT !!!

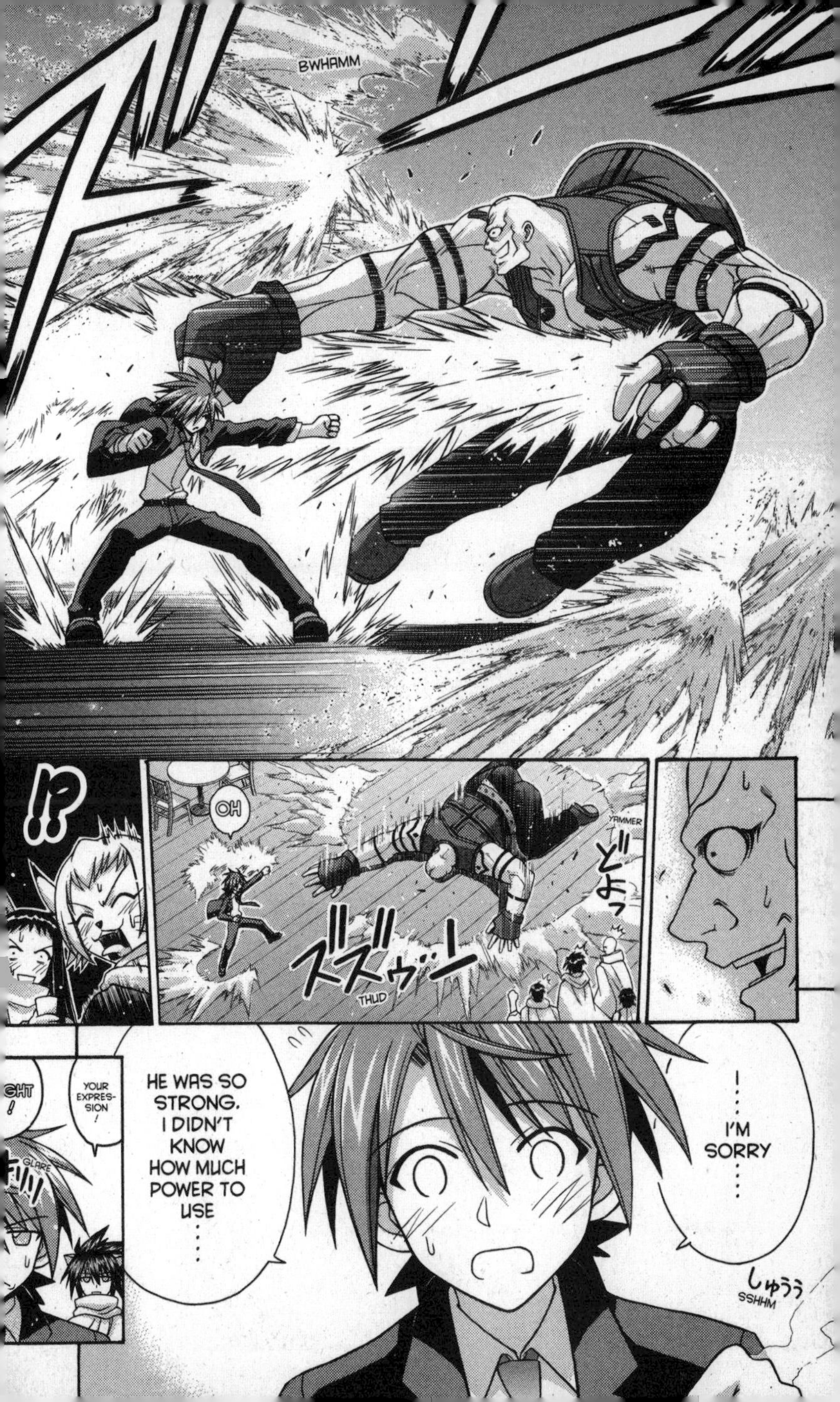
BWHAMM
OH
どよっ
YAMMER
ズズゥ…ン
THUD
!?
……I'M SORRY……
HE WAS SO STRONG. I DIDN'T KNOW HOW MUCH POWER TO USE……
しゅうう
SSHHM
YOUR EXPRES-SION!
GLARE

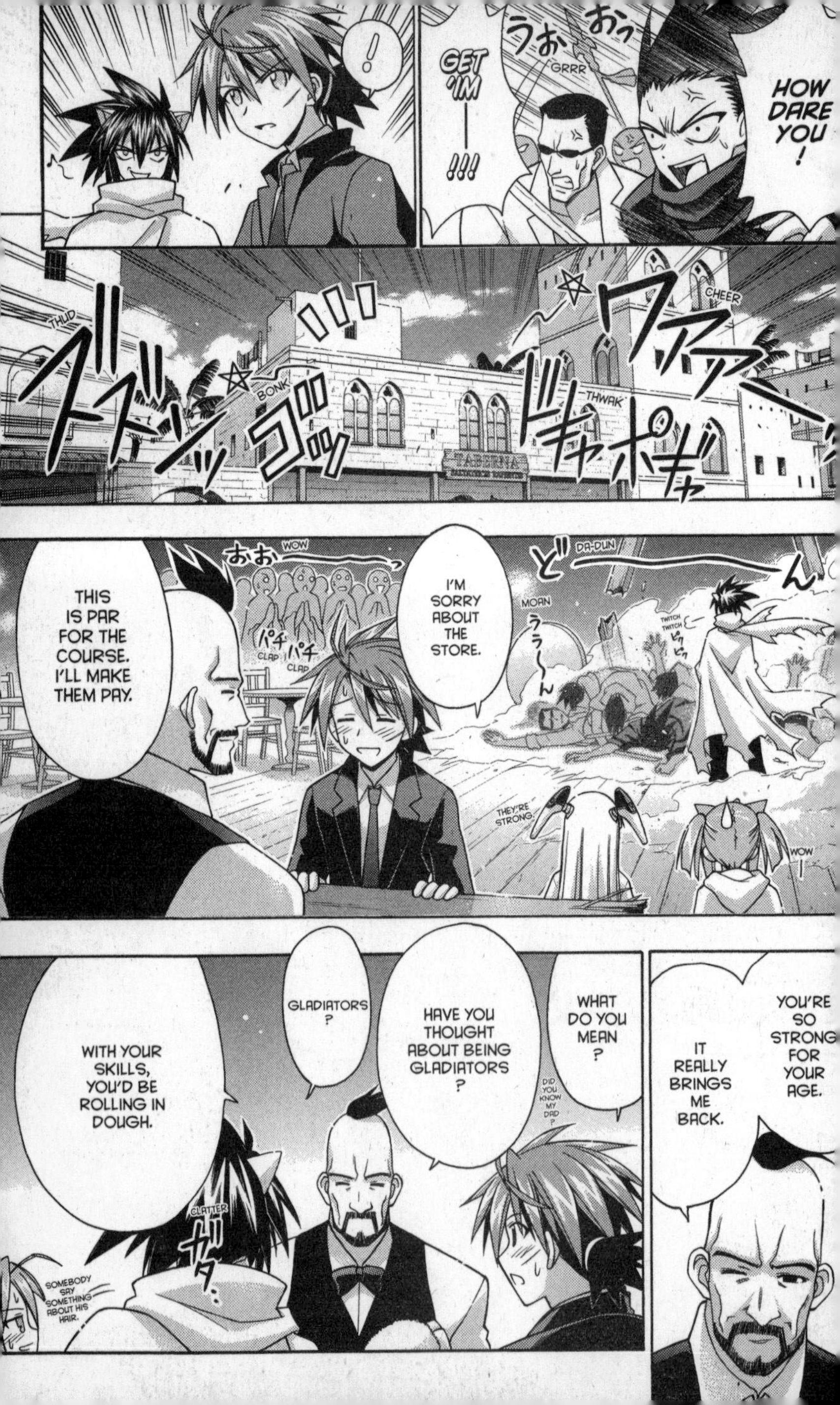
HOW DARE YOU!
うおおっ
GRRR
GET 'IM——!!!
!
CHEER
ワアア〜
THWAK
ドギャポギャ
TABERNA
BONK
ゴッ
!!!
THUD
ズドンッ
DA-DUN
どーーん
TWITCH TWITCH
ピクピク
MOAN
うう〜ん
WOW!
THEY'RE STRONG.
I'M SORRY ABOUT THE STORE.
おお
WOW
パチパチ
CLAP CLAP
THIS IS PAR FOR THE COURSE. I'LL MAKE THEM PAY.
YOU'RE SO STRONG FOR YOUR AGE.
IT REALLY BRINGS ME BACK.
WHAT DO YOU MEAN?
DID YOU KNOW MY DAD?
HAVE YOU THOUGHT ABOUT BEING GLADIATORS?
GLADIATORS?
WITH YOUR SKILLS, YOU'D BE ROLLING IN DOUGH.
CLATTER
ガタ
SOMEBODY SAY SOMETHING ABOUT HIS HAIR.

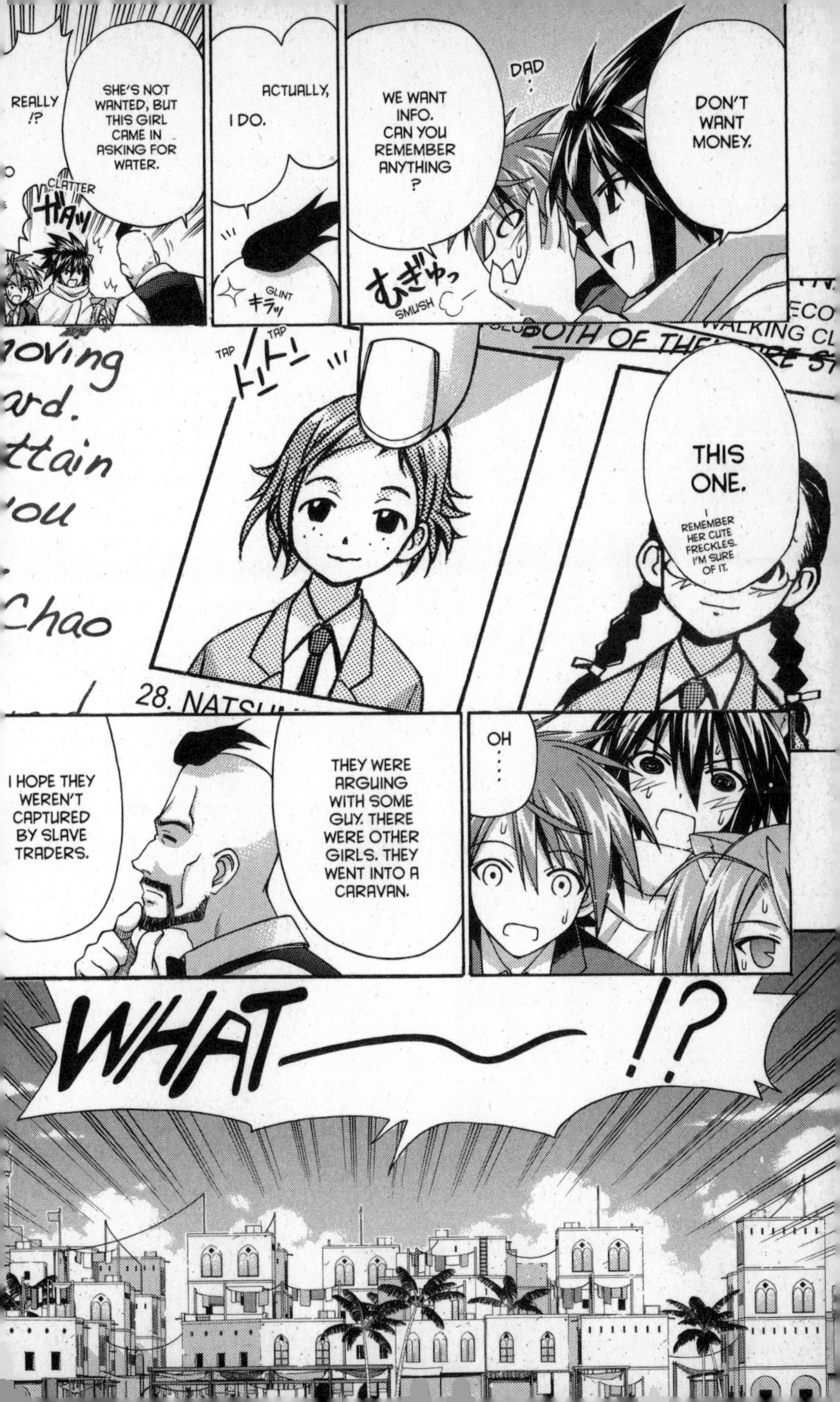

DAD...
DON'T WANT MONEY.
WE WANT INFO. CAN YOU REMEMBER ANYTHING?
むぎゅっ SMUSH
ACTUALLY, I DO.
キラッ GLINT
SHE'S NOT WANTED, BUT THIS GIRL CAME IN ASKING FOR WATER.
REALLY!?
ガタッ CLATTER
THIS ONE.
I REMEMBER HER CUTE FRECKLES. I'M SURE OF IT.
トントン TAP TAP
OH...
THEY WERE ARGUING WITH SOME GUY. THERE WERE OTHER GIRLS. THEY WENT INTO A CARAVAN.
I HOPE THEY WEREN'T CAPTURED BY SLAVE TRADERS.
WHAT——!?

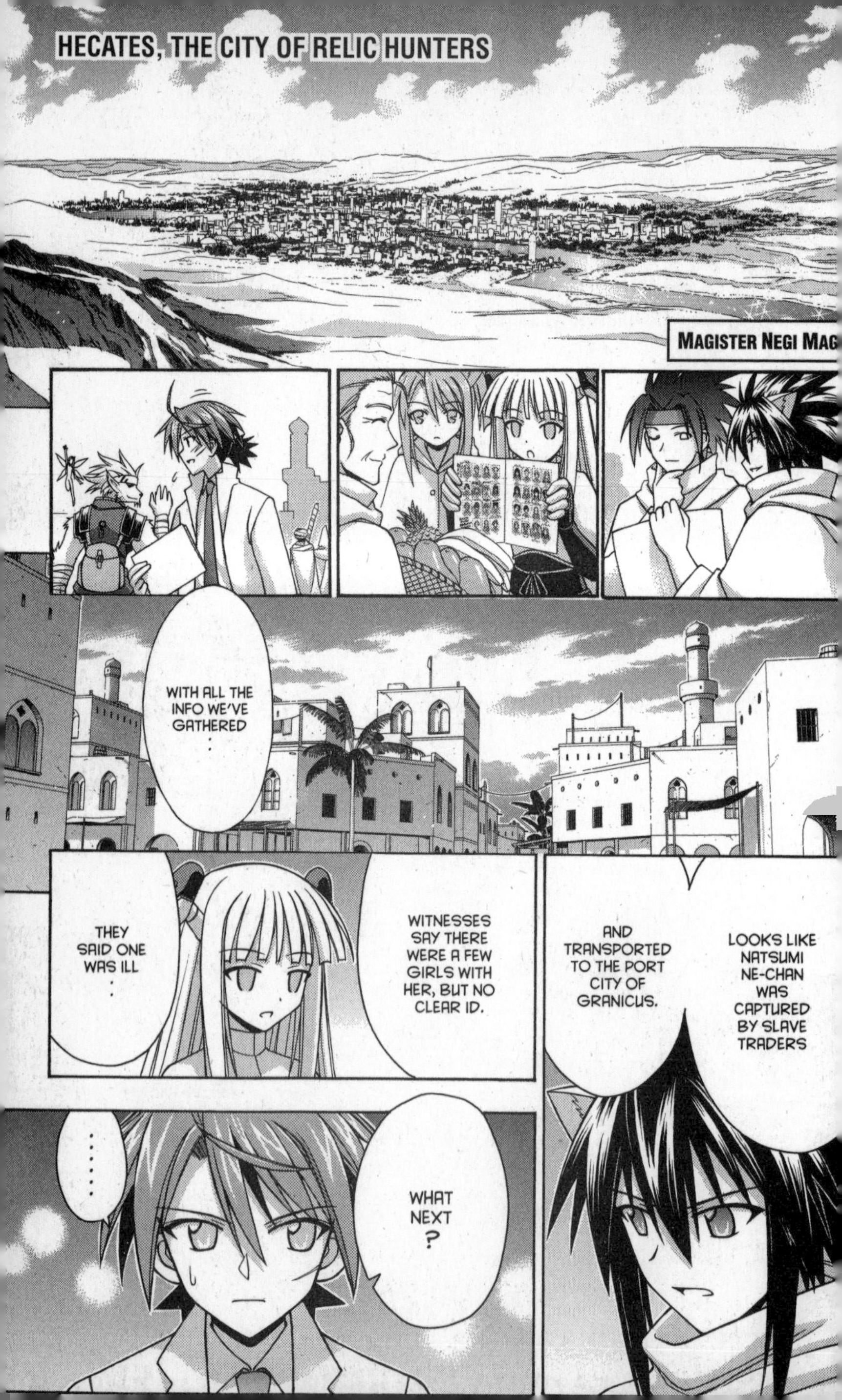
HECATES, THE CITY OF RELIC HUNTERS
MAGISTER NEGI MAG
WITH ALL THE INFO WE'VE GATHERED . .
LOOKS LIKE NATSUMI NE-CHAN WAS CAPTURED BY SLAVE TRADERS
AND TRANSPORTED TO THE PORT CITY OF GRANICUS.
WITNESSES SAY THERE WERE A FEW GIRLS WITH HER, BUT NO CLEAR ID.
THEY SAID ONE WAS ILL . .
WHAT NEXT ?
......

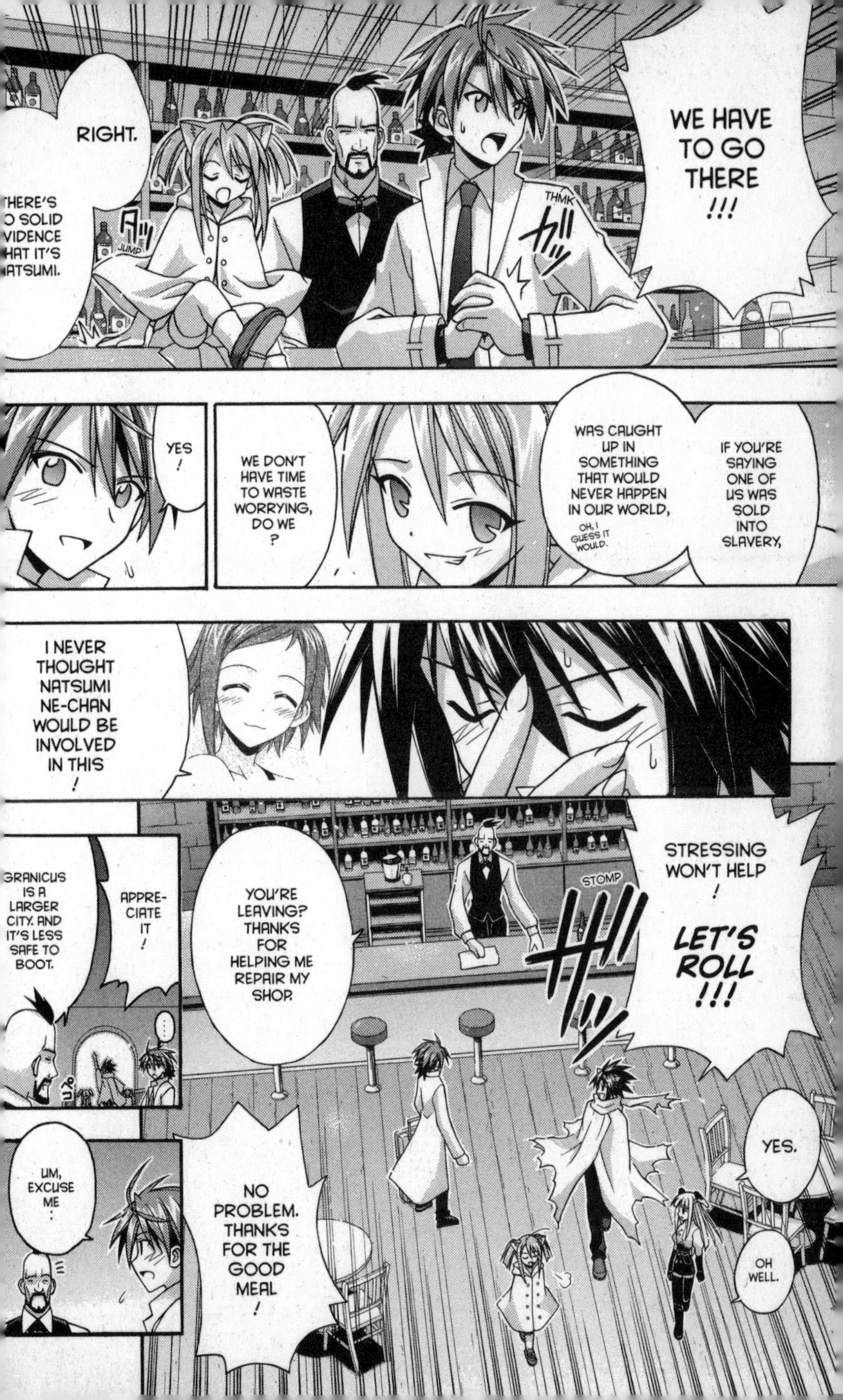

WE HAVE TO GO THERE!!!
THMK
RIGHT.
THERE'S O SOLID VIDENCE HAT IT'S ATSUMI.
JUMP
IF YOU'RE SAYING ONE OF US WAS SOLD INTO SLAVERY,
WAS CAUGHT UP IN SOMETHING THAT WOULD NEVER HAPPEN IN OUR WORLD,
OH, I GUESS IT WOULD.
WE DON'T HAVE TIME TO WASTE WORRYING, DO WE?
YES!
I NEVER THOUGHT NATSUMI NE-CHAN WOULD BE INVOLVED IN THIS!
STRESSING WON'T HELP!
LET'S ROLL!!!
STOMP
YOU'RE LEAVING? THANKS FOR HELPING ME REPAIR MY SHOP.
NO PROBLEM. THANKS FOR THE GOOD MEAL!
YES.
OH WELL.
APPRE-CIATE IT!
GRANICUS IS A LARGER CITY. AND IT'S LESS SAFE TO BOOT.
...
UM, EXCUSE ME:

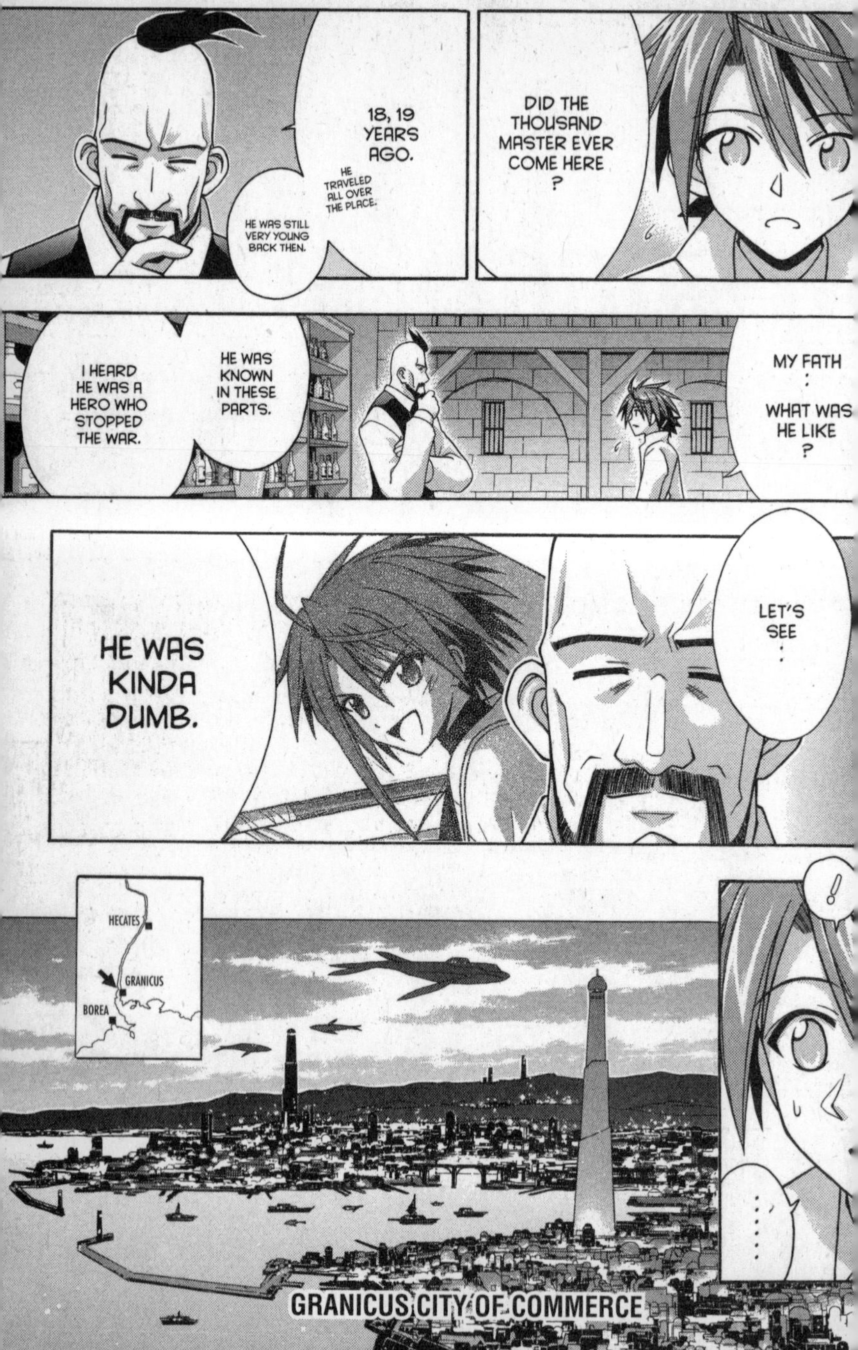
DID THE THOUSAND MASTER EVER COME HERE ?
18, 19 YEARS AGO.
HE TRAVELED ALL OVER THE PLACE.
HE WAS STILL VERY YOUNG BACK THEN.
MY FATH : WHAT WAS HE LIKE ?
HE WAS KNOWN IN THESE PARTS.
I HEARD HE WAS A HERO WHO STOPPED THE WAR.
LET'S SEE . . .
HE WAS KINDA DUMB.
!
. . . . . .
HECATES
GRANICUS
BOREA
GRANICUS CITY OF COMMERCE

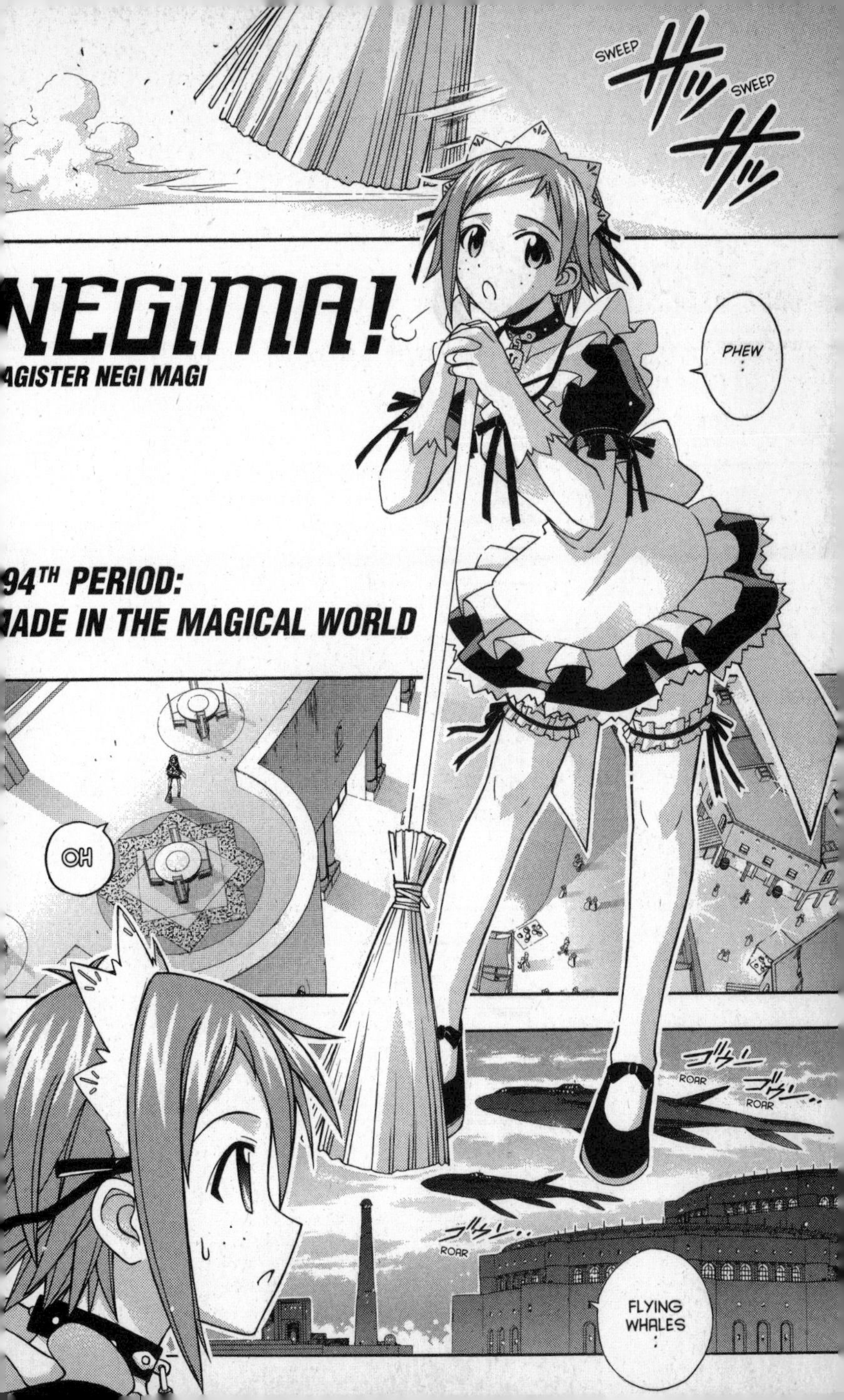
SWEEP
SWEEP
PHEW
NEGIMA!
AGISTER NEGI MAGI
94TH PERIOD:
ADE IN THE MAGICAL WORLD
OH
ROAR
ROAR
ROAR
FLYING WHALES

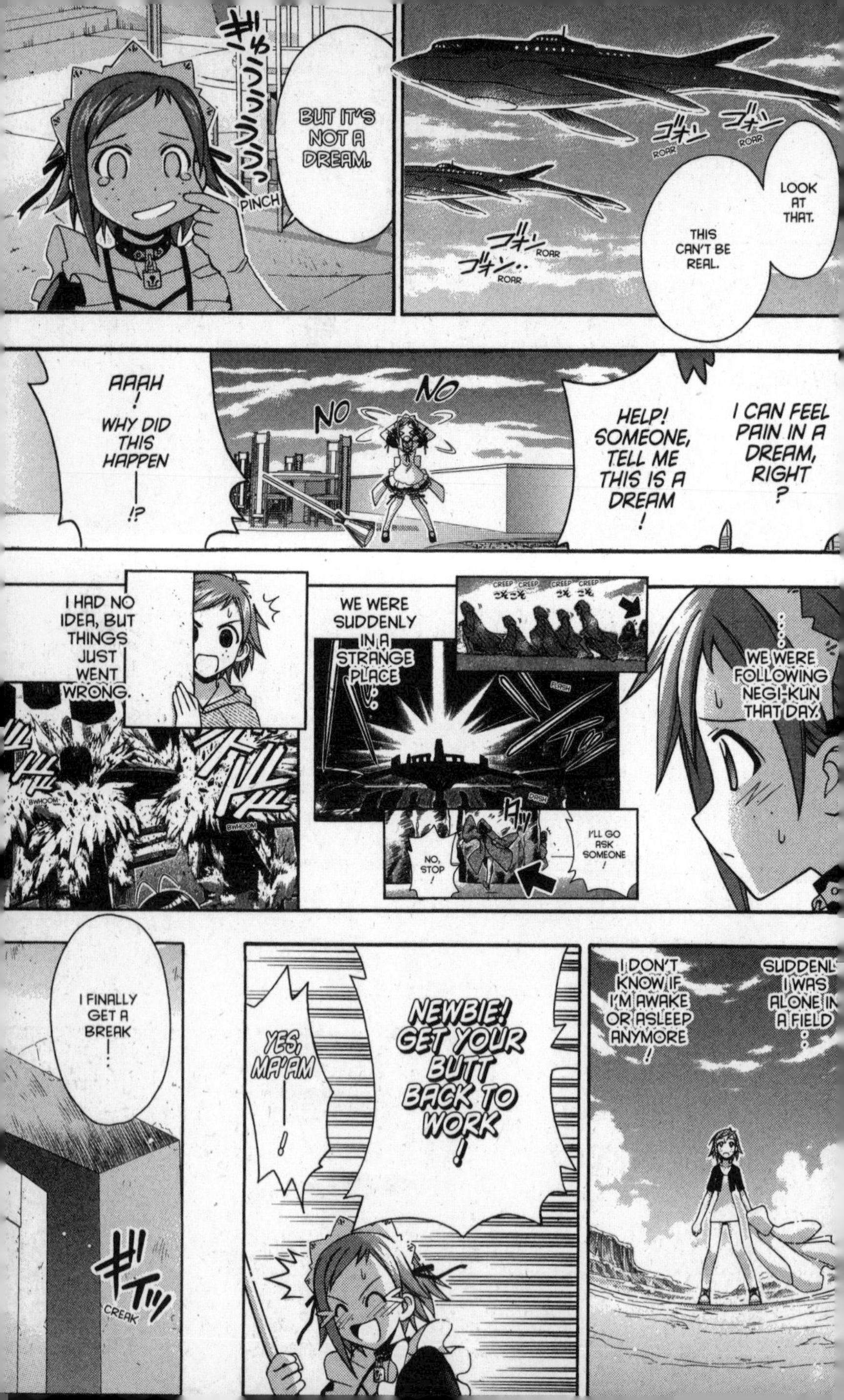
ROAR
ROAR
LOOK AT THAT.
THIS CAN'T BE REAL.
ROAR
ROAR
BUT IT'S NOT A DREAM.
PINCH
I CAN FEEL PAIN IN A DREAM, RIGHT?
HELP! SOMEONE, TELL ME THIS IS A DREAM!
NO
NO
AAAH! WHY DID THIS HAPPEN—!?
...WE WERE FOLLOWING NEGI-KUN THAT DAY.
CREEP CREEP CREEP CREEP
WE WERE SUDDENLY IN A STRANGE PLACE...
FLASH
DASH
I'LL GO ASK SOMEONE!
NO, STOP!
I HAD NO IDEA, BUT THINGS JUST WENT WRONG.
BWHOOM
BWHOOM
SUDDENL I WAS ALONE IN A FIELD...
I DON'T KNOW IF I'M AWAKE OR ASLEEP ANYMORE!
NEWBIE! GET YOUR BUTT BACK TO WORK!
YES, MA'AM—!
I FINALLY GET A BREAK!
CREAK

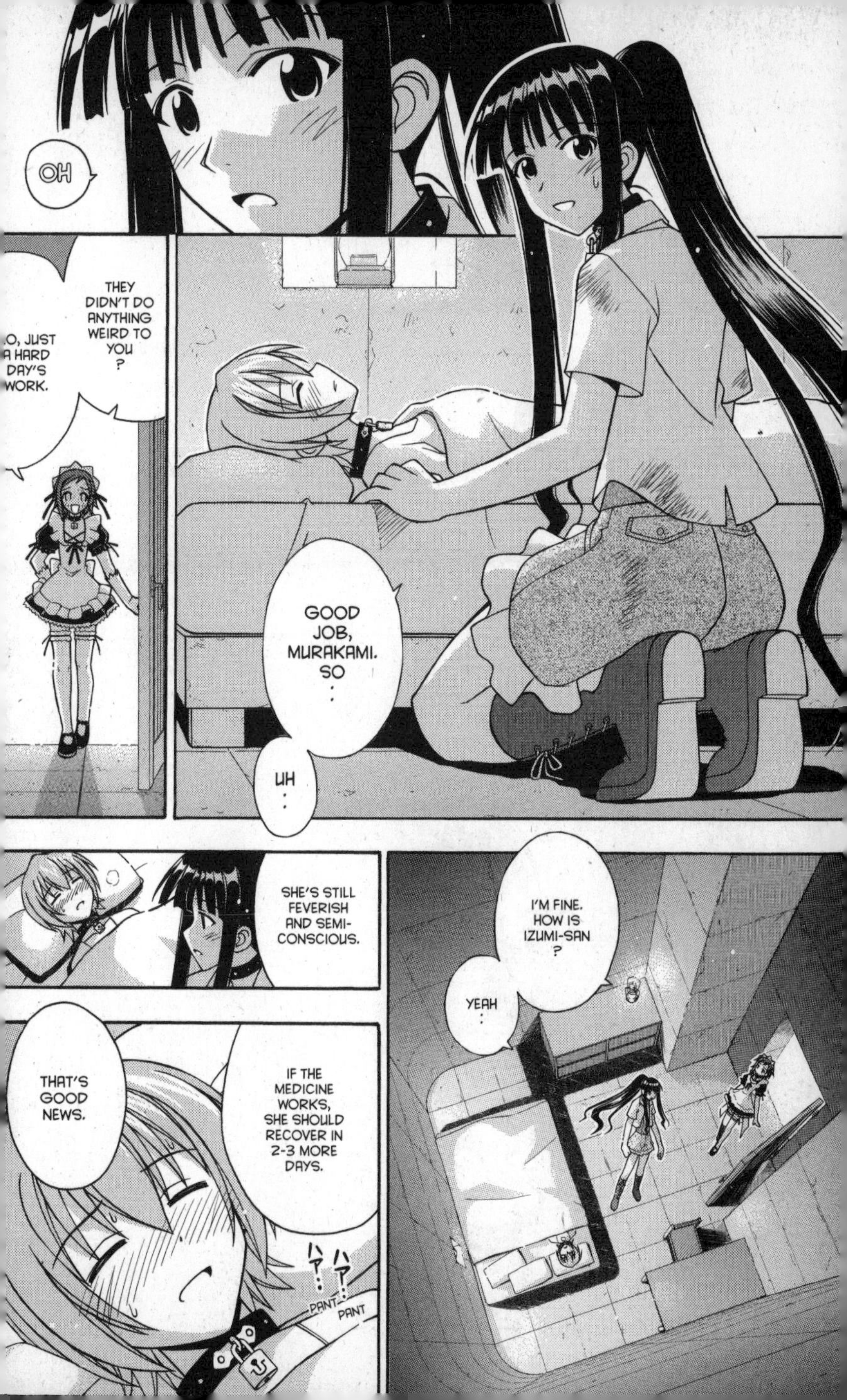
OH
GOOD JOB, MURAKAMI. SO...
UH...
THEY DIDN'T DO ANYTHING WEIRD TO YOU?
O, JUST A HARD DAY'S WORK.
I'M FINE. HOW IS IZUMI-SAN?
YEAH...
SHE'S STILL FEVERISH AND SEMI-CONSCIOUS.
IF THE MEDICINE WORKS, SHE SHOULD RECOVER IN 2-3 MORE DAYS.
THAT'S GOOD NEWS.
ハァ… ハァ…
PANT PANT

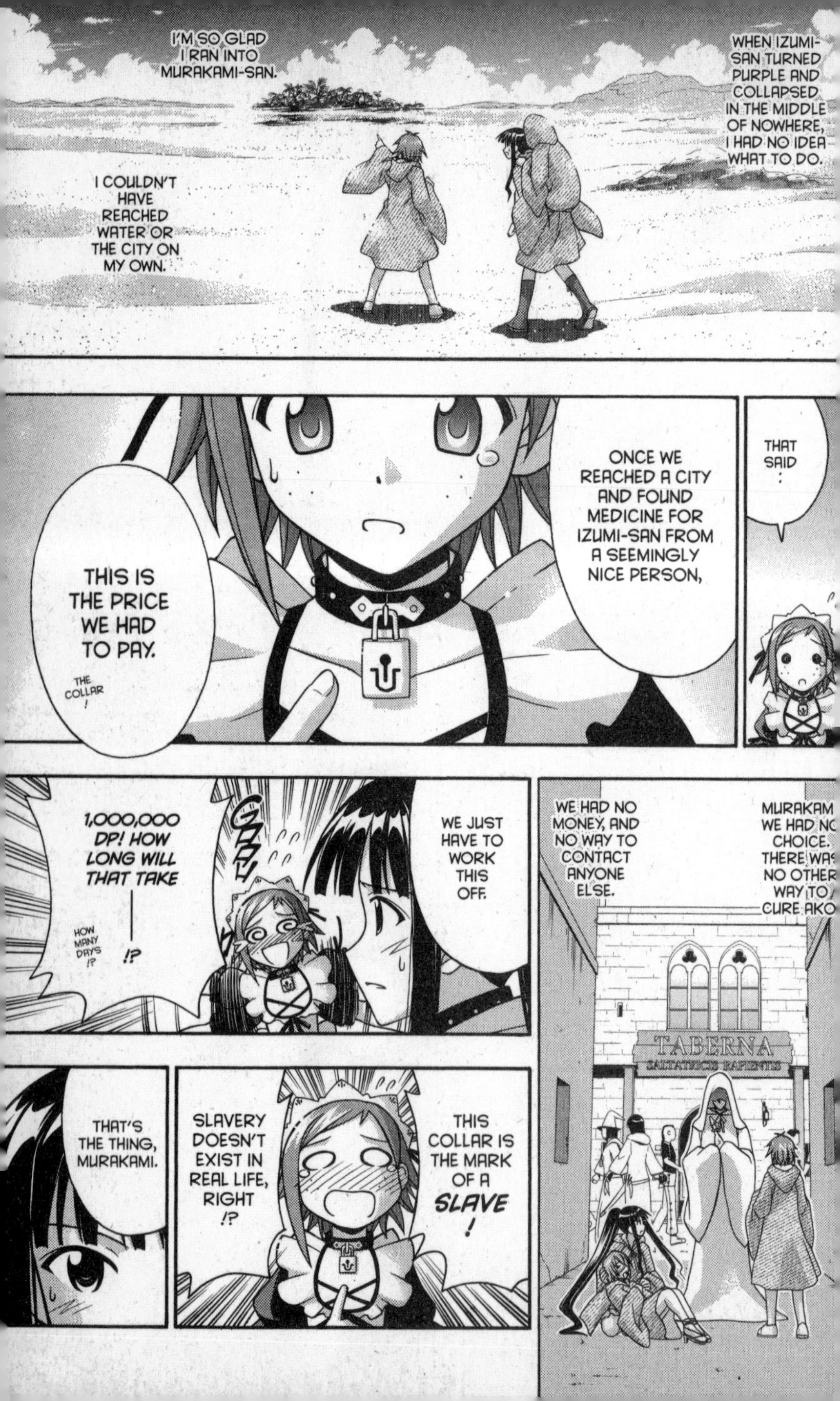
WHEN IZUMI-SAN TURNED PURPLE AND COLLAPSED IN THE MIDDLE OF NOWHERE, I HAD NO IDEA WHAT TO DO.
I'M SO GLAD I RAN INTO MURAKAMI-SAN.
I COULDN'T HAVE REACHED WATER OR THE CITY ON MY OWN.
THAT SAID :
ONCE WE REACHED A CITY AND FOUND MEDICINE FOR IZUMI-SAN FROM A SEEMINGLY NICE PERSON,
THIS IS THE PRICE WE HAD TO PAY.
THE COLLAR !
MURAKAM WE HAD N CHOICE. THERE WAS NO OTHER WAY TO CURE AKO
WE HAD NO MONEY, AND NO WAY TO CONTACT ANYONE ELSE.
TABERNA
SALTATRICIS RAPIENTIS
WE JUST HAVE TO WORK THIS OFF.
1,000,000 DP! HOW LONG WILL THAT TAKE —— !?
HOW MANY DAYS !?
THIS COLLAR IS THE MARK OF A SLAVE !
SLAVERY DOESN'T EXIST IN REAL LIFE, RIGHT !?
THAT'S THE THING, MURAKAMI.

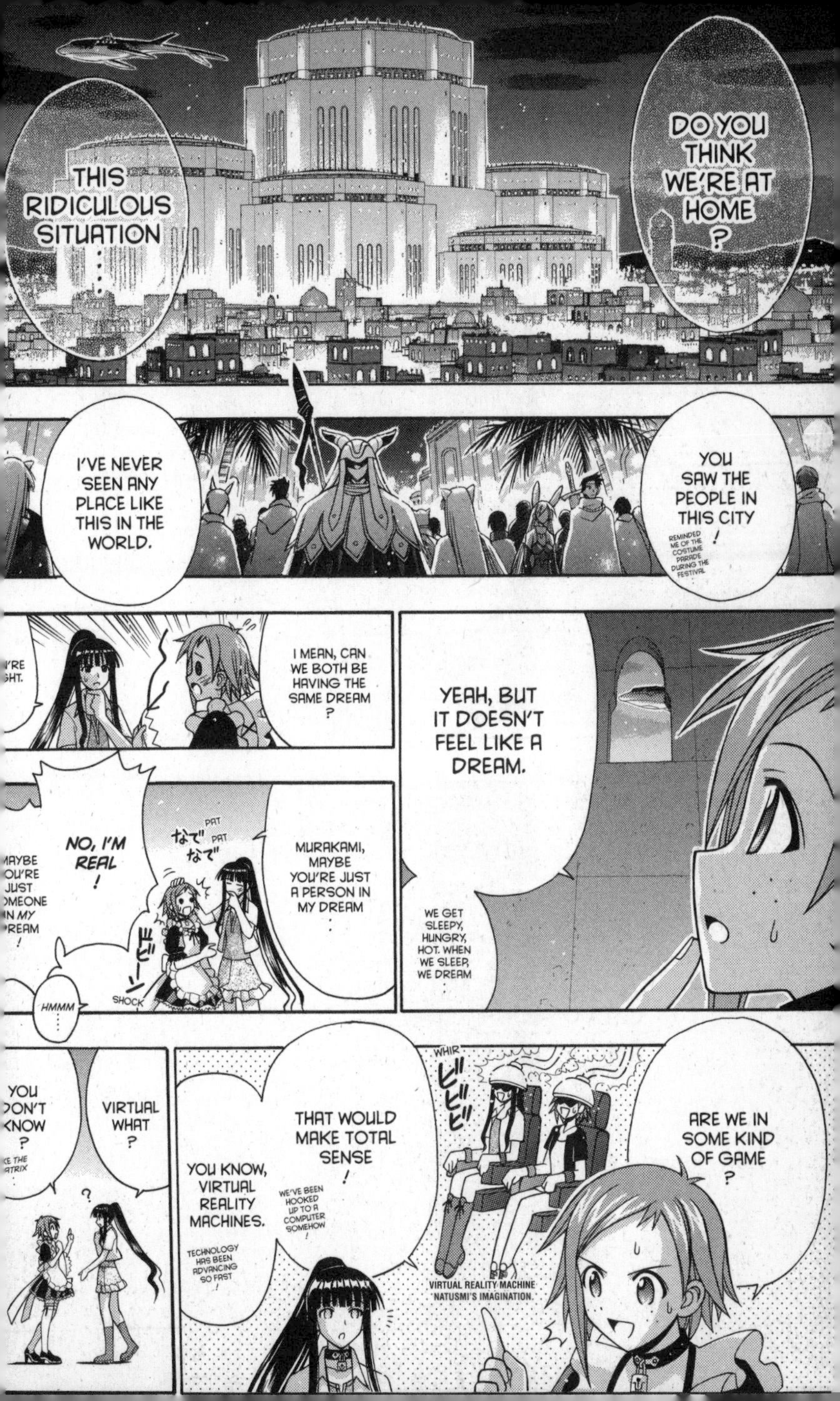

DO YOU THINK WE'RE AT HOME?
THIS RIDICULOUS SITUATION......
YOU SAW THE PEOPLE IN THIS CITY!
REMINDED ME OF THE COSTUME PARADE DURING THE FESTIVAL
I'VE NEVER SEEN ANY PLACE LIKE THIS IN THE WORLD.
YEAH, BUT IT DOESN'T FEEL LIKE A DREAM.
WE GET SLEEPY, HUNGRY, HOT. WHEN WE SLEEP, WE DREAM...
I MEAN, CAN WE BOTH BE HAVING THE SAME DREAM?
MURAKAMI, MAYBE YOU'RE JUST A PERSON IN MY DREAM...
なで なで
PAT PAT
NO, I'M REAL!
ビビーン
SHOCK
HMMM......
ARE WE IN SOME KIND OF GAME?
ビビビ
WHIR
VIRTUAL REALITY MACHINE NATUSMI'S IMAGINATION.
THAT WOULD MAKE TOTAL SENSE!
WE'VE BEEN HOOKED UP TO A COMPUTER SOMEHOW!
YOU KNOW, VIRTUAL REALITY MACHINES.
TECHNOLOGY HAS BEEN ADVANCING SO FAST!
VIRTUAL WHAT?

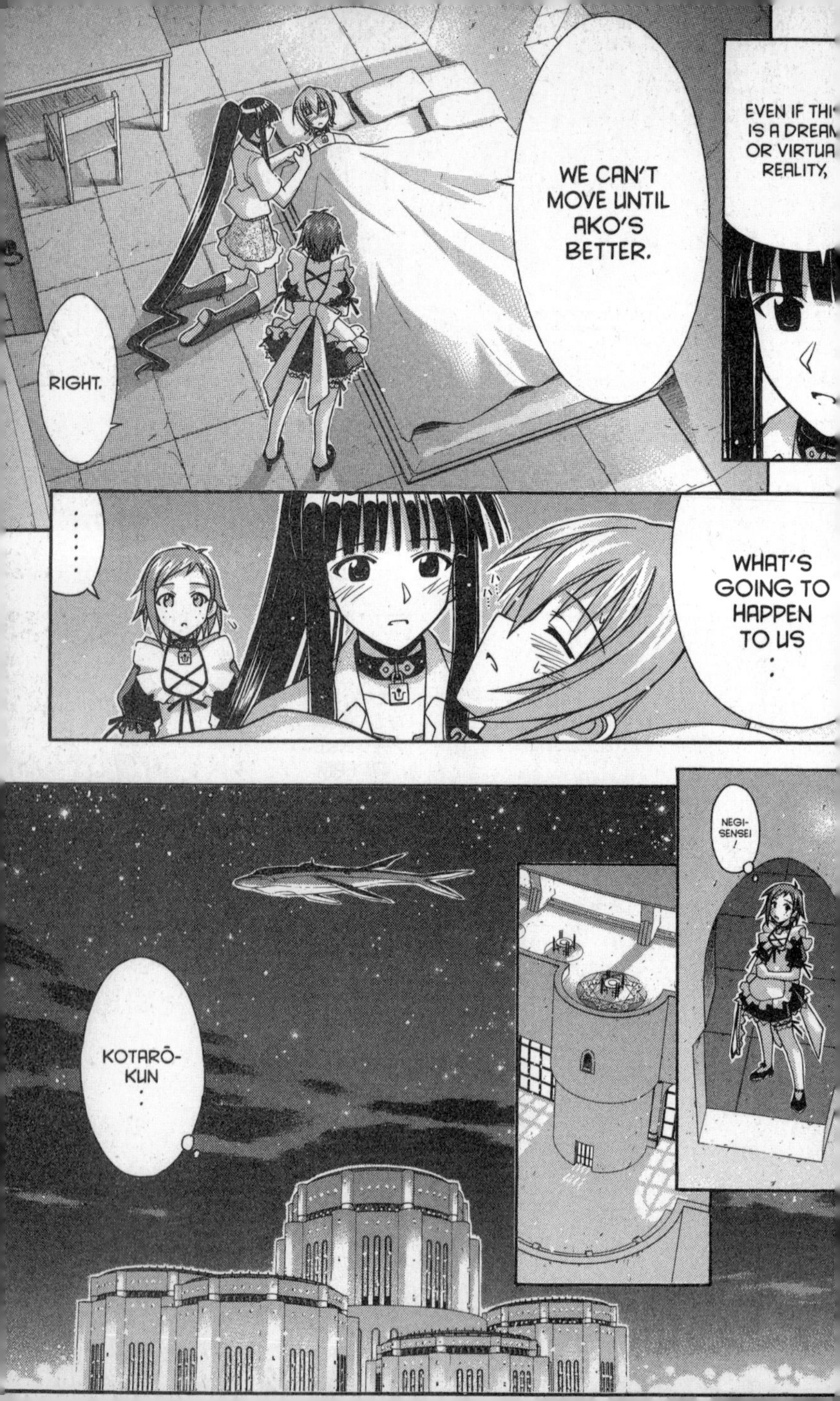
EVEN IF THI
IS A DREAM
OR VIRTUA
REALITY,
WE CAN'T MOVE UNTIL AKO'S BETTER.
RIGHT.
WHAT'S GOING TO HAPPEN TO US
:
......
NEGI-SENSEI
!
KOTARŌ-KUN
:

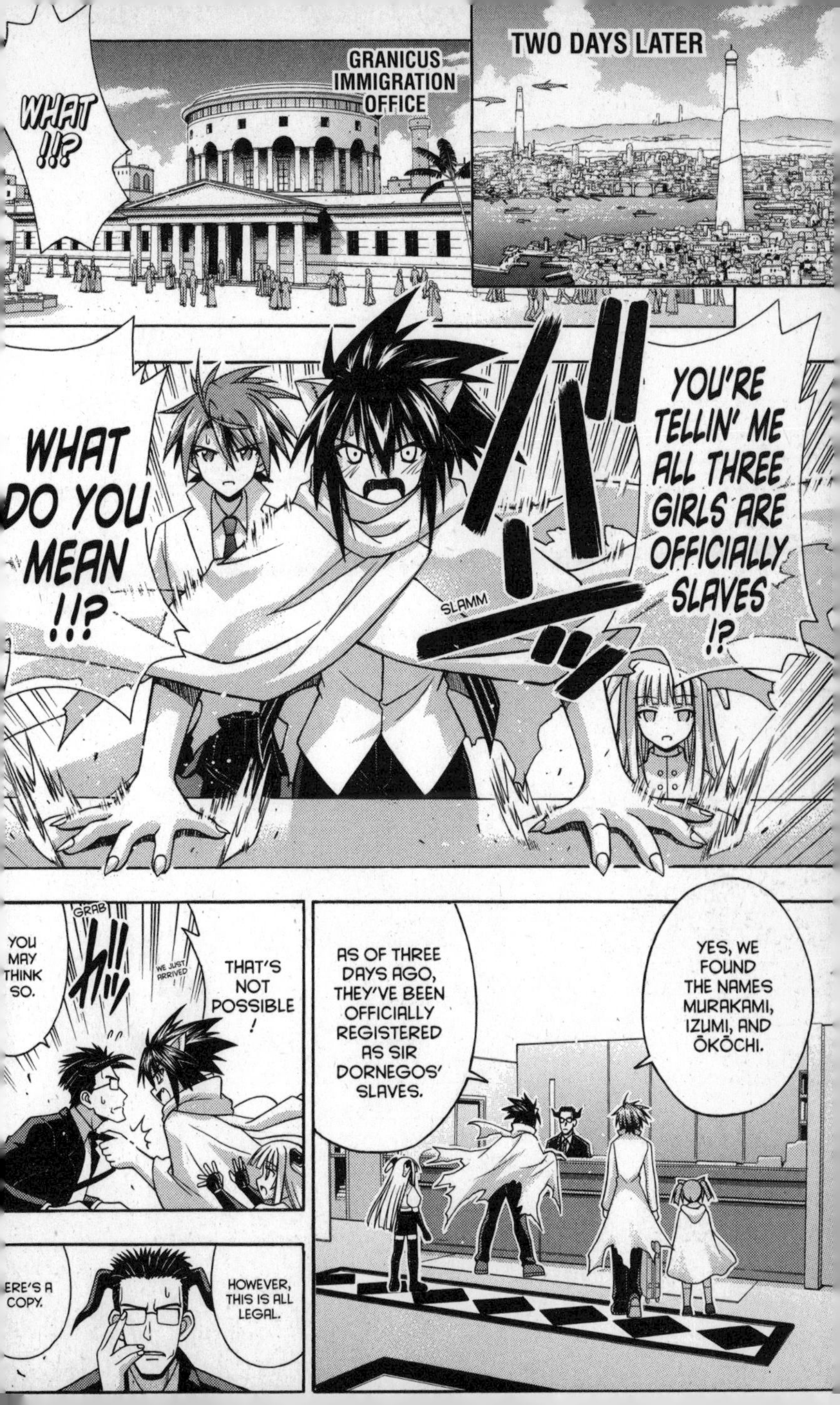

TWO DAYS LATER
GRANICUS IMMIGRATION OFFICE
WHAT !!?
YOU'RE TELLIN' ME ALL THREE GIRLS ARE OFFICIALLY SLAVES !?
SLAMM
WHAT DO YOU MEAN !!?
YES, WE FOUND THE NAMES MURAKAMI, IZUMI, AND ŌKŌCHI.
AS OF THREE DAYS AGO, THEY'VE BEEN OFFICIALLY REGISTERED AS SIR DORNEGOS' SLAVES.
THAT'S NOT POSSIBLE !
WE JUST ARRIVED
GRAB
YOU MAY THINK SO.
HOWEVER, THIS IS ALL LEGAL.
ERE'S A COPY.

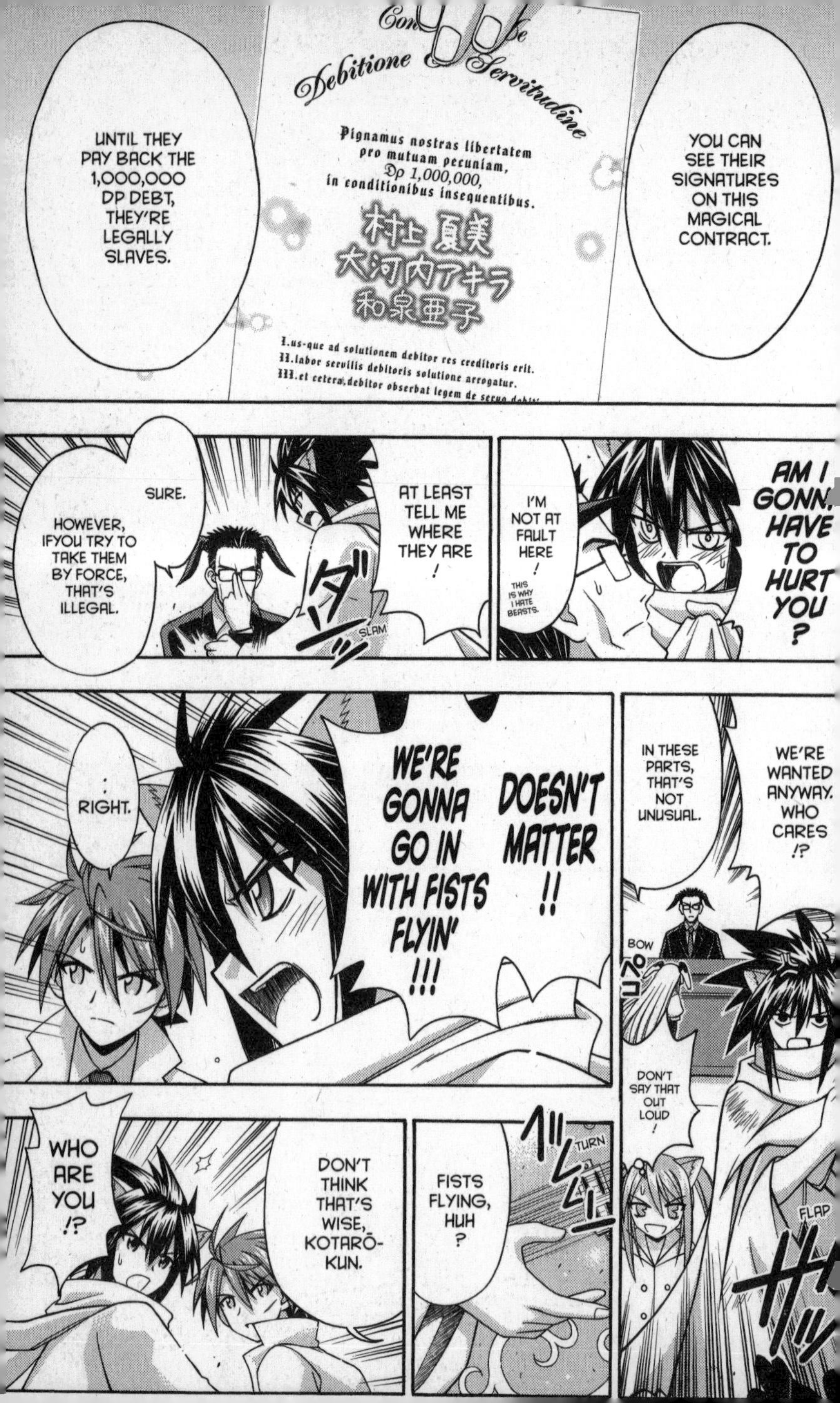
YOU CAN SEE THEIR SIGNATURES ON THIS MAGICAL CONTRACT.
Con... de Debitione & Servitudine
Pignamus nostras libertatem pro mutuam pecuniam, Dp 1,000,000, in conditionibus insequentibus.
村上 夏美
大河内アキラ
和泉亜子
I.us-que ad solutionem debitor res creditoris erit.
II.labor servilis debitoris solutione arrogatur.
III.et cetera,debitor obserbat legem de servo debit
UNTIL THEY PAY BACK THE 1,000,000 DP DEBT, THEY'RE LEGALLY SLAVES.
AM I GONNA HAVE TO HURT YOU?
I'M NOT AT FAULT HERE!
THIS IS WHY I HATE BEASTS.
AT LEAST TELL ME WHERE THEY ARE!
SLAM
SURE.
HOWEVER, IFYOU TRY TO TAKE THEM BY FORCE, THAT'S ILLEGAL.
WE'RE WANTED ANYWAY. WHO CARES!?
IN THESE PARTS, THAT'S NOT UNUSUAL.
BOW
DON'T SAY THAT OUT LOUD!
FLAP
DOESN'T MATTER!!
WE'RE GONNA GO IN WITH FISTS FLYIN'!!!
: RIGHT.
FISTS FLYING, HUH?
TURN
DON'T THINK THAT'S WISE, KOTARŌ-KUN.
WHO ARE YOU!?

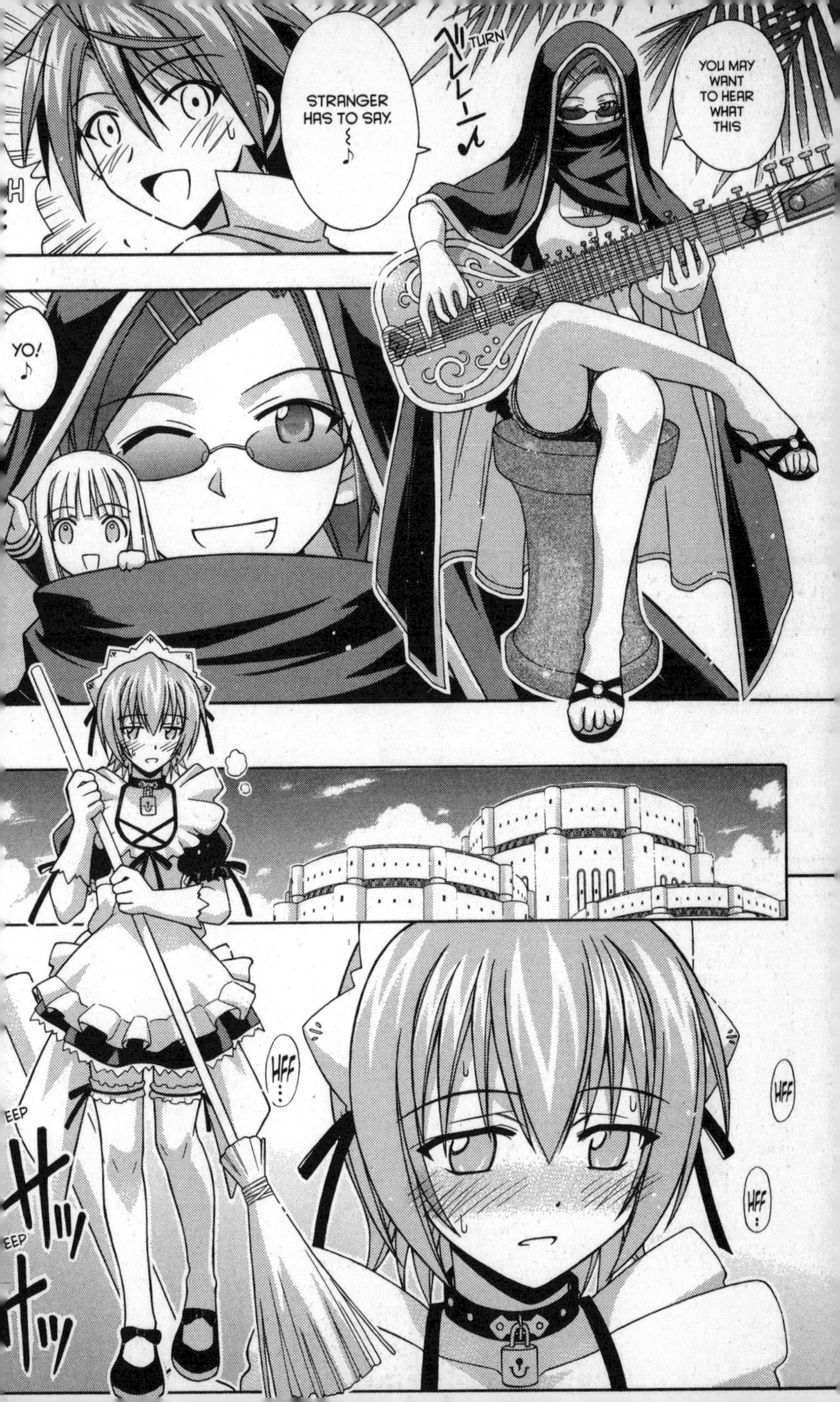
YOU MAY WANT TO HEAR WHAT THIS
TURN
STRANGER HAS TO SAY. ♪
YO! ♪
HFF
HFF
HFF...
EEP
EEP

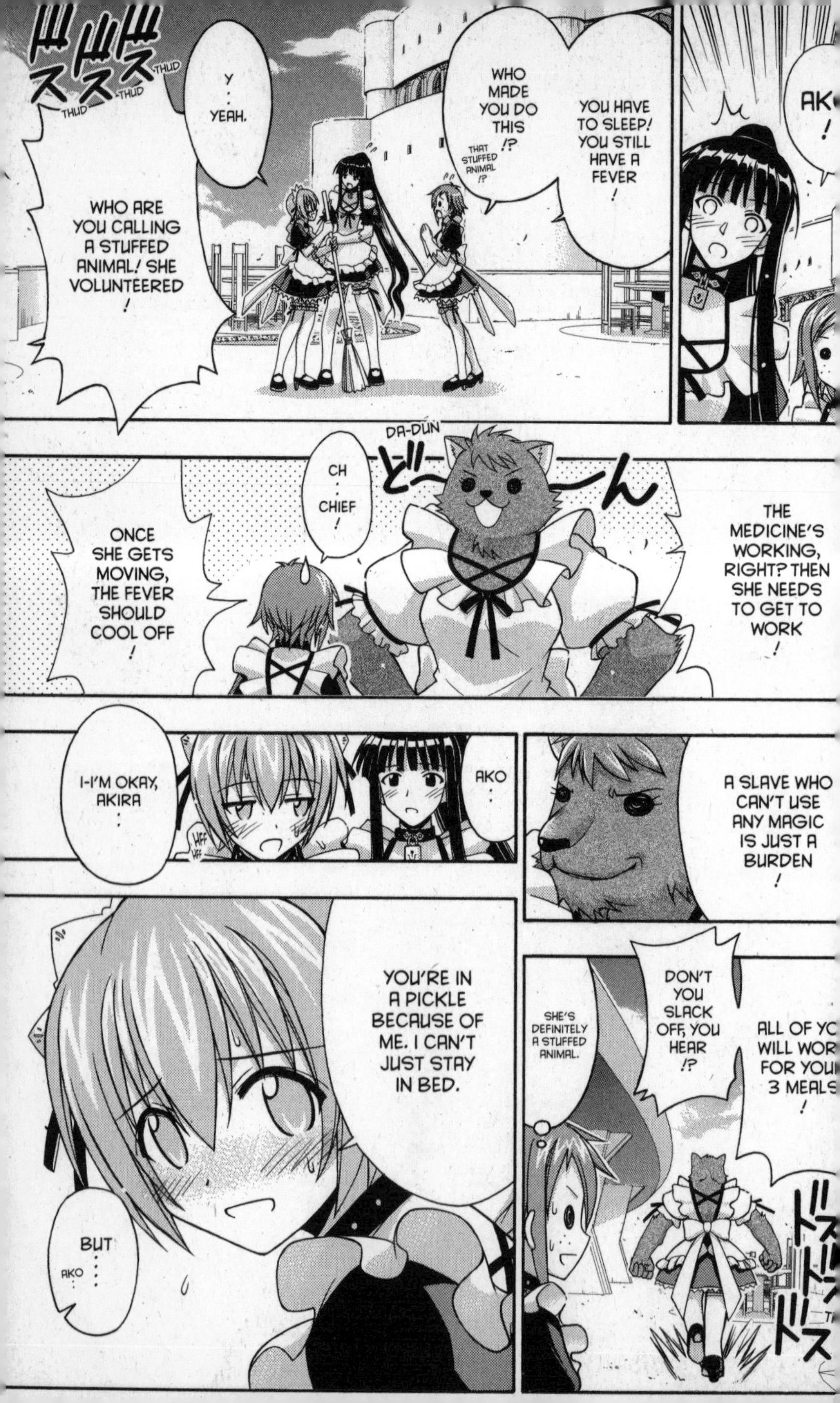
AK!
YOU HAVE TO SLEEP! YOU STILL HAVE A FEVER!
WHO MADE YOU DO THIS!?
THAT STUFFED ANIMAL!?
Y... YEAH.
THUD THUD THUD
WHO ARE YOU CALLING A STUFFED ANIMAL! SHE VOLUNTEERED!
THE MEDICINE'S WORKING, RIGHT? THEN SHE NEEDS TO GET TO WORK!
DA-DUN
CH... CHIEF!
ONCE SHE GETS MOVING, THE FEVER SHOULD COOL OFF!
A SLAVE WHO CAN'T USE ANY MAGIC IS JUST A BURDEN!
AKO...
HFF HFF
I-I'M OKAY, AKIRA...
ALL OF YO WILL WOR FOR YOU 3 MEALS!
DON'T YOU SLACK OFF, YOU HEAR!?
SHE'S DEFINITELY A STUFFED ANIMAL.
YOU'RE IN A PICKLE BECAUSE OF ME. I CAN'T JUST STAY IN BED.
BUT...
AKO...

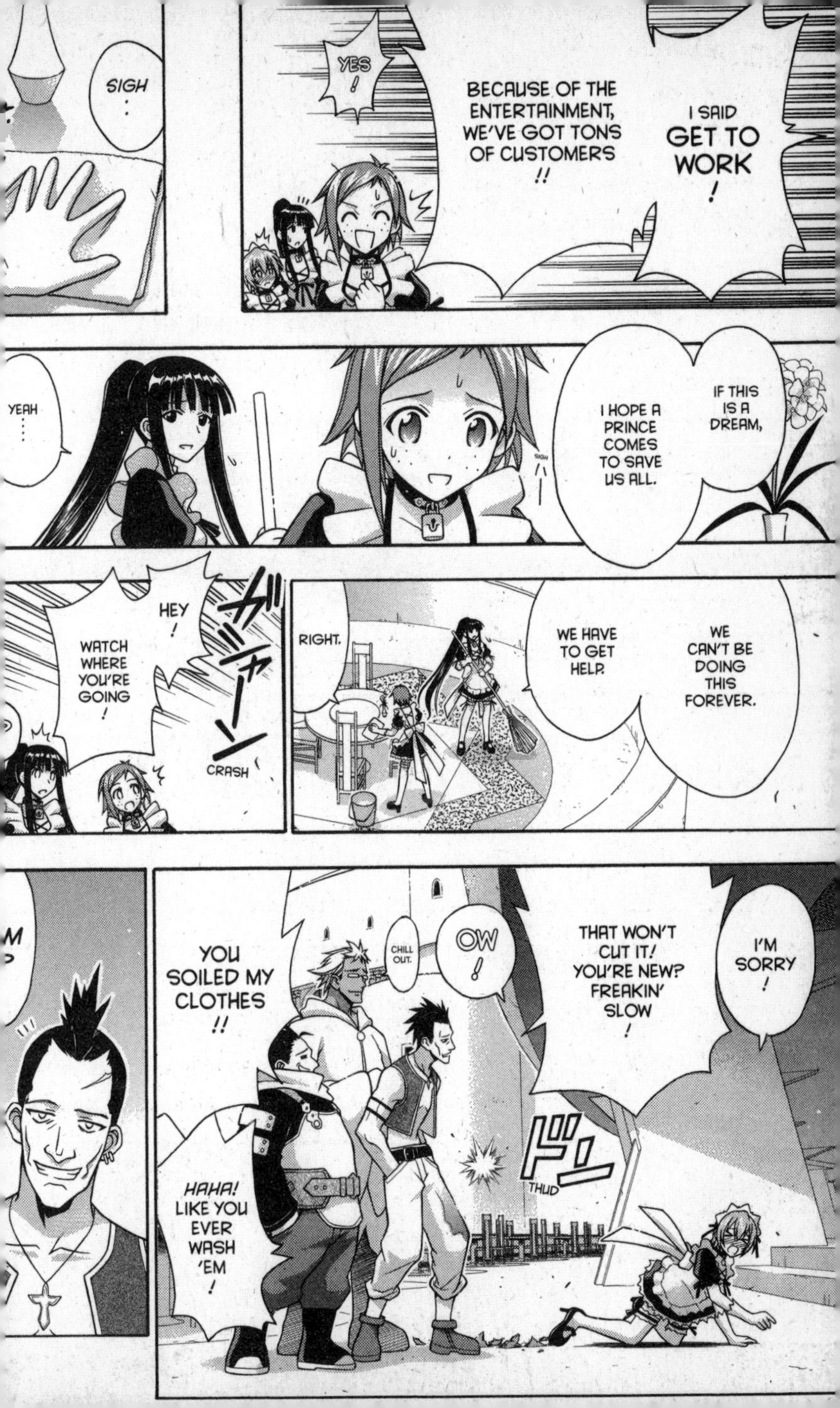
I SAID GET TO WORK!
BECAUSE OF THE ENTERTAINMENT, WE'VE GOT TONS OF CUSTOMERS!!
YES!
SIGH...
IF THIS IS A DREAM,
I HOPE A PRINCE COMES TO SAVE US ALL.
SIGH
YEAH...
WE CAN'T BE DOING THIS FOREVER.
WE HAVE TO GET HELP.
RIGHT.
HEY!
WATCH WHERE YOU'RE GOING!
CRASH
I'M SORRY!
THAT WON'T CUT IT! YOU'RE NEW? FREAKIN' SLOW!
OW!
CHILL OUT.
YOU SOILED MY CLOTHES!!
THUD
HAHA! LIKE YOU EVER WASH 'EM!

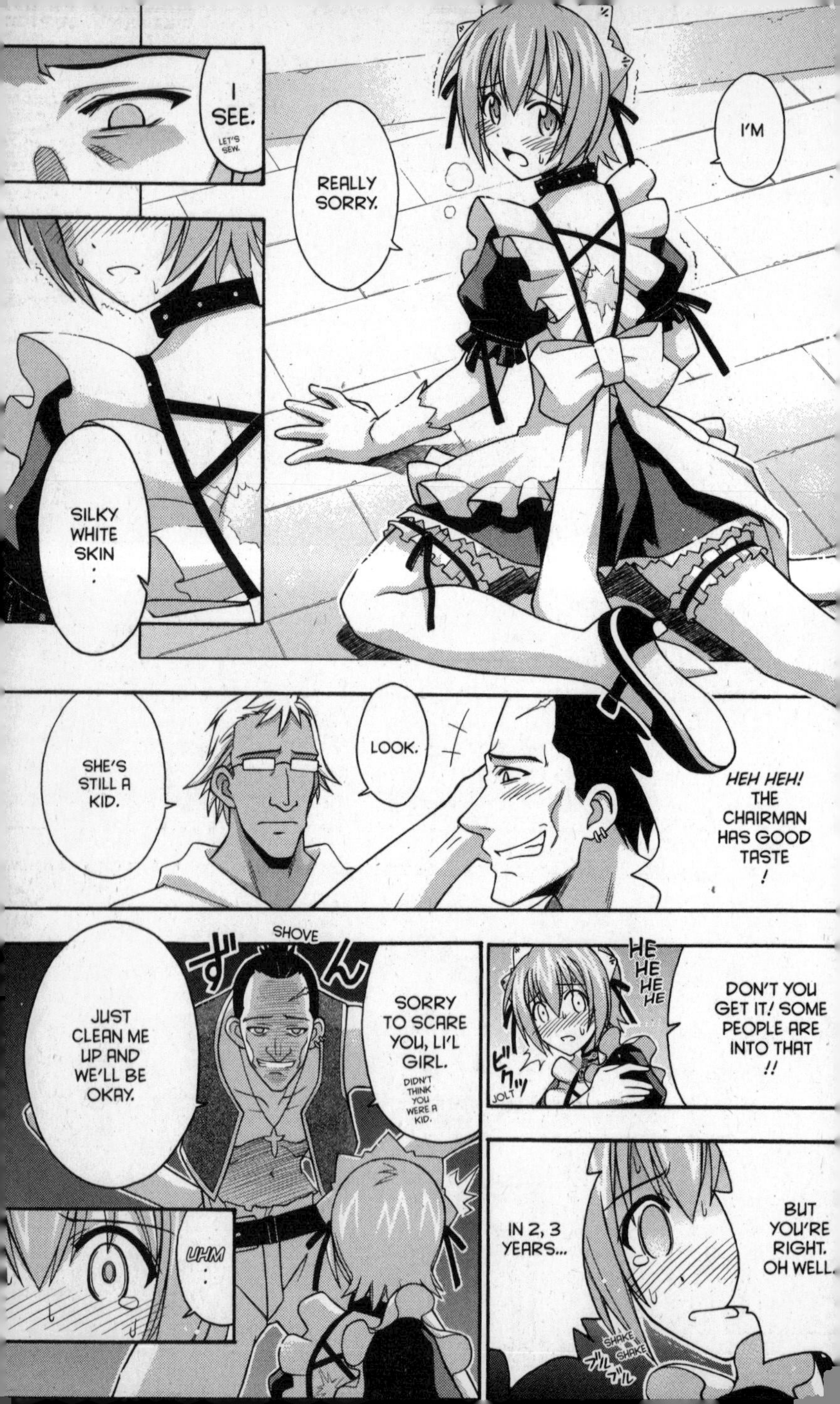
I'M
REALLY SORRY.
I SEE.
LET'S SEW.
SILKY WHITE SKIN . . .
HEH HEH! THE CHAIRMAN HAS GOOD TASTE !
LOOK.
SHE'S STILL A KID.
HE HE HE HE
DON'T YOU GET IT! SOME PEOPLE ARE INTO THAT !!
JOLT
BUT YOU'RE RIGHT. OH WELL.
IN 2, 3 YEARS...
SHAKE SHAKE
SHOVE
SORRY TO SCARE YOU, LI'L GIRL.
DIDN'T THINK YOU WERE A KID.
JUST CLEAN ME UP AND WE'LL BE OKAY.
UHM . .

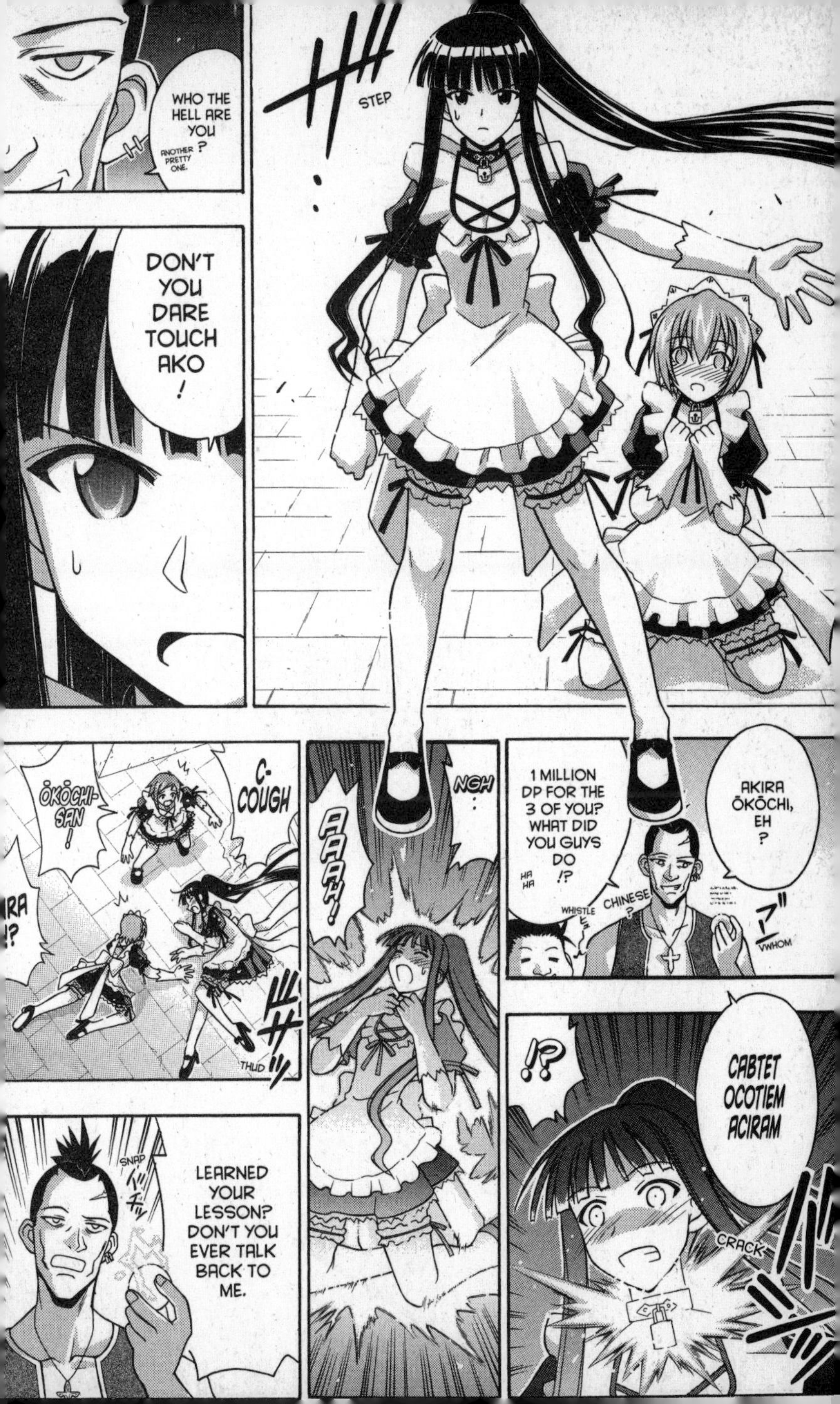
STEP
WHO THE HELL ARE YOU?
ANOTHER PRETTY ONE.
DON'T YOU DARE TOUCH AKO!
AKIRA ŌKŌCHI, EH?
VWHOM
1 MILLION DP FOR THE 3 OF YOU? WHAT DID YOU GUYS DO!?
HA HA
CHINESE?
WHISTLE
CABTET OCOTIEM ACIRAM
!?
CRACK
NGH
AAAAH!
ŌKŌCHI-SAN!
C-COUGH
THUD
SNAP
LEARNED YOUR LESSON? DON'T YOU EVER TALK BACK TO ME.

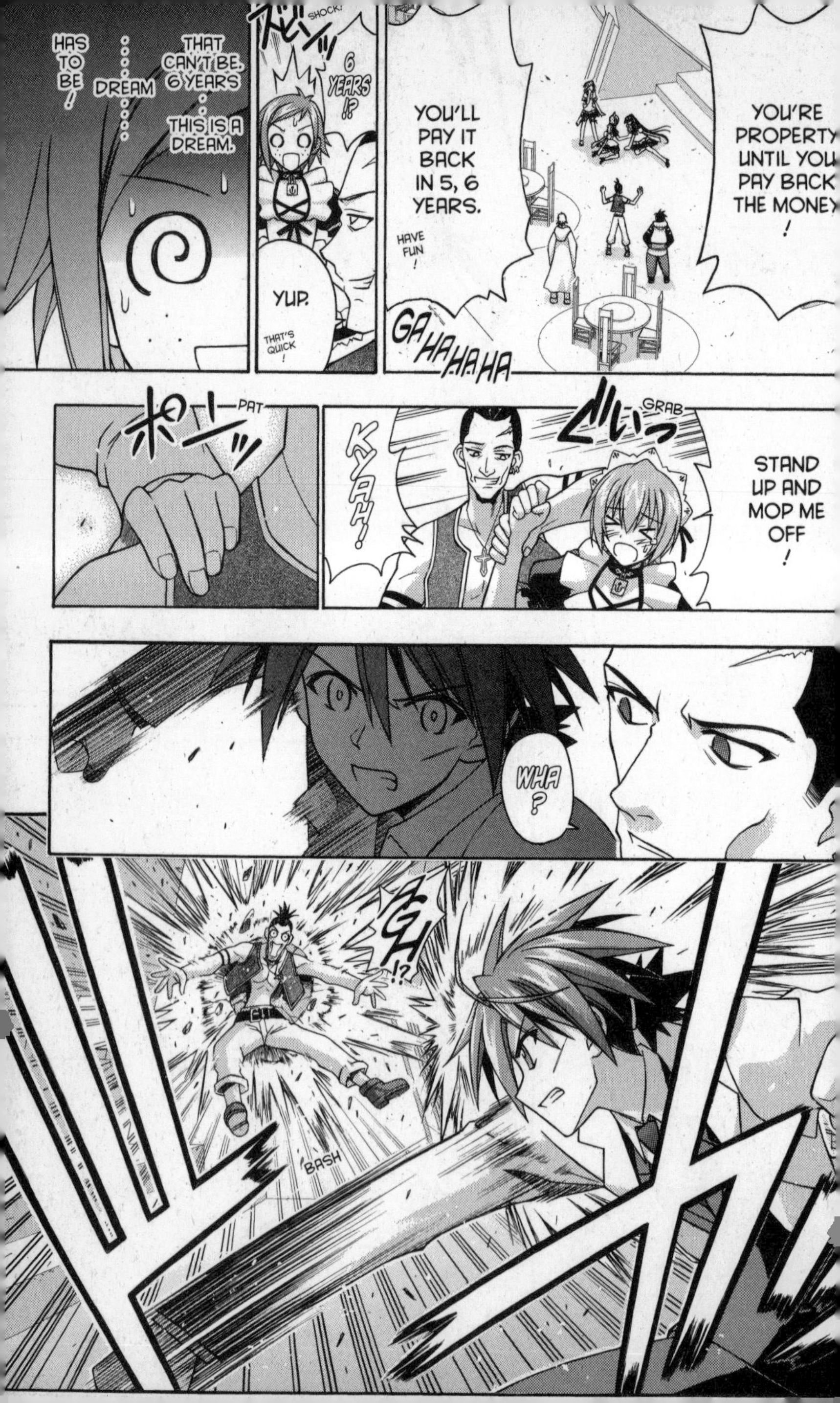
YOU'RE PROPERTY UNTIL YOU PAY BACK THE MONEY!
YOU'LL PAY IT BACK IN 5, 6 YEARS.
HAVE FUN!
GAHAHAHAHA
SHOCK!
6 YEARS!?
YUP.
THAT'S QUICK!
THAT CAN'T BE. 6 YEARS...
THIS IS A DREAM.
DREAM......
HAS TO BE!
GRAB
STAND UP AND MOP ME OFF!
KYAAH!
PAT
WHA?
AGH!?
BASH

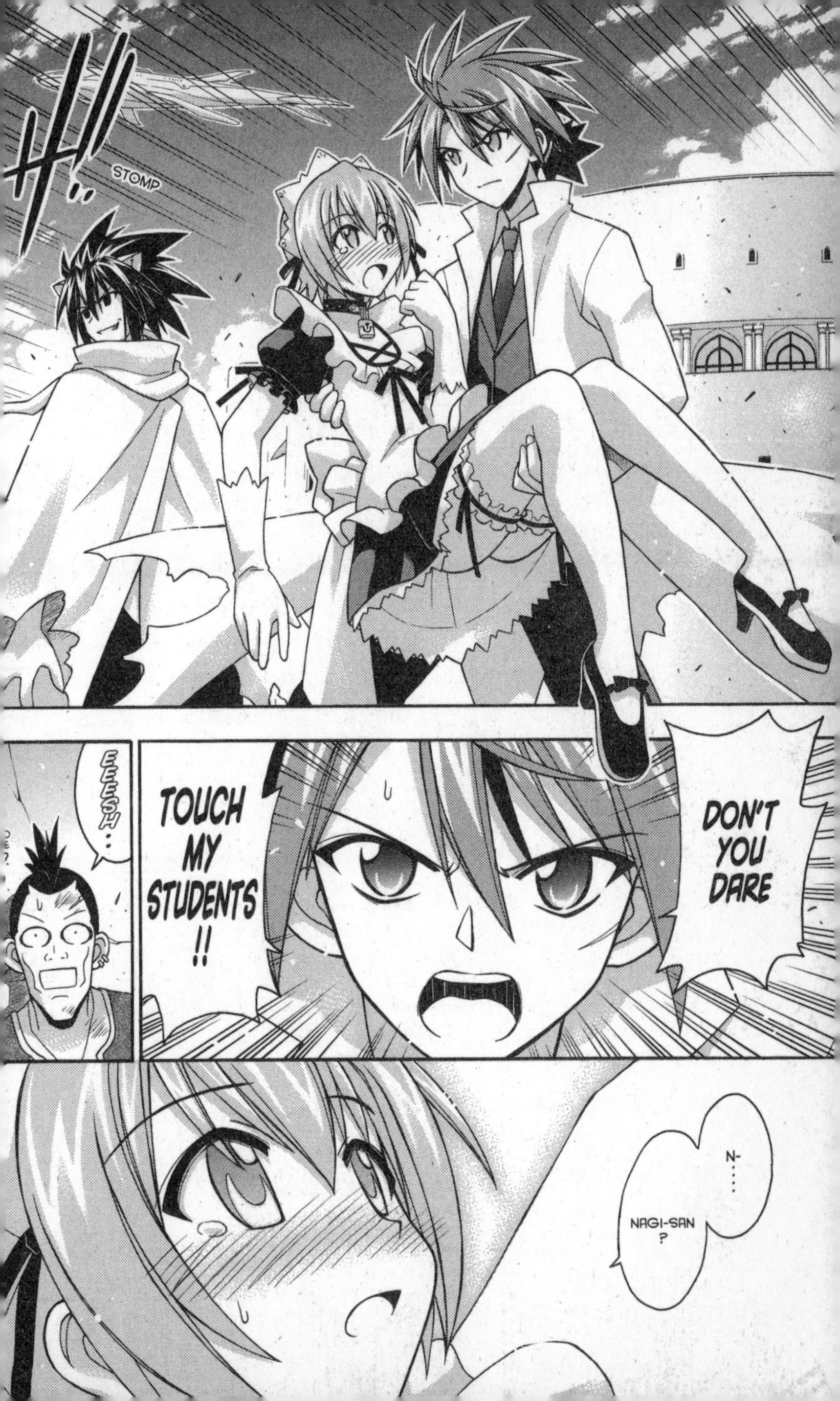
!!
STOMP
DON'T YOU DARE
TOUCH MY STUDENTS !!
EEESH...
N-.....
NAGI-SAN ?

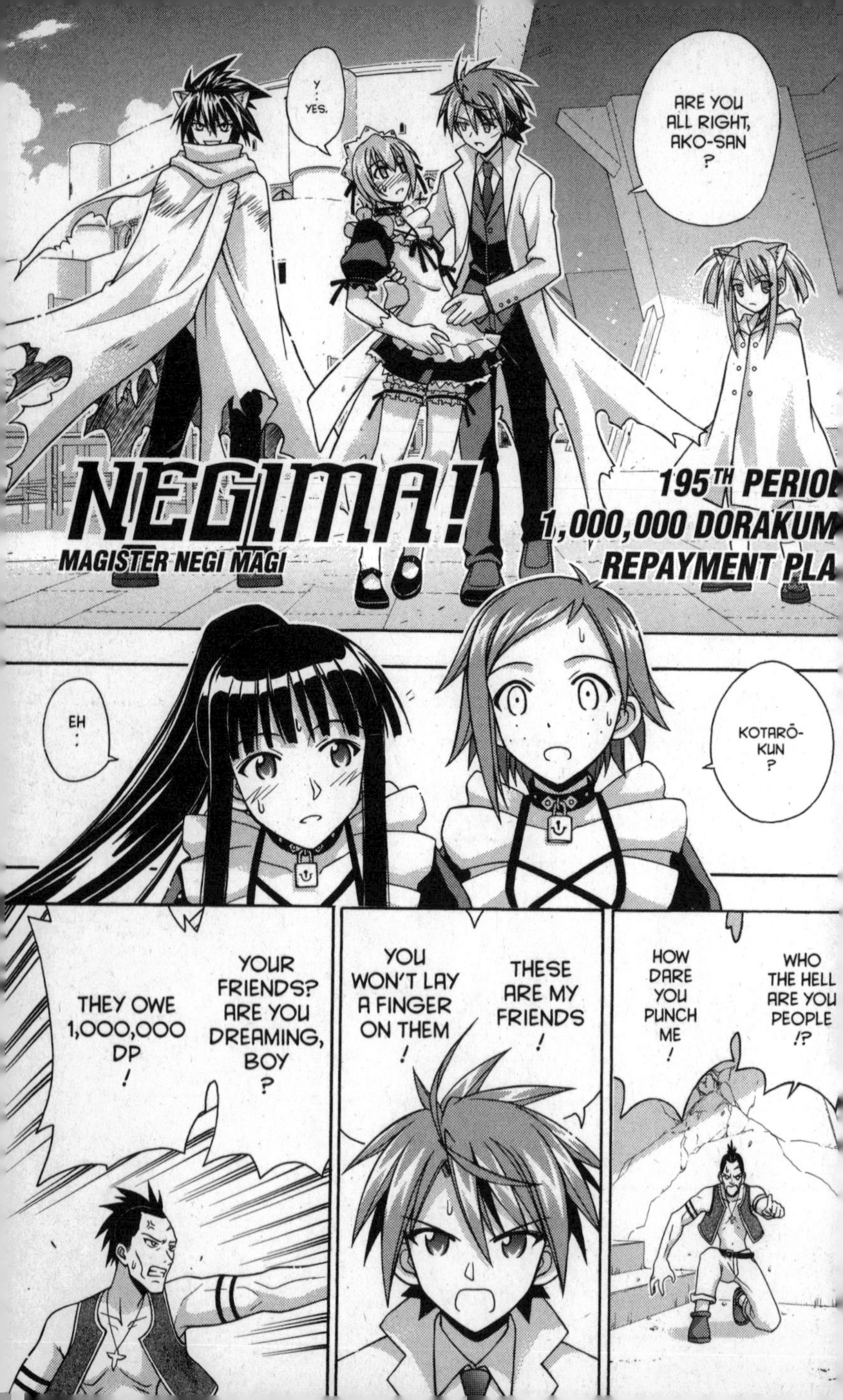
ARE YOU ALL RIGHT, AKO-SAN ?
Y... YES.
NEGIMA!
MAGISTER NEGI MAGI
195TH PERIO
1,000,000 DORAKUM
REPAYMENT PLA
KOTARŌ-KUN ?
EH...
WHO THE HELL ARE YOU PEOPLE !?
HOW DARE YOU PUNCH ME !
THESE ARE MY FRIENDS !
YOU WON'T LAY A FINGER ON THEM !
YOUR FRIENDS? ARE YOU DREAMING, BOY ?
THEY OWE 1,000,000 DP !

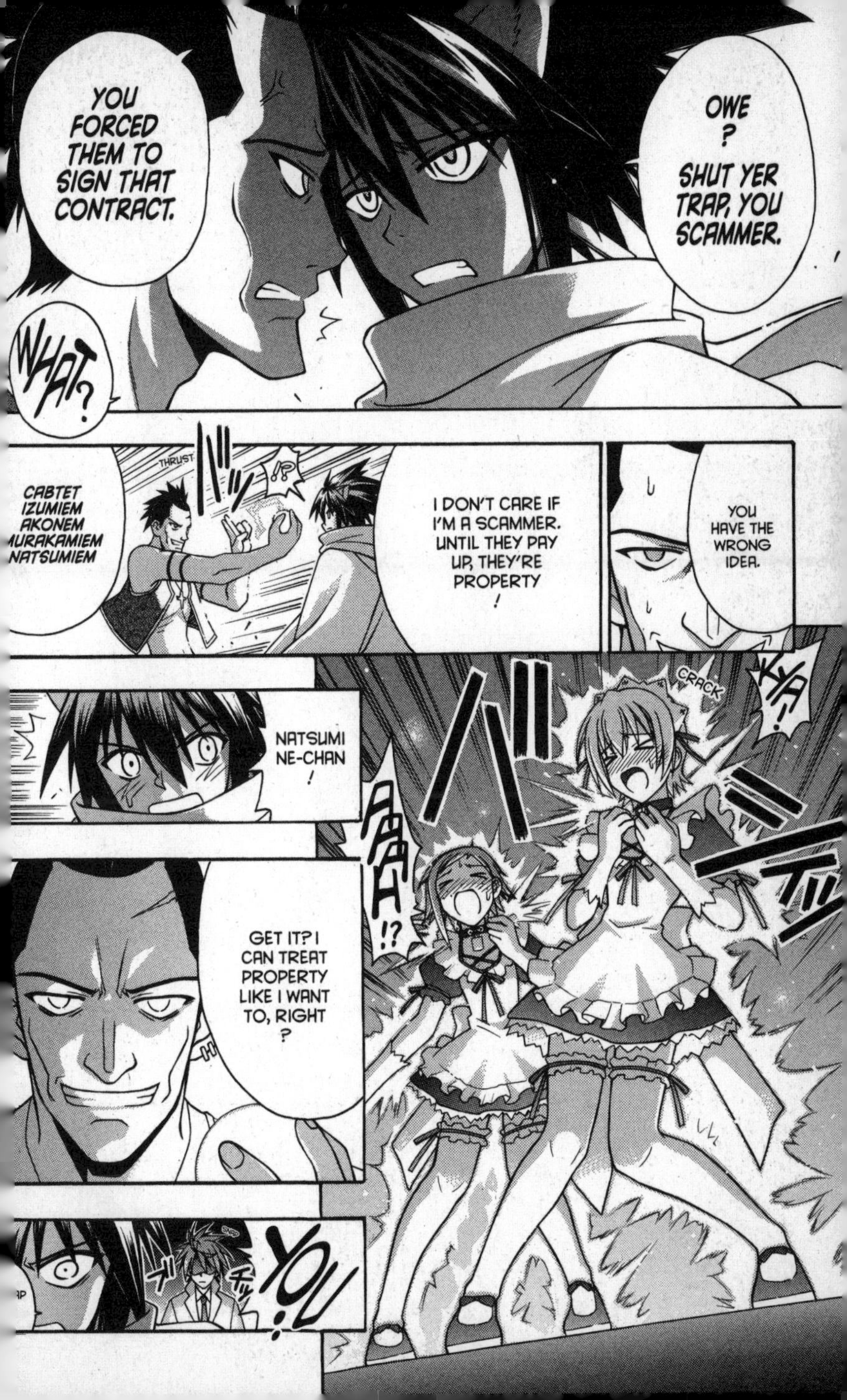
OWE? SHUT YER TRAP, YOU SCAMMER.
YOU FORCED THEM TO SIGN THAT CONTRACT.
WHAT?
YOU HAVE THE WRONG IDEA.
I DON'T CARE IF I'M A SCAMMER. UNTIL THEY PAY UP, THEY'RE PROPERTY!
THRUST
!?
CABTET IZUMIEM AKONEM MURAKAMIEM NATSUMIEM
CRACK
KYA!
AAAH!?
NATSUMI NE-CHAN!
GET IT? I CAN TREAT PROPERTY LIKE I WANT TO, RIGHT?
SNPP
YOU!

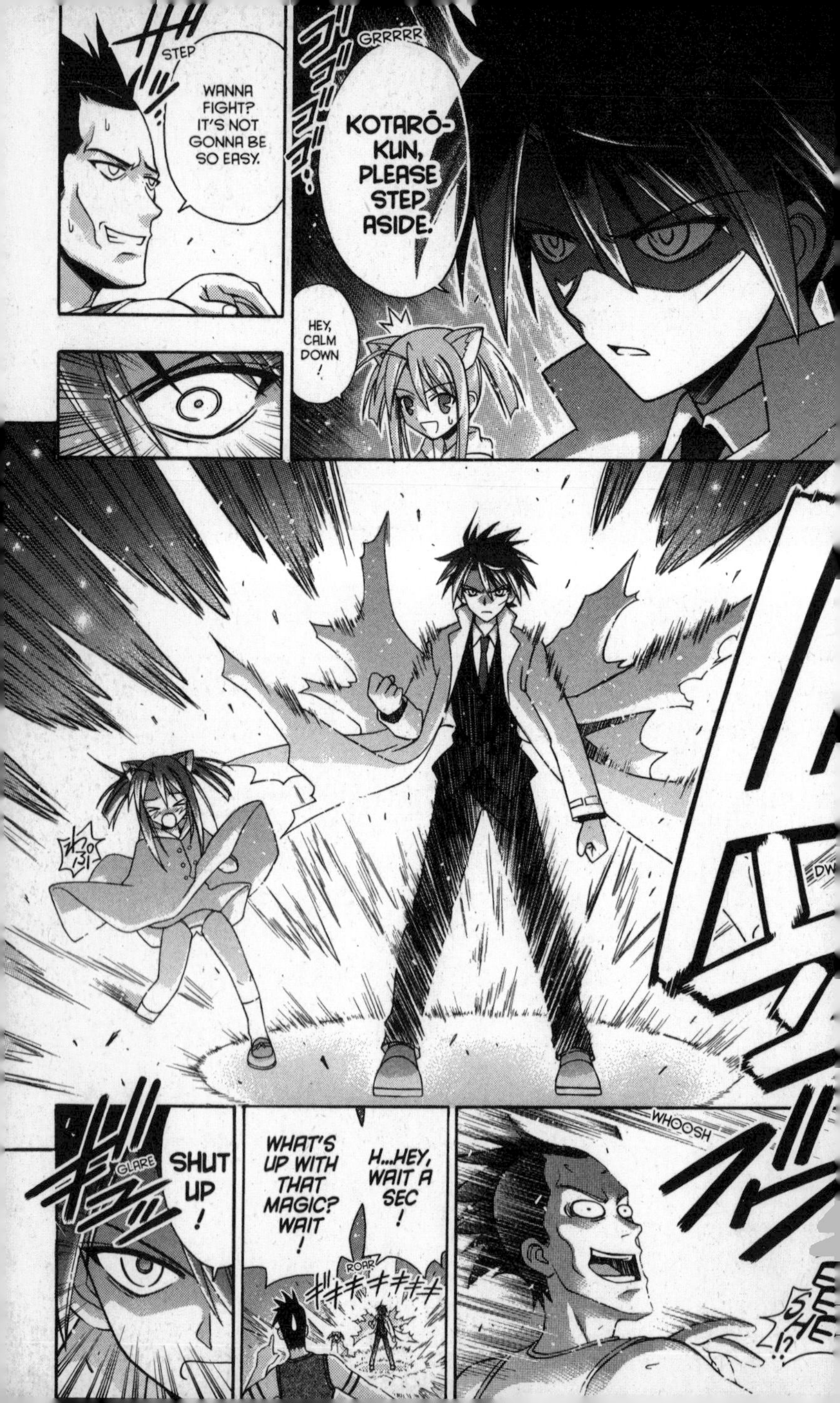
GRRRRR
KOTARŌ-KUN, PLEASE STEP ASIDE.
HEY, CALM DOWN!
STEP
WANNA FIGHT? IT'S NOT GONNA BE SO EASY.
DW
WHOOSH
SHE!?
H...HEY, WAIT A SEC!
WHAT'S UP WITH THAT MAGIC? WAIT!
ROAR
GLARE
SHUT UP!

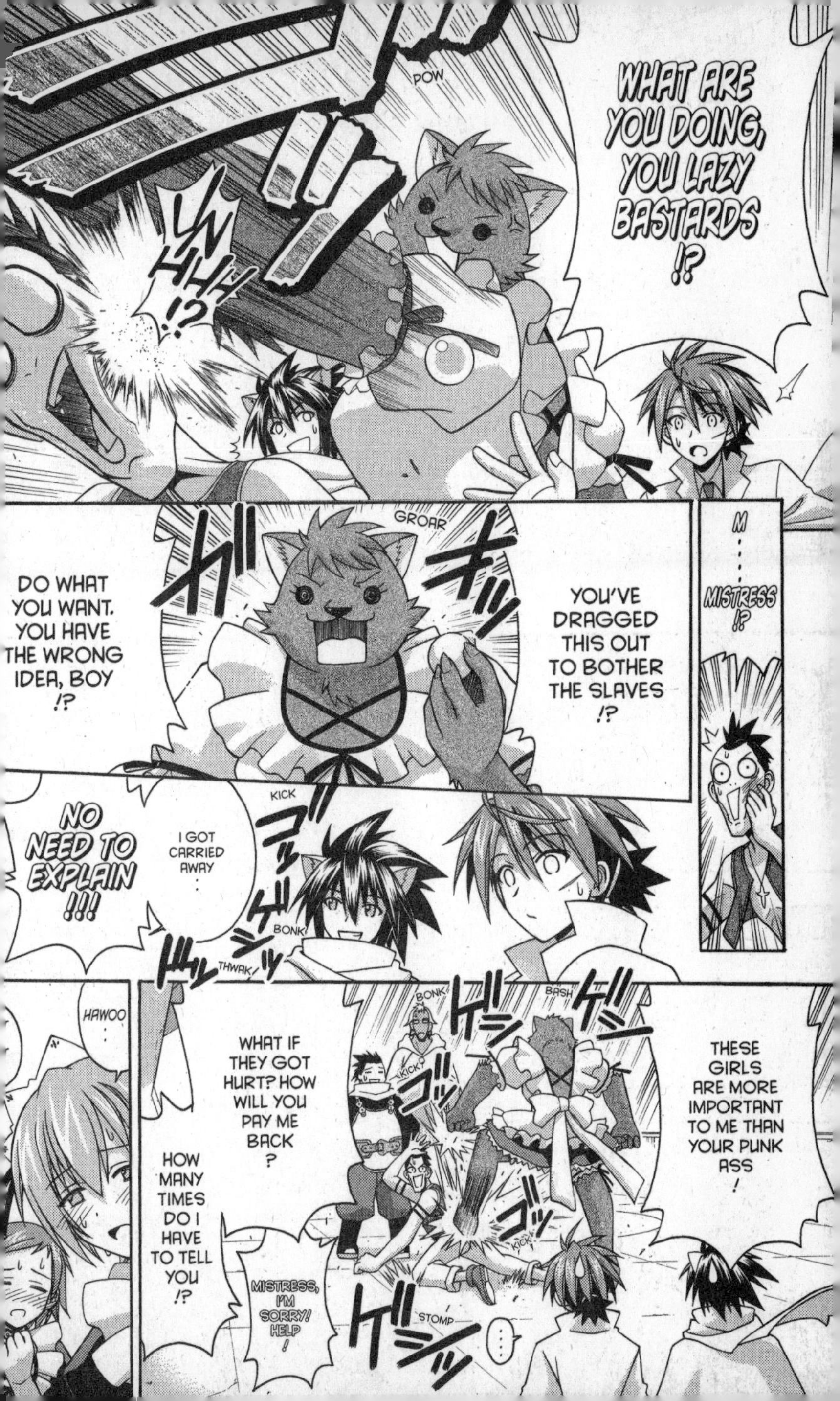
WHAT ARE YOU DOING, YOU LAZY BASTARDS !?
POW
UNHHH !?
M... MISTRESS !?
GROAR
YOU'VE DRAGGED THIS OUT TO BOTHER THE SLAVES !?
DO WHAT YOU WANT. YOU HAVE THE WRONG IDEA, BOY !?
I GOT CARRIED AWAY ...
NO NEED TO EXPLAIN !!!
KICK
BONK
THWAK
THESE GIRLS ARE MORE IMPORTANT TO ME THAN YOUR PUNK ASS !
BASH
BONK
WHAT IF THEY GOT HURT? HOW WILL YOU PAY ME BACK ?
KICK
KICK
HOW MANY TIMES DO I HAVE TO TELL YOU !?
MISTRESS, I'M SORRY! HELP !
STOMP
...
HAWOO ...

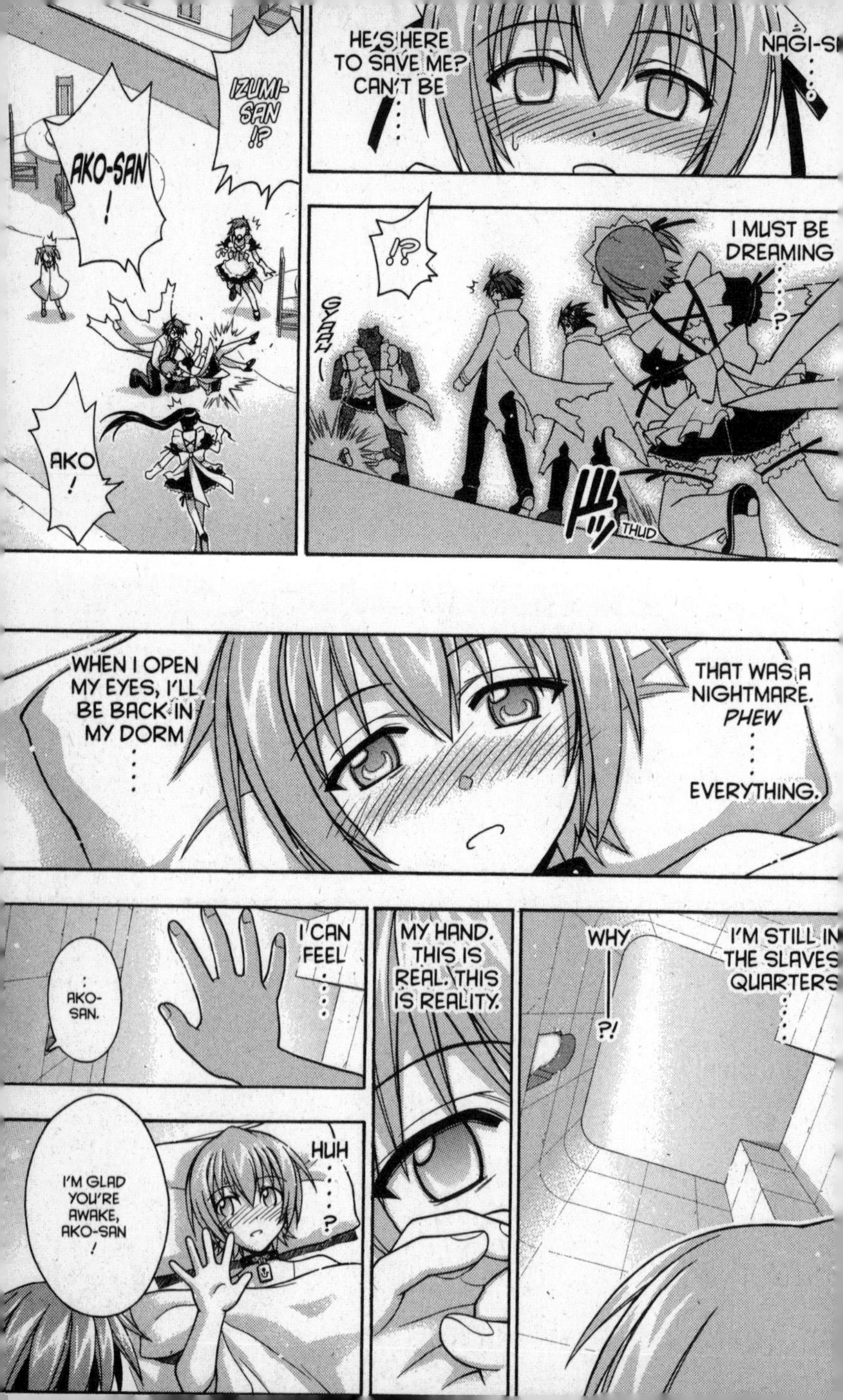

NAGI-S…
HE'S HERE TO SAVE ME? CAN'T BE…
I MUST BE DREAMING…?
!?
GYAAH
THUD
IZUMI-SAN !?
AKO-SAN !
AKO !
THAT WAS A NIGHTMARE. PHEW… EVERYTHING.
WHEN I OPEN MY EYES, I'LL BE BACK IN MY DORM…
I'M STILL IN THE SLAVES QUARTERS…
WHY—?!
MY HAND. THIS IS REAL. THIS IS REALITY.
I CAN FEEL…
…AKO-SAN.
HUH…?
I'M GLAD YOU'RE AWAKE, AKO-SAN!

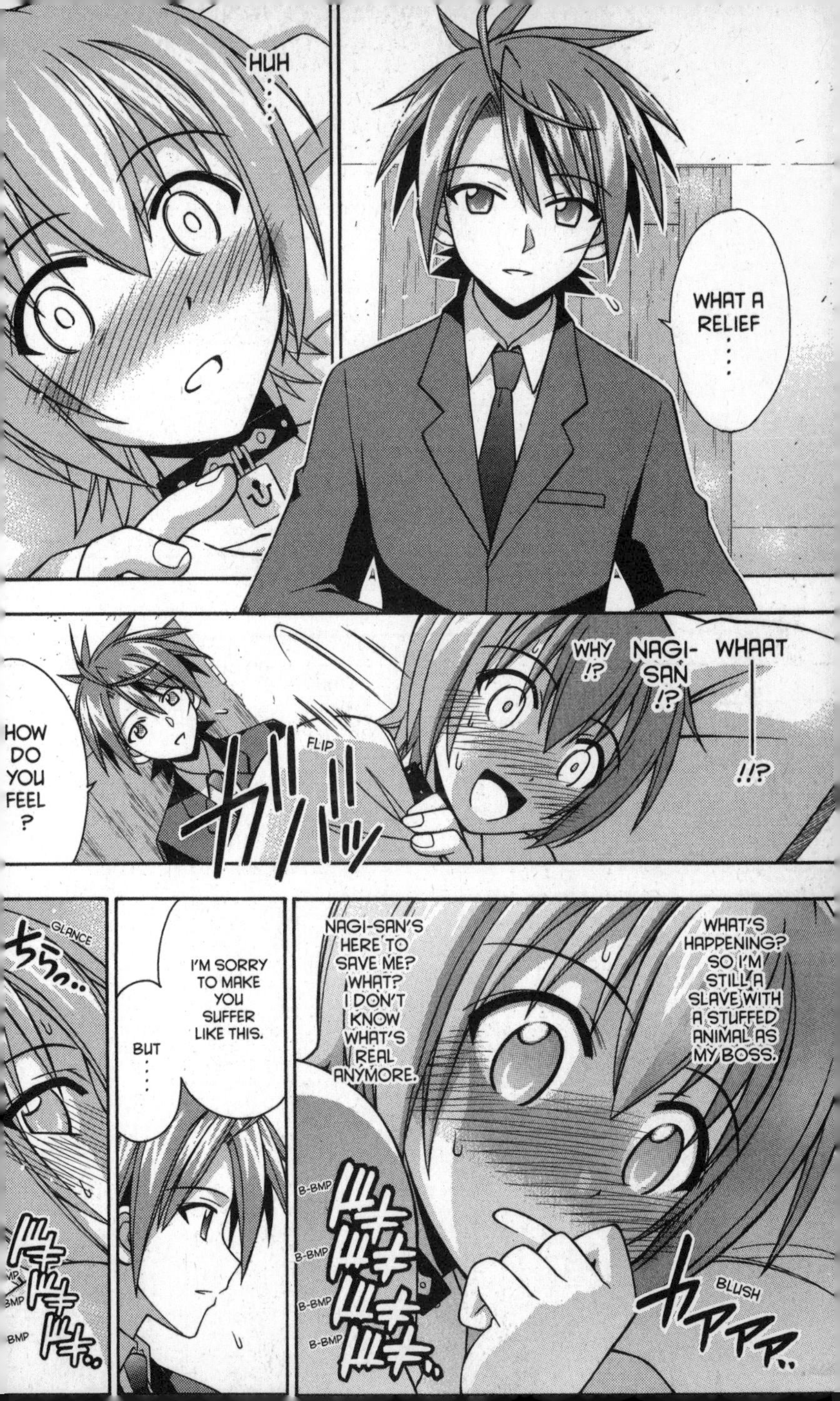
WHAT A RELIEF ....
HUH ...
WHAAT —— !!?
NAGI-SAN !?
WHY !?
FLIP
HOW DO YOU FEEL ?
WHAT'S HAPPENING? SO I'M STILL A SLAVE WITH A STUFFED ANIMAL AS MY BOSS.
NAGI-SAN'S HERE TO SAVE ME? WHAT? I DON'T KNOW WHAT'S REAL ANYMORE.
BLUSH
B-BMP
B-BMP
B-BMP
B-BMP
I'M SORRY TO MAKE YOU SUFFER LIKE THIS.
BUT ...
GLANCE
BMP
BMP
BMP

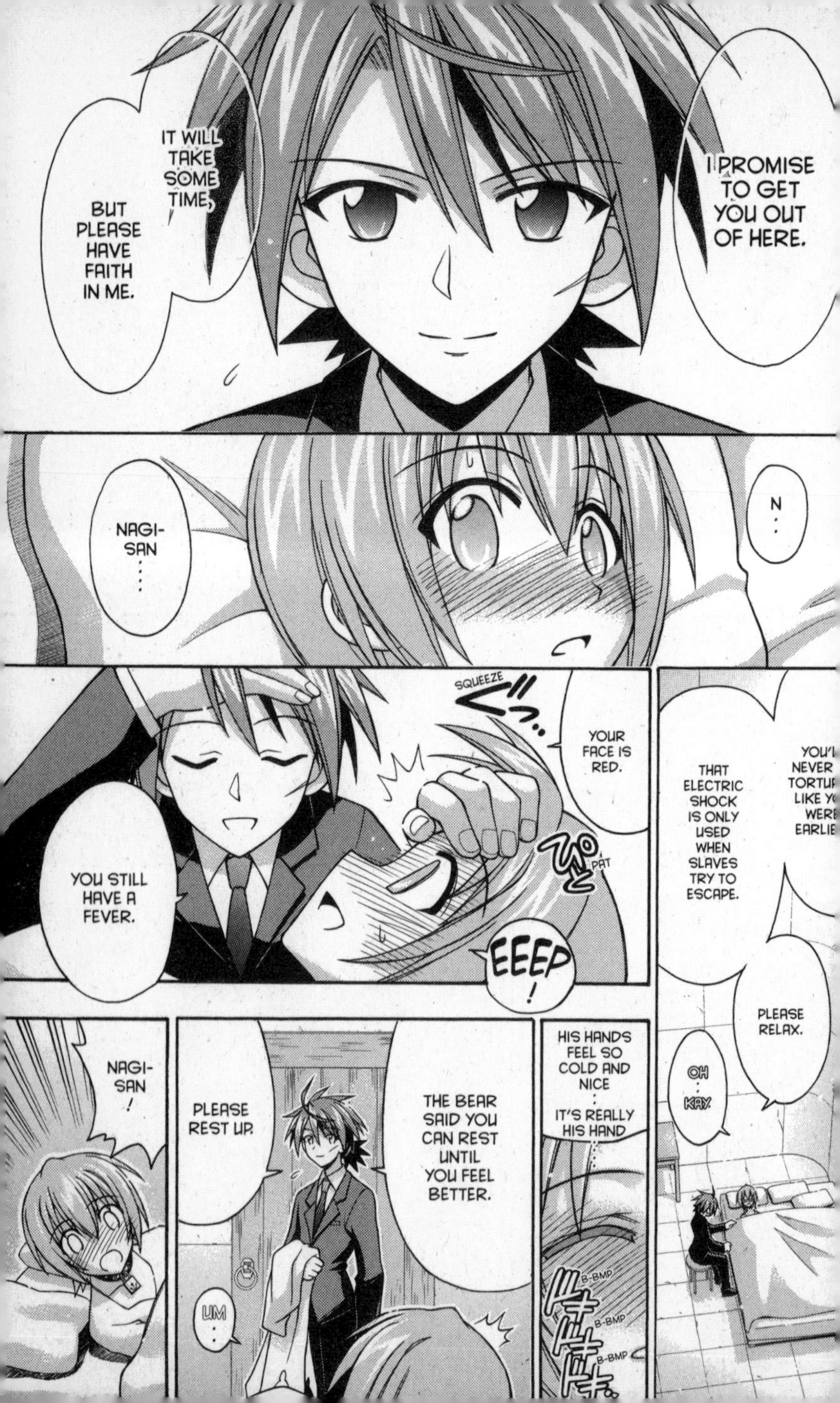
I PROMISE TO GET YOU OUT OF HERE.
IT WILL TAKE SOME TIME,
BUT PLEASE HAVE FAITH IN ME.
N...
NAGI-SAN.....
YOU'L NEVER TORTUR LIKE YO WERE EARLIE
THAT ELECTRIC SHOCK IS ONLY USED WHEN SLAVES TRY TO ESCAPE.
PLEASE RELAX.
OH... KAY.
SQUEEZE
YOUR FACE IS RED.
PAT
EEEP!
YOU STILL HAVE A FEVER.
HIS HANDS FEEL SO COLD AND NICE...
IT'S REALLY HIS HAND...
B-BMP
B-BMP
B-BMP
THE BEAR SAID YOU CAN REST UNTIL YOU FEEL BETTER.
PLEASE REST UP.
UM...
NAGI-SAN!

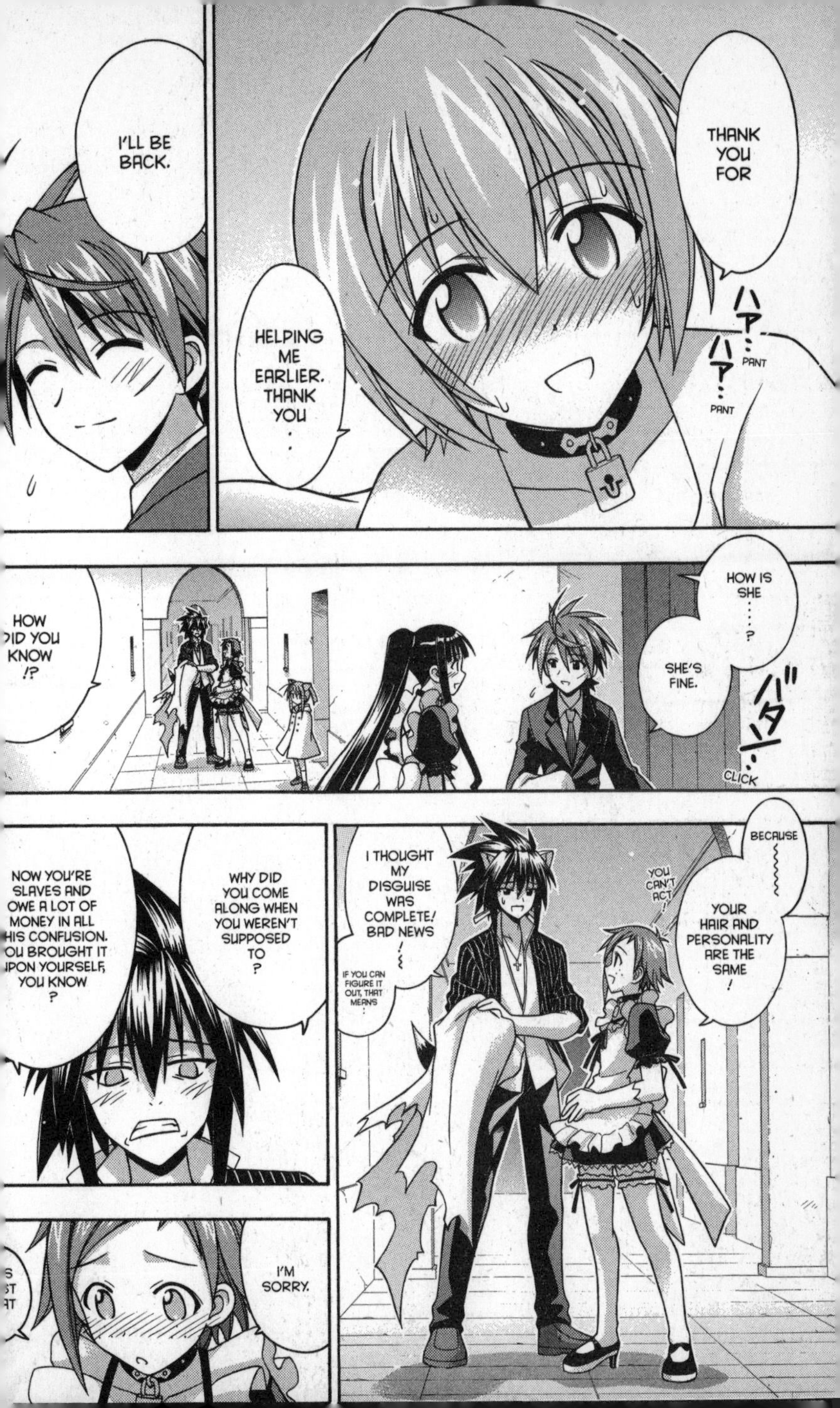
THANK YOU FOR
HELPING ME EARLIER. THANK YOU...
ハア… PANT
ハア… PANT
I'LL BE BACK.
HOW IS SHE...?
SHE'S FINE.
バタン CLICK
HOW DID YOU KNOW!?
BECAUSE~~
YOUR HAIR AND PERSONALITY ARE THE SAME!
YOU CAN'T ACT!
I THOUGHT MY DISGUISE WAS COMPLETE! BAD NEWS!
IF YOU CAN FIGURE IT OUT, THAT MEANS...
WHY DID YOU COME ALONG WHEN YOU WEREN'T SUPPOSED TO?
NOW YOU'RE SLAVES AND OWE A LOT OF MONEY IN ALL THIS CONFUSION. YOU BROUGHT IT UPON YOURSELF, YOU KNOW?
I'M SORRY.

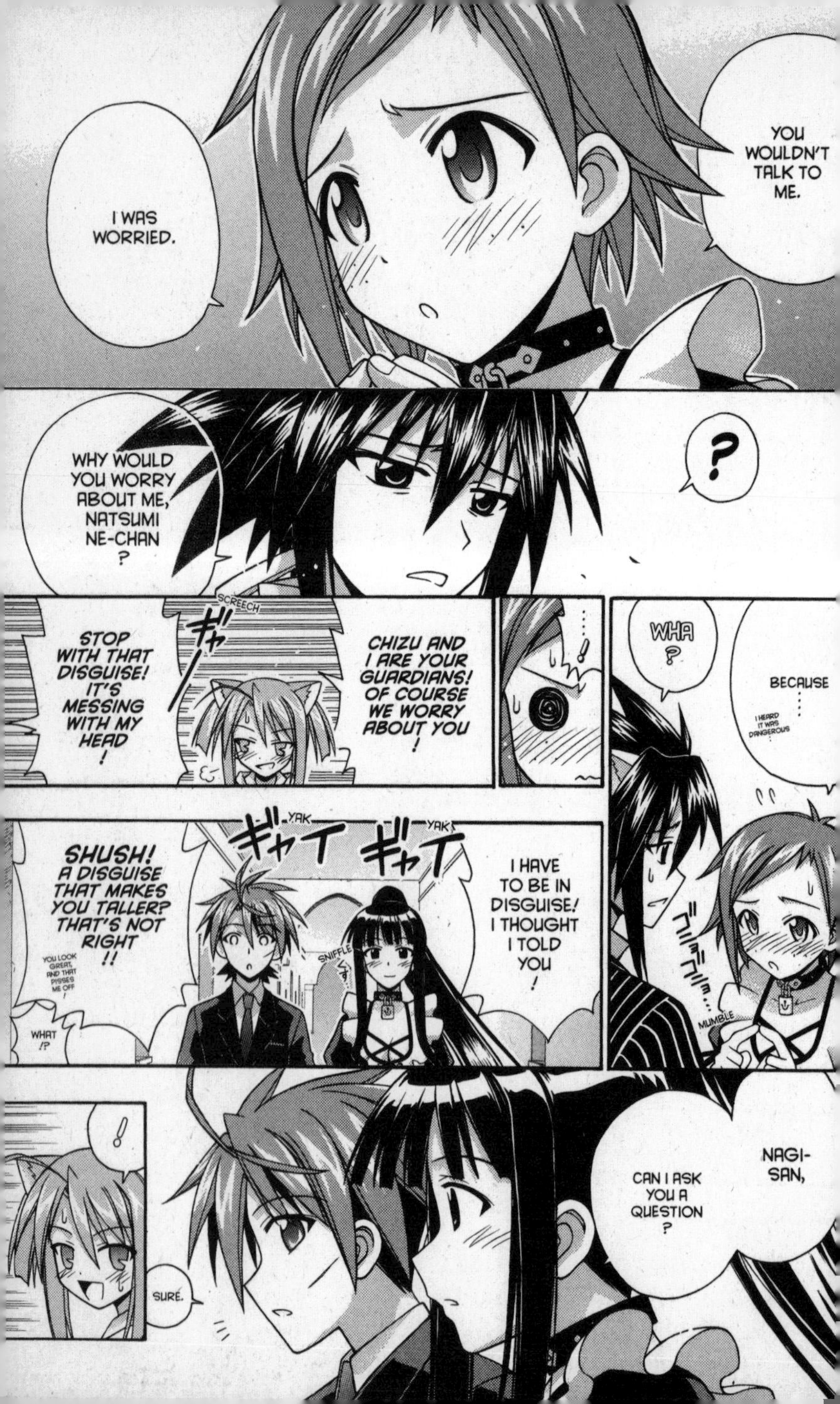
YOU WOULDN'T TALK TO ME.
I WAS WORRIED.
?
WHY WOULD YOU WORRY ABOUT ME, NATSUMI NE-CHAN?
WHA?
BECAUSE......
I HEARD IT WAS DANGEROUS
MUMBLE
...!
SCREECH
CHIZU AND I ARE YOUR GUARDIANS! OF COURSE WE WORRY ABOUT YOU!
STOP WITH THAT DISGUISE! IT'S MESSING WITH MY HEAD!
YAK
YAK
I HAVE TO BE IN DISGUISE! I THOUGHT I TOLD YOU!
SNIFFLE
SHUSH! A DISGUISE THAT MAKES YOU TALLER? THAT'S NOT RIGHT!!
YOU LOOK GREAT, AND THAT PISSES ME OFF!
WHAT!?
NAGI-SAN,
CAN I ASK YOU A QUESTION?
!
SURE.

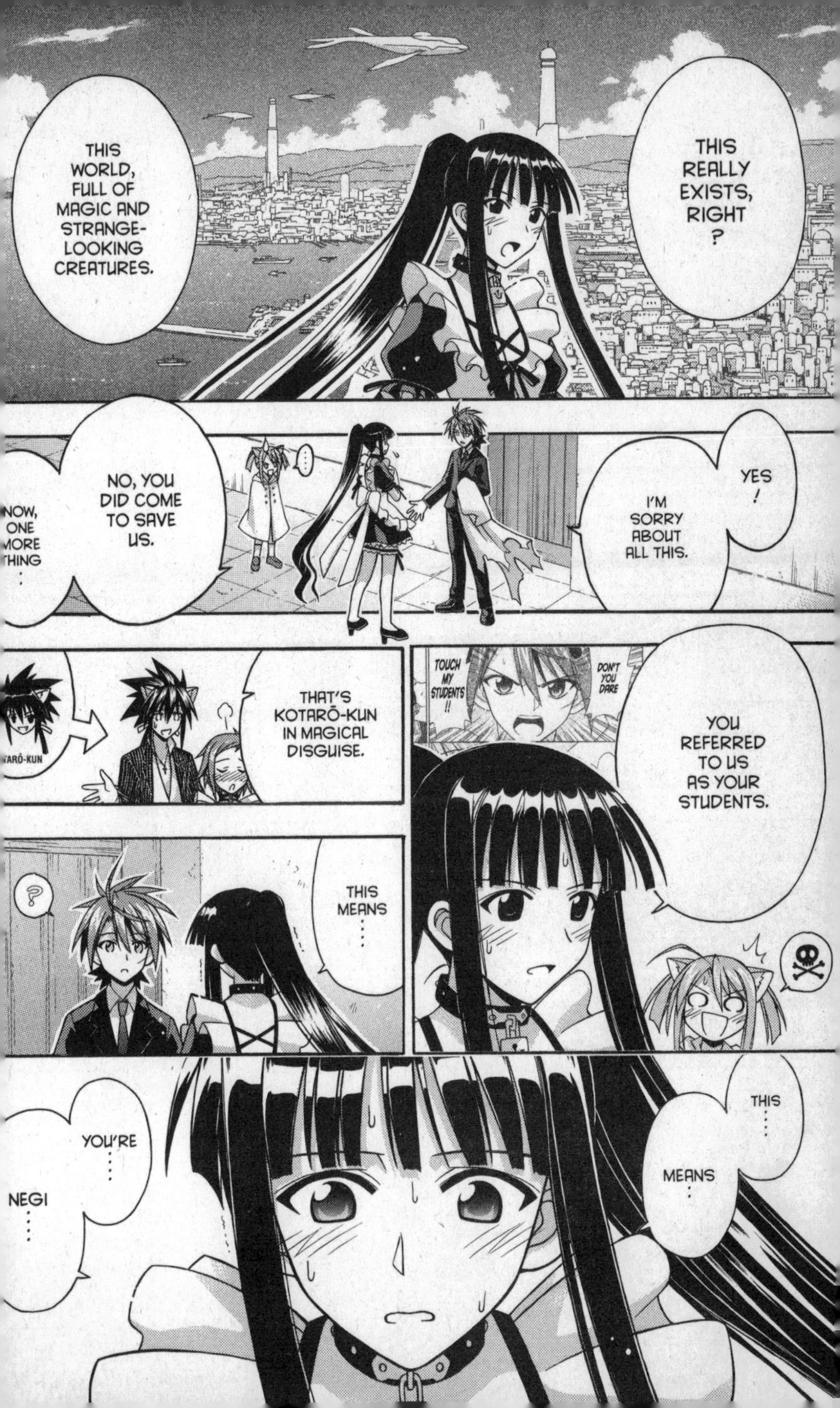
THIS REALLY EXISTS, RIGHT?
THIS WORLD, FULL OF MAGIC AND STRANGE-LOOKING CREATURES.
YES! I'M SORRY ABOUT ALL THIS.
...
NO, YOU DID COME TO SAVE US.
NOW, ONE MORE THING...
DON'T YOU DARE
TOUCH MY STUDENTS!!
YOU REFERRED TO US AS YOUR STUDENTS.
THAT'S KOTARŌ-KUN IN MAGICAL DISGUISE.
THIS MEANS...
?
THIS... MEANS...
YOU'RE... NEGI...

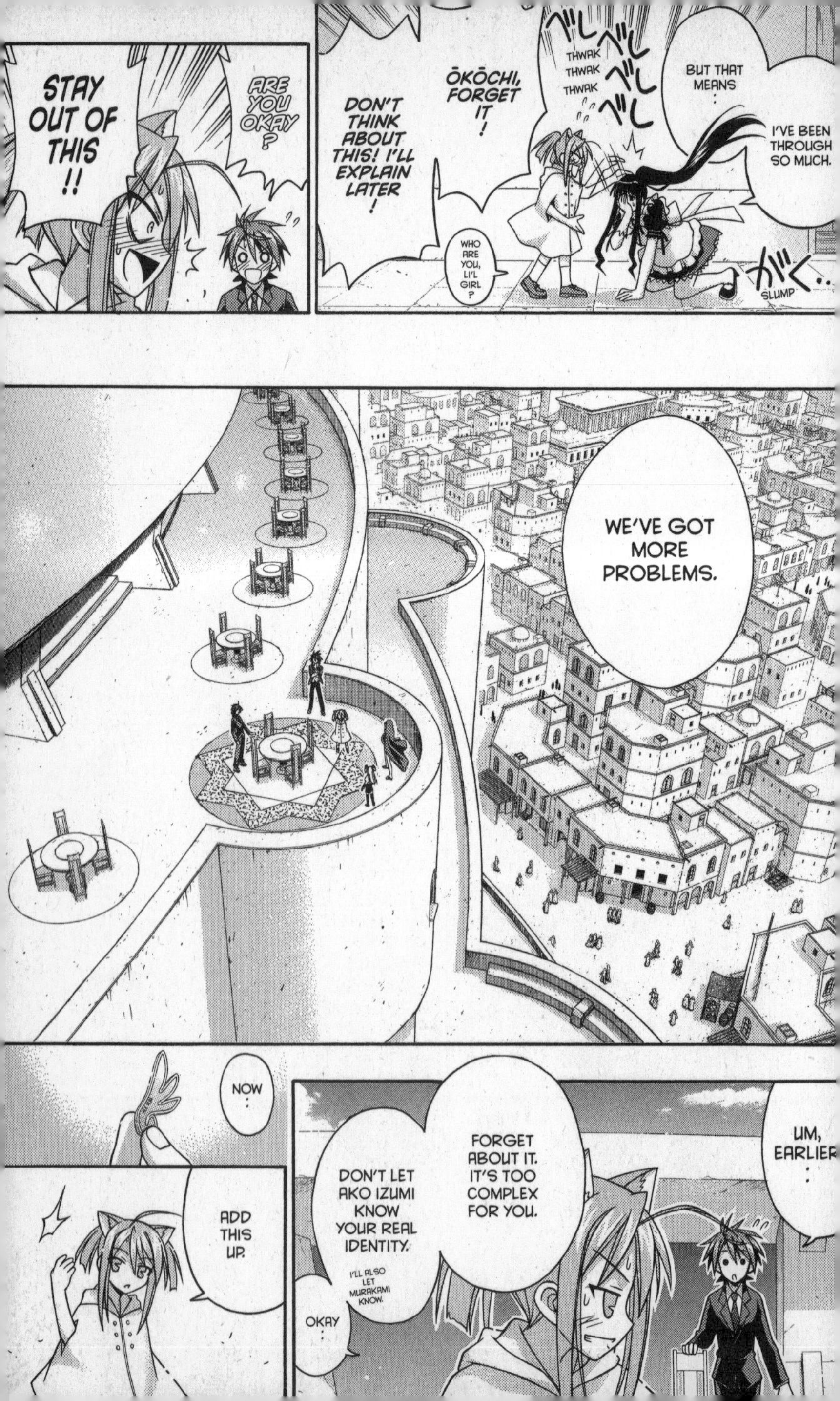

BUT THAT MEANS :
I'VE BEEN THROUGH SO MUCH.
THWAK THWAK THWAK
SLUMP
ŌKŌCHI, FORGET IT!
DON'T THINK ABOUT THIS! I'LL EXPLAIN LATER!
WHO ARE YOU, LI'L GIRL?
ARE YOU OKAY?
STAY OUT OF THIS!!
WE'VE GOT MORE PROBLEMS.
UM, EARLIER :
FORGET ABOUT IT. IT'S TOO COMPLEX FOR YOU.
DON'T LET AKO IZUMI KNOW YOUR REAL IDENTITY.
I'LL ALSO LET MURAKAMI KNOW.
OKAY :
NOW :
ADD THIS UP.

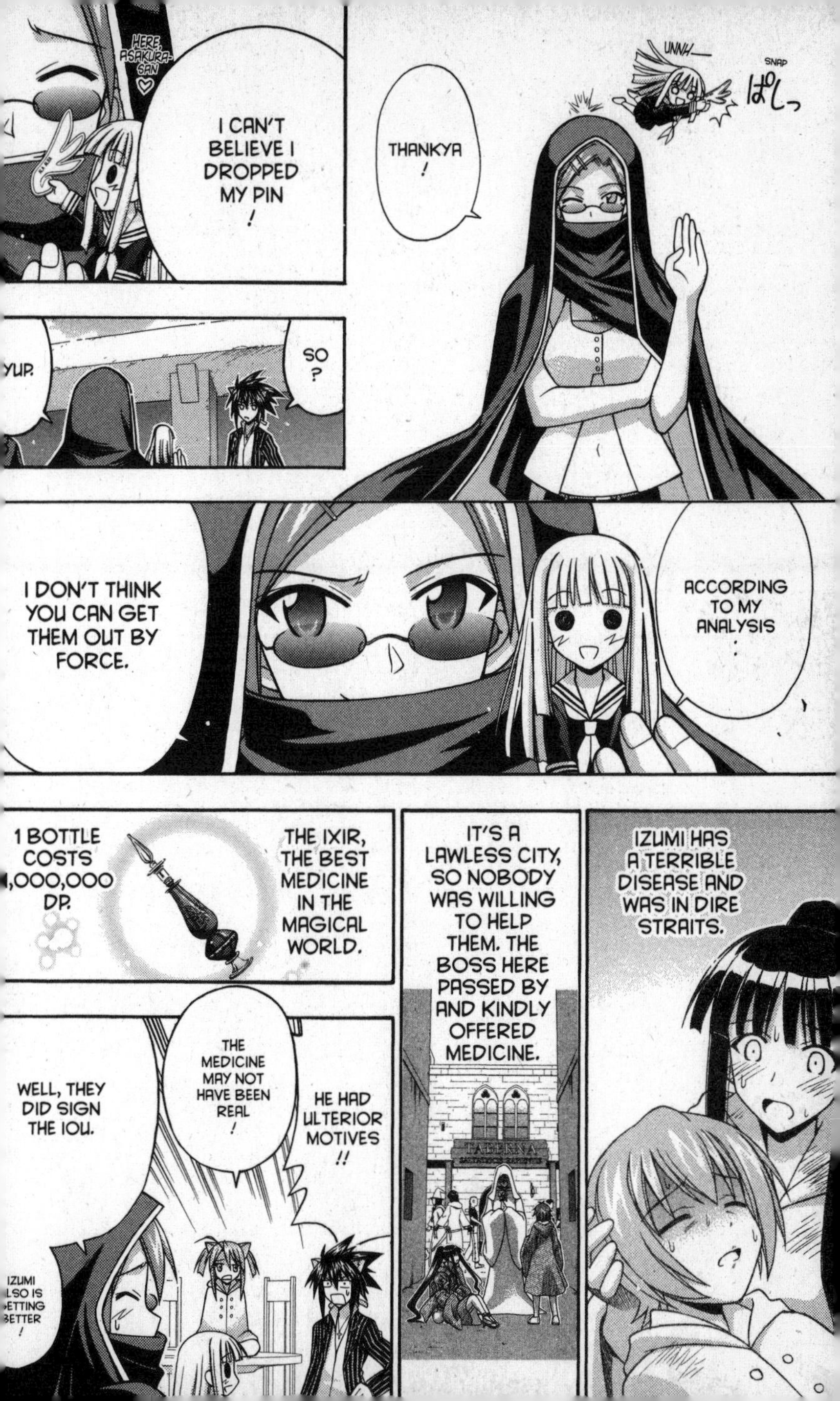
UNNH—
SNAP
ぱしっ
THANKYA!
HERE, ASAKURA-SAN ♥
I CAN'T BELIEVE I DROPPED MY PIN!
SO?
YUP.
ACCORDING TO MY ANALYSIS...
I DON'T THINK YOU CAN GET THEM OUT BY FORCE.
IZUMI HAS A TERRIBLE DISEASE AND WAS IN DIRE STRAITS.
IT'S A LAWLESS CITY, SO NOBODY WAS WILLING TO HELP THEM. THE BOSS HERE PASSED BY AND KINDLY OFFERED MEDICINE.
TABERNA
THE IXIR, THE BEST MEDICINE IN THE MAGICAL WORLD.
1 BOTTLE COSTS ,000,000 DP.
HE HAD ULTERIOR MOTIVES!!
THE MEDICINE MAY NOT HAVE BEEN REAL!
WELL, THEY DID SIGN THE IOU.
IZUMI LSO IS ETTING BETTER!

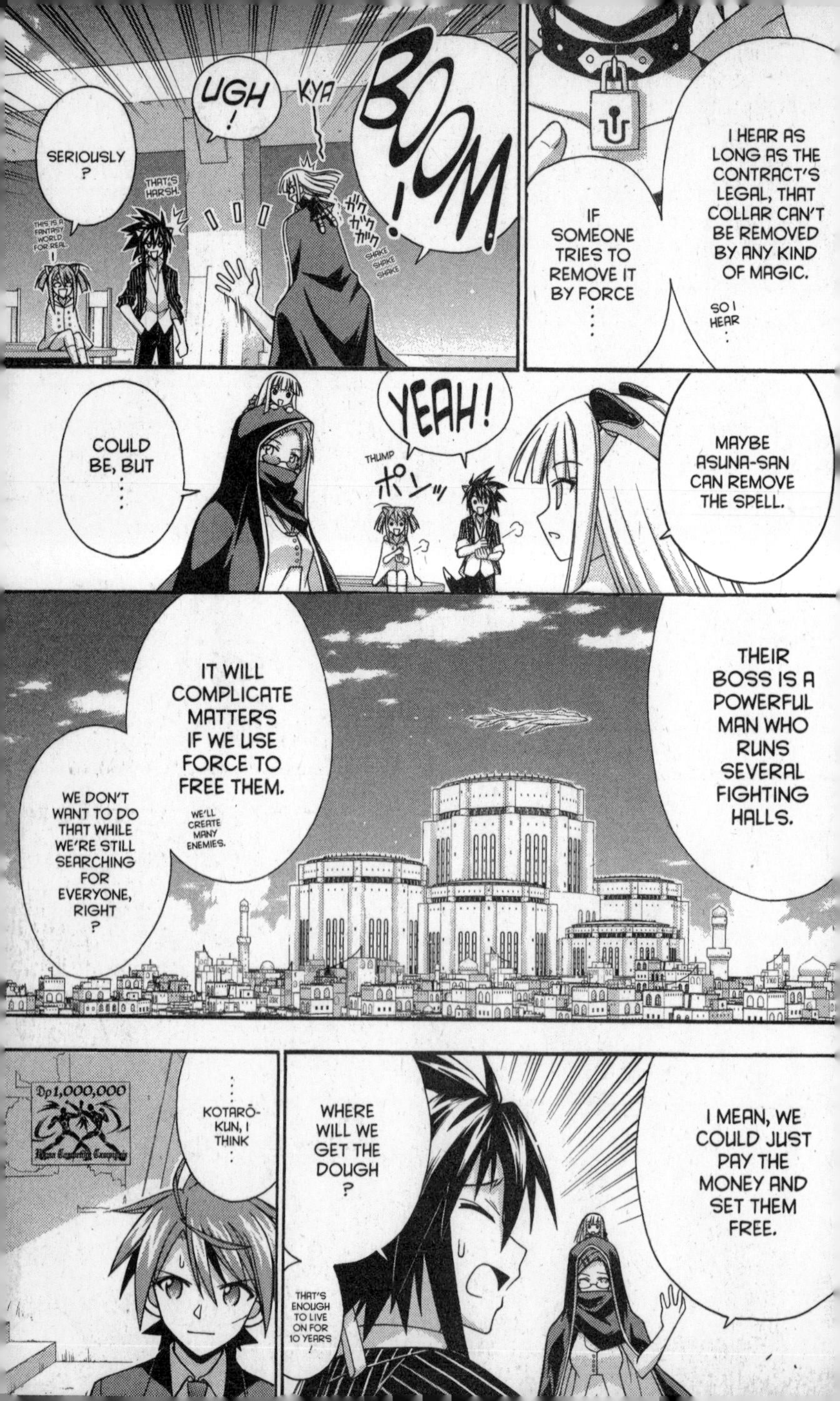
I HEAR AS LONG AS THE CONTRACT'S LEGAL, THAT COLLAR CAN'T BE REMOVED BY ANY KIND OF MAGIC.
SO I HEAR...
IF SOMEONE TRIES TO REMOVE IT BY FORCE...
BOOM!
KYA
UGH!
ガクガクガク
SHAKE SHAKE SHAKE
THAT'S HARSH.
SERIOUSLY?
THIS IS A FANTASY WORLD FOR REAL!
MAYBE ASUNA-SAN CAN REMOVE THE SPELL.
YEAH!
THUMP
ポンッ
COULD BE, BUT...
THEIR BOSS IS A POWERFUL MAN WHO RUNS SEVERAL FIGHTING HALLS.
IT WILL COMPLICATE MATTERS IF WE USE FORCE TO FREE THEM.
WE'LL CREATE MANY ENEMIES.
WE DON'T WANT TO DO THAT WHILE WE'RE STILL SEARCHING FOR EVERYONE, RIGHT?
I MEAN, WE COULD JUST PAY THE MONEY AND SET THEM FREE.
WHERE WILL WE GET THE DOUGH?
THAT'S ENOUGH TO LIVE ON FOR 10 YEARS!
...KOTARŌ-KUN, I THINK...
Dp1,000,000

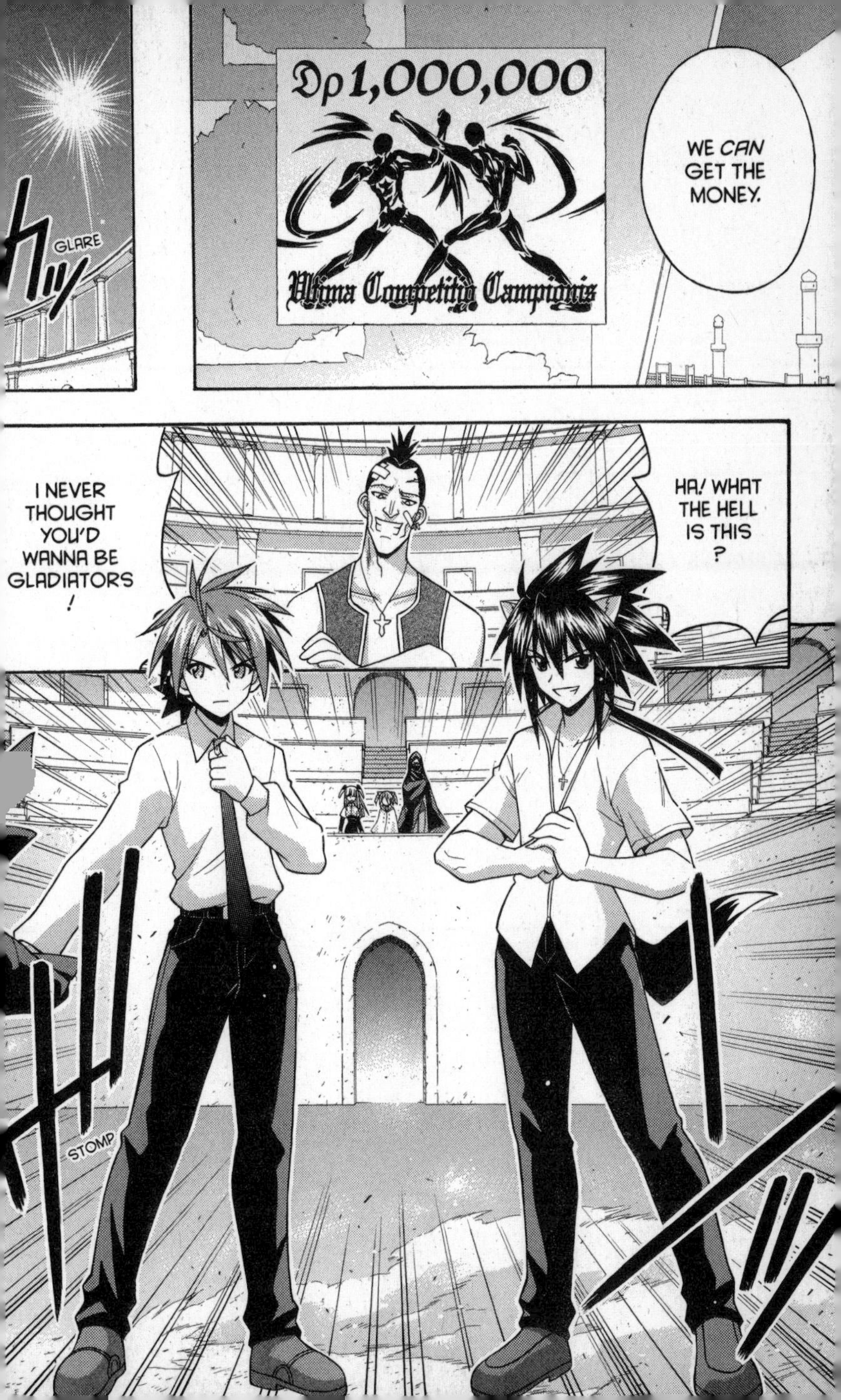
Dp1,000,000
Ultima Competitio Campionis
WE CAN GET THE MONEY.
GLARE
HA! WHAT THE HELL IS THIS?
I NEVER THOUGHT YOU'D WANNA BE GLADIATORS!
STOMP

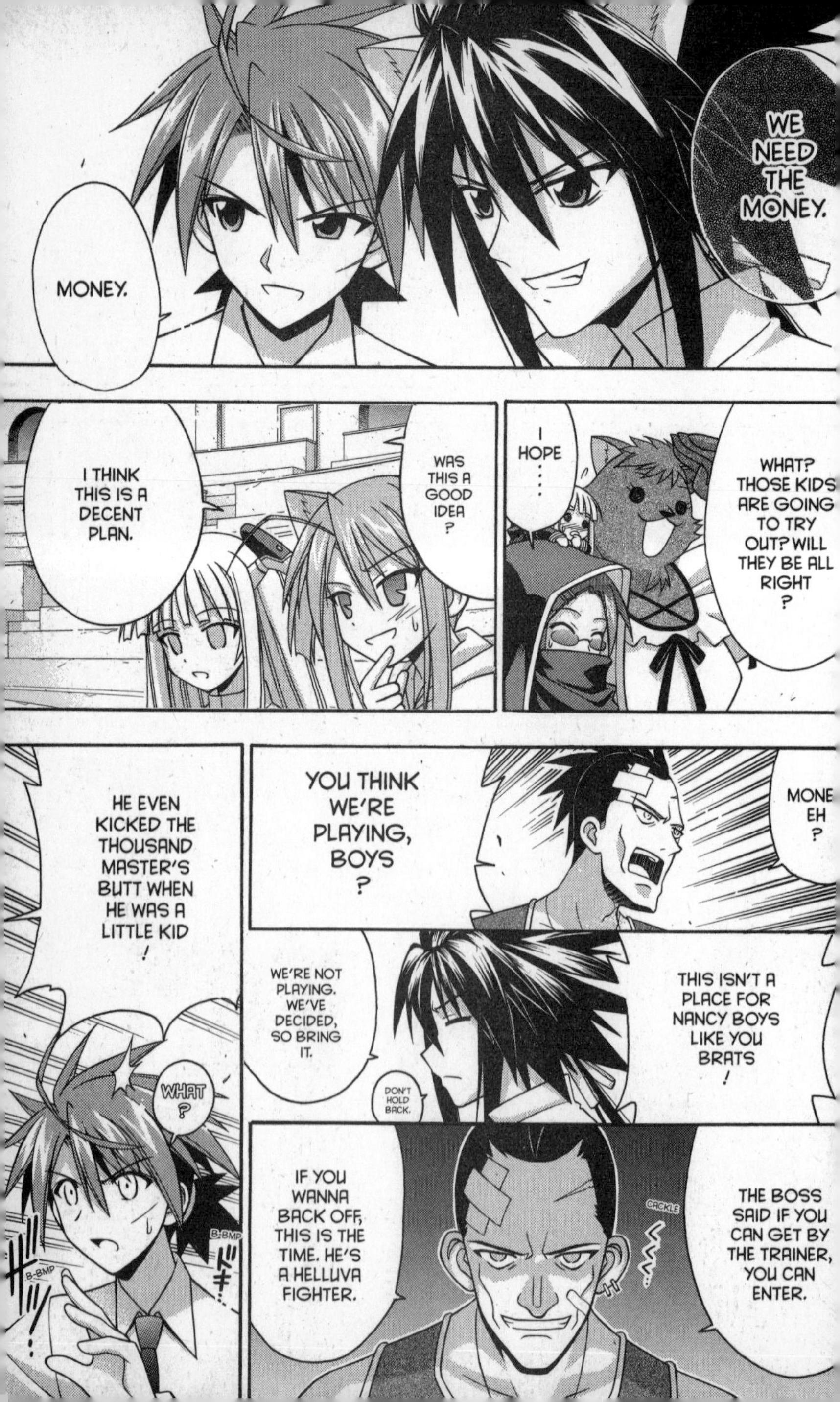
WE NEED THE MONEY.
MONEY.
WHAT? THOSE KIDS ARE GOING TO TRY OUT? WILL THEY BE ALL RIGHT?
I HOPE....
WAS THIS A GOOD IDEA?
I THINK THIS IS A DECENT PLAN.
MONE EH?
YOU THINK WE'RE PLAYING, BOYS?
THIS ISN'T A PLACE FOR NANCY BOYS LIKE YOU BRATS!
DON'T HOLD BACK.
WE'RE NOT PLAYING. WE'VE DECIDED, SO BRING IT.
THE BOSS SAID IF YOU CAN GET BY THE TRAINER, YOU CAN ENTER.
CACKLE
IF YOU WANNA BACK OFF, THIS IS THE TIME. HE'S A HELLUVA FIGHTER.
HE EVEN KICKED THE THOUSAND MASTER'S BUTT WHEN HE WAS A LITTLE KID!
WHAT?
B-BMP
B-BMP

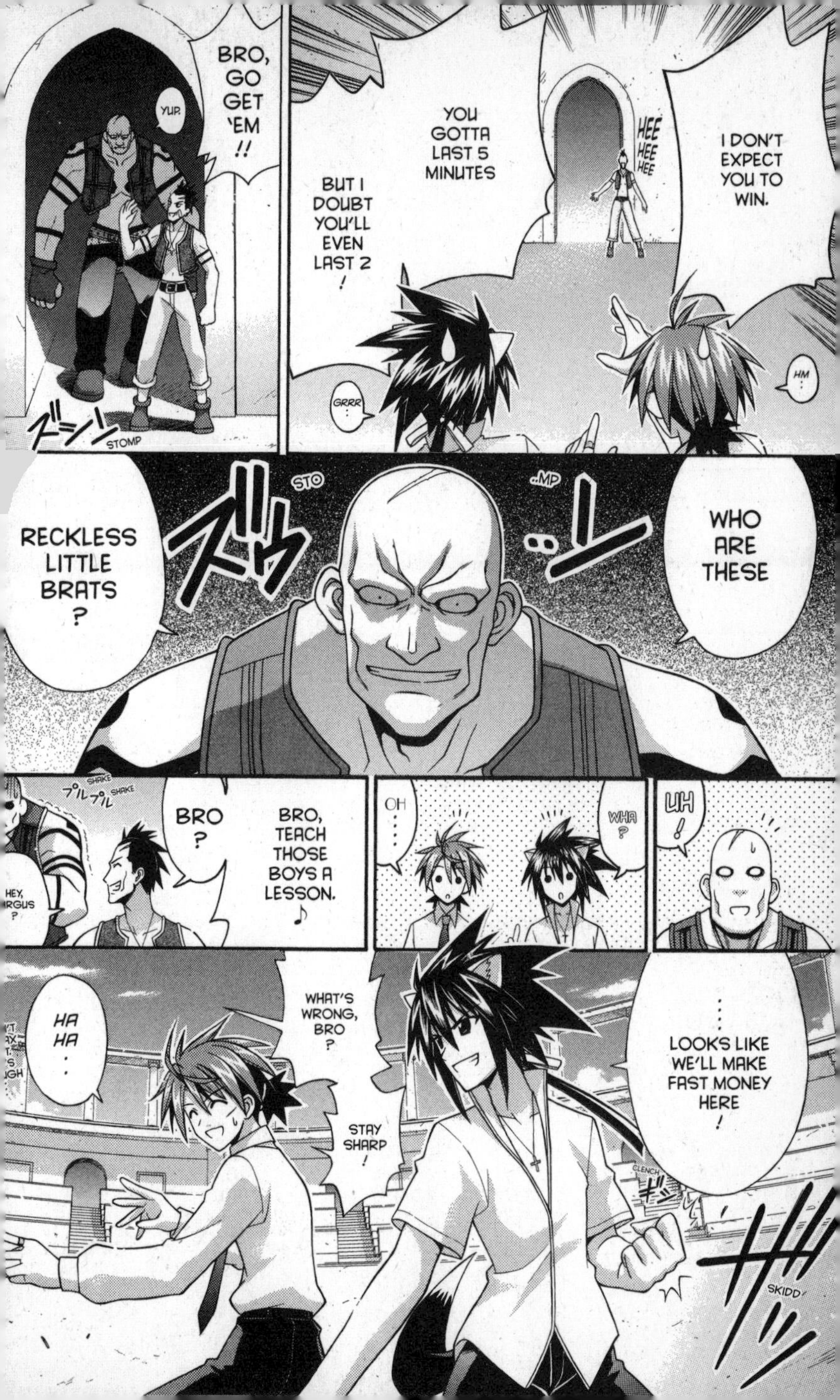
I DON'T EXPECT YOU TO WIN.
HEE HEE HEE
YOU GOTTA LAST 5 MINUTES
BUT I DOUBT YOU'LL EVEN LAST 2!
HM...
GRRR...
BRO, GO GET 'EM!!
YUP.
STOMP
WHO ARE THESE
..MP
STO
RECKLESS LITTLE BRATS?
UH!
WHA?
OH...
BRO, TEACH THOSE BOYS A LESSON. ♪
BRO?
SHAKE SHAKE
HEY,
...LOOKS LIKE WE'LL MAKE FAST MONEY HERE!
CLENCH
SKIDD
STAY SHARP!
WHAT'S WRONG, BRO?
HA HA...

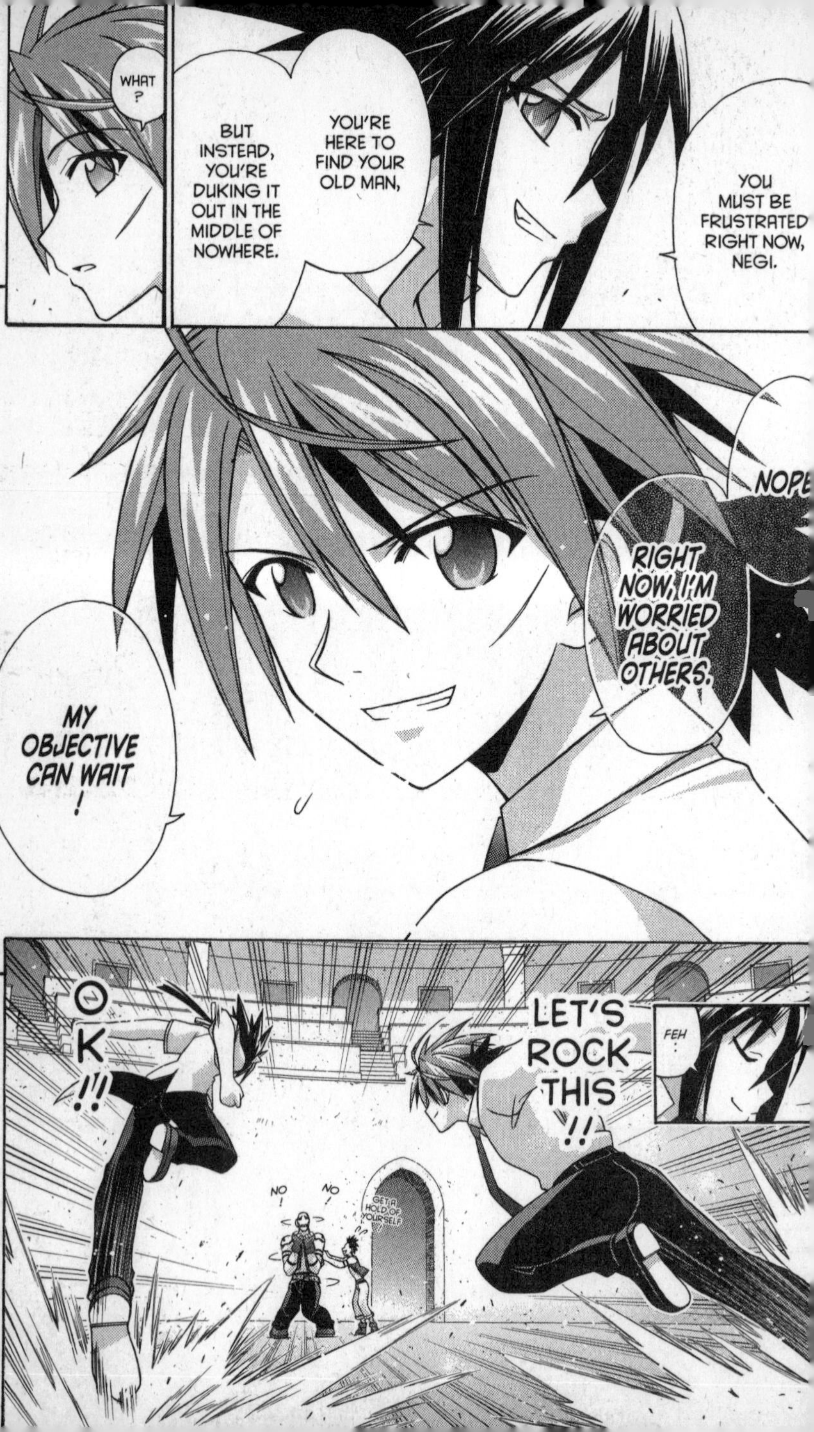
YOU MUST BE FRUSTRATED RIGHT NOW, NEGI.
YOU'RE HERE TO FIND YOUR OLD MAN,
BUT INSTEAD, YOU'RE DUKING IT OUT IN THE MIDDLE OF NOWHERE.
WHAT?
NOPE
RIGHT NOW, I'M WORRIED ABOUT OTHERS.
MY OBJECTIVE CAN WAIT!
FEH
LET'S ROCK THIS!!
OK!!
GET A HOLD OF YOURSELF
NO!
NO!

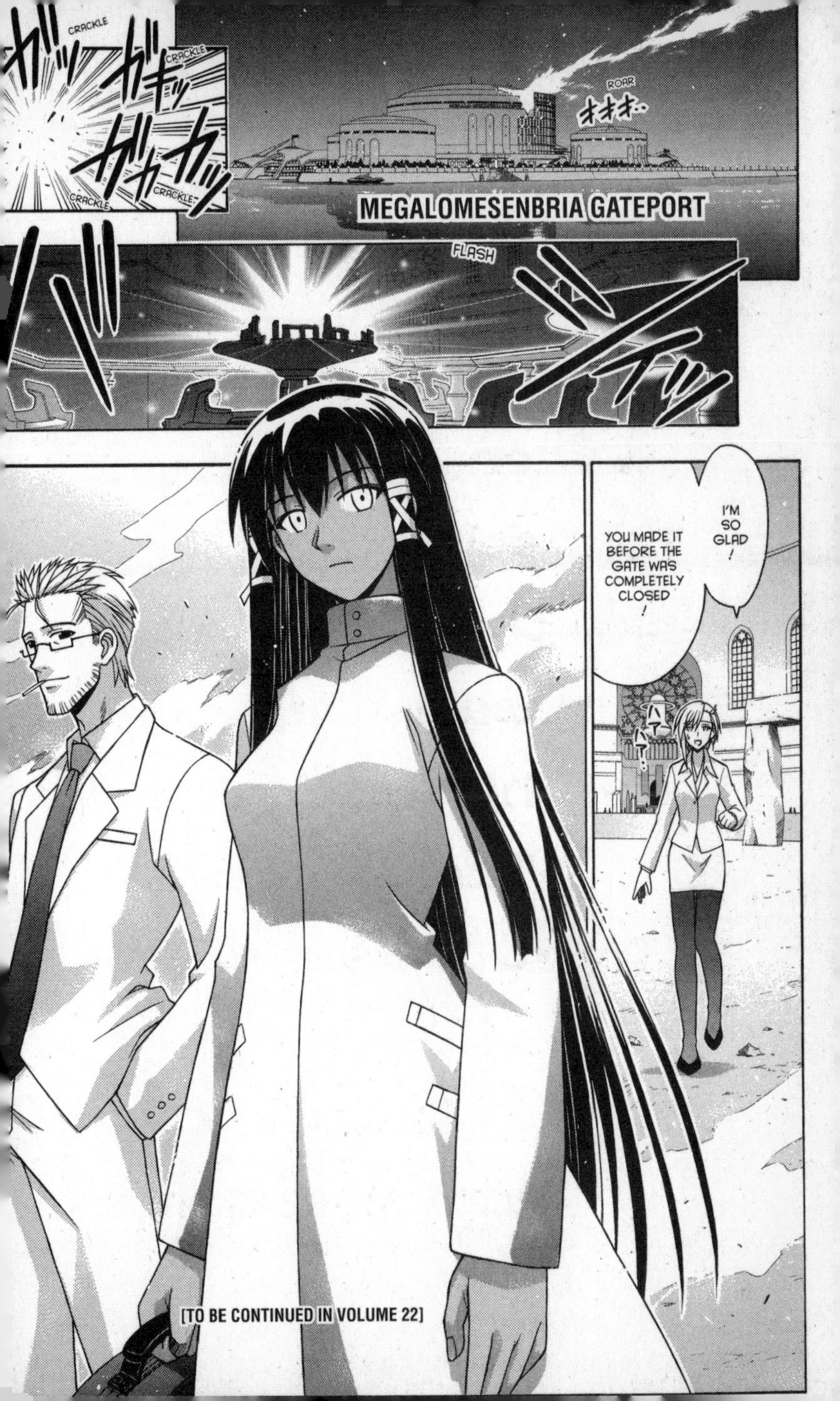
ROAR
MEGALOMESENBRIA GATEPORT
CRACKLE
CRACKLE
CRACKLE
CRACKLE
FLASH
I'M SO GLAD!
YOU MADE IT BEFORE THE GATE WAS COMPLETELY CLOSED!
[TO BE CONTINUED IN VOLUME 22]

–STAFF–

Ken Akamatsu
Takashi Takemoto
Kenichi Nakamura
Masaki Ohyama
Keiichi Yamashita
Tadashi Maki
Tohru Mitsuhashi

Thanks to
Ran Ayanaga

NEGI MA!

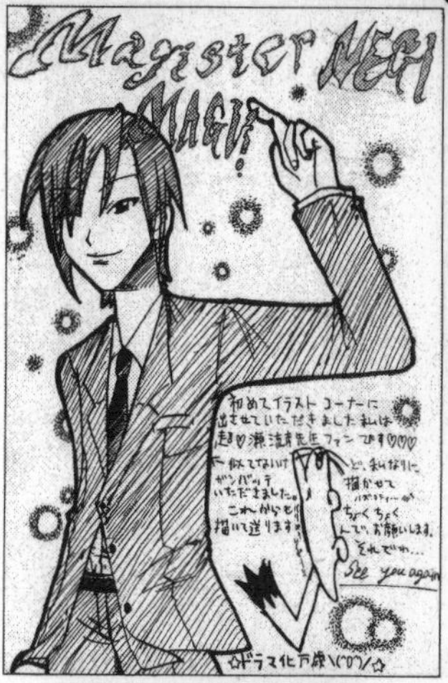

Magister NEGI MAGI!
初めてイラストコーナーに出させていただきました私は超♡瀬流彦先生ファンです♡♡
See you again
☆ドラマ化万歳\(^O^)/☆

HE'S SO COOL!

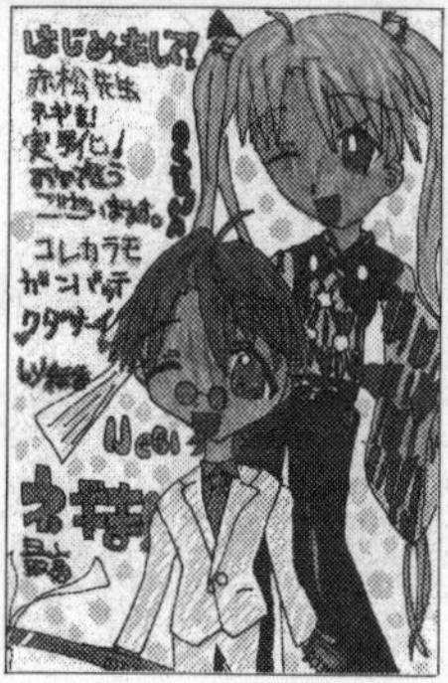

はじめまして!! 赤松先生、ネギま!実写化!おめでとうございます。
コレカラモガンバッテクダサイ
Negi

THANKS FOR THE COLORFUL ARTWORK.

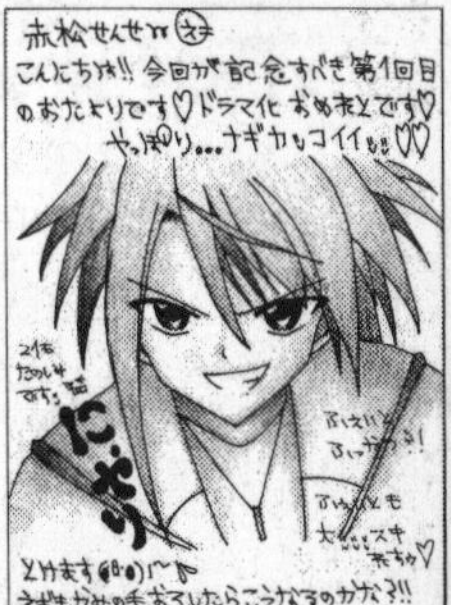

赤松せんせい
こんにちは!! 今回が記念すべき第1回目のおたよりです♡ドラマ化おめでとうです♡
やっぱり…ナギカッコイイ…♡♡
ネギもカみのもおろしたらこうなるのカナ?!!
これからも頑張って下さい♡
P.N まきすぷりんぐ

NAGI'S ALSO IN THE LIVE-ACTION DRAMA!

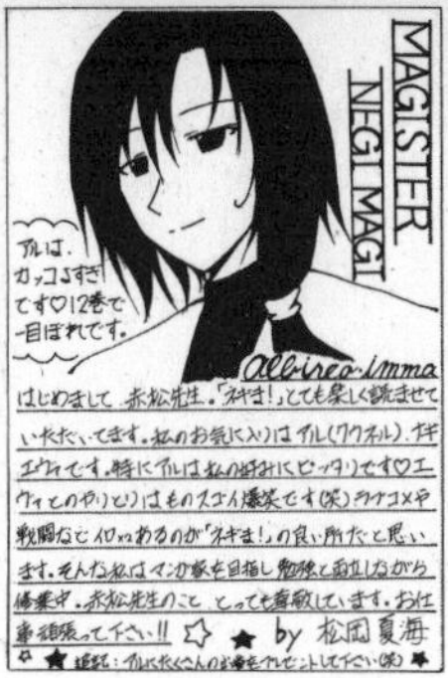

MAGISTER NEGI MAGI
アルは、カッコよすぎです♡12巻で一目ぼれです。
Albireo-imma
はじめまして 赤松先生。「ネギま!」とても楽しく読ませていただいてます。私のお気に入りはアル(クウネル)、ナギ、エヴァです。特にアルは私の好みにピッタリです♡エヴァとのやりとりはものスゴイ爆笑です(笑)ラブコメや戦闘などイロイロあるのが「ネギま!」の良い所だと思います。そんな私はマンガ家を目指し勉強と両立しながら修業中。赤松先生のこと とっても尊敬しています。お仕事頑張って下さい!!
by 松岡夏海

SO HANDSOME!

NEGIMA!
FAN ART CORNER

FATE AND NAGI'S ARE BECOMING MORE AND MORE POPULAR FROM THE LOOKS OF IT (IN SECRET? (LAUGHS)) ASUNA IS AS POPULAR AS USUAL ★ HERE WE GO AGAIN FOR TODAY (^^)
★ BANA CREAM PUFF'S ILLUSTRATION FROM LAST TIME CAPTURED THE ESSENCE OF HAKASE. (^^; I'M SORRY FOR THE MISTAKE.

TEXT BY ASSISTANT MAX

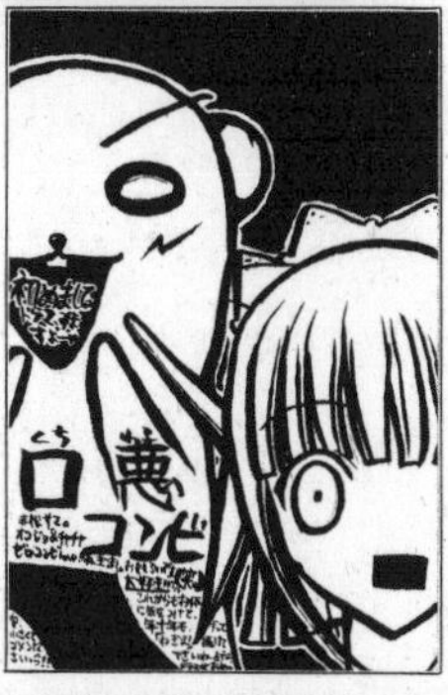

口悪コンビ

GREAT COMBO

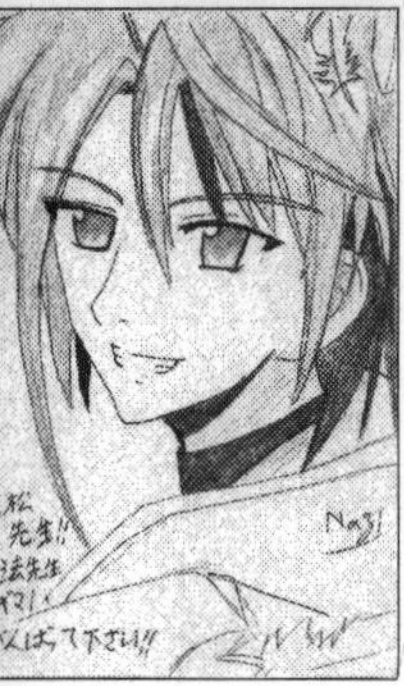

Nagi

PRETTY BOY!

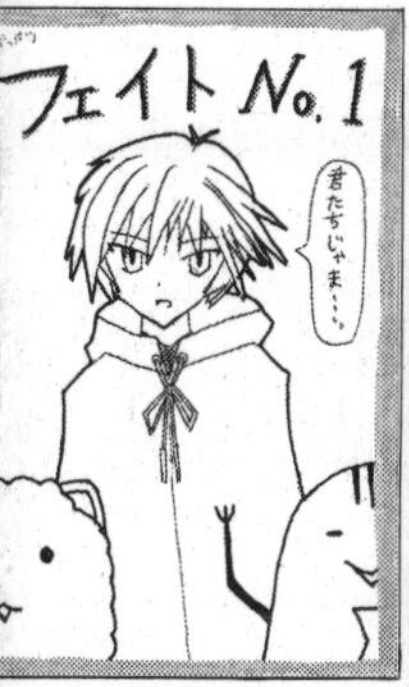

フェイト No. 1
君たちじゃま…。

HE'S POPULAR.

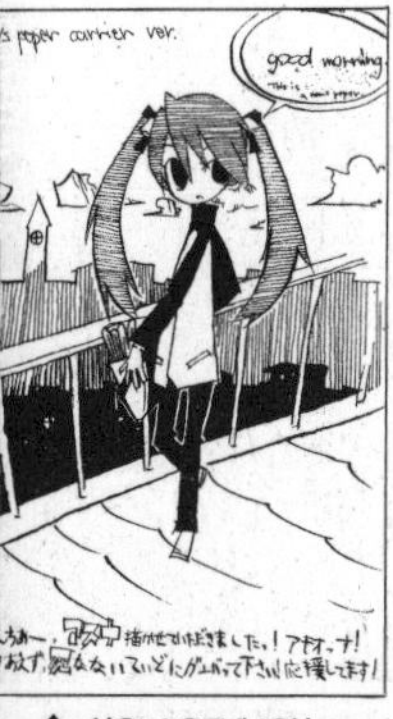

good morning

HOW STYLISH

MAGISTER NEGI MAGI

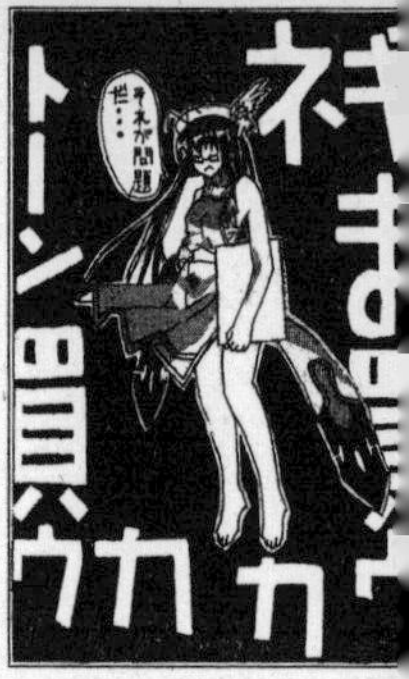
それが問題だ…

▲ LOOKS WORRIED

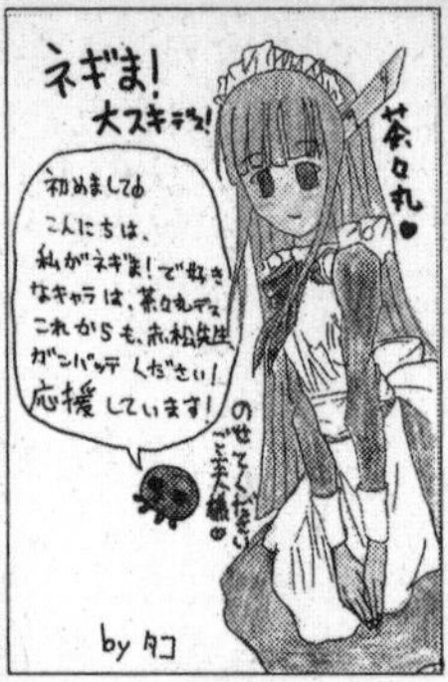
ネギま! 大スキデス!
茶々丸♥
初めまして。こんにちは、私がネギま!で好きなキャラは、茶々丸デス これからも、赤松先生ガンバッテください! 応援しています!
のせてください ご主人様
by タコ

▲ I WANT HER TO POUR MY TEA!

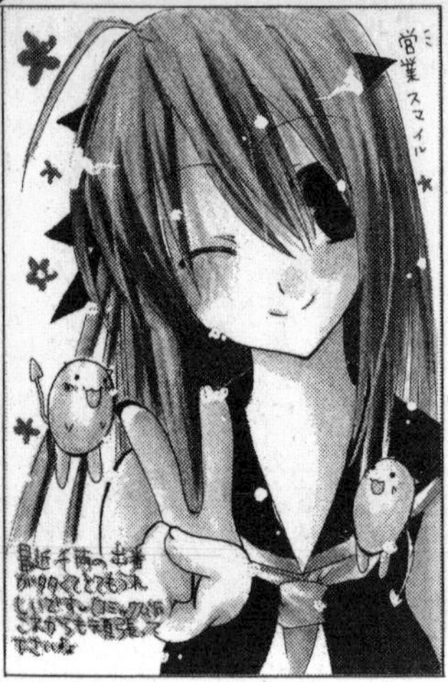
営業スマイル

▲ SUPERCUTE!

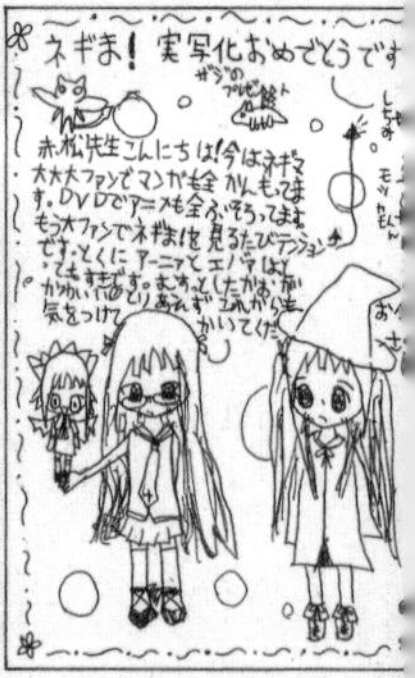
ネギま! 実写化おめでとうです

▲ ADORABLE★

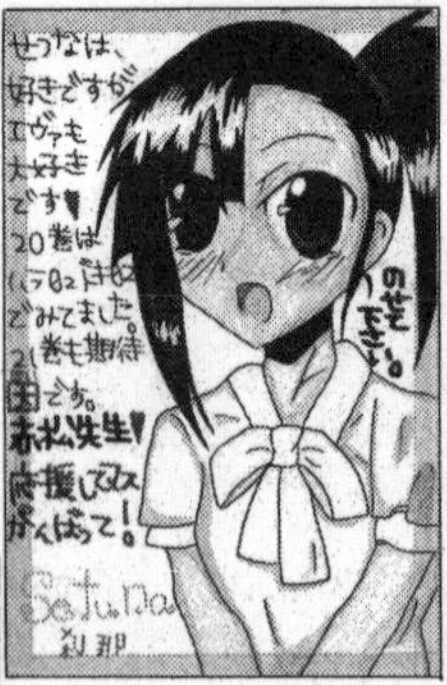
のせて下さい。
赤松先生! 応援してマス がんばって!
Setsuna
刹那

▲ SETSUNA-SAN LOOKS SO POLITE.

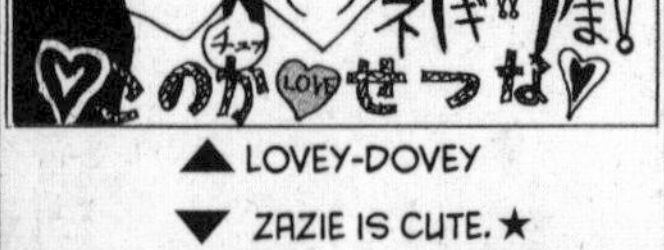
がんばって下さい!! 赤松先生!!
ネギま!
このか LOVE せつな

▲ LOVEY-DOVEY

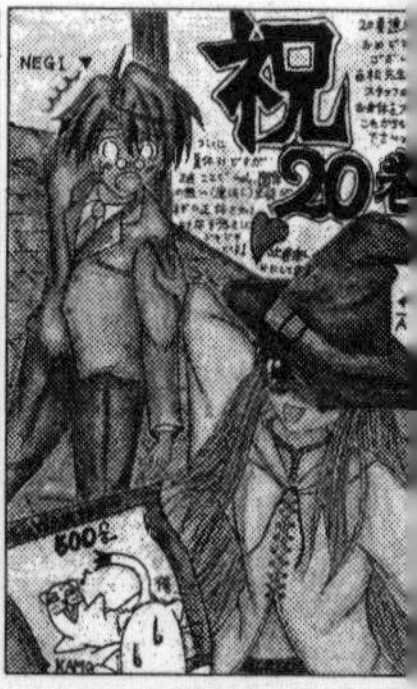
祝 20巻
NEGI

▲ FRIENDS★ (^^)

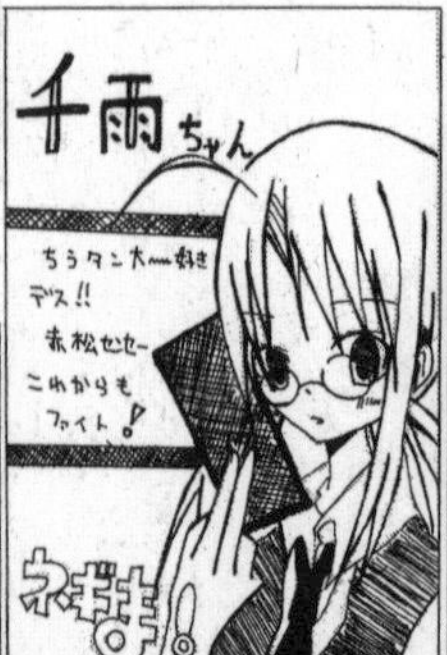
千雨ちゃん
ちうタン大〜好きデス!! 赤松セセー これからもファイト!
ネギま!

▲ SHE'S A COOL BEAUTY (^^).

▼ ZAZIE IS CUTE.★

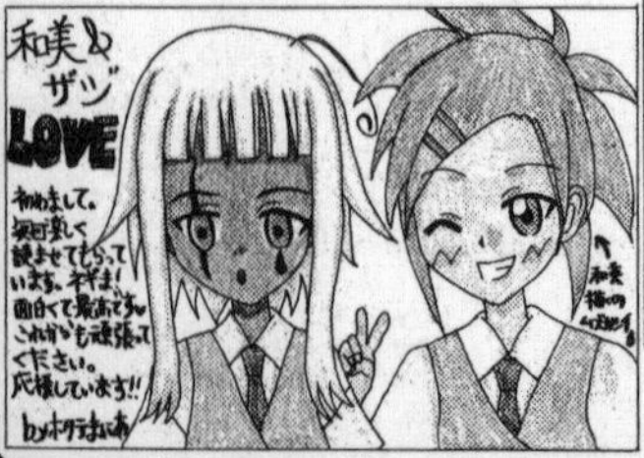
和美&ザジ LOVE
応援しています!!

NEGI MA!

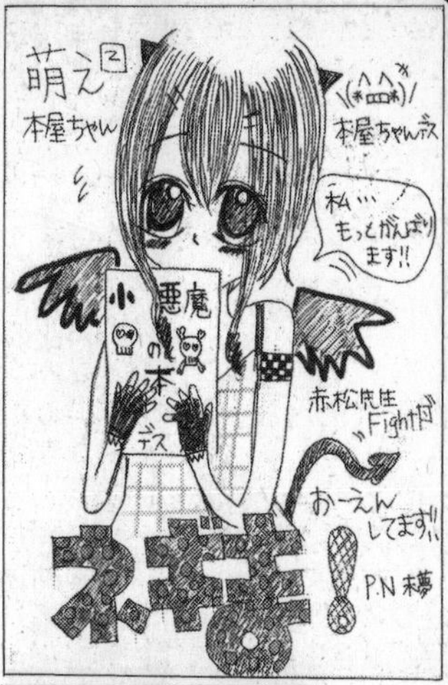
萌え
本屋ちゃん
本屋ちゃんデス
私… もっとがんばります!!
小悪魔の本デス
赤松先生Fight!!
おーえんしてます!!
ネギま!
P.N 未夢

GOOD BOOK (LAUGHS)

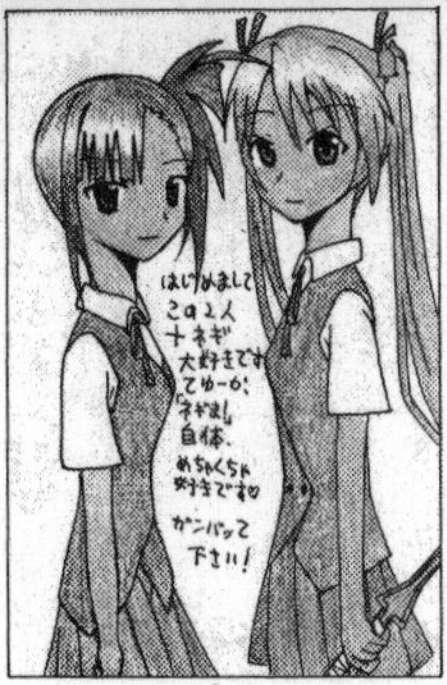

▲ THEY'RE BOTH SO STRONG (^^).

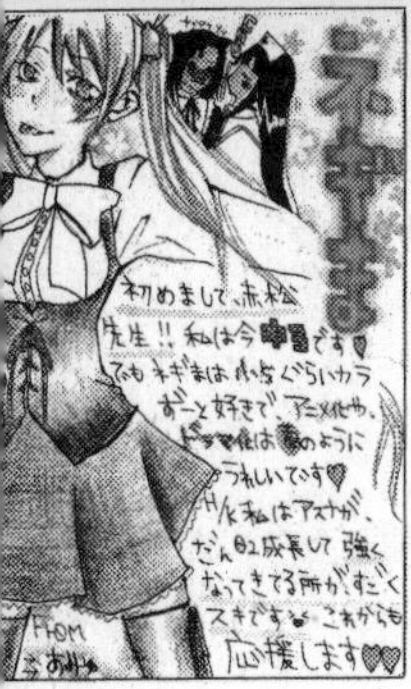

▲ FLIRTY ASUNA (^^)

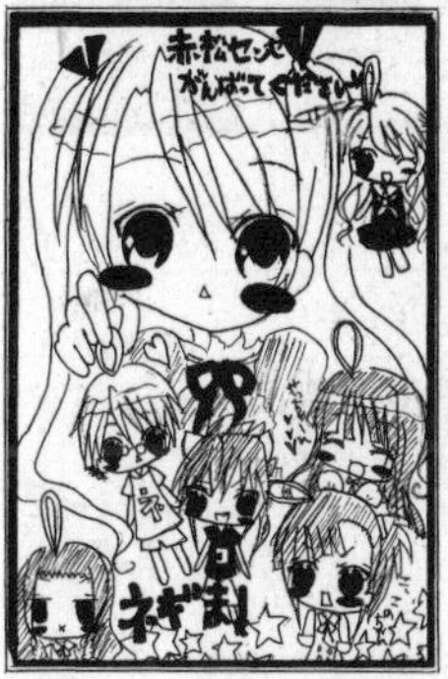
ネギま!

ASUNA'S CUTE. ▲

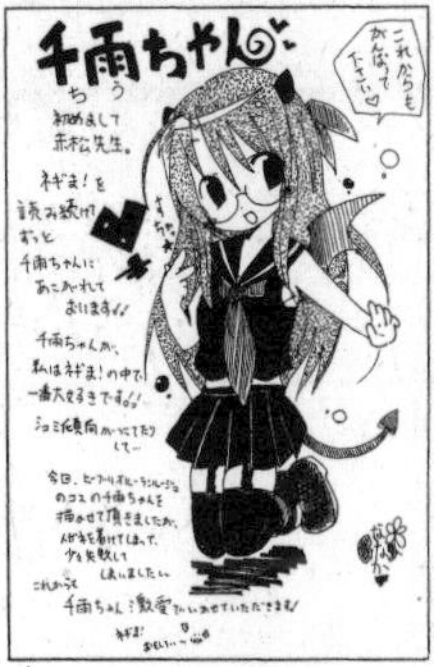
千雨ちゃん
初めまして 赤松先生。

▲ LOVE THE TAIL

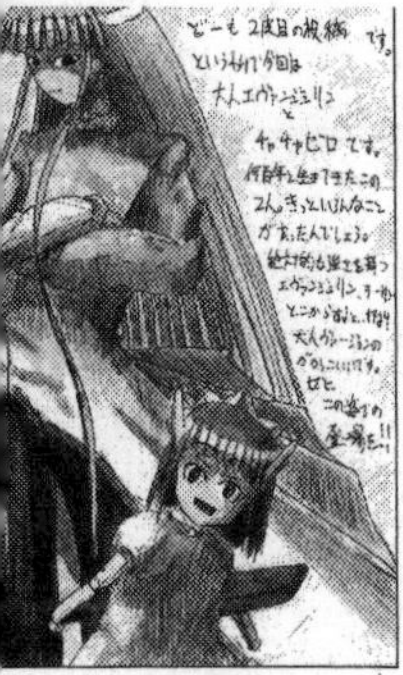

▲ SERIOUS CHACHAZERO★

▼ HOT AND COOL (^^)

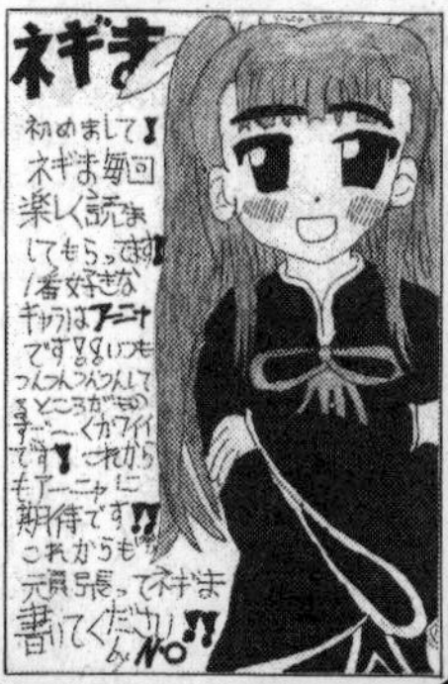
ネギま
初めまして
ネギま毎回楽しく読ましてもらってます

▼ SHE'LL BE ACTIVE.★

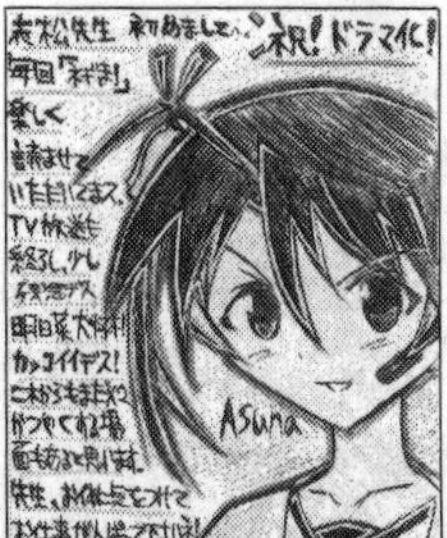
赤松先生 初めまして。
祝!ドラマ化!
Asuna

▼ NO NEED TO CRY (LAUGHS)

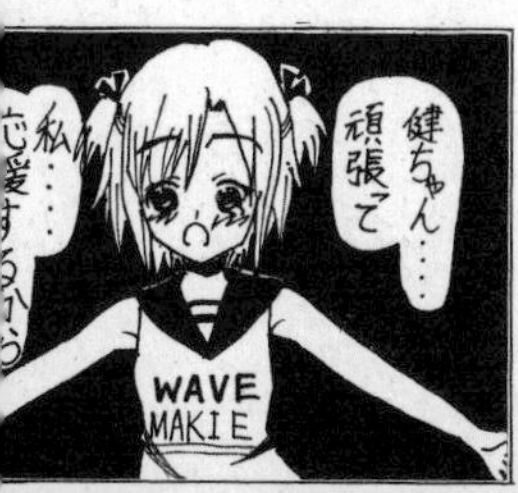
健ちゃん…頑張って
私…応援するから
WAVE
MAKIE

今回の

FEATURED CHARACTER

KAEDE NAGASE RANKING

NEGI MAGI MAGISTER

FIRST PLACE

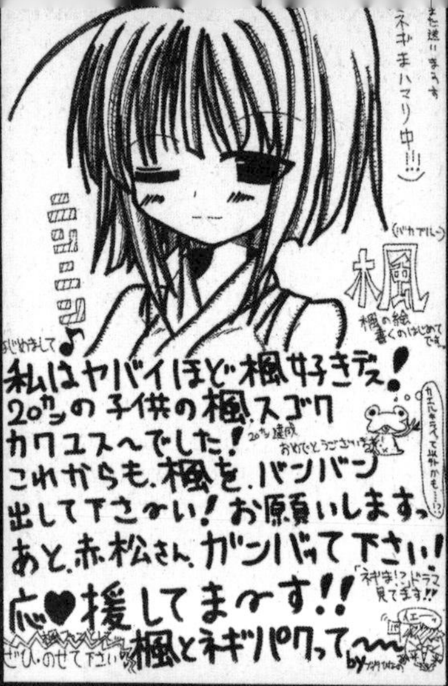

ネギまハマリ中!!!
楓
私はヤバイほど楓好きデス！
20巻の子供の楓スゴクカワユスーでした！
これからも、楓を、バンバン出して下さ～い！お願いします。
あと、赤松さん、ガンバって下さい！
応♥援してま～す！！
楓とネギパクって～

WHAT AN ADORABLE KAEDE. A PACTIO WITH NEGI, EH... DON'T YOU THINK THAT WOULD MAKE HER TOO STRONG? (LAUGHS)

SECOND PLACE

KAEDE'S IMAGE ABOUT SUMMER THE MOUNTAINS. SD IS ADORAB

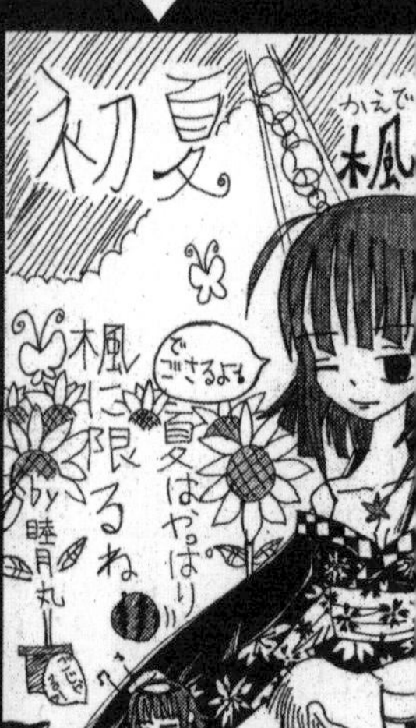

初夏
でござるよ。
楓に限るね
夏はやっぱり

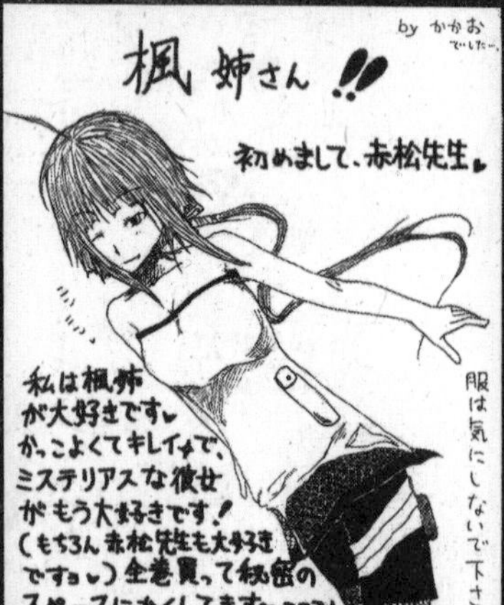

楓姉さん!!
初めまして、赤松先生。
私は楓姉が大好きです。かっこよくてキレイで、ミステリアスな彼女がもう大好きです！（もちろん赤松先生も大好きですよ）全巻買って秘密のスペースにかくしてます。これからもずっとおうえんしてます。なので、無理せずに、お体に気を付けてがんばって下さいね。
ドラマ化おめでとうございます。見ます
服は気にしないで下さい。

THIRD PLACE

WHY DO YOU HIDE THEM IN A SECRET PLACE? (LAUGHS) IS IT TOO SEXY?

LEXICON NEGIMARIUM

[*Negima!* 187th Period Lexicon Negimarium]

■ **Μελαω Και Σφαιοιρικον Δεσμωτηριον**
 • This is a spell that confines an object within a powerful boundary. It means "a black, round prison" in ancient Greek. The purpose of this magic is not for standard restraint, but rather to contain highly spiritual objects such as dragons and giants. Asphalt will be poured over the object, and it will be suffocated within the spheric borders. It looks like Kaede narrowly escaped. Unless the confined object has special magical survival abilities, it will suffocate to death.

[*Negima!* 188th Period Lexicon Negimarium]

■ **Ibukidono ōharahe**
 Takamagahara ni kamuzumarimasu
 kamuro ki kamuro minomikotowomochite
 sumegamitachino maeni mausaku
 kurushimiuefu wagatomoyo
 mamorimegumahi sakiwaetamaheto
 • Konoka Konoe's personal magical spell.
 This spell activates the power of Kochinohiougi. This spell is incanted in the old Yamato dialect of Japanese. Magicians were given personalized spells that reflected their quality and character.
 According to the Shinto ritual prayer in volume 8 of "Engishiki" called "Minazukinotsugomorioooharae" (what is called Nakatominoharae), "Ibukido" is a location where sin is dispersed to "Nenokuni" or "Sonokuni" by the "ibukidonushi," which is one aspect of the Haraedo Yohashi Ookami, a god. It's a place where all sins were erased. However, in ancient Japanese culture, sin is described more as corruption and catastrophe. In "Minazukinotsugomorioooharae," misfortune and vice are erased through the "Ibukido." Injuries and illness fall into this category and can also be erased through the "Ibukido."

During the Kamakura Era, in the sacred texts "Yamatohimenomiko" and "Nakatominoharahekunge," "Ibukidonushi" is the "Kamunahobinokami," a deity, in ancient Japanese mythology. An Edo era philosopher and scholar, Norinaga Omoto, felt that in order for any healing to occur, one must think straightforwardly. This honesty can purge uncleanliness or misfortune and will the spirit from calamity to purification ("Kojikiden," volume 6). According to norinaga, the "Ibukidonushi," aka "Kamunahobinokami," is a deity that "repairs" calamity. In the Yamato dialect, "to repair" also means "to heal." Therefore, the "Ibukidonushi" is also a healer.

Konoka's personalized spell is influenced by her teacher's magic (as a result, an inexperienced magician can still possess power similar to magic). However, Konoka's magical power exceeds that of Negi in this case, so her control over "Kochinohiougi" is rather unstable.

■ **The Palace of the dead, deep within the wombs of the Earth...(appear below us) The Stone Pillar of Hades**
(ω Ταρταρω κειμενον Βασιλειον νεκρων [Φαινσαοθω ημιν] Ο ΜΟΝΟΑΙΘΟΣ ΚΙΩΝ ΤΟΥ ΑΙΔΟΥ)
•This spell gives the ability to move enormous pillars of stone. A high-ranking mage can move and attack with this object via psychokinesis. Each pillar is enormous, hence the devastation is incredible. While these stones are moving through magic, magical barriers cannot prevent the damage due to the massive amount of energy produced by their impact.

[*Negima!* 193rd Period Lexicon Negimarium]

■ **Melodia Bellax De Bi-Festinando**
•A high-level magic used during close-contact fighting. It gives great agility to every movement of the mage's body.

■ **Sagitta Magica Series Sabulonis**
•An offensive magical spell that utilizes sand. The magical arrows created by sand are blasted shotgun style, spewing sand everywhere. It's nearly impossible to deflect the multiple sand projectiles. The sand granules are infused with magical power; hence, they have the ability to penetrate metal.

■ Iksir
(الإكسير, al-iksir)

•"Iksir" is an Arabic word referring to secret medicines used in alchemy. The word comes from the ancient Greek ξήριον (kseriou, medicinal powder for drying wounds) and originally meant nothing more than a powdered medicine. When given the Arabic article [الإكسير] al, "iksir" becomes "al-iksir," which then becomes the Latin "elixir."

A politician and historian active in North Africa, Ibn Khaldun (1332–1406), wrote the following in his book *The Muqaddimah: An Introduction to History*:

"Great alchemists consider iksir to be a substance composed of the four elements. When one applies special alchemic treatments, this substance gains specific traits and various natural powers. These powers cause anything the substance touches to assimilate with it, and change the thing, giving it the same traits and form as the substance. The powers transmit their various properties and powers to whatever they touch. It is exactly like the yeast in bread assimilating the dough, giving it its own traits, and making the bread loose and fluffy" (chapter 6, section 32[1]).

In regards to the effects of iksir, there are various alchemic theories, such as turning base metals into precious metals or granting ageless immortality, but it would seem that its essential function is to assimilate what it touches with its own traits. Then what are the traits of this iksir?

According to Ibn Khaldun, iksir is refined from a "noble stone" (ibid. ibidem). In layman's terms, this noble stone is the "wise man's stone (lapis sophorum)" or the "philosopher's stone (lapis philosophorum)," but these terms had not yet been coined in Ibn Khaldun's time. The reason the "stone" from which the iksir is derived is called the philosopher's stone is that the Spanish philosopher Maslama al-Majriti (approximately tenth century) and others considered alchemic knowledge to be absolutely essential to philosophy (ibid. section 29).

According to the written works of a pupil of Maslama al-Majriti, cited by Ibn Khaldun, as things created in the natural world go in order from mineral (earth) to vegetable to animal, their degree of purity goes up and they become higher quality (ibid. ibidem). This is because plants absorb their essence from the earth and animals

---

1. Section numbers in chapter 6 are from the Parisian edition (rev. by Quatremère, 1858).

prey upon those plants. And the philosopher's stone is inside the highest level of natural creations—namely, animal—and taking it apart would yield the four elements.

This work by Maslama al-Majriti's pupil gives a fascinating explanation about a treatment of a philosopher's stone:

"Take the noble stone. Place it in a cucurbit and an alembic. Divide it into the four elements: water, air, earth, and fire. Those are substance, spirit, soul, and dyeing. Once the water is separated from earth and the air from fire, keep them in their own individual containers. Take the dregs—that is, the sediment—from the bottoms of the containers. Purify in a hot flame until the blackness is removed and its coarseness and hardness disappear. Carefully bleach and evaporate the excess moisture hidden inside. Then it will become a white water, with no kind of darkness, dregs, or disharmony" (ibid. ibidem).

Here we can see the idea of "albedo," known by later generations as one of the four major stages of alchemy. This work does not clarify what the white liquid that is obtained after extracting the four elements from the philosopher's stone, but based on the fact that it is a substance gained from the philosopher's stone, assuming that it is iksir would not contradict Ibn Khaldun's report that iksir is refined from the philosopher's stone.

Nevertheless, even assuming that this white liquid is iksir, all we know is that it is a substance of extremely high purity, and it is still unclear what effects it has when used on other things. However, Ibn Khaldun says that iksir's power and the traits it transmits are not one, but many. It is possible that iksir does not have only one specific use but is used in many different ways. Therefore, it may not only change the qualities of minerals, but also function as a panacea to heal human flesh. This is because as long as alchemy is said to directly alter the elements, it would not only change the properties of minerals, but also of vegetables and animals.

Furthermore, Ibn Khaldun gives a stern warning that alchemy is harmful to monetary economies (ibid. section 32). Taking this into account, that is reason enough for the iksir to be extremely expensive. This is because if the iksir were to be sold at a low price, the value of precious metals such as gold and silver would plummet, throwing the economy into confusion. If the price of iksir was not set higher than the value of the precious metals that can be refined by it, the economy could fail.

2. There are strong suspicions that this work is apocryphal.

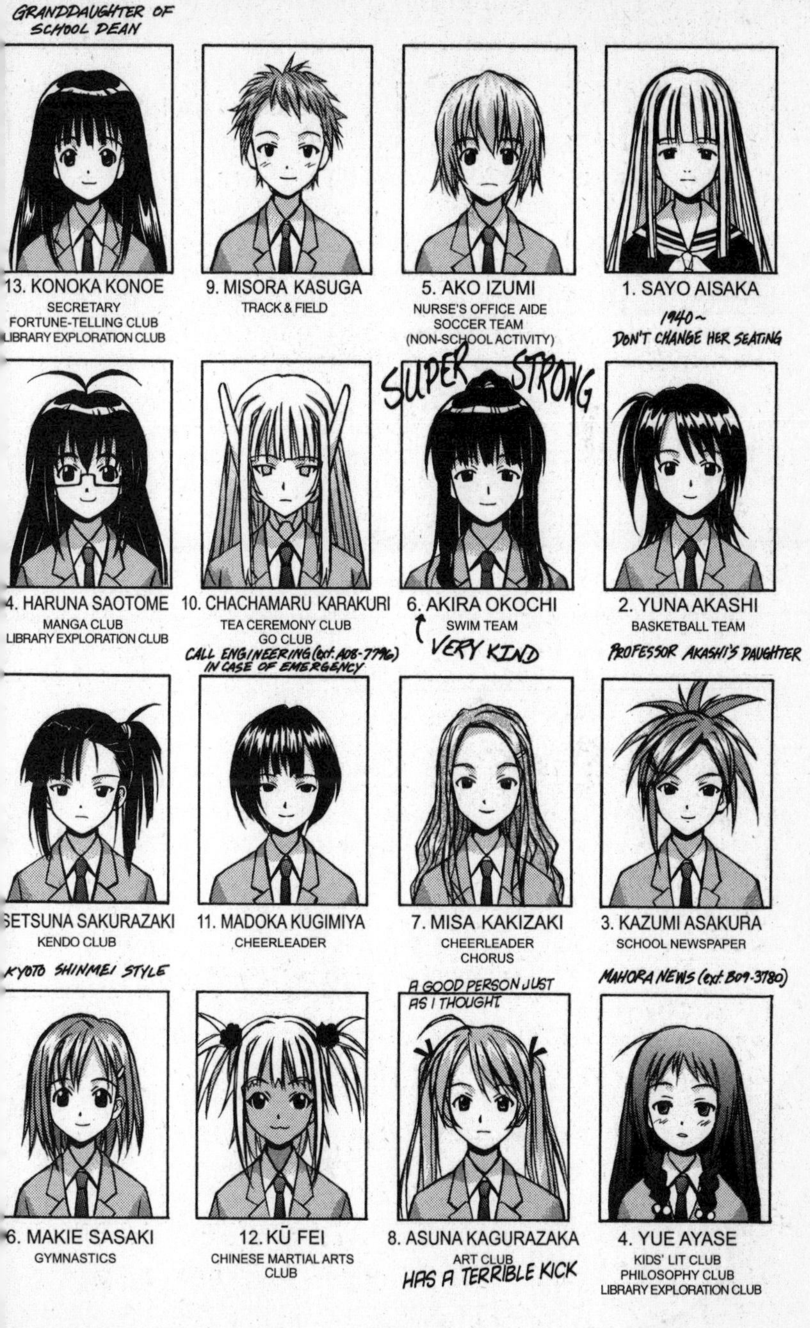

1. SAYO AISAKA
1940~
DON'T CHANGE HER SEATING
5. AKO IZUMI
NURSE'S OFFICE AIDE
SOCCER TEAM
(NON-SCHOOL ACTIVITY)
9. MISORA KASUGA
TRACK & FIELD
GRANDDAUGHTER OF SCHOOL DEAN
13. KONOKA KONOE
SECRETARY
FORTUNE-TELLING CLUB
LIBRARY EXPLORATION CLUB
2. YUNA AKASHI
BASKETBALL TEAM
PROFESSOR AKASHI'S DAUGHTER
SUPER STRONG
6. AKIRA OKOCHI
SWIM TEAM
VERY KIND
10. CHACHAMARU KARAKURI
TEA CEREMONY CLUB
GO CLUB
CALL ENGINEERING (ext. A08-7796) IN CASE OF EMERGENCY
4. HARUNA SAOTOME
MANGA CLUB
LIBRARY EXPLORATION CLUB
3. KAZUMI ASAKURA
SCHOOL NEWSPAPER
MAHORA NEWS (ext. B09-3780)
7. MISA KAKIZAKI
CHEERLEADER
CHORUS
11. MADOKA KUGIMIYA
CHEERLEADER
SETSUNA SAKURAZAKI
KENDO CLUB
KYOTO SHINMEI STYLE
4. YUE AYASE
KIDS' LIT CLUB
PHILOSOPHY CLUB
LIBRARY EXPLORATION CLUB
A GOOD PERSON JUST AS I THOUGHT.
8. ASUNA KAGURAZAKA
ART CLUB
HAS A TERRIBLE KICK
12. KŪ FEI
CHINESE MARTIAL ARTS CLUB
6. MAKIE SASAKI
GYMNASTICS

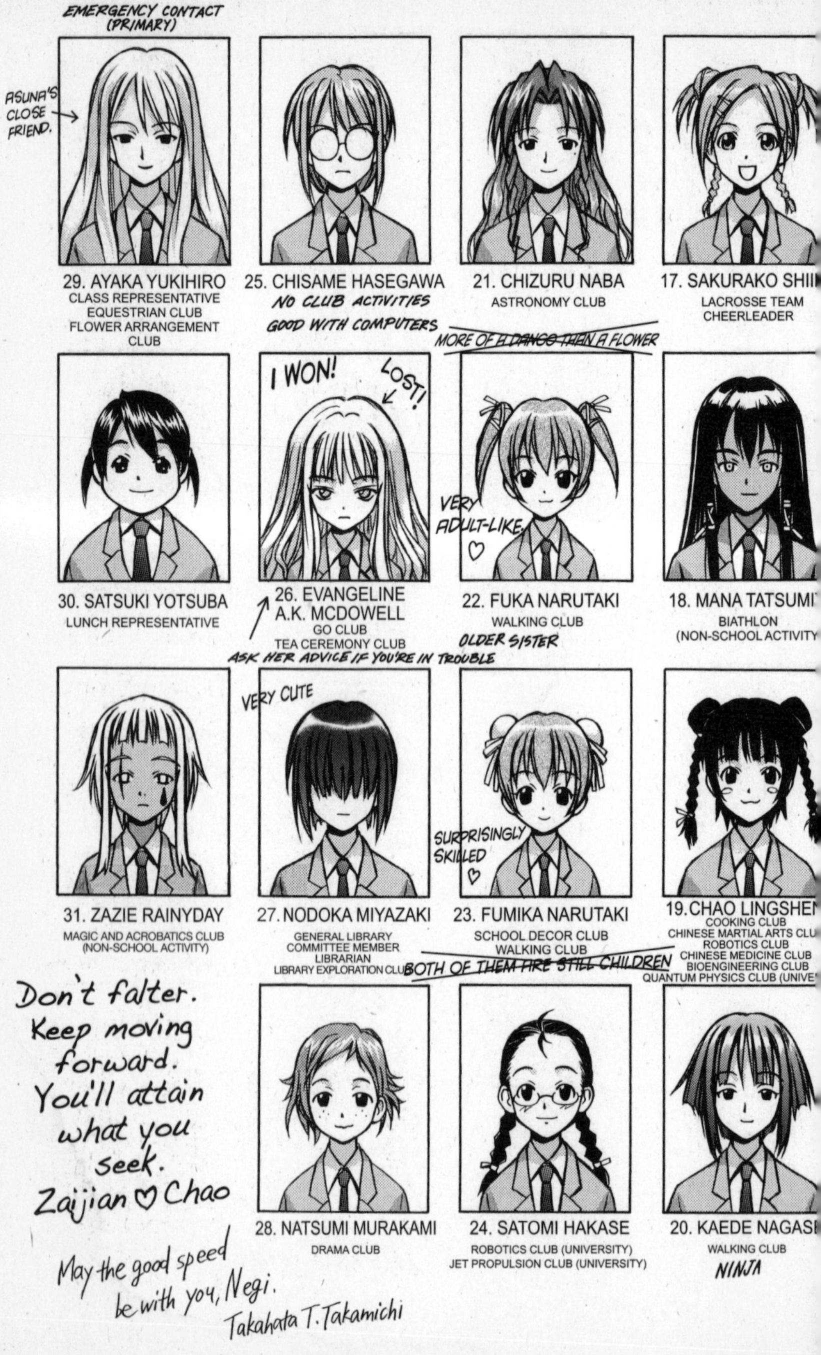

17. SAKURAKO SHII
LACROSSE TEAM
CHEERLEADER
21. CHIZURU NABA
ASTRONOMY CLUB
MORE OF A DANGO THAN A FLOWER
25. CHISAME HASEGAWA
NO CLUB ACTIVITIES
GOOD WITH COMPUTERS
EMERGENCY CONTACT (PRIMARY)
ASUNA'S CLOSE FRIEND.
29. AYAKA YUKIHIRO
CLASS REPRESENTATIVE
EQUESTRIAN CLUB
FLOWER ARRANGEMENT CLUB
18. MANA TATSUMI
BIATHLON
(NON-SCHOOL ACTIVITY
VERY ADULT-LIKE ♡
22. FUKA NARUTAKI
WALKING CLUB
OLDER SISTER
LOST!
I WON!
26. EVANGELINE A.K. MCDOWELL
GO CLUB
TEA CEREMONY CLUB
ASK HER ADVICE IF YOU'RE IN TROUBLE
30. SATSUKI YOTSUBA
LUNCH REPRESENTATIVE
19. CHAO LINGSHEN
COOKING CLUB
CHINESE MARTIAL ARTS CLU
ROBOTICS CLUB
CHINESE MEDICINE CLUB
BIOENGINEERING CLUB
QUANTUM PHYSICS CLUB (UNIVE
SURPRISINGLY SKILLED ♡
23. FUMIKA NARUTAKI
SCHOOL DECOR CLUB
WALKING CLUB
BOTH OF THEM ARE STILL CHILDREN
VERY CUTE
27. NODOKA MIYAZAKI
GENERAL LIBRARY COMMITTEE MEMBER
LIBRARIAN
LIBRARY EXPLORATION CLUB
31. ZAZIE RAINYDAY
MAGIC AND ACROBATICS CLUB
(NON-SCHOOL ACTIVITY)
20. KAEDE NAGAS
WALKING CLUB
NINJA
24. SATOMI HAKASE
ROBOTICS CLUB (UNIVERSITY)
JET PROPULSION CLUB (UNIVERSITY)
28. NATSUMI MURAKAMI
DRAMA CLUB
Don't falter. Keep moving forward. You'll attain what you seek.
Zaijian ♡ Chao
May the good speed be with you, Negi.
Takahata T. Takamichi

魔法先生ネギま!

MAGISTER NEGI MAGI

赤松 健 SHONEN MAGAZINE COMICS

KEN AKAMATSU

21

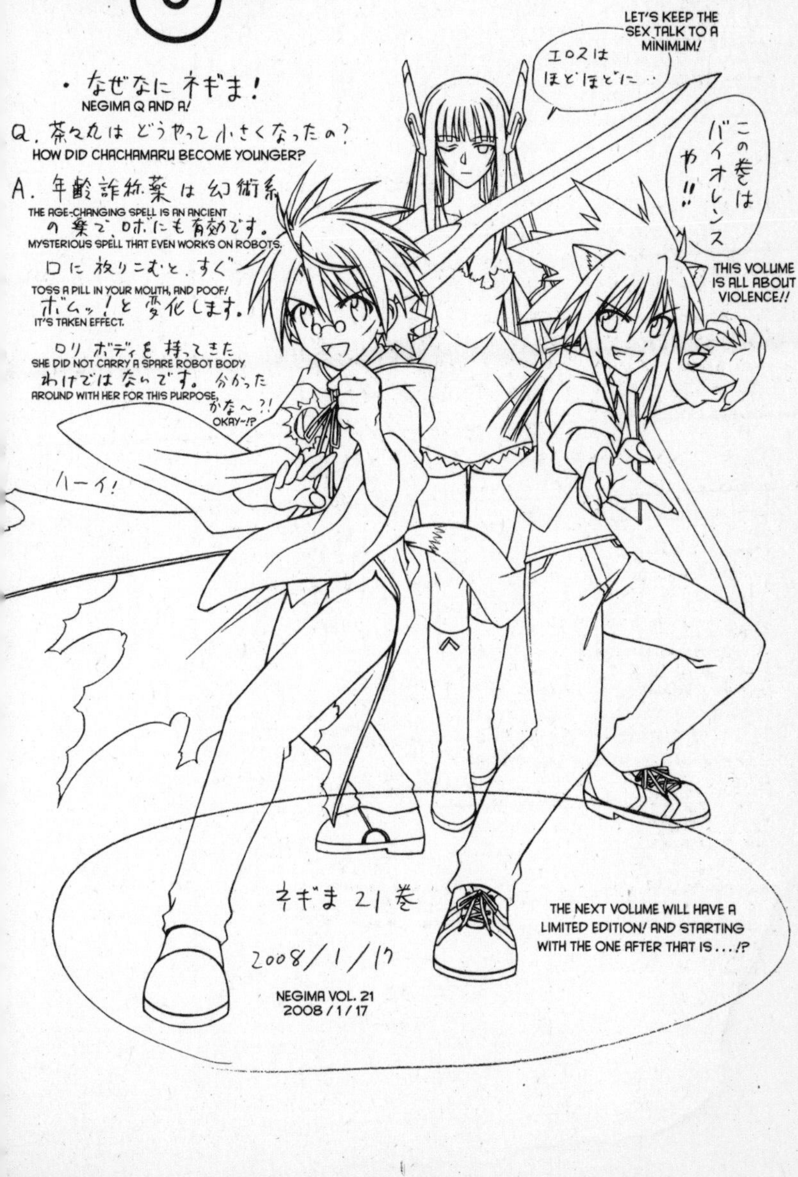

LET'S KEEP THE SEX TALK TO A MINIMUM!
エロスはほどほどに・・
この巻はバイオレンスや!!
THIS VOLUME IS ALL ABOUT VIOLENCE!!
・なぜなにネギま!
NEGIMA Q AND A!
Q. 茶々丸はどうやって小さくなったの?
HOW DID CHACHAMARU BECOME YOUNGER?
A. 年齢詐称薬は幻術系の薬で、ロボにも有効です。
THE AGE-CHANGING SPELL IS AN ANCIENT MYSTERIOUS SPELL THAT EVEN WORKS ON ROBOTS.
口に放りこむと、すぐボムッ!と変化します。
TOSS A PILL IN YOUR MOUTH, AND POOF! IT'S TAKEN EFFECT.
ロリボディを持ってきたわけではないです。分かったかな~?!
SHE DID NOT CARRY A SPARE ROBOT BODY AROUND WITH HER FOR THIS PURPOSE, OKAY~!?
ハーイ!
ネギま 21巻
2008/1/17
NEGIMA VOL. 21
2008/1/17
THE NEXT VOLUME WILL HAVE A LIMITED EDITION! AND STARTING WITH THE ONE AFTER THAT IS . . .!?

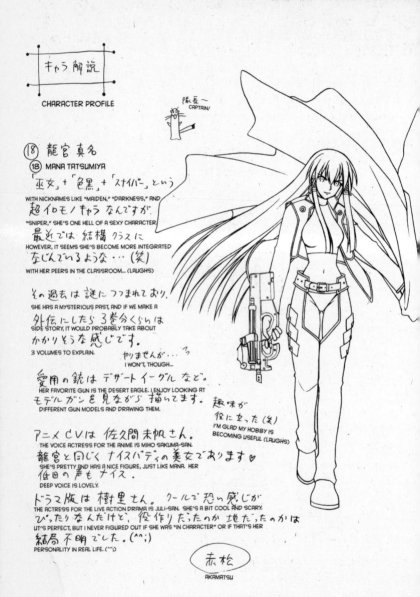

キャラ解説

CHARACTER PROFILE

隊長～
CAPTAIN!

⑱ 龍宮真名

⑱ MANA TATSUMIYA

「巫女」+「色黒」+「スナイパー」という

WITH NICKNAMES LIKE "MAIDEN," "DARKNESS," AND

超イロモノキャラ なんですが、

"SNIPER," SHE'S ONE HELL OF A SEXY CHARACTER.

最近では 結構 クラスに

HOWEVER, IT SEEMS SHE'S BECOME MORE INTEGRATED

なじんでいるような…(笑)

WITH HER PEERS IN THE CLASSROOM... (LAUGHS)

その過去は 謎に つつまれており、

SHE HAS A MYSTERIOUS PAST, AND IF WE MAKE A

外伝にしたら 3巻分くらいは

SIDE STORY, IT WOULD PROBABLY TAKE ABOUT

かかりそうな 感じです。

3 VOLUMES TO EXPLAIN.

やりませんが…?

I WON'T, THOUGH...

愛用の銃は デザートイーグル など。

HER FAVORITE GUN IS THE DESERT EAGLE. I ENJOY LOOKING AT

モデルガンを 見ながら 描いてます。

DIFFERENT GUN MODELS AND DRAWING THEM.

趣味が

役に立った(笑)

I'M GLAD MY HOBBY IS

BECOMING USEFUL (LAUGHS)

アニメCVは 佐久間末帆さん。

THE VOICE ACTRESS FOR THE ANIME IS MIHO SAKUMA-SAN.

龍宮と同じく ナイスバディの美女であります♡

SHE'S PRETTY AND HAS A NICE FIGURE, JUST LIKE MANA. HER

低田の声も ナイス。

DEEP VOICE IS LOVELY.

ドラマ版は 樹里さん。 クールで恐い感じが

THE ACTRESS FOR THE LIVE ACTION DRAMA IS JULI-SAN. SHE'S A BIT COOL AND SCARY.

ぴったりなんだけど、役作りだったのか 地だったのかは

IT'S PERFECT, BUT I NEVER FIGURED OUT IF SHE WAS "IN CHARACTER" OR IF THAT'S HER

結局 不明でした。(^^;)

PERSONALITY IN REAL LIFE. (^^;)

赤松

AKAMATSU

Translation Notes

Japanese is a tricky language for most Westerners, and translation is often more an art than a science. For your edification and reading pleasure, here are notes on some of the places where we could have gone in a different direction or where a Japanese cultural reference is used.

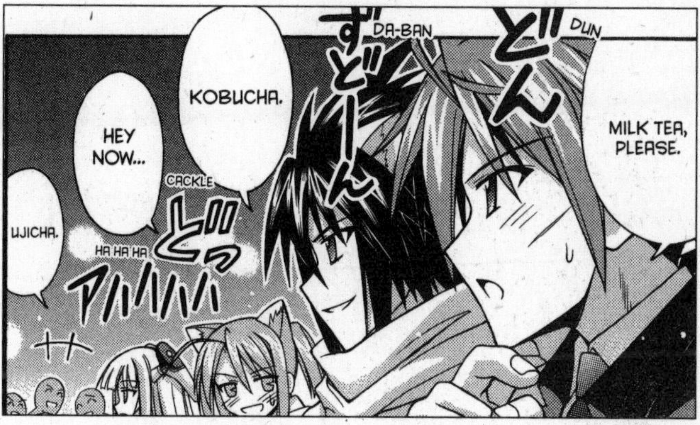

どん
DUN
MILK TEA, PLEASE.
ずどーん
DA-BAN
KOBUCHA.
HEY NOW...
どっ
CACKLE
UJICHA.
アハハハ
HA HA HA

Kobucha and Ujicha, page 120

The Japanese kobucha is very different from what is known (and often mistakenly assumed to be the same) in the West as "kombucha." Kombucha is a sweetened tea made from bacteria and yeast fermentation. Kobucha is a slightly salty tea made from a type of kelp called konbu.

Ujicha is a type of green tea and one of the most popular green teas in Japan. The leaves are not covered by shade, so it has high quantities of caffeine and tannins. It is the most common type of tea produced in Japan.

Uji is a Southern city located in Kyoto Prefecture. Ever since Shigun Yoshimitsu encouraged tea cultivation in the city, Uji has been known as the Japanese epicenter for fine green tea.

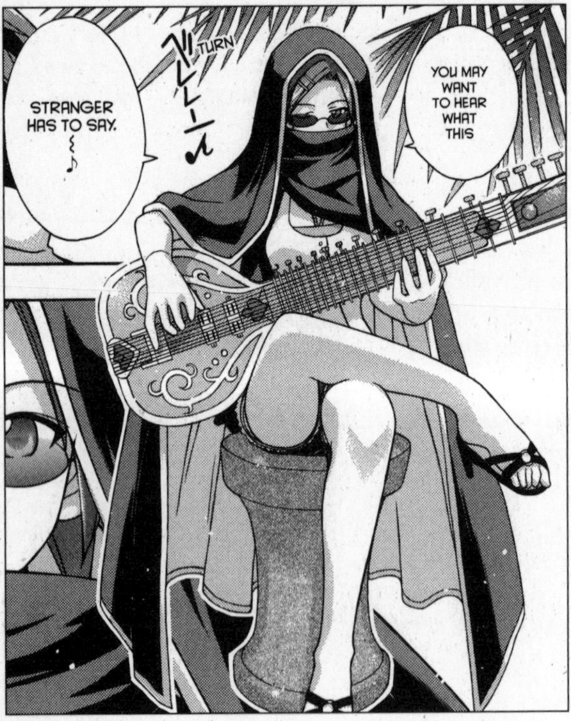

YOU MAY WANT TO HEAR WHAT THIS
TURN
STRANGER HAS TO SAY.

Sitar, page 138

The instrument that Kazumi is playing on page 138 is very similar to a traditional Indian instrument called the sitar. The sitar has been present in India since the twelfth century. The instrument gained international attention through the work of Mr. Ravi Shankar, a prominent virtuoso. The sitar can be heard in popular music by artists such as the Beatles, Rolling Stones, and Metallica.

About the Creator

Negima! is only Ken Akamatsu's third manga, although he started working in the field in 1994 with *AI Ga Tomaranai* (released in the United States with the title *A.I. Love You*). Like all of Akamatsu's work to date, it was published in Kodansha's *Shonen Magazine*. *AI Ga Tomaranai* ran for five years before concluding in 1999. In 1998, however, Akamatsu began the work that would make him one of the most popular manga artists in Japan: *Love Hina*. *Love Hina* ran for four years, and before its conclusion in 2002, it would cause Akamatsu to be granted the prestigious Manga of the Year award from Kodansha, as well as going on to become one of the bestselling manga in the United States.

Preview of *Negima!* Volume 22

We're pleased to present you with a preview of volume 22. Please check our website (www.delreymanga.com) to see when this volume will be available in English. For now you'll have to make do with Japanese!

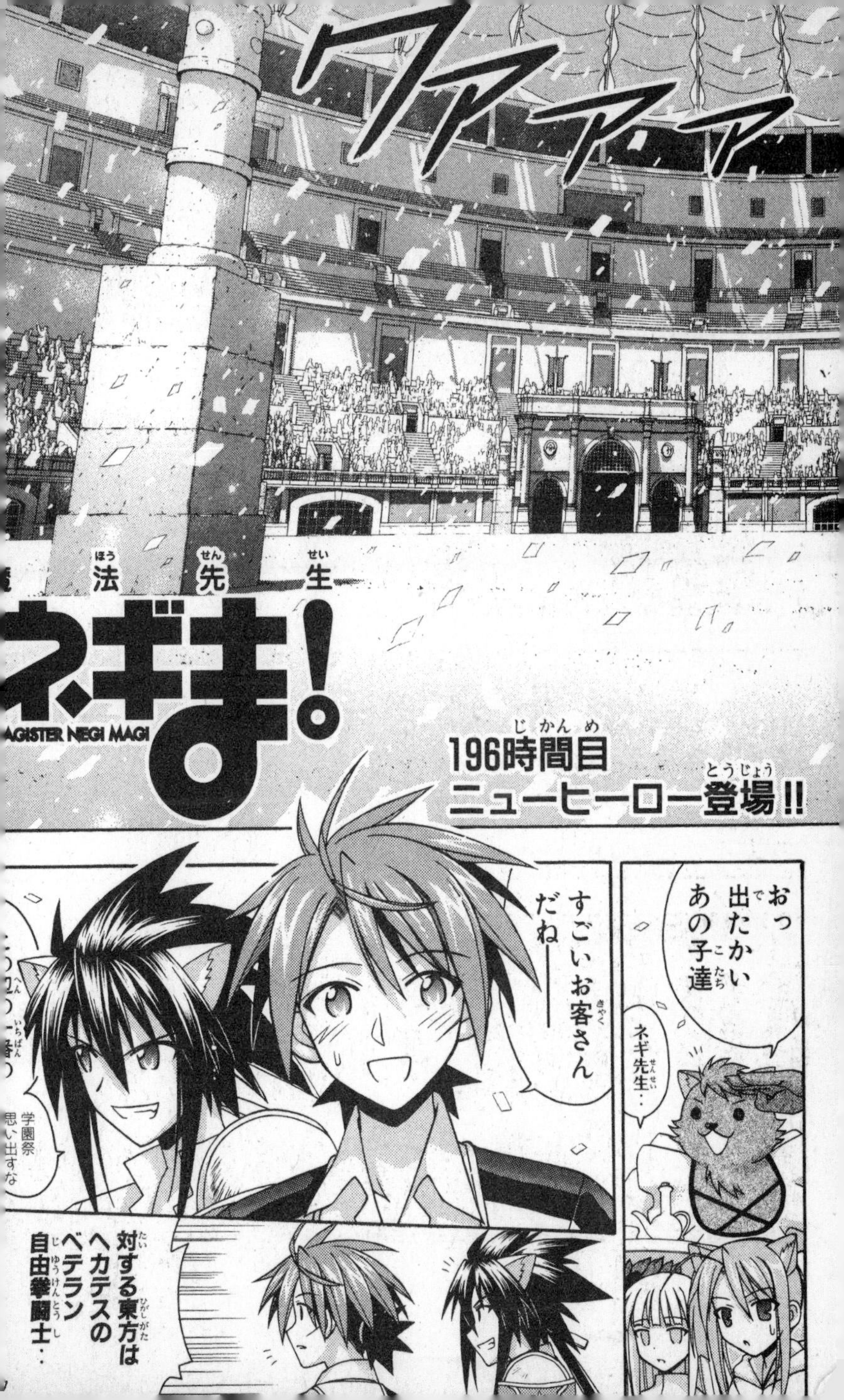
ワァァァ
法先生
ネギま!
AGISTER NEGI MAGI
196時間目
ニューヒーロー登場!!
おっ 出たかい あの子達
ネギ先生‥
すごいお客さんだねー
学園祭思い出すな
対する東方はヘカテスのベテラン自由拳闘士‥

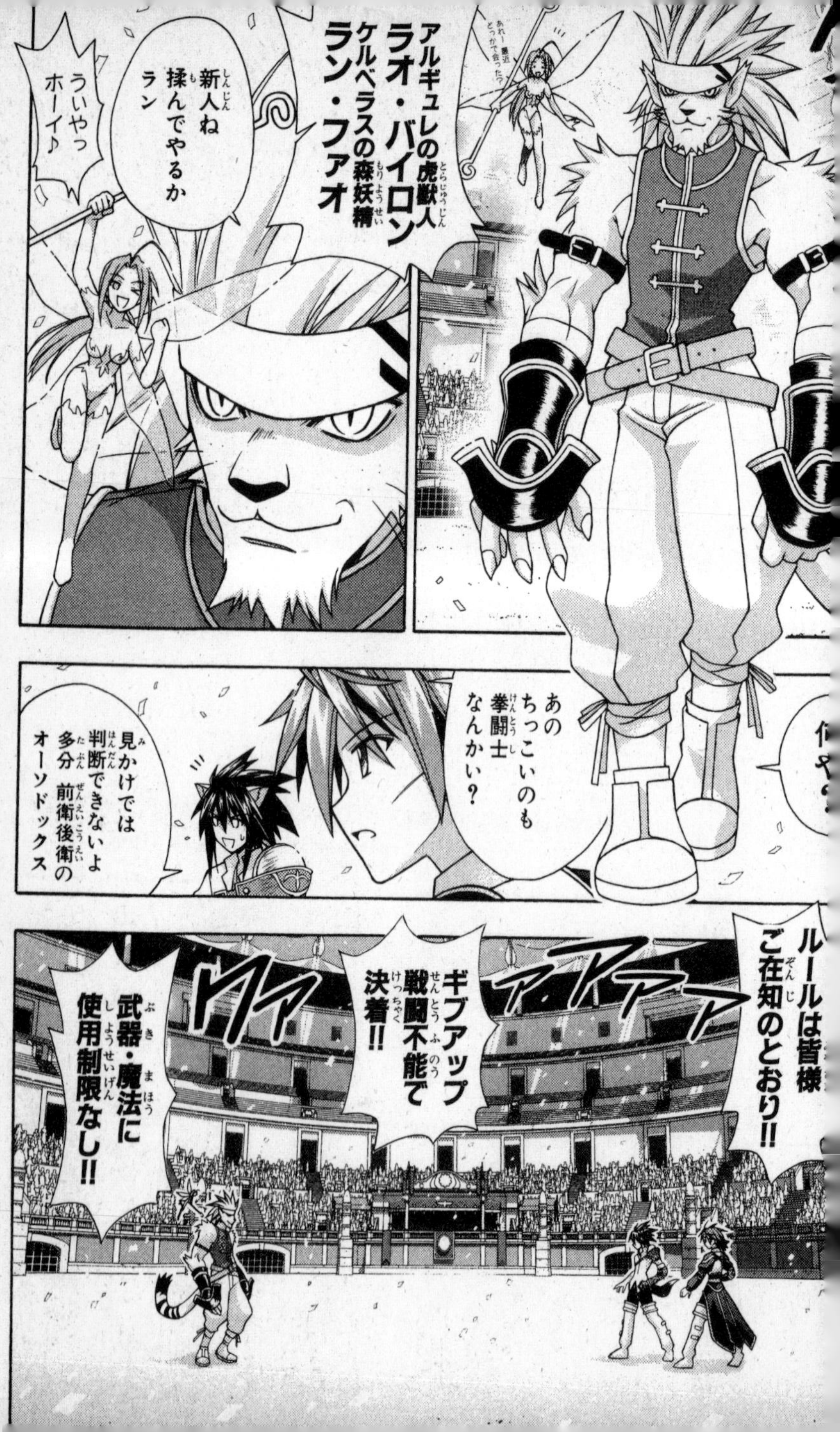
あれー最近どっかで会った？
アルギュレの虎獣人
ラオ・バイロン
ケルベラスの森妖精
ラン・ファオ
新人ね 揉んでやるか ラン
ういやっ ホーイ♪
あの ちっこいのも 拳闘士なんかい？
見かけでは 判断できないよ 多分 前衛後衛の オーソドックス
ルールは皆様 ご存知のとおり!!
ワァァアァァ
ギブアップ 戦闘不能で 決着!!
武器・魔法に 使用制限なし!!

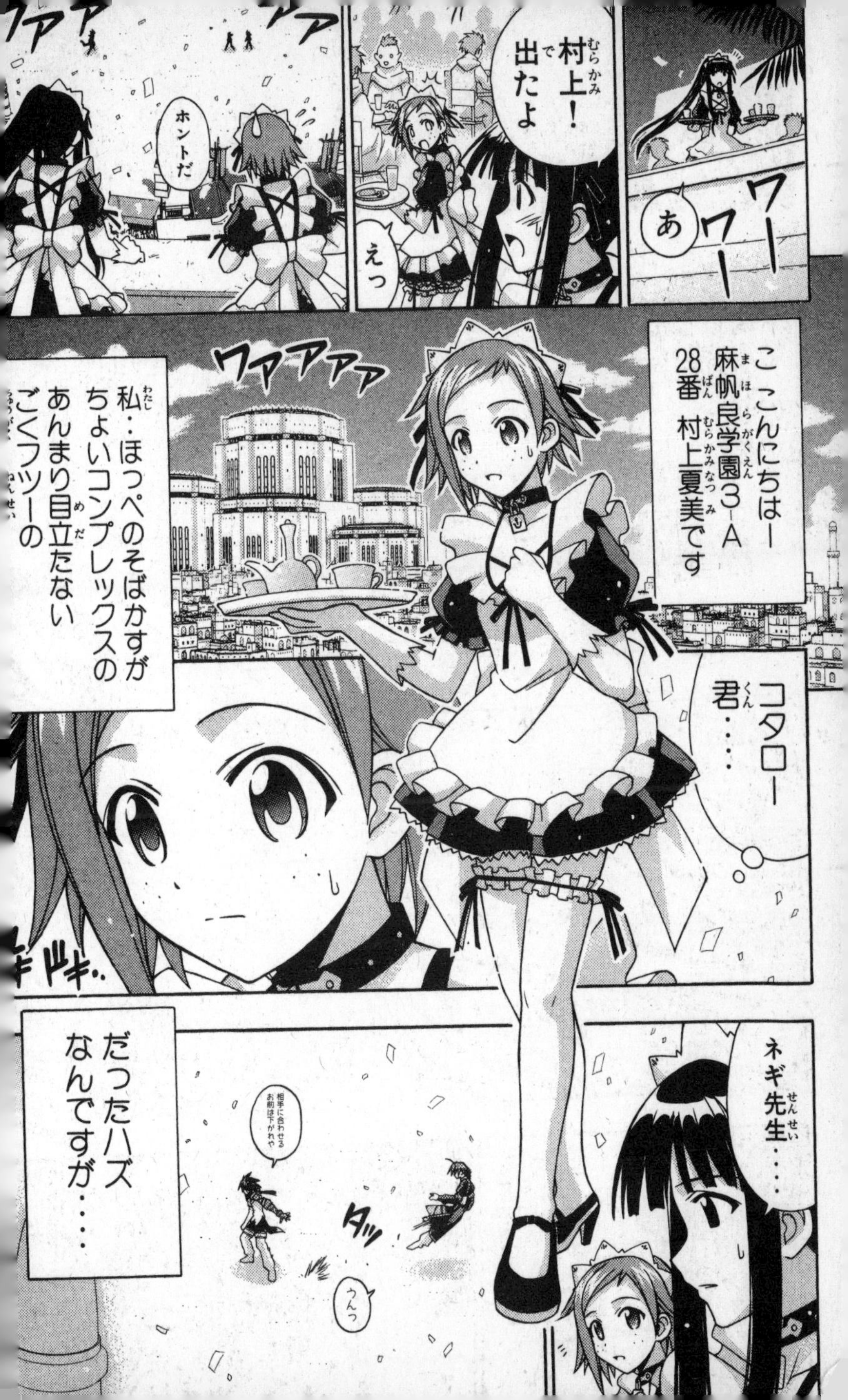
ワーワー
あ
村上！出たよ
えっ
ワァア
ワァア
ホントだ
こ…こんにちはー
麻帆良学園3-A
28番 村上夏美です
ワァアアァ
私：ほっぺのそばかすが
ちょいコンプレックスの
あんまり目立たない
ごくフツーの
コタロー君…
ドキドキ..
ネギ先生…
相手に合わせる
お前は下がれや
タッ
うんっ
だったハズ
なんですが…

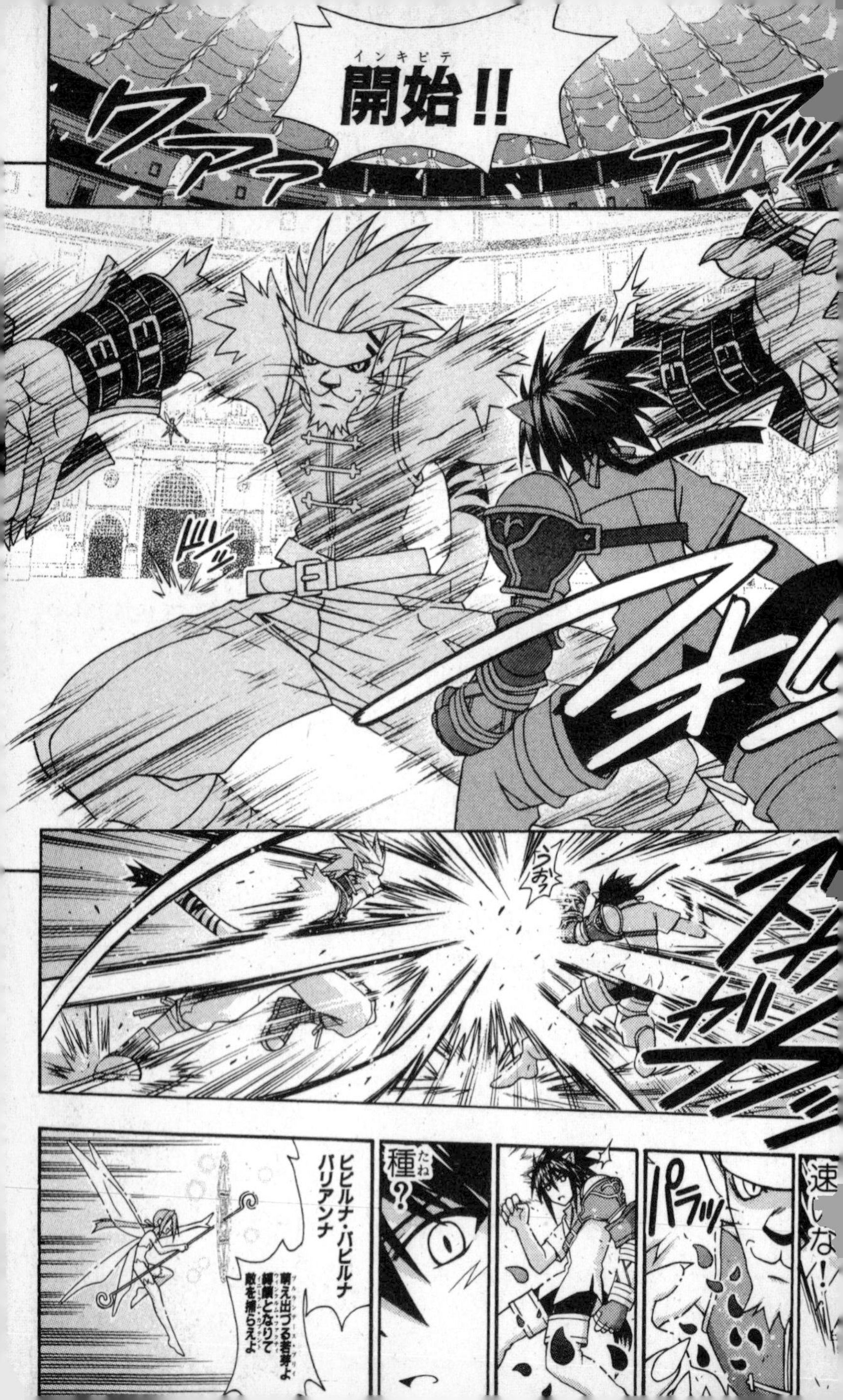
開始!!
ワァァァ
ァアッ!!
ドッ
うおっ
速いな…!
パラッ
種?
ビビルナ・バビルナ バリアンナ
萌え出づる若芽よ 綱鎖となりて 敵を捕らえよ

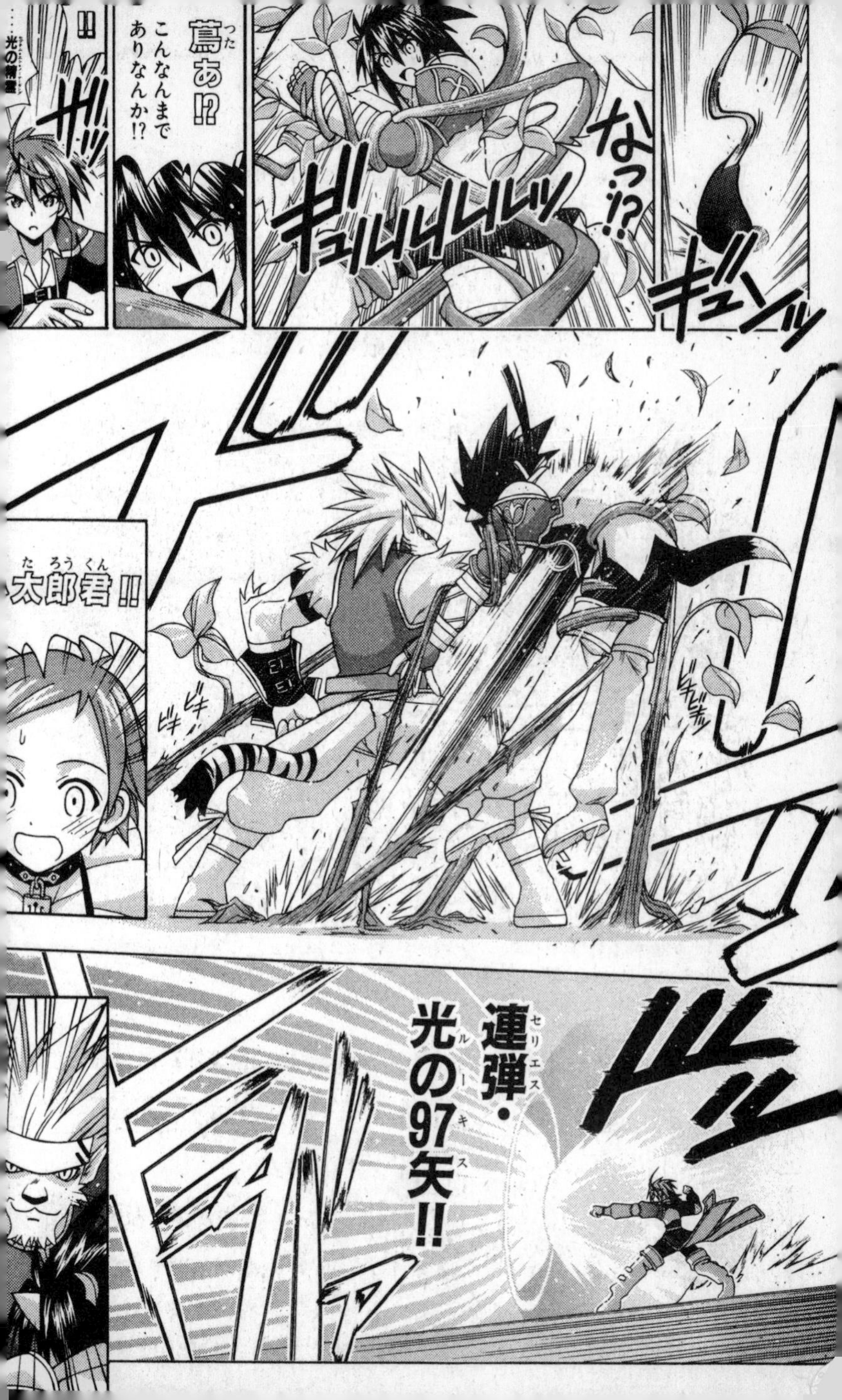

ギュンッ
なっ⁉
ギュルルルルッ
蔦あ⁉
こんなんまでありなんか⁉
!!
ザッ
・・・・光の精霊
太郎君!!
ビキビキ
ビキビキッ
ドッ
連弾・光の97矢!!

TOMARE!

[STOP!]

You're going the wrong way!

Manga is a completely different type of reading experience.

To start at the *beginning*,
go to the *end*!

That's right! Authentic manga is read the traditional Japanese way—from right to left, exactly the *opposite* of how American books are read. It's easy to follow: Just go to the other end of the book, and read each page—and each panel—from right side to left side, starting at the top right. Now you're experiencing manga as it was meant to be.